Crossword

Play these other fun puzzle books by *USA TODAY*:

USA TODAY Sudoku

USA TODAY Everyday Sudoku

USA TODAY Mini Sudoku/Sudoku X

USA TODAY Word Roundup/Word Search

USA TODAY Word Play

USA TODAY Logic Puzzles

CROSSWORD

200 Puzzles
from The Nation's No. 1 Newspaper

**Andrews McMeel
Publishing, LLC**
Kansas City • Sydney • London

Andrews McMeel Publishing, LLC
an Andrews McMeel Universal company
1130 Walnut Street, Kansas City, Missouri 64106

www.andrewsmcmeel.com
puzzles.usatoday.com

11 WKT 10 9 8 7

ISBN: 978-0-7407-7032-6

Crosswords edited by Tim Parker

CROSSWORD

1
WORLDWIDE WOOF
By Fran & Lou Sabin

ACROSS

1 Villa d'___
5 Decorates a cake
9 Large spread
14 Sudden transition
15 It's sometimes a drag
16 Stan's sidekick
17 Tijuana toy?
20 La Scala's city
21 NHL Hall-of-Famer
22 Ready to be tied?
23 Mixed dish
25 Storm preceder, it's said
28 Brussels barker?
35 LAX listings
36 Novel
37 Tara deed-holder
38 Cries of surprise
39 Cager's credits
42 Get out of Dodge
43 Ascended, as from the grave
45 Base address
46 "Little Man ___" (Jodie Foster film)
47 Highland howler?
51 Where to find a relief of Lincoln
52 Morales of "NYPD Blue"
53 CD follower
56 Russian blue, e.g.
58 It's shy of a treaty
61 Sitka sled-puller?
66 Range dwelling, once
67 Certain sugar source
68 Cattle goad
69 Ralph Waldo Emerson piece
70 Goes no further
71 Pullets

DOWN

1 A samara source
2 Apparently are
3 Kind of dancer or stand
4 Actor's last words (Var.)
5 Shiraz citizens
6 Item kicked by kids in a game
7 It will return your calls
8 Kind of party
9 Favoring
10 Building extension
11 Hebraic alphabet opener (Var.)
12 Emphatic foreign affirmation
13 Word with driving or rabbit
18 Colombian city since 1536
19 "Dies ___" (hymn)
24 Rightmost math column
26 Summer birthday boys
27 Ticket abbr.
28 The Refrigerator's team
29 Code of conduct
30 Stock-acquisition aid?
31 Sound made by taffeta
32 Part of a religious title
33 Deliver a declamation
34 Scrappy competitor
39 Dealer's request
40 Put in place
41 Bridge supports
44 All-encompassing abbr.

46 Defeat all comers
48 Quechua
49 Position on an issue
50 ___ avis
53 Charge per unit
54 Some shouts of support
55 Travelers' checks?
57 Counterfeiter's nemesis

59 Treat meat
60 College since 1440
62 Vast area
63 "Defense of Fort M'Henry" author
64 "After that . . . ?"
65 They make periodical changes, briefly

2
ZOOM ZOOM ZOOM
By Alan Olschwang

ACROSS

1 Impertinence
4 "___ at 'em!"
9 Scour
14 Clear start?
15 Exemplar
16 Boor
17 Hannah of "Hannah and Her Sisters"
18 Type of artist
20 Louisiana feature
22 Do-well intro
23 Partner of sex and videotape
24 Diva's offering
26 Topples
28 Commuter's alternative
33 Subject of King Fahd bin Abdul Aziz
34 Emissary of the pope
35 Kind of sister or story
38 Beautiful and graceful girls
40 Long, fluffy scarf
41 Leaf aperture
43 Wasn't used
44 Potbelly
47 Bator's beginning
48 Harvard's theater award
50 Right-triangle reciprocal
53 Palindromic sound effect
54 Uzbekistan sea
55 Silence between notes
59 Deliver an impassioned presentation
62 Use a remote, in a way

65 Euripides drama
66 Aromatic compound
67 A form of defamation
68 Disencumber
69 Gangling
70 Musical study
71 Ernie of the PGA

DOWN

1 Symbol of obedience
2 Pelvis parts
3 Act
4 Readily convertible to cash
5 An Internet address ender
6 Chinese chow
7 Medieval war club
8 Actress Sommer
9 MIT, for one
10 Swiss Alps residence, perhaps
11 Altercation
12 Goaded
13 Sanctify
19 Bread end
21 Small African antelope
25 E. Coast ocean
27 Pizza orders
28 Prison terms
29 Kind of rug
30 Counter
31 Opposite of ecstasy
32 Anti-discrimination org.
35 PC diversion
36 Arabian Sea nation
37 Report of a shooting?

39 Bridge part
42 English ruling dynasty
45 The Jetsons' dog
46 Shanty
48 Obeyed the sentry
49 Scribble
50 Less hazardous
51 Clear the whiteboard

52 Class of Hindu society
56 Della's creator
57 Farr co-star
58 Forbidden perfume?
60 Plug away
61 Breaks off
63 Word with fish or small
64 Kind of carpet

3
GET HIGH
By James Page

ACROSS

1 Name at the pumps
6 Ma holds one
11 Kind of scores
14 Johannesburg coins
15 Bubbling over
16 Literary initials
17 Like Mr. America
19 "I thought so!"
20 Keyboard key
21 Scott Turow novel
22 Kappa's preceder
24 Cape of Good Hope navigator
26 Olympic event
30 Hook, line and sinker types
32 Flat fillers
33 Camping stuff, e.g.
34 Mississippi mud, e.g.
35 Radical '60s org.
36 "Let it go!" (and hint to this puzzle's theme)
41 Big embrace
44 Simple dwelling
45 Musical finale
48 Best Picture of 1984
51 Posh
54 Planting season
56 Rice of literature
57 Chi paper (with "The")
58 Degrees for execs, perhaps
60 Hardly a mark of distinction
61 Firm head
62 Trusting act
66 Like Gen. Clark

67 Looks up and down
68 Greek isle
69 White bill in Monopoly
70 Barbecue needs
71 Fling

DOWN

1 Fleet
2 Overwhelming defeat
3 Currently in the limelight
4 Atlanta-based public health agcy.
5 Holmenkollen overlooks it
6 Highland games poles
7 "Christ Stopped at ___"
8 "Buck Privates" first name
9 "Moment in Peking" author Yutang
10 All 45s, now
11 Rodin created some
12 Not exactly proud
13 Nonalcoholic brew
18 ___'acte
23 Some IHOP orders
25 Blast furnace byproduct
27 Ballet bend
28 Evil glance
29 Letter afterthoughts letters
31 Before, in rhyme
34 Ryan's rank, briefly
37 Bully
38 Force from office
39 It may be found in a sheet
40 "Animal House" frock

	41 Calls one's own	52 Book sheet
	42 A whole bunch	53 Subdued chuckle

41 Calls one's own
42 A whole bunch
43 Infamous Spanish collar
46 More first-rate
47 Warren's wife
49 Half of MIV
50 As a whole group
51 Mold in relief

52 Book sheet
53 Subdued chuckle
55 Force forward
59 Army NCOs
61 ___-Magnon man
63 Hot dog's problem
64 Mode lead-in
65 Dada sculptor

4
VOID

By Mengel & Gianette

ACROSS

1 Cryptographer
6 Plan ahead, for short
10 Seed of an Asiatic legume
14 It may be light or grand
15 Wasp's nest location, perhaps
16 Help in a way one shouldn't
17 It may be advertised
20 Forest denizen
21 Launderer's step
22 Seville ritual
23 Brit's air arm
24 Standoff, of a kind
25 Organ near the temple
26 Mother Hubbard had one
32 Smart follower
33 Borrower's burden
34 Brother of Fidel
38 Where most strikes occur
39 Flight coordinators (Abbr.)
40 One less than hexa-
41 Notorious pirate captain
42 "___ boy!" ("Nice going!")
43 Like most films
44 Bad thing to hold on to
47 "Blame It on ___" (Caine film)
50 Time for les vacances
51 Be decisive
52 Not spotted
54 Man from U.N.C.L.E.
56 He had 37 KOs
59 Deadpan
62 ___ di Como, Italia
63 Tibet explorer Hedin

64 Driveway part
65 Balls with lids
66 Competing team
67 Shoe shapes

DOWN

1 Sheltered bay
2 Geyserite, e.g.
3 Place for two black suits
4 Newsworthy time
5 Turns inside out
6 Certain body shape
7 Transfixed
8 "Die Meistersinger" heroine
9 Rug type
10 Copycat's request
11 Too big for one's britches?
12 Annoying gossip
13 Fragrant oil
18 Sukiyaki ingredient
19 Tower part
23 Inch back
24 Shoe adornment
26 Pitching error
27 Kyrgyz mountain range
28 A way to rupture
29 County in Missouri or Nebraska
30 Itty-___
31 Like nightmares
35 Kind of matter
36 North American Indians
37 Put aboard
40 Business plan
42 Relevance

45 Proverbial heirs (with "the")
46 You get a credit for it
47 Russian coin
48 Do parquetry
49 Type of orange
53 TV spinoff of 1980
54 Earned a citation, maybe

55 Department of France
56 Puts on the small screen, e.g.
57 Swag
58 Hostelries
60 Sweet age in old Roma
61 Masseur's milieu

5

NARROW FOCUS

By V. Fleming and B. Venzke

ACROSS

1 Movie mutt
6 Virus prefix
10 Imbibes slowly
14 Use a blender, in a way
15 Nail anagram
16 College credit
17 Surface extents
18 It may get the brush-off
19 Barker of filmdom
20 Focal point of a weighty matter?
23 It takes things to the extreme
24 Preschooler
25 Took much too much, briefly
26 Bender
27 "Casablanca" character
29 Certain leather source
32 Linebacker Junior
35 ___ Reader (former magazine name)
37 Boy toy
39 Focal point of the politically moderate?
42 Find diverting
43 Natural table
44 Some old laptops
45 Job listing letters
46 Tail end
48 They're inhuman
50 Gas or elec., e.g.
52 Alphabetic run
53 Fleur-de-___
56 Focal point of a politician?

61 Lovers' place
62 Small and weak
63 Played-out
64 Slight interruption
65 Emmy-winning Falco
66 Available for occupation
67 Turkeys
68 Weightlifters' iterations
69 Despots

DOWN

1 Maneuvering room
2 Antidotes
3 Word separating looks and everything
4 Entree item, often
5 It carries the words "Rey de Espana"
6 Shell out
7 Babe in the woods
8 Soft bell sound
9 Emcees' deliveries
10 Charmingly sophisticated
11 What employee theft is
12 "Kalifornia" star
13 Dog show command
21 Noxious elephant, e.g.
22 Poor Richard's forte
26 One of the martial arts
27 Extrapolate
28 "I'm game!"
30 The good earth
31 Reebok competitor
32 Hook hand

33 One in Hanover
34 More than recessed
36 1970s TV detective
38 Bearded bloom
40 Type of poetry
41 The Santa Maria landed here
47 One not getting any reception
49 Expression of disapproval
51 Is overrun

52 They may appear on lids
53 Bizet opera priestess
54 ___ alia (among other things)
55 Printers' retentions
56 Iron follower
57 Home of Iolani Palace
58 In the altogether
59 Quick cut
60 Some still-life subjects

6

COOL IT!

By Fran & Lou Sabin

ACROSS

1 Type of track
6 Stinging blow
10 Bit of praise
14 Kegler locale
15 Take on
16 China placement
17 "Cool it!"
20 House vote
21 Where many arrive just to split
22 Fussy couple?
23 "___ She Sweet"
24 Tuning fork's output
26 "Cool it!"
32 Police blotter types, slangily
33 Texas hold 'em holding, perhaps
34 Penultimate letter
35 Vientiane is its capital
36 "Fantasia" dancer
38 Young salmon up to two years old
39 It may have several cups of coffee
40 Retina receptor
41 Letter flourish
42 "Cool it!"
46 Artificial bait
47 Worrysome thing
48 First-stringers
51 Small town
52 PC alternative
55 "Cool it!"
59 Definitely not well-done
60 Word with throat or loser

61 Bat maker's machine
62 Puppies' plaints
63 Clark of the comics
64 Command on 52-Across

DOWN

1 Duke's daughter
2 Cosmetics additive, often
3 Humerus neighbor
4 Garner
5 They are of mixed origin
6 Japanese religion
7 CEO carrier, perhaps
8 Dada co-founder
9 It can be split
10 Type of roll
11 Applications
12 Eat by candlelight, perhaps
13 Stable fare
18 Start of a counting-out rhyme
19 Certain voice range
23 Mann's "The Magic Mountain" locale
24 Word with fly or speed
25 17th of 50
26 What the Tin Man wanted
27 Home of Maine's Black Bears
28 Good hand to have
29 Hive activity
30 Condor's nest (Var.)
31 One in a condition of servitude
32 "What's more . . ."
36 Billing unit, for some
37 Heading for a memo subject

38 Wooden pins
40 Good buddies
41 Cuddle together
43 Dental items
44 "Absolutely!"
45 Cross inscription
48 Twisted
49 Chiang Mai citizen, often

50 Holliday partner
51 Capital on the Aare
52 Jeff's sidekick
53 U.S. court star
54 "Half-Breed" singer
56 Word of reproval
57 Long-handled tool
58 Displayed fear, in a way

7
PUZZLE TIME
By Barry C. Silk

ACROSS
1 St. John's bread
6 Imposture
10 Roman Senate garb
14 Warm welcome?
15 It springs eternal
16 He was terrible
17 It ends ". . . shall not be infringed"
20 Tongue-clucking sound
21 Dumbfound
22 Traffic sign
23 Hummus accompaniment
24 Word with snow or snap
26 Branded product that may be apple or grape
33 "Golden Boy" dramatist Clifford
34 Cribbage piece
35 Choice assignment
36 Slangy denial
37 2004 contender
39 Canton that borders Bern
40 "Comin' ___ the Rye"
42 Steamed state
43 Orange variety
45 What a corset may provide
49 Seemingly forever
50 Glazier's item
51 Wing it
54 Wasp's nest site, perhaps
55 Paltry amount
58 It begins in the spring
62 "American ___ "
63 Line of clothing?

64 Wicked ways
65 Skateboarder Hawk
66 Leatherworking tools
67 Bouncing off the walls

DOWN
1 Playbill listing
2 Draft selections
3 Music style
4 "Now I get it!"
5 Outlaws
6 Magician's word
7 Pentagonal plate
8 Do an impression of
9 Chess pieces
10 Number of at-bats
11 Concluded
12 Word with motorcycle or street
13 Up-front poker payment
18 Social engagement
19 Same key signature as B min.
23 Stock option
24 Quay
25 Anxious
26 Billing cycle, often
27 43rd state
28 India's first prime minister
29 ___-ski
30 "P.S.___" ('90s detective series)
31 Doctor, one would hope
32 French novelist Zola
37 Pottery oven
38 Paleozoic and Mesozoic
41 FOX News show host

43 Capital of ancient Assyria
44 of Reason
46 Mongolian expanse
47 Muscle twitches
48 Bean variety
51 Shaft entrance
52 Woodworking groove
53 City on the Rhone

54 Abbr. in a footnote, perhaps
55 Use scissors
56 Gawk
57 Letters on an old Asian map
59 Fed. property manager
60 Cut with an ax
61 It climbs the walls

8
BEST FRIENDS
By Alan Olschwang

ACROSS
1 Prepared to fire
6 French states
11 Passing fancy
14 Kind of jump
15 Cuban export
16 Initials in lending
17 Orchestral instruments
19 Born as
20 Needle case
21 1953 baseball AL MVP Al
22 MC less XXXIX
23 Jennifer Lopez role
25 Mysteriously spooky
27 Someone Guinness is interested in
32 ___ Mochis of Mexico
35 First name in horror flicks
36 Tale starter
37 Some sow wild ones
39 Flow out
41 Ms. Ward
42 Smarts
45 Shindig
48 Spectrum color
49 Good 30-foot jumper
52 "I Love Lucy" episode, e.g.
53 Single-cell protozoans
57 Mouse manipulator
59 Sinatra song
62 Chesterfield, e.g.
63 Symbol of punishment
64 Alternative to briefs
66 Pac 10 sch.

67 Awkward
68 Medicinal plants
69 Cut short
70 Piths
71 He made heads roll

DOWN
1 French clerics
2 Fuming
3 Iraq city on the Tigris
4 Less complicated
5 ETO commander
6 Mimic
7 Barcelona uncles
8 Came to terms
9 Most envied at the beach, perhaps
10 Alums to be
11 Star reading?
12 It's at the very top
13 Ein, zwei, ___
18 Vestige
22 Catchers and chefs have them
24 Bird's beak
26 "The Crying Game" star
28 Ringside cheer
29 Browning's Ben Ezra, e.g.
30 Nice lady?
31 Frequent auditions
32 Sort of soul
33 Office entry requirement, perhaps
34 Motivated
38 Villainous expression

40 Prohibit
43 Neighbor of Lux.
44 Italian dessert
46 Judges' orders
47 It may be around a woman's knees
50 Some cameo stones
51 Work on shoes
54 Nonmetallic element

55 Subsequently
56 Pert
57 Russian river
58 Mediocre
60 What Carroll's walrus did
61 They may be fine and you may support them
64 Magnanimous
65 "That'll show 'em!"

USA TODAY.

9

TALK UNDER PRESSURE

By B. Venzke and V. Fleming

ACROSS

1 Toothpaste style
4 Three, per an adage
9 Fawning toon?
14 "What ___, a bank?"
15 Comic Mandel
16 Lionize
17 Uncomfortable humidity
19 Pole staff?
20 Start of an Abraham Lincoln quotation
22 Deep-voiced songstress
24 Connect with, in a way
25 Part 2 of the quotation
30 Call a turkey?
31 His work with couples is legendary
32 Jock's cable choice
36 Sun Devils' letters
37 Part 3 of the quotation
41 Boo or bally attachment
42 Not just listening
44 Scan or peruse
45 "That's so-o-o-o cute!"
46 Part 4 of the quotation
51 Treelike cactus
54 Dinghy
55 End of the quotation
60 Absent from
61 Worth zero
64 Inviting odor
65 Pals of sultans
66 Knock on wood
67 Adjust, as sails
68 Theater capacity
69 Berkshire abode

DOWN

1 School of whales
2 Avian that's swift afoot
3 "Don't act so serious!"
4 Currently fashionable
5 Columnist Barrett
6 First name in an Irving title
7 Cheesehead's st.
8 Bygone car
9 Went off, as a timer
10 "Sweet Child o' Mine" singer
11 Whiz
12 Like food after grace
13 Linda Ronstadt's "___ Easy"
18 A branch of math.
21 Former space docking site
22 How some securities are priced
23 Tibet's capital
26 Clandestine maritime org.
27 Ham, to 31-Across
28 Tit for ___
29 Fingerprint feature
33 Followers
34 Kind of surge
35 "As if!"
38 Golfer's device
39 In possession of
40 Summer hrs. in N.Y.C.
43 Wave of destruction
47 Appliance brand
48 Extension

49 Bread units
50 Revered figure
51 Echo finder
52 In advance of, poetically
53 University of Florida footballer
56 It's given to a newborn

57 Pelvic bones
58 Writer Vonnegut
59 Untouchable Eliot
62 Stood no more
63 Seek intelligence, in a way

10
ON THE BRIGHT SIDE
By Diane C. Baldwin

ACROSS
1 Man of means
6 Sanction in wrongdoing
10 Kind of roll or shot
14 Pacific salutation
15 Interoffice communique
16 Verve
17 Fluctuates wildly
18 Grievously injure, in a way
19 Bona ___ (authentic)
20 One way to follow a pattern
21 Clever one
24 Bermuda border
26 Some bits
27 Least loony
29 Primitive shelters
31 Verdi heroine
32 Riding whip
34 "Roll 'em!" followers
39 March middle
40 It has an S-shaped neck
42 Delicate cut
43 Yankee first name
45 Poet St. Vincent Millay
46 Shredded, as lettuce
47 Type of chatter
49 Reprimanded (with "out")
51 She's a college grad
55 Lamb Chop's friend
56 Savvy individual
59 Harbor craft, perhaps
62 Word with "American" or false
63 Be fervid
64 Buy alternative
66 River duck
67 Word before or after where
68 Little screecher
69 Pangolin's diet
70 Children's connectibles
71 Some construction junctions

DOWN
1 Some floor votes
2 Natural emollient
3 Amazing lad
4 "What have we here!"
5 Quarters of some quartets
6 Capital on the Jabbok
7 Part of the California flag
8 Throw off
9 F-14, e.g.
10 Obfuscate
11 Similar
12 Lowest point
13 They may buckle
22 Item in a book
23 Give the boot
25 Desist partner
27 Not tacit
28 Adjutant
29 Vast multitude
30 Current with
33 Virginia dance
35 Michaelmas daisy
36 One needing no advice
37 Irish Republic
38 Made haste
41 Chip variety

44 Genial
48 Versatile piece of furniture
50 Consecrate
51 Brookner or Ekberg
52 Fabric for cold climates
53 Lusitania sinker
54 Gangsters' gals

55 They may hit the ground running
57 Go it alone
58 Kind of fight
60 Secondhand
61 Picks up on
65 A wool producer

11
CLEAN LIVING
By Raymond Hamel

ACROSS

1 Someone you may see after class
6 Candid
10 Raisin rum cake
14 A Pointer sister
15 Address forthrightly
16 Exiled Roman poet
17 Defeat handily
20 Deputized group
21 Add an explanation to
22 Jimmy Carter's daughter
24 London baby carriage
27 Grandparent, sometimes
28 Issue, as an insult
31 Oyster's place
33 Obsolete palindromic preposition
34 Cabbage
35 Bad way to be at the wheel
38 Feature of some watches
43 She gave us "Heartburn"
44 Italian port city
45 Envoy XL maker
48 Yang counterpart
49 Tin alloy
50 Not as plentiful
53 Scandinavian epic
55 Creature on Michigan's state flag
56 Concurrence
58 Less cordial
61 1939 John Garfield drama
66 Certain facial expression

67 St. James' Piccadilly designer
68 When penitents convene?
69 Ultimatum ender, often
70 Old TV knob
71 Merchandise

DOWN

1 Flat cap
2 Family card game
3 Move stealthily
4 Camp Swampy dog
5 Some cheers
6 Make available
7 Member of one's coterie
8 Green prefix?
9 Element number 10
10 Greet with ceremony
11 Do the Wright thing
12 Like one who cannot let it go
13 Cleave
18 Catch sight of
19 Fish stick?
22 Something for the poor
23 Catty remark
25 Skip town
26 Succulent fruit
29 Cut and run
30 Northern nomad
32 Feral shelter
35 Where the eagle has landed
36 Advantage
37 Exclamation of relief
39 Diffident
40 Front tooth

41 Coward of England
42 What nyctophobes fear
45 Kind of match
46 Technical reading
47 British potato chips
49 Rate of work
51 Lauder of cosmetics
52 Laura Petrie's TV hubby
54 Common contraction
57 Former House Speaker Gingrich
59 "___ What You Did Last Summer"
60 Legendary singer James
62 Picture of health
63 Japanese capital
64 L.A.-to-Boise dir.
65 "By all means!"

12
HOUSEWARES DEPARTMENT
By Fran & Lou Sabin

ACROSS
1 Tarzan, ___ Greystoke
5 "This way" indicator
10 Negri of "Forbidden Paradise"
14 Reed under Maazel
15 Linney of "Kinsey"
16 Ice Capades leap
17 Nightcaps, e.g.?
19 Rough-terrain vehicle
20 Peeper prettifier
21 26-time champs
22 "Hail, Caesar!"
23 Tennyson creation
25 Give the willies
28 Place for chips and drinks
33 Casual goodbye
34 Spyri young heroine
35 Terhune's admirable dog
36 They're under exclamation points
37 Where the Styx flows
38 Type of package
39 Alphabet train
40 Something to drum up
41 Khartoum is its capital
42 Bridal cache
44 Part of a chignon
45 Painter's application
46 Browning's "___ Lippo Lippi"
47 Something to behold
50 Goats, sheep, etc.
55 Seraphic topper
56 Certain meeting leader
58 Curved molding
59 Like the designated driver
60 Latvian's capital
61 Fishing hole
62 Mighty small
63 It may lead up or down

DOWN
1 Earring site
2 Follow instructions
3 Teased mercilessly
4 States emphatically
5 Isolated
6 Inn posting
7 German mining region
8 It may pan out
9 "... flag ___ still there"
10 Kind of party
11 Plow pullers
12 Onion's kin
13 Hannibal's challenge
18 Iron-rich food
21 Hirsute legend
23 Chasuble wearer
24 Bookie's figure
25 Walk through water
26 Bel ___ (operatic style)
27 Devoured
28 Mountaineer's dwelling
29 Culex's cousin
30 Cutting edge
31 "___ Theme" ("Doctor Zhivago")
32 Paradisal spots
37 Tee-hee relative
38 Museum supervisors

40 Macbeth or Duncan, e.g.
41 It can make a sucker out of you
43 Repeated exactly
46 River transport
47 High school class
48 The Moor's envier
49 Hidden valley
50 Subject of the Red Sox curse, pre-2004

51 Mortgagee's obligation
52 Discharge
53 "In" thing
54 Variety of pea
56 Ill. clock setting
57 Cabbage patch tool

13
PARTING SHOTS
By James E. Buell

ACROSS

1 It should make you pause
6 Legendary centerfielder
10 Tap the brakes
14 Common computer font
15 Muscat's country
16 Temporary superstar
17 What you may do for laughs
19 Sanction misdeeds
20 Flop's opposite
21 The Bard's river
22 Kind of witness
24 Pave the way for
26 Whatsis
28 Gruyere coat
30 Inventor of an alcohol thermometer
34 Hunter's quarry
37 Nerd kin
39 One way to be conspicuous
40 Lamb of literature
41 Dot com letters
43 One of Chekhov's "Three Sisters"
44 Some oxygen sources
46 Tuscany river
47 Hightailed it
48 Tons in a Tennessee Ernie Ford song
50 Far Eastern desert
52 They create applause
54 Where to pack up your troubles
58 Climb

61 Woeful expression
63 Wine consideration
64 French Sudan, now
65 Make petty distinctions
68 Colonizer of Greenland
69 Celestial bear
70 Keeps an eye on the figures?
71 Nucha
72 It's shaped like a bell
73 Former Toyota model

DOWN

1 Hiding place
2 Hatch of politics
3 Mazda model
4 Slangy name for a stranger
5 Acid neutralizer
6 Magic power or spell
7 In the company of
8 Beast of burden
9 Merit a blessing?
10 "Cheer up!"
11 Occipital ___
12 Superior to
13 Unit of power
18 Requite
23 Dec. highlight
25 Overcome unfamiliarity
27 Exasperating
29 Union issue
31 Symbol of suburbia
32 More than suggest
33 Try for a part

34 Fathoms
35 Mountain range of southwest Kyrgyzstan
36 Coquette
38 Acoustic organ
42 Observe
45 Yoko's son
49 Ultimately becomes
51 Miter wearer
53 Certain condiment

55 Leaves the groom at the altar, e.g.
56 Nod in unison
57 Plasterlike preparation
58 Congregational response
59 "Two Mules for Sister ___"
60 Kind of joint
62 Mendacious one
66 Start for school
67 Eastern honorific

14
UMBRELLA REQUIRED
By Victor Fleming

ACROSS

1 Has to
5 Off one's trolley
9 Card player's headwear, perhaps
14 0 on a phone
15 Lake in four states
16 Foreword, e.g.
17 Kiev resident
19 Insertion mark
20 Escort to the living room, say
21 Env. abbreviation
23 Enticing sign word
24 Medicinal herbs
26 Egypt's Mubarak
28 Three-sided sword
29 "Bad Moon Rising" band, briefly
32 1936 and 1937 Best Actress Luise
35 Daylong marches
38 In ___ (unborn)
39 Hardly old-fashioned
42 Bopped on the noggin
44 One end of the spectrum
45 Television announcer Don
47 Inactiveness
49 Rice and wheat, e.g.
51 Relaxing resort
52 Charter
56 Get slick, in a way
58 Meteorologist's line
60 Jonathan Larson's musical
62 Place for a crow's-nest

65 "All that I am I ___ thee"(Psalms)
66 TV studio sign
68 With 48-Down, theme of this puzzle
70 Start an Internet session
71 Scale deduction
72 Scrambler, e.g.
73 Likhovtseva of women's tennis
74 Kitty starter
75 Doesn't hold up well?

DOWN

1 Chilled dessert
2 Household expenses
3 Unflappable
4 Instructor's charge
5 Bear lair
6 Solo for Renata Scotto
7 Auto that debuted in 1899
8 Certain decimal fraction
9 Singer Damone
10 Visibly peeved
11 Chef's gadget
12 Southern Russian city
13 Boring way to learn, to some
18 Words with pickle or minute
22 Negative joiner
25 Battle memento
27 Nejd native
30 Capital examiners, briefly
31 Land-related portfolio items
33 Prior to, poetically

34 Towel site
36 Steakhouse order, perhaps
37 Succumb to stress
39 Automobile sticker fig.
40 Trireme tool
41 Kind of ditch
43 Morales of "La Bamba"
46 Articulation
48 See 68-Across
50 Object to find in Kakuro
53 Land on the Bay of Biscay

54 OK for the rugrats
55 Chips away at
57 An Italian cuisine
59 Tippler
60 Thing to play
61 Hydroxyl compound
63 Observatory function
64 Fruity pastry
67 Some strands in a cell
69 Something to drive off

15
WHAT'S YOUR HURRY?
By Andy Pinner

ACROSS

1 Speaks hoarsely
6 George Takei role
10 First born
14 More than required
15 Opposed to, in Dogpatch
16 Start with European or China
17 Lose one's cool
20 What an F may indicate
21 Skull and Bones member, e.g.
22 Formidable opponents
23 Renders senseless
25 Intention
26 Plundered treasure
29 Line from an operator?
31 Liberal follower
35 Like a green banana
37 They may be against you
39 Shade
40 Jump all over a person
43 King that brought fame to Howard Carter
44 Obviously carefully written
45 Automobile part
46 Fencer's selection
48 Kicked oneself
50 Prepares a cannon
51 Drag one's feet
53 Holders of many frames
55 Turpentine, e.g.
59 Contessa portrayer
60 Word with poison or solid
63 Bodyguard or decoy's task, sometimes

66 "Magnet and Steel" singer Walter
67 More than a star
68 Winery process
69 Bingo kin
70 Buffalo Bill, formally
71 Shoppers' bags

DOWN

1 Some whistle-blowers, briefly
2 Toll unit
3 It ran around Hades
4 More than a dabbler
5 Certain fastener
6 Companion of silks
7 Exclamation of disgust
8 What a title search may uncover
9 Unprecedented
10 Mall feature, often
11 "No ifs, ___ or buts . . ."
12 At leisure
13 Uh-uh and nay
18 Why you need a shot in the arm?
19 "What ___, chopped liver?"
23 Cookbook direction
24 Kid's vehicle, perhaps
26 Steep-sided hill
27 Put down, in a way
28 Make an allocution
30 Word with want or personal
32 Mary's sidekick
33 Made a grand grander

34 Soothsayers
36 Full of pep
38 Suspect something's amiss
41 Sigma follower
42 Adam's grandson
47 Meteorological menace
49 Without listening
52 Abby's twin
54 Name in a Bette Davis film title

55 Arduous voyage
56 Bigger than the both of us
57 ___ instant (suddenly)
58 Make over
60 "Put a lid ___!"
61 Dermatologist's concern
62 They're tapped
64 16.5 feet
65 Attitude of self-importance

16
THE SHADOW KNOWS
By James E. Buell

ACROSS
1 Possessive pronoun
5 Some recyclables
9 Cheer for Pavarotti
14 Vaulted space
15 Substitute spread
16 Secondhand tire, perhaps
17 Stay in the shadows
20 Qualm
21 By what means
22 Snuggery
23 Green peg
24 Ivory ticklers
26 Stay in the shadows (with 45-Across)
30 Former first lady's maiden name
31 Part of a royal flush
32 Utility company's measurement
36 Word with shell or on
37 Tenderfoot's org.
38 Demolitionist's charge
40 ___, Daman and Diu (until 1987)
41 Check line
43 "Well, lookee here!"
44 Forfeiture
45 See 26-Across
49 Monte Carlo game
52 Cohort of Luke and Leia
53 Historical period
54 Ms. Vance, to Lucy
55 Word in some newspaper names

59 Stay in the shadows
62 Explorer Polo
63 Muck
64 Goofs up
65 Comparatively cagey
66 Means justifiers
67 Inadvisable action

DOWN
1 Tibetan oxen
2 Cartel since 1960, briefly
3 Mouse manipulator
4 Purported
5 Is successful in a lawsuit
6 Natural balm
7 Spanking follower
8 First name among Italian leading ladies
9 Certain power failure
10 Rink whistle-blower, briefly
11 Hydrochloric and boric
12 Gentleman's gentleman
13 Begins admitting customers
18 Mimicker
19 Loud burst of laughter
24 Autograph hound's necessity
25 Unknown factors
26 It's part of the flight
27 Roman raiment
28 Uptight
29 Grassy field
33 Atwitter
34 "Jeepers!"
35 Steinbeck title direction

37 Comportment
38 Howe'er
39 Polite decline
42 And so on, for short
43 Pick a card, say
44 Centers and guards, e.g.
46 Filmdom's Brockovich
47 Barbaric
48 Work-shy

49 Road shoulders
50 "It's been ___ pleasure"
51 Toyota model
55 Benevolent
56 Bilbao bull
57 Reason for signaling
58 Exxon precursor
60 Snoopy, in his fantasies
61 Alternative to "smoking"

17
BODY LANGUAGE
By Fran & Lou Sabin

ACROSS

1 Victorian and Romantic, for two
5 Brat's Christmas present
9 ___ patriae (patriotism)
13 Baronet's bride
14 Actress Braga
15 "Venus de ___"
16 Gardener's gift
18 Termini
19 Languish
20 Brief investments?
21 Great surge
23 Word with brain or price
24 It may be forbidden
25 Emulated Huck Finn
28 Margaret or Diana, e.g.
31 Ohio Indians, in the past
32 Avoided bloodshed, in a way
33 Interjection to express doubt
34 Horton's worry
35 Many are broadcast
39 Had something
40 Stentorian
42 It's Grande
43 Nina's traveling companion
45 Harpist or guitarist, at times
47 Straight talk
48 Film maven Roger
49 Cutty ___ (historic ship)
50 Natural gas component
52 A relative of mine?
53 ___ Dolorosa
56 Offensive expression
57 0.0929 square meter

60 Type of hug
61 Tuck site
62 Palindromic emperor
63 Mickey's character
64 Dips in gravy
65 Gymnast's perch

DOWN

1 On tenterhooks
2 Nearly extinct
3 "Lilies of the Field" song
4 Look or must adjunct
5 "Over There" penner
6 Unpleasant task
7 Deadeye's forte
8 Doing arduous work
9 North or South ending
10 It's on the watch
11 Pioneer automaker
12 ___ Hashanah
14 Guarneri's kin, for short
17 Most pleasant
22 Wimpled woman
23 Sault ___ Marie
24 Kukla and Ollie's friend
25 Studio stock
26 Vernacular
27 Part of some sailing vessels
28 Previous arrest
29 Words with music or work
30 Type of campaign
36 Airplane seat features
37 Artist Mondrian
38 Meager

41 Louis XV's madame
44 Press agent's goal
46 John's sign, sometimes
47 Keep in stock
49 Rock layers
50 Where Napoleon was exiled
51 Parent's challenge, stereotypically

52 Brahman feature
53 Show of hands, e.g.
54 Modicum
55 Subject of a split
58 Status ___
59 Watch pocket

18
SLAPSTICK
By Ben Tausig

ACROSS

1 It's a sign
6 Navy noncoms
10 Trident-shaped letters
14 German sub
15 Singer of the cinema
16 Active Italian volcano
17 Send payment
18 Move slowly, as goo
19 Graceland middle name
20 Larry
23 Part of a G&S title
24 Once named
25 Chore at hand
26 Palm Pilot, e.g.
27 Just for men
29 Slithery swimmer
32 Company patronized by Wile E. Coyote
35 Overseas greeting
37 Barely winning, in volleyball
39 Curly
42 Dustin's role in "Midnight Cowboy"
43 Reason for a parental reprimand
44 Therewithal
45 Be obliged to
46 Not forthwith
48 Doesn't lack
50 Payroll datum, often
52 UK lexicon
53 Words with nose or hair
56 Moe
61 Quickly, quickly

62 Handle adversity
63 Minuscule amounts
64 Gollywobbler, e.g.
65 The world, to Atlas
66 Treat like dirt
67 Park in Chicago or London
68 What one little piggy had
69 They're often out on a limb

DOWN

1 Sitcom butler
2 Heavy construction piece
3 Fails, as a comedian
4 Travel choice
5 Show up at
6 Garlic unit
7 Literary honey-lover
8 Rice-shaped pasta
9 Rest of the afternoon?
10 Achieves top performance
11 Find crude stuff?
12 Aware of
13 Named names
21 Show how
22 Prepare to score on a fly ball
26 What great crossword-solvers use
27 That's a wrap!
28 Contents of some chests
30 Abel's nephew
31 Billy Crystal was his first guest
32 It may be picked out
33 Sticking point
34 The Beatles' Rita, e.g.

36 "In that case . . ."
38 They have open houses, briefly
40 They are often checked
41 Milo of "The Verdict"
47 Modern Republican, perhaps
49 Mrs. Rocky Balboa
51 Waldorf salad ingredient
52 With a lot to lose?

53 Some test versions
54 Dough-raiser
55 Church recesses
56 "Miss America" accessory
57 Old chap's exclamation
58 Inadvisable action
59 Created a web site?
60 Type of beef

19
CASINO CALLS
By Carol Lachance

ACROSS

1 International Tennis Hall of Fame inductee, 2004
5 Simpsons' syllables
9 Popular font
14 Klinger's state
15 Needlecase
16 Knight stick
17 Those that are 35 today, e.g.
18 A boxer makes it
19 Nimble
20 Some hockey feats
22 Play worker
23 Pass on
24 Garfield's sidekick
25 Opening off a larger room
28 Tracy of films
31 Love of antiques
32 Auction, e.g.
34 Site of a memorable Beatles concert
35 Chateau d'If setting
36 Surprise fare
39 Annoy
40 Fashion designer Gucci
42 Wharf
43 "Silas Marner" character
45 Nor partner
47 Strong points
48 You may hit the ground with it
49 ___ Ste. Marie, Mich.
51 Walked nervously
53 Extremely trivial
57 Europe-Asia divide
58 Miss Bagnold
59 Builder's need
60 Thomas of "That Girl"
61 Wine-producing province
62 With great expectations
63 Supplementary feature
64 When it's saved, it's taken
65 It holds the team together

DOWN

1 Vincent Van ___
2 Moon of Saturn
3 Grammarian's eyebrow-raiser
4 Ballroom dance
5 Sully
6 City on the Mohawk
7 Sled dog, often
8 Is on the bottom?
9 Advert
10 Babka need
11 Wealthy, slangily
12 Throb
13 Scornful expression
21 Increase, as production
24 Oil cartel letters
25 Pertaining to birds
26 City north of Paris
27 It has purchasing power
28 Innuendo
29 Causing goosebumps
30 Tools for croupiers
32 Culinary directive
33 Seidel filler, sometimes
37 Columnist's page

38 Gene of dancing
41 Desdemona's husband
44 Save for a rainy day
46 North American river
47 Expert commentator
49 Feeling or hearing, e.g.
50 "Dolly" novelist Brookner

51 Ranch menace
52 Romanian city on the Mures
53 Like two ___ in a pod
54 NASA scratch
55 Borrowed without permission
56 Slight advantage

20
OUT FOR A SPIN
By Lynn Lempel

ACROSS
1 Purplish hue
6 Child's query
9 Horseshoes, e.g.
14 Political sphere, e.g.
15 Vin alternative
16 Jungle painter Rousseau
17 Some root vegetables
18 It rode out the storm
19 Moved hesitantly
20 Start of a quip about roulette
23 "Fire away"
26 Packed away
27 Wagner heroine
28 Quip (Part 2)
32 USSR news agency
33 Noted spokescat
34 Frat recruiting event
36 Kind of geometry
37 Visceral
38 Campus near Mt. Holyoke
43 World Series of Poker airer
45 Film about teeth?
46 "Blue Tail Fly" singer Burl
50 Quip (Part 3)
52 Good test grade
54 "Ixnay"
55 Sailor's back
56 End of the quip
60 Select group
61 Geisha's tie
62 Sex appeal
66 Kitchen device
67 Impair

68 God-loving
69 Cause of a rude awakening?
70 Last word, often
71 Wasn't vigilant

DOWN
1 Spot for a rat race?
2 Rage
3 Farrah's one-time husband
4 Naysaying
5 Discard
6 Pop goer
7 Snowshoe, e.g.
8 Hearty laughs
9 Masticates
10 Extremely popular
11 Bassett of "Waiting to Exhale"
12 Engenders
13 Moves like a crab
21 Western Indians
22 Sets one's sights
23 They give you your money's worth
24 "Skedaddle!"
25 Wallenda family patriarch
29 Start for a threesome
30 Under the table
31 Word with dry or flat
35 Hip toys?
37 Dean's List meas.
39 It may clean your sole
40 Prefix with lung or marine
41 Hang ten
42 Word with heaven

44 Eye nuisance
45 College Board exam
46 Draws conclusions
47 String quartet string
48 Met legend Caruso
49 Trend ending
51 Complete

53 Limerick starter
57 Flop
58 Where the auction is
59 Stir up
63 Curly and Shemp's brother
64 White-furred seal, perhaps
65 V-E Day president

21
SALUTE
By Alex Cole

ACROSS

1 Epistles writer
5 Deli creations
9 Rose oil, e.g.
14 Korbut of gymnastics
15 Siouan
16 Aquatic bird
17 Whiskey ingredient
18 Ice sheet asea
19 Ear-related
20 Sign at many a driveway
23 Bitsy opening
24 Stocking stuffer
25 Certain bank quote
28 Professional org. since 1847
30 Entranced
34 Man-mouse link
35 Darned introduction?
37 Prefix meaning "one thousandth"
38 Padres, e.g.
41 Silly
42 Barely sufficient
43 Way to go, briefly
44 Haggling topic
45 Mouse's reception
46 Great depression
48 Bygone school event
50 Skitter
51 You may have a vote in it
59 Notched, as a leaf
60 They may inhibit sound thinking
61 Harmless, as threats

62 Danny's daughter, Phil's wife
63 Water, in Seville
64 Common mixer
65 Sojourns
66 Frat alternative
67 Hysteria curber, sometimes

DOWN

1 Ceremonial elegance
2 Pertaining to wings
3 Certain large fruit
4 View from the Baltic Sea
5 Easygoing marketing technique
6 Newsman Garrick
7 Fleischer's Betty
8 Divination practitioner
9 Visibly shocked
10 John Wayne classic
11 Guam, for one (Abbr.)
12 Blind as ___
13 Be dependent (on)
21 Dress-code concern
22 Pay attachment
25 "Doonesbury" or "Garfield," e.g.
26 You may pour it down the sink
27 Hindu princes (Var.)
28 One way to be taken
29 Prefix with byte or buck
31 On one's toes
32 Word with fashion or dinner
33 Kitchen counter?
36 ___ majeste
37 Measuring system
39 Furtively

40 Well-known recruiter
45 Clean-air org.
47 Overhead storage sites
49 Snacks with three layers
50 Bakery staple
51 Some are priceless
52 Middle of QED

53 Writer/director Ephron
54 Balloon variety
55 Breakfast food brand
56 "American ___"
57 Spicy Spanish stew
58 Less-than-average tide

22
END OF TIME
By Scot Ober

ACROSS

1 Eyeball
5 Skeptic's grain
9 Mister's analogue
14 Verifiable
15 Lobster portion
16 Fight site
17 What a busboy clears?
20 "Intimations of Immortality," e.g.
21 Orthopedist's tool
22 Initial start
23 Does likewise
24 Worst kind of loser
25 Didn't merely grow
28 Mother follower
29 Gallivant
32 Pertaining to an arm bone
33 Part of an old phone
34 What's more
35 Not quite a ten
38 Hits the road
39 Fine finish
40 Bert's buddy
41 More than -er
42 Quarry
43 Handsome lad of myth
44 Bricklaying gear
45 Semicircles
46 Reliquary, perhaps
49 Icelandic literary work
50 Forbiddance
53 Marshal's duty
56 Fit to be tied

57 Unnamed auth.
58 One is "Come here often?"
59 Some shirts
60 Warsaw, for one
61 Skedaddled

DOWN

1 Sgt. Snorkel's dog
2 Deg. holder
3 Service-station service
4 River in Northern California
5 Reached home
6 Sporty cars, familiarly
7 Like some petticoats
8 A quarter of eight
9 With little potential for further growth
10 Rugged ridge
11 Iniquitous places
12 Pay to hold hands
13 It holds a yard
18 Maven
19 Noggin
23 Build a reserve of
24 Wet bars?
25 1944-45 battle
26 Bread spreads
27 Commencement
28 Like a dryer's trap
29 1962 and 1998 orbiter
30 PC character set
31 Lavishes affection
33 Has the courage to try
34 Spherical coifs

36 Set, as cement
37 Terminal figure?
42 Deliverers of express mail?
43 Zealous
44 Aware of, slangily
45 Like some committees
46 Pass over
47 Apt lunch for Superman

48 Kind of number
49 Sicilian mount
50 It's often posted
51 Embarrassing problem to face?
52 Have to have
54 It may be between your teeth
55 Polar assistant

23
IN THE ALLEY
By Cathy Kline

ACROSS

1 Hippocratic pronouncement
5 Type of whale
10 Contents of some banks
14 Nolo contendere, e.g.
15 Indoor plant areas, perhaps
16 Exuberance
17 Evidence of a poor assembly
19 Suffer from lack of water
20 Kind of talk or rally
21 Reversals of fortune
23 Some don't leave work without it
26 Table prop
28 Joan of Arc's crime
29 Nottingham nemesis
31 One's Big, another's Little
34 Type of rug
35 Place to pass the baton
40 Some labor union ultimatums
43 In an extremely large manner
44 Aegean and Beaufort
45 St. Paul's birthplace
47 Life of Riley
48 Whalebone
52 Certain brain size
54 T. follower
55 Trojan War hero
58 Mao ___-tung
60 Exclude
61 Be minutely precise
66 Number of muses
67 Sam or Alistair
68 Laugh-a-minute

69 Could be chem. or mech.
70 Put into a database
71 Stead

DOWN

1 Saturn's spouse
2 Gran Paradiso, for one
3 Sympathy partner
4 King David's instrument
5 Drained of energy
6 Link between home and school, briefly
7 Gets it all wrong
8 Ceremonial event
9 Editorial-page feature
10 Thermos inventor James
11 Carroll character
12 Some diplomatic doings
13 Unable to sit still
18 Dragon roll ingredient
22 Transparent gem
23 Deep divide
24 Large artery
25 Dutch South Africans
27 Construction site sight
30 Awards-night platform
32 Pizzeria shovels
33 Emphasize
36 Be revolting?
37 Lend ___ (pay close attention)
38 Type of fire
39 Historical region of England
41 March fliers
42 Dissipate

46 Irish dog
48 Daniel or Pat
49 Kind of asst.
50 Breaking a commandment
51 Perfumer's compound
53 Bone china component
56 "... ___ a midnight dreary"

57 It welcomes change
59 Sandwich man?
62 Part of Tina Turner's revue
63 "Rocky ___" (1982)
64 Caviar, literally
65 Alphabet trioacross

24
DRIVE ON
By Allan E. Parrish

ACROSS
1 Entrance for extraction
5 LeBron James' team, in brief
9 One-time Turkish title
14 Jean Renoir's "La ___ Humaine"
15 1973 embargo org.
16 Antonym of love
17 Allege as fact
18 Barr, ___, Ashcroft
19 Put forth minimal effort
20 Investor's purchase, perhaps
23 ___ Moines, Iowa
24 Safe at home
25 Exercise based on karate
27 Wedding reception tradition
30 Movie credit displays
33 Misanthrope, e.g.
36 "Salvation" novelist
38 Lie alongside
39 Havana residue
40 Drank copiously
43 Cheer for the torero
44 Military transportation, perhaps
46 Lotion ingredient
47 Prepare a surfboard, e.g.
49 Buffoonery
51 Item on a rod
53 Much-discussed layer
55 Provides with an office
59 Hoedown date
61 Perry Mason's secretary
64 Clerical vestment
66 Erratic evasive movements
67 Poi source

68 State tree of Texas
69 Bit of chatroom shorthand
70 "Happy motoring!" was its slogan
71 Wield
72 Israeli statesman
73 Filled with import

DOWN
1 Precalculator calculators
2 English cattle
3 Gossipy squibs
4 Little housewrecker
5 Pupil covering
6 Bronx Zoo denizens
7 Unburden oneself
8 Move along quickly
9 Green Bay celebrity
10 All of the blood-type letters
11 Spar without a partner
12 Stockings
13 A&E word
21 They mingle at landfills
22 Secret stockpile
26 Pasture plaint
28 Jib, for example
29 Letter-shaped opening
31 "To Sir, With Love" vocalist
32 Procedure part
33 Muslim pilgrimage
34 Perplexed
35 One-time Sting operation?
37 Role for Liz
41 "True Grit" Oscar winner

42 Resided
45 Dispensed candy
48 Gave a warning
50 Squirrel or porcupine, e.g.
52 Smith's partner
54 Segar who created Popeye
56 Put a halt to
57 Brusque

58 Urban social site
59 Rubberneck
60 Wall St. acronym
62 Souvlaki ingredient
63 Turkish title
65 End for 20, 61-Across, and 11, 29, 35-Down

25
FASTEN YOUR SEATBELT
By Alan Olschwang

ACROSS
1 Greedy sort
4 Tossed dishes
10 In vigorous health
14 Enero to diciembre
15 Tamable cat
16 Norway's patron saint
17 It may be used to get things started
19 Exude slowly
20 Sanyo competitor
21 Boggy wasteland
22 Primp
23 Certain diacritical mark
25 Driver's helper, briefly
26 The Apennines, for one
33 Zeroed (in)
35 Royal races locale
36 Powerful lobbying org.
37 "Time's Arrow" novelist
38 "The In-Laws" actor
39 Mayberry character
40 A place to spend the night
41 Ink ingredient
42 Damp
43 Storm phenomenon, sometimes
46 Galena or mispickel
47 Indian nursemaids
49 Baked brick
52 It gets marked up
55 A Cobb
57 Run or hide, e.g.
58 Medicine chest item
60 If not

61 Depression vendors' wares
62 Noted TV cousin
63 Some classic cars
64 Gets a new lawn
65 Mayday! Mayday!

DOWN
1 One bear
2 Alaskan native
3 Take a dip
4 Word with sister or story
5 Sagacity
6 Apollo's mother
7 A choir member
8 Site for a bell
9 RR stop
10 Old-fashioned "Yippee!"
11 Cosmetic ingredient, often
12 Pass the time idly
13 Without advantage or disadvantage
18 Circles in some religious paintings
22 Diplomatic accomplishment
24 Flop
25 Soon, ere now
27 Tibia connections
28 Invite to enter
29 ___ on the cake
30 Exact opposite
31 Eye membrane
32 Boss Tweed's lampooner
33 Salute with enthusiasm
34 It means everything

38 First-rate
39 "C'est magnifique!"
41 To be, in Toulon
42 Everyone has one
44 Watterson tiger
45 Surrounded, as with light
48 Altercation
49 Declare

50 Mark for removal
51 Approximately
52 Make do
53 It may precede a crash
54 WWII battle locale
56 Whirlpool outlets
58 Road cover
59 Ltr. addenda

26
LETTERS TO ROME
By Elizabeth C. Gorski

ACROSS

1 J. Fred Muggs was one
6 Cried "uncle!"
10 Old hands
14 Eagle's destination, sometimes
15 Man who made cars for indoors
16 It was once circulated
17 Nudges
18 Grommet
19 Hungry for more
20 Golf great, in Old Rome?
22 Show respect, in a way
23 Work after hours
25 Kind of dog
26 Famed movie studio
29 Dog days mo.
30 Boutique
32 Periods of note
34 Some appliances
36 Sponsorships (Var.)
40 Go yachting in Old Rome?
43 Waterborne
44 Game with 108 cards
45 Corn syrup brand
46 Type of school
48 Scorpius' heavenly neighbor
50 He's under wraps?
51 Wood cutter
54 Some fast planes
57 Chuckleheads
59 They may be smiling in a song, in Old Rome?
63 Violist's clef, perhaps

64 "Oh, sure, that could really happen!"
65 Units in physics
66 Neatnik's opposite
67 Site of a wreck, perhaps
68 Pertaining to birth
69 See at a distance
70 Mini-whirlpool
71 Serious play

DOWN

1 Spit relative
2 Mister, in Mainz
3 Word with will or fist
4 Calf-length skirts
5 100 centimos
6 "Aw shucks!"
7 Ring around a lagoon
8 Some chamber music instruments
9 Clairvoyance initialism
10 Scheme
11 Splits apart
12 Bracket-braced window
13 Despondently
21 It's known as the best medicine
22 IRA's kin
24 Tipper and Al, in invitations
26 Black Hills formation
27 1999 French Open champ
28 It may be registered
31 Stop on "moe"
33 Trough fill

35 Moo ___ pork
37 Jazz singing style
38 Earth tone
39 Kilt-wearer
41 Waterproof canvases, e.g.
42 When to tell the boss you'll be there
47 Composed
49 Within easy reach
51 Defame

52 They wear very little clothing?
53 "Legs" rock trio
55 Jimmied
56 Ravi's instrument
58 "___ Dooby" (Roy Orbison hit)
60 Teensy bit
61 Mosque man
62 Spanish isle
64 Common verb conjugation

27
DOLLARS AND SENSE
By Lynn Lempel

ACROSS

1 Swell reason to stay in bed?
6 Bell or shell start
10 Genghis or Kublai
14 Garret
15 Title character in a Tom Hanks film
16 Fabled loser
17 Start of a quip about financial planning
20 It may be over your head
21 Illumination unit
22 Tackle box contents
23 Bethlehem sellout
24 Persnickety one
26 Caroline, to Ted
29 Obedience-school word
31 Katmandu's country
33 Ooze
34 Sawbones' gp.
36 King who Christianized Norway
38 Legacy from an X and Y
39 Middle of the quip
43 "The Daily Show" host Stewart
44 Microscope part
45 Stretch with no fed. holidays
46 Political competition, e.g.
48 Single-masted vessel
50 Peace of mind
54 Kind of pad
56 Dissertation forerunner
58 Remiss
59 Dolt
61 Tigger's pal

62 Color additive
63 End of the quip
67 Frame of mind
68 Person with a list
69 Skirt style
70 Claim on some orange juice cartons
71 Stupefy, in a way
72 Man of La Mancha

DOWN

1 Singer Johnny
2 Hammarskjold's successor
3 Sicilian tourist lure
4 Thanksgiving finale
5 It may itch
6 Hi and Lois' baby
7 Vote from a pro
8 Deal you'll get no credit for?
9 Aware of
10 Casual slacks
11 Yokels
12 Creative output
13 New beginning?
18 Family identifiers
19 Carried the day
25 Program-provider
27 It was made of steel in 1943
28 Gov. air-monitor
30 Chew the fat
32 Scheme
35 Blanc of cartoons
37 Grippe
39 Drawbridge site

40 One known for forbearance
41 One on the sidelines
42 Period
43 Some namesakes, for short
47 Make hard to figure out
49 Propelling with poles
51 Second man on the moon
52 Refuses, in a way

53 Tolkien's college at Oxford
55 Electrical resistance unit
57 Some are sleepers
60 Anti-drinking gp.
63 Young rascal
64 Old French coin
65 Artesian water
66 Stopover in la mer

28
STATUE CREATION
By Raymond Hamel

ACROSS

1 Softball officials, briefly
5 Lacking imagination
10 Lumpy mass
14 Digit end
15 Borscht server
16 Like edible fruit
17 Step one of an invention
18 Frank option
19 It may be upped
20 Not easily changed
23 One who rules the roast
24 Carpentry tool
27 Mortgage points, e.g.
28 "Green Acres" wife
32 Arboreal snake
33 Goal of crunches
36 Film lioness
40 Hoover handle?
41 Break cleanly
42 JELL-O dish
45 Apple's G4, perhaps
46 Mme. Bovary
47 Some notebooks, briefly
50 Cure baldness?
53 Koran creed
55 Cooking device
59 Striker's anathema
61 "Survivor" unit
62 Definitely not good
63 Participate in an ice sport
64 Visibly elated
65 Marsala meat
66 ___ dixit

67 Take on a new resident
68 Makes a mistake

DOWN

1 Worldwide relief org.
2 Tussauds' title
3 14th U.S. president
4 "Amistad" extra
5 Walk with weariness
6 Wife of a rajah
7 Mythical creator of the cosmos
8 Make use of boots
9 Gossipy gal
10 Some family reunion members (Var.)
11 Umpire's assistant
12 Be decisive
13 Domesticated insect
21 They may be shocking
22 Part of a big spender's phrase
25 Palindromic pop group
26 Tarantula's nemesis
29 Glaciated
30 Dishwasher's sinkful
31 Plankton components
34 Source of dates
35 Car on rails
36 Arab royalty
37 Temporal ___
38 Racing collectibles
39 Cute
43 Gets through great effort
44 Award delivery site
47 Certain wading bird

48 Expensive eggs
49 Is repulsive, in a way
51 Oil from flower petals
52 Sad song
54 Canyon of the comics

56 Small brook
57 Double-reed instrument
58 Colorful salamander
59 ___-fi
60 Cake or board starter

29
BUY, BUY, BUY
By Diane C. Baldwin

ACROSS
1 Skirt-chaser
5 Hardy heroine
9 Dog-tired
14 Samson's pride
15 Beehive State
16 By-the-fireside drink
17 Podded vegetable
18 Microwave, colloquially
19 Brought on board
20 Ad enticement
23 Magic bullet
24 Fail to keep
25 Bright, as a pupil
28 Hybrid fuel
31 Good buddies' gear
34 Speak ugly of
36 Speak lovingly
37 Borscht veggie
38 Ad warning
42 Service sign-off
43 Stick in a hall?
44 Limiting word
45 Pretty pitiful
46 Station-house reading
49 Lead-in to a sheepish excuse
50 Pod spherule
51 Succulent emollient
53 Ad come-on
60 Jaw protrusion
61 Leif's pa
62 Type of bargain
63 Rock concert venue
64 Clear breach
65 Duffer's handful
66 Fake drake
67 Gridiron officials
68 It can pull a team together

DOWN
1 Stop, on the trail
2 Trees sacred to Druids
3 Former Italian currency
4 Former French currency
5 Arctic treeless plain
6 Some musical compositions
7 Rice beverage
8 Jettison
9 Grouper assembly
10 Essential meaning
11 Linen hue
12 Turn-downs
13 Shaver
21 Goose egg
22 It works when pushed
25 Brother of Menoetius
26 Word with donna or ballerina
27 Brought under control
29 Double quartet
30 ___ polloi
31 Word on a nickel
32 Contradict
33 Kind of manual
35 Be gluttonous, e.g.
37 Voyage preceder
39 Brilliant success
40 Batman and Robin, e.g.
41 They replaced guilders

46 Double-cross
47 Duty
48 Votes in
50 Cliburn's instrument
52 Drain to the bottom
53 Abraded
54 Novelist Waugh

55 Title for Helmut Kohl
56 Superior neighbor
57 Ersatz butter
58 Smell to high heaven
59 Life of Riley
60 Certifiable

30
HOME OF THE BRAVE
By Elizabeth C. Gorski

ACROSS
1 Trappist, e.g.
5 They're on the books
9 Chicago daily, familiarly
13 "Take ___ leave . . . "
14 Oahu adieu
16 Improve, as skills
17 City southeast of Milan
18 Descend into dementia
19 It can be private
20 Serves more than one purpose
23 Makes jubilant
24 Assumed command
25 "___ Clown" (Porter)
27 Archaeologist's find
28 Al Fatah's gp.
30 Radial footprint
32 Like the things that belong to us
35 Protagonist
36 Promise
39 En route to England, maybe
41 Recorded
42 Their dishes may be fancy
44 Olive that goes with a little salt?
45 It was tested on Bikini, 1954
50 "Say what?"
51 Water, to Monet
53 Inquiry for a lost package
54 Lifestyle magazine
58 Troupe's itinerary
59 Exceedingly caustic
60 All atwitter
61 Ambiance

62 Defense grp. abolished in 1977
63 It's within your range
64 ___-bitsy
65 Canonized femmes, briefly
66 Word with chin or head

DOWN
1 Less sharp, as cheese
2 "Lord Jim" star Peter
3 "The agreement's off"
4 Olympian Yamaguchi
5 Nigerian city
6 Baseball's Felipe or Moises
7 Where something wonderful is created
8 Gwyneth Paltrow film
9 Traffic sign word
10 Pop flavor
11 12 months from today
12 Night spot
15 "Zip-___-Doo-Dah"
21 Interior design
22 Banned pesticide
26 "Much ___ About Nothing"
28 Articulates
29 High, as goals
31 P, in the Greek alphabet
33 Japanese salad ingredient
34 Alphabetic run
36 1 and 2, e.g.
37 Stumblebum
38 '60s jacket style
39 German exclamation
40 Allow no runs in a victory

43 Clinton, e.g., briefly
46 Maine metropolis
47 Pianist's span
48 Mixes, as companies
49 Bear of Alabama football
52 Some batteries

53 Brouhahas
55 "King Kong" headliner
56 "Phooey!"
57 Allude to
58 ___ chi chu'an

31
NOW'S THE TIME
By Everette Hastings

ACROSS

1 Wan
6 Robinson of song
9 They're kept under wraps
14 The Gold Coast, now
15 Thee, now
16 Sea interrupter
17 Now's the time for . . .
19 Like caramel
20 First name in a Lloyd Webber work
21 Thumb or throat condition, perhaps
22 Weave partner
23 One of a score's two
25 Now's the time for . . .
30 "And hast thou ___ the Jabber-wock?"
32 Sweet sherry
33 Fragrant loop
35 Cupid's mo.
36 Family docs
37 Now's the time for . . .
42 Word with up, out or down
43 Dipsomaniac
44 Surname ascribed to an un-known
45 Legendary
48 Type of cavity
52 Now's the time for a . . .
56 Greek salad ingredient
57 Frequently, poetically
58 Airhead's lack?
60 Word with blind or the cradle

61 Florida bay
64 Now's the time for . . .
66 Completely unfamiliar
67 Word with dry or flat
68 Standard of excellence
69 Common contraction
70 Accolade for a bullfighter
71 Spring features

DOWN

1 Shoelace ends
2 Beach toy
3 Largest city of the West Indies
4 L.A.-to-N.Y. flight path
5 Catches in a dragnet, e.g.
6 Gift to the baby Jesus
7 Beverly Hills Drive
8 Pension beginning?
9 Male for sale
10 Barometric line
11 Worker at Mel's diner
12 Golf hole start
13 Type of pen
18 Five-ring org.
22 Failed miserably
24 Place for a cooling pie
26 Normandy city
27 Chant at a fraternity party?
28 Glimpse
29 Dashed-off message?
31 Born, on the society pages
34 Enclosure
35 Belong
37 A presidential power

38 The whole nine yards
39 Compulsive's list-heading
40 Ampersand follower, often
41 Unlistening
42 What a hippie may have dropped
46 Begin again, as a debate
47 Pablum consumer
49 Composer Rachmaninoff
50 Lacking a musical quality

51 Mailing supply
53 Synagogue
54 Send to seventh heaven
55 Bottom-line amount
59 Grand in scope
61 Wee bit
62 He worked on canvases
63 Halfway
64 Lover's sound
65 "Much ___ About Nothing"

32
MONEY MATTERS
By Robert H. Wolfe

ACROSS

1 Like some hard-to-reach goals
6 Large combo
11 Golden Fleece source
14 First name among noted artists
15 Chicken part
16 Words at a union meeting?
17 Tiny alteration?
19 One way to follow a pattern
20 Stick like glue
21 Lowdown joint?
23 Nocturnal observer
26 Melody
27 Added pizzazz to
28 Hunter's supply, perhaps
30 Singer Easton
32 "Love Story" author
33 Word with "imagine" or "fancy"
34 Monumental
37 Lake Urmia locale
38 Enjoys a sloop
39 Marceau, for one
40 Slippery and slithery
41 "But only God can make a ___" (Kilmer)
42 Forget-me-not feature
43 One who hems but doesn't haw
45 Printed page count
46 Caterer's warmer
48 Charge
49 Tennis stratagem
50 Chinese herbivore
51 Bullfighter
54 "Go on . . ."

55 Latex restaurant bill?
60 It changes locks
61 American carrier
62 Boredom
63 It's part of a head
64 To the point
65 Gave medicine

DOWN

1 Good times
2 Former war zone, familiarly
3 Corp. job requirement, often
4 First lady of scat
5 Blabbed
6 Questionnaire option
7 Burn a bit
8 Pea picker?
9 You can beat it
10 1940 Karloff film
11 Perilous seat of government?
12 Fred's sister
13 Leveled a lawn
18 Greek letters
22 What the Padres start
23 Late actor Davis
24 Reporter's word
25 Legitimate barkeeper?
27 Mathematical groups
29 Whistle cord
30 More timid
31 In vigorous health
33 Pacific island herb
35 Insect stage
36 Famous person, briefly

38 D-Day town
42 Like some navels
44 Getting nowhere fast
45 Offensive expression
46 Garden tool
47 Tucker or Roberts
48 French brother

51 Outdoor lift
52 Sashes
53 "It can't be!"
56 Take advantage of
57 Two of nine?
58 Shuffleboard stick
59 Joke around

33
IN THE PAN

By Fred Jackson III

ACROSS

1 Letters on a radio
5 Nasal membranes
10 Typical Three Stooges response
14 Festive soiree
15 Committee type
16 Architect Saarinen
17 Desktop object
18 Impossible to miss
20 Rifles
22 Member of the 500-homer club
23 Playbook play
25 Conversation filler
26 Some surgical tools
28 Winter vehicle
33 Smith biopic
35 They start
37 "Doctor Zhivago" heroine
38 Enter cyberspace
40 Fruity quaff suffix
41 Henry Wells' partner
42 Turkish general (Var.)
43 Kind of decoration or arrangement
45 Permissable actions
46 Parlor piece, perhaps
48 Send back to a lower court
50 High marks?
52 Bad thing to be at the wheel
55 Subscription cards, e.g.
59 "I ___ Rhapsody"
60 Out-of-date magazine issue
64 McLean's sitcom co-star

65 Mercury's ankle attachments
66 Worker's wish
67 Theatrical trappings
68 Some lab stock
69 Advanced with care
70 Famed ancient metropolis

DOWN

1 Gracefully athletic
2 Georgia city
3 Driveway accessory, perhaps
4 Incantatory word
5 One easily taken in
6 Tokyo, once
7 21st Greek letter
8 Hinged implement
9 Caster's selection
10 Word with taught or effacing
11 Table section
12 "Comus" composer
13 Slammer
19 It's well for the French
21 She can be lazy
24 It's not quite gross
25 1968 title role for Vanessa
27 Not so-called
29 Pay stub?
30 He'll give you a hand
31 Mythical sea vessel of note
32 New Mexico art colony
33 Word for Yorick
34 Orchestra alternative
36 Word with pittance or formality

39 Neigh sayer's treat
41 It could precede 18, 60-Across and 3, 30-Down
43 Main attraction
44 Professional org. since 1847
47 Garner
49 N.Y. Mets division
51 Comparable to a wet hen
53 Poetry muse

54 Type of violet
55 Support beam
56 Simba's love in "The Lion King"
57 Singing style
58 Barely makes (with "out")
61 Humongous
62 Compass dir.
63 It stops traffic

34
MOMENT OF TRUTH
By Carol Lachance

ACROSS

1 Ham operator's letter
6 Calf exposure?
10 Greeting from Gleason's bartender
14 Standoffish
15 Latin quarters, perhaps
16 They may get you the upper hand
17 Source of problems
19 Greek letter
20 Seamy matter
21 Fuzzy fruit
22 Porker's haunch
24 Clapper's place
25 Located the source of
29 Cyclops feature
32 Actor's love, perhaps
34 "Shepherd Moons" Grammy winner
35 Tierra del ___
36 "Who, me?"
37 What things may be as much fun as
41 "... boy ___ girl?"
42 Prepares for washing
43 "How now! ___?" (Hamlet)
44 Vichyssoise base
46 Utterances of disapproval
48 Gotland's land
49 Not petit
50 "Get your hands off me!"
51 Melville's curmudgeon
52 Notable 1860s nickname

55 Benefit
58 King novel
61 The Munsters' pet bat
62 Currier's partner
63 Finds favorable
64 Yup's counterpart
65 Something to feather
66 Bring up?

DOWN

1 Folded tortilla
2 Banned McIntosh application
3 Word for the wiser
4 Schmaltz
5 How Alfalfa sings
6 Nasty frown
7 Suborder of gulls
8 An end to sex?
9 The Pequod's harpooner
10 Ecological disaster team
11 Block in a restaurant?
12 "Are we there ___?"
13 Busy ___ bee
18 Crafty Coyote
23 Felonious flames
24 Withstand
26 Land development?
27 "The Sweet Hereafter" director
28 Believers, kinda
29 Dances to jazz
30 Lined up
31 Spin around
32 Clumps
33 Skirt's outskirts

35 Cry while holding an iron?
38 Cosmetologist Lauder
39 Booby hatch
40 "Get Smart" enemy org.
45 Stay attached to
46 International Tennis Hall of Fame inductee
47 Unruly crowd
49 Phantom

51 Grows old gracefully
52 "Puppy Love" singer
53 Sugar source
54 Latin being
55 Fall from grace
56 Way back when
57 Keystone player
59 Forum greeting
60 Black gold

35
PHYSICS LESSON
By Robert H. Wolfe

ACROSS

1 Chimney chaser
6 Dramatic work
10 Lead
14 Pelts
15 Speed competition
16 Cordoba cash
17 ___ the Giant
18 "___ La Douce"
19 From the top
20 Question Isaac Newton may have asked
23 Summer at MIT, e.g.
24 Certain English assignment
25 John Boy, for one
29 "Huh?"
32 Minor area
33 Japanese ancestor worship
38 Newton's question (Part 2)
41 Masseur's concern
42 April 1st victim
43 Isn't wrong?
44 Doesn't possess
46 Inappropriate
50 Three-strikes result
51 Newton's question (Part 3)
59 Culture developer
60 Crooner Paul
61 Choreographer Alvin
62 "Sommersby" star
63 Large juicy fruit
64 Bozo, famously
65 A great lake

66 Bender
67 Fonda film

DOWN

1 Food fish
2 Sot
3 Whirlpool
4 Architect Saarinen
5 False start?
6 Write like a small child
7 Pork fat
8 Apex
9 Orbital period
10 Does an usher's job
11 Albacore and yellowfin
12 Sports venue
13 Rambunctious
21 An ens. may be in it
22 Words with music or work
25 Word on bulbs
26 Late, great netman
27 Property encumbrance
28 Labels
29 Bridge ancestor
30 Top 40 songs
31 Word with takers or day now
33 Explorer Hedin
34 Slays, mob-style
35 "Go Tell ___ the Mountain"
36 "Vamoose!"
37 Thaw
39 Ranch in a Ferber novel

40 "Wheel of Fortune" request, perhaps
44 Follower of Mao
45 Go on the offensive
46 Grammarian's concern
47 African nation
48 Video-game pioneer
49 Blender setting

50 Broadcasting sign
52 Stretched tight
53 "Bus Stop" writer
54 St. of the union
55 Mound
56 Matty, Felipe or Moises
57 Salamander
58 A bit of force

36
SOUNDS GREAT!
By Ron Halverson

ACROSS
1 Word with who, what or where
5 Subdued
10 Pump, e.g.
14 Completely convinced
15 Model's asset
16 Grabbed by force
17 "Smoking hasn't affected me a bit . . ."
20 Basis of reasoning
21 Lightens the load
22 Choice words?
23 Iron attachment
25 Thunderstruck
29 Serb or Croat, e.g.
30 War stat
33 Loathsome one
34 Nonchalant
35 Auberge
36 "Hand me that fly swatter . . ."
40 Lemon addition
41 Polly and Rhody
42 "The Magic Mountain" locale
43 Abe's son
44 ___ ex machina
45 Loss of the certifiable
47 Be nostalgic for
48 That lady yonder
49 Poker phrase
52 Prevent from being seen
56 "Let's see your swan dive . . ."
60 Sacrum or radius
61 Place for a Chicago touchdown?
62 Kind of pool

63 City north of Des Moines
64 Zephyrs, e.g.
65 Carangid fish

DOWN
1 Computer key
2 Closed circuit
3 Talk like a toper
4 Drop-off spot
5 Casual garment
6 Accrue
7 They might squeak by
8 Antlered critter
9 Morning deposit
10 Home extension
11 Tills the soil
12 Flow oh so slowly
13 ___ out (barely gets)
18 Med. insurance groups
19 Billows
23 Where one makes the grade
24 Secure with cord
25 Casey was here
26 Mild Holland cheese
27 Terrorized pledges, in a way
28 Wood-shaping tool
29 Taj Mahal attractions?
30 Vanilli's partner
31 Unfitting
32 Fidgety
34 Additional remuneration
37 Kind of pool
38 Spectrum bands
39 No-star review

45 Common, horse and sixth
46 Spot for a keystone
47 Lode abodes
48 Hidden cache
49 Benny and three others
50 Hover threateningly
51 Script unit

52 Family group
53 Roe
54 Baldwin or Waugh
55 Russian spacecraft series
57 Farm mother
58 Upsilon follower
59 River bottom

37
TAX CREDITS
By Randall J. Hartman

ACROSS

1 Commit a coup d'etat
6 Preamble
11 Court bisector
14 Come to a point
15 Five of a kind
16 Words with pickle or jam
17 Start of a quip
19 Avenue of exposure for many artists
20 Mother ptarmigan, e.g.
21 Chihuahua cash
22 Church pinnacle
24 First name in life vests
25 Rock on the edge
26 More of the quip
32 Colorful chalcedony
33 Some fallout
34 Global extreme
35 Where jewelry is often exchanged
36 It may have fallen on a foot
40 Much-impersonated star
41 Configuration
42 More of the quip
47 Cheep substitutes?
48 "I object!"
49 Calgary Stampede, for one
50 Ship of the desert
53 ___-mo replay
56 Have title to
57 End of the quip
60 Seek redress

61 They're in the banks along the Seine
62 Letter on a screen
63 Engage in espionage
64 Some paper quantities
65 Dustin's role in "Midnight Cowboy"

DOWN

1 Where many Mormons live
2 Wise person
3 Abreast of
4 M.L.K. title
5 Get ready
6 Fleming and Paisley
7 Captain of the Nautilus
8 Family follower
9 Howard of "American Graffiti"
10 Kickoffs
11 Aircraft fleet named after an admiral
12 Dining selection
13 Cheers, notably
18 Swamp thing
23 Architect of the Rock and Roll Hall of Fame
24 Adam, to Eve
25 Hippodrome section
26 Emulate Nelly
27 It may be inflated with hot air
28 Guy's companion
29 Round of applause, e.g.
30 Sean of "The Lord of the Rings"

31 Many a climactic movie scene
35 Some microbrewery offerings
36 Bounty bellow
37 Cheerleader's cry
38 Big Four firm employee (Abbr.)
39 "For ___ a jolly good fellow"
40 Endue
41 Storm protection
42 Not like this clue
43 Outperform
44 Poitier of film
45 Bauxite or galena
46 Stimulate
50 "Fame" singer Irene
51 Elemental building block
52 Feel the lack of
53 Type of card game
54 Maui necklaces
55 Capital on a fjord
58 Chromaticity
59 Doctors' org.

38
SLUGFEST
By Bonnie L. Gentry

ACROSS

1 Pisan pronoun
5 Substantive part
9 Dome-shaped do
13 Subject of introspection
14 Top-flight
15 Hardly colorful
16 It often ends with a pun
19 It may be hitched
20 -osis : -oses :: -y : -___
21 Tyrolean refrain
22 John's dance partner in "Pulp Fiction"
23 It's pressed for cash
24 Based on theory
26 Completely wasted
29 Say one's piece
30 Heroine of "Last Days of Pompeii"
31 It's dropped
34 Trevi filler, once
35 Fashionable Geoffrey
37 Sociologist Shere
38 Agent's due
39 Only about 10 percent of it is visible
40 Whoop it up
41 Dawdle
44 List for hubby
47 Collector's suffix
48 Kidnapping org. of 1974
49 Seat of Marion County, Florida
50 Babylonian god of the sky
51 What Simon does

52 Without a clue
56 Symbol of silence
57 Burns' hillside
58 Luke's sister
59 Duffer's target
60 Some are jam-packed
61 Dentist's request

DOWN

1 Frozen snack
2 Use Western Union, say
3 Type of plum
4 Texans' org.
5 Bully's dare
6 Geologic divisions
7 Year, south of the border
8 Gumshoe
9 Append
10 Ringbearer of film and fiction
11 Autumn toiler
12 Old manuscript markings
17 Kin kin
18 Mr. Mister song named after a prayer
19 Nureyev or Friml
23 Took in a poor boy
24 The King's middle name
25 You can see right through it
27 Compass hdg.
28 San follower
31 Pretends to be something one's not
32 "Rikki Don't Lose That Number" group

33 River formations
35 It's drawn with a rifle?
36 "In conclusion"
37 Playboy Hugh, familiarly
39 Scopes prosecutor
40 Pretoria's land (Abbr.)
41 Remove, as a calcium compound
42 Port in the Loire Valley
43 Sufficient, in Dogpatch

44 Moonshiner's wares
45 Prefix for "eye"
46 Present at birth
50 At some distance
51 Penetrate slowly
53 Pres. with a ranch
54 A strike-out makes it go down
55 U.N. agcy. promoting social justice

39
UNEQUAL SEQUELS
By Eugene Newman

ACROSS
1 Aggressively virile
6 Around the bend
10 Didn't merely pass
14 Sharp-tongued
15 Notion
16 Dress type
17 Film about the Von Trapp family dog?
20 First word of "Nowhere Man"
21 Wayside places
22 Gladden
23 Noble Italian family
24 Burroughs' heroine
26 Film about a failed surgery?
33 Cyberperiodicals, familiarly
34 More than intuition
35 Commotion
36 Bygone auto adornment
37 Powerful blows
39 UV index monitor
40 ___ about (approximately)
42 Word with shaving or mess
43 Makes out
45 Film about the great Chianti caper?
49 Moving vehicles
50 Effectively treat
51 Taunted
54 It may be saved for you
55 Money's money source
58 Film about a career janitor?
62 Iron and Bronze, e.g.
63 Male raccoon

64 Miss Doolittle
65 Orbital point
66 Mollycoddle
67 Bill addendum

DOWN
1 Calculating subject
2 Word with neck or belly
3 Civic boundaries?
4 Elizabeth II's monogram
5 Some wind players
6 Old World finch
7 Payout determiner, perhaps
8 Top exec
9 Dunderhead
10 Talismans
11 Durango dwelling
12 It's taken when leaving
13 High roller's need
18 Biblical preposition
19 A choice location
23 Cardiologist's instrument (Abbr.)
24 Be jocular
25 Creatures on some Egyptian relics
26 Cloud
27 Acid type
28 Church regulation
29 Former British PM
30 Gestation stations
31 Become edible, in a way
32 Eliminate
37 Shirt opponent

38 Humorists
41 PRNDL pick
43 Exemplar of lightness
44 Piercing tool
46 Dry streambed
47 Working hypothesis
48 Preliminary contest
51 FBI agent
52 Shakespearean villain
53 Sired
54 Wild guess
55 In the thick of
56 Sleep lightly
57 Rigging support
59 Wane
60 Words with "number on"
61 First name in pharmaceuticals

40
MENSWEAR
By Gary Cooper

ACROSS
1 Hotel section
6 Athletes look for it
10 Renowned pole explorer
14 Busy American airport
15 Major in astronomy?
16 Beastly bellow
17 Last layer of paint
19 Change for Chirac
20 Glad rags
21 The 12th of 26
22 Netanyahu's predecessor
23 They run and leap in Portland
27 Like some motors
30 Thumbs-up review
31 Balanchine's specialty
32 Junior, e.g.
36 "What was ___ think?"
37 Corn holder, perhaps
38 Amy's sister
39 In the next place
43 Under par
46 Steady
47 Gives abilities to
48 Entomologist's apparel?
52 At full speed
53 "___ death do us ..."
54 Shoe saver
58 Emulated Quasimodo
59 Apollo 13 gear
62 Monopoly components
63 Blow the whistle
64 Idolized sports figures
65 Luge, e.g.
66 Master of locks
67 Plant parts

DOWN
1 Choir perch
2 Mississippi tributary
3 Loud noise
4 English seaport
5 Toady's answer
6 Big name in geometry circles
7 Whimsically humorous
8 Fed. purchasing org.
9 "Mangia"
10 They blow through the jasmine of my mind
11 "___ Sixteen" (Ringo Starr)
12 Less plentiful
13 Smelting refuse
18 Valentine's Day symbol
22 Surface
24 Field part
25 Muffin option
26 Crook's escape
27 Heron's relative
28 NBA great Thurmond
29 United nations, e.g.
32 Aye alternative
33 "Jake's Thing" writer Kingsley
34 County on the Strait of Dover
35 Popover ingredients
37 ___-Napoca, Romania
40 "Thanks" (with "much")
41 Atomic number 10
42 Thieving bird

43 Tarsus site
44 Common contraction
45 Iceberg is one type
47 Site of a cold snap?
48 Fabric measures
49 Virus carrier, sometimes
50 One of a knight's arms

51 Even a bit
55 Run rampant
56 Sicilian landmark
57 Start of North Carolina's motto
59 Unkempt abode
60 Fairy tale veggie
61 "___ boom bah!"

41
BOO!
By Randall J. Hartman

ACROSS
1 Jacket border
4 Completely change
10 "Fernando" singers
14 He sits on the bench in L.A.
15 Aviator Earhart
16 One of three squares
17 Campfire tale
19 Scat queen Fitzgerald
20 Fit as a fiddle
21 Understands
22 Crater mouths
23 Captures
26 Squad car
28 Longtime Pennsylvania senator
34 Minor worker
37 Time's Man of the Year, 1977
38 He gets lost in the crowd
39 Creole cookery pod
41 Add a lane to
43 ". . . would thou hadst ___ been born" ("Othello")
44 Serengeti antelope
46 Spent
48 Curve of a ship's planking
49 Nickelodeon series
52 Point-of-honor settler
53 Eclipse phenomenon
57 Mean business?
59 Invisible emanation
63 Bring up
64 Merino's coat
65 It's at the foot of Mount St. Helens

68 Additional
69 Role for Courteney Cox
70 Large cask
71 Sax object
72 Fished with a hook
73 "___ Pinafore"

DOWN
1 States of euphoria
2 Green Mountain Boys leader Allen
3 Simoleons
4 Betrayer
5 Middle of summer?
6 Examines, as a contract
7 Skin cream ingredient, often
8 Bog
9 Settles a debt
10 League of Angels
11 Puts down
12 Soothing ointment
13 Expression of pity
18 Antitoxins
24 Where MDs and RNs stay busy
25 Cabbage side
27 Just in
29 Mike's mother-in-law
30 Gymnast Comaneci
31 Back in the navy
32 Haydn's "The Creation" setting
33 Calhoun of filmdom
34 What Vassar became in 1969
35 Kan. neighbor
36 Extravagant

40 Declared invalid
42 They catch acrobats
45 Change bland to blond?
47 Homer Simpson expletive
50 Type of TV
51 Earthy deposit
54 Browne's "cure of all diseases"
55 Plumber's filler

56 Small songbirds
57 Ablutionary vessel
58 Mouse's cousin
60 Fairy tale's second word
61 It holds the key
62 Seed integument
66 Water you may walk on
67 Shaver

42
WITHHOLDING JUDGMENT
By Ben Tausig

ACROSS
1 Kramer of "Seinfeld"
6 Utility abbr.
10 Navy noncoms
14 Type of cuisine
15 Dinner side
16 Tops
17 Antiquing agents
18 Caucus site
19 Attack, as a fly
20 Quote from "The Philadelphia Story"
23 Rock layers
24 Chimney coat
25 "Stop!" graphically
28 Wind up or down
30 Who and Howser, briefly
31 James Clavell's "____-Pan"
32 Bungee jumper's feeling
36 Clumsy one
38 Display histrionics
40 Middle of the quote
44 Triple trio
45 Bridal bio word
46 Swiss giants
47 Corp. conclusion?
48 "The Polar Express" extra
51 Helium, e.g.
53 Prefix with con
54 Police action
56 Up-to-the-minute
61 End of the quote
64 Bit of wampum, perhaps
66 Knight fight

67 Name on many gimme caps
68 Husband or wife
69 Stable staples
70 They help you get a leg up
71 Small songbird
72 It's often staged
73 Cathedral features

DOWN
1 Fireside followers
2 "There ___ to be a law!"
3 Elvis expression
4 Santa ___, Colombia
5 Type of inspection
6 Cleveland's body of water
7 Plunders
8 A Blues Brother
9 Racket
10 Bourbon barrel
11 Chainsaw, e.g.
12 Man-mission link
13 Doing fine
21 Lord's lodging
22 Cruising, e.g.
26 Believe without question
27 Loses on purpose?
29 Water container?
32 Take downtown, say
33 Leading 3-2, e.g.
34 Accent the off-beats
35 Toolshed item, perhaps
37 Bygone auto ornament
39 CEO's deg., perhaps
41 In ___ (unborn)

42 Car battery abbr.

43 They may be fair or square

49 Business traveler's accessory

50 Daughterly, e.g.

52 Actress Bullock

55 Triangular river formation

57 Prepare to drive?

58 Some roulette bets

59 Suit material

60 Head lock

62 First place?

63 Teensy

64 Pricey wheels

65 Musical aptitude

43
MASTER CHEF
By Mark Milhet

ACROSS
1 One with designs on Jackie?
5 Use a divining rod
10 Overhead predator
14 Sugar substitute?
15 Heat center
16 Wise-owl link
17 Desperate, as a situation
18 "Bonanza" first name
19 Take a shine to
20 Hazelnut or Irish cream, e.g.
23 Knight's title
24 Big bang letters
25 Poisonous snake
28 Where the successful go
31 Point toward, as with a gun
35 Wrath
36 Secured a profit
39 Statistics calculation
40 One with much experience
43 Machu Picchu builder
44 Livestock lunch site
45 It may come after long
46 They get a paste in the mouth?
48 Aluminum source
49 Dog tag datum
51 Apt first name for a lawyer?
53 Eight bits
54 Made more interesting
62 Scratch, at NASA
63 Instance of clemency
64 Heinz's nvmber?
66 "___ out?" (pet's choice)
67 Use, as china

68 Sargasso swimmers
69 Funeral fire
70 Pass bills
71 Master of locks

DOWN
1 Unusual
2 Erik the Red's son
3 Viscount's superior
4 Word with monkey or gun
5 Grief
6 ___ about (legalistic phrase)
7 Existed
8 Quick follower
9 Put in office
10 When the band performs
11 "Yeah, right!"
12 "Finnegans ___" (Joyce)
13 Cap site
21 Sign of late August
22 Words with roll or leash
25 Drop in on
26 Castle with a lot of steps?
27 Timeless Christmas wish
28 Sporty Pontiac
29 Combo conjunction
30 Variety show
32 Erin of "Happy Days"
33 "Time is money," e.g.
34 Enrico Caruso, for one
37 Social bug
38 Fahrenheit figure, briefly
41 College entrance consideration
42 Type of sandal

47 Shade
50 Methodism's founder John
52 Tidies up the lawn
53 Continuously
54 Cutting sound
55 Small whiskey glass
56 Humpbacked helper

57 Word with fly or clap
58 Bigot's emotion
59 Desktop image
60 Eye membrane
61 It may be hard to swallow
65 ___ Bay (Honshu inlet)

44
HIGHER EDUCATION
By Fred Jackson III

ACROSS
1 Sci-fi landing site, perhaps
5 Transfer design
10 It can be checked
14 Big name in cosmetics
15 It may precede other things
16 Hunter's need
17 Overhaul
18 John for Janes
20 Thames team
21 Abbr. with Shaker or Brooklyn
22 Came around
23 Express a view
25 Cape near Lisbon
27 Drop back
29 Arthur Miller protagonist
33 Island dances
34 In the thick of
35 Hearty partner
36 Nobel-winning U.N. agency
37 It could precede the last word
    of 18-, 56-Across, 3-, 30-Down
38 Word heard at boot camp
39 Worthy starter
41 Bring on board
42 Like most films
44 Hood attachment
46 Chalice mates
47 Reveal
48 Seed spreader
49 Beautify
52 Actor Mineo
53 Victor's cry, perhaps
56 Vessel for underwater work

59 It really smells
60 Uniform
61 Rub out
62 Branch location
63 Darling dog
64 29-Across
65 Approved

DOWN
1 Latin singer Anthony
2 State point-blank
3 It diverts the bull
4 Chinese vegetable
5 Nymph loved by Apollo
6 Get carried away in Hollywood
7 Some elephants or whales
8 It divided Martin from Lewis
9 Shirt size, briefly
10 Blazer cleaner
11 Melville novel
12 Out of control
13 Weighty book
19 Word with arms or foot
24 Picks out of a lineup, briefly
25 Worker's reward
26 Auto pioneer
27 Thick-skinned behemoth
28 Swiss mathematician Leonhard
29 Eligible for Mensa
30 Pinnacle of fine art
31 Completely unfamiliar
32 The socially lost, in stereotypes
34 Skirt style
37 "Moonstruck" star

40 Audrey Hepburn role

42 Like some deals

43 Corroded

45 Jazz flutist Herbie

46 Hay fever cause

48 Taco topper, perhaps

49 Yemeni port

50 Prima donna

51 Hot spot

52 Clothes line

54 Words of understanding

55 Require

57 Salon stuff

58 Sib for sis

45
SO WHAT?
By Robert H. Wolfe

ACROSS
1 Style for a haircut or a rug
5 Truisms
10 Old press group
14 Scenes of action
15 ___ ease (uncomfortable)
16 Eye with ideas
17 Start of a "So what?" quip
20 Assailed
21 Zoophagous cravings
22 Gray gradually
23 Churn
25 Quip (Part 2)
30 Early second-millennium date
33 Utter impulsively
34 Author Joyce Carol
35 Actress Longoria
36 Mischievous evil spirit
37 Plucked instruments
38 Matinee subject
39 Biblical ending
40 Council of Trent, e.g.
41 Tangle
42 Grounded flier, briefly
43 Quip (Part 3)
45 Grass appendages
46 It's often found with order
47 Made an oath
50 Completely reorganizes
55 End of the quip
58 Comic Johnson
59 Travel like gnats
60 One answer to "Should we?"
61 Predicament

62 Desktop publisher's choices
63 Domestic squabble

DOWN
1 Use a letter opener
2 Sounds from Santa
3 "___ in every garage"
4 Make an attempt
5 Albert of "Erin Brockovich"
6 Oodles
7 Muse of history
8 Boy
9 Fr. holy woman
10 Swimmer's accessory
11 Turkish title
12 Bed support
13 Hardens
18 Octet number
19 Out of proper order
23 Like gory films
24 They're small and tender
25 French clerics
26 Novel ideas
27 Goose egg
28 Hills
29 "Ye shall not ___ every tree . . ." (Genesis)
30 Olympic success
31 Illegal hunters seek it
32 Singer Frankie
37 She's a coal miner's daughter
38 Accountants used to dip into them
40 Worked in a lumber mill

41 Plumber's device
44 Fire and burglar, e.g.
45 French city
47 Fraudulent scheme
48 Had on
49 Inning stats
50 Observatory function

51 Male red deer
52 Drip through
53 Arthur Ashe Stadium org.
54 "Hey you!"
56 Rubber-check letters
57 Jefferson bill

46
REDUNDANT?
By Alan Olschwang

ACROSS
1 Some pomes
6 One-time econ. yardstick
9 Act part
14 Bayou or fjord, e.g.
15 One in a pack?
16 Revamp
17 Some are heard on Broadway
20 Addendum conjunction
21 Ho head?
22 Commanded
23 ___ Dolorosa
25 Hot times in Le Havre
27 Tools of one pro's trade
35 Gesture-based communication (Abbr.)
36 Singer McEntire
37 Land of photography
38 Happy start
40 Mark of repetition
43 Tolstoy heroine
44 Inventor Nikola
46 What many sushi bars offer
48 Brain wave test
49 Namesake's collection of flops?
53 Afflicts
54 System starter
55 OT prophet
58 Time partner
61 First-century date
65 Noted spy's holdings?
68 Age-old expression
69 A third of 100?
70 Con men?

71 A noble gas
72 Beyond help in the ER
73 Disco era phrase

DOWN
1 Gyro bread
2 Organic compound
3 Some donations
4 Expunge
5 Place for shoats
6 What models need
7 Part of a 1492 trio
8 Aggravated
9 Made a lap
10 It may be behind the bar
11 Eruptive Italian landmark
12 Require
13 Scottish Gaelic
18 Prepared for cooking, in a way
19 They may be matched
24 Like some vbs.
26 Cote dweller
27 Savor
28 Placed on Capri, e.g.
29 Sand product
30 Sapporo sash
31 Western flick
32 Lawful possessor
33 Was fed by Wolfgang Puck, say
34 Hosiery mishaps
39 A polite dismissal
41 Knight of classic TV
42 Ashley and Mary-Kate
45 2001 sports biopic

47 Certain NCO
50 Dieter's target
51 Newsman Charles
52 Type of tea
55 Comet competitor
56 Fabricated
57 Middle Eastern sultanate

59 ___ Domini
60 Sneaking suspicion
62 Enthusiastic about
63 "Understood," hippie-wise
64 Playground comeback
66 D.C. VIP
67 Sheepish sound

47
SLIPPERY SLOPE
By Lynn Lempel

ACROSS
1 Some carpets
6 Morgue bed
10 Snowball
14 Seat separator
15 Dust Bowl figure
16 Ethiopian slave of opera
17 Beginning of a chilly definition
20 Intensifies
21 Development divisions
22 A way to enlightenment
23 Control mechanisms
24 Coast Guard ally
27 Bjorn Borg, for one
29 Foolish fellow
33 "... what a good boy ___"
34 Mall occupant
35 Alpine moppet
36 Middle of the definition
40 Place for a strike
41 Printed material
42 Fingerstall
43 Direct
44 Embarrassing display
46 Track records?
47 Didn't just stand there
49 Hua's predecessor
51 What you work for
53 Spot for 24-Across or 6-Down
57 End of the definition
59 Composer Stravinsky
60 Ball for the fans
61 Equine comment
62 Huff and puff

63 Green-eyed monster
64 Like Montmartre

DOWN
1 Buckleless belt
2 It's heard before a snap
3 It's about 17,000,000 sq. miles
4 Ostentatious
5 Have a hunch
6 Scholar's conclusion?
7 Acapulco article
8 Degraded
9 Pee-wee Herman trademark
10 Mob member
11 Solemn observance
12 Some Horace works
13 Major undertaking?
18 Hesitant
19 James' creator
23 Generally believed
24 Type of spray
25 Copious
26 "Twelfth Night" heroine
28 Pursue lovingly
30 React to pain
31 Village figure?
32 Color gradations
34 Pig's digs
35 Monopoly token choice
37 Imminent-danger warning
38 Thriller author Deighton
39 Freed from obligation
44 Attack from the air
45 Sri Lanka, once

46 More gaunt

48 Horse supplanter

50 Health insurer

51 Nintendo rival, once

52 River that joins the Severn

53 Like brilliantine

54 Dither

55 Short-order order

56 Cinderous

57 Savor, as a cocktail

58 Guzzler at the pump

48

BEFORE THE CART

By B. Venzke & S. Daily

ACROSS

1 Notary's tool
5 Dinner that's dipped
11 Clock change inits.
14 River flowing to Rennes
15 Marco Polo's destination
16 Miracle observer's feeling
17 Ready for presentation, in a way
19 Pink Panther series actor Herbert
20 Aristide's land
21 Off-road wheels, briefly
22 Senior's org.
23 Monogram of "The Waste Land" poet
24 Cord in some backyards
28 "There's more than one way to skin ___!"
29 Terrestrial mollusk
30 Lay into
34 Big name in steaks
37 Second-longest Polish river
38 It could follow the first word of 17-, 24-, 50- and 61-Across
41 Fail to include
42 Petty officer
44 Chew over
46 Old Russian rulers
49 It has its limits
50 Fast-paced card game
53 NFL signal-callers
56 Prefix with port or pad
57 Day follower?
58 Diddly-___

60 Lead-in for verse or cycle
61 Missive to a 1-A
64 Treat leather
65 Get back
66 Hemoglobin component
67 It follows ka in the Spanish alphabet
68 "Tristram Shandy" author
69 Authors

DOWN

1 A sense
2 Sewing machine innovator Howe
3 1966 role for Michael Caine
4 Riga resident
5 On the side of
6 Words between man and mouse
7 Attack like a puppy
8 Despair locale
9 Like 1, 3 and 5
10 Train schedule abbr.
11 Tibetan bigwig
12 Type of enemy
13 Home of Arizona State
18 Nature worship
22 Money derived from an old union
25 Mascara target
26 Palindromic emperor
27 ___ Paulo
28 Region of Italy
30 Tennis shot

31 Shakespeare title word
32 Peyote
33 Behave humanly
35 Flop's opposite
36 Had a repast
39 It may precede or follow "as"
40 Give off
43 Senate vote
45 "___ Easy" (Ronstadt song)
47 Wish undone
48 Stored fodder

50 Waterslide feature
51 Relating to the kidneys
52 Make it big
53 1/20th of a ream
54 Breakfast staple
55 British submachine guns
59 Double-swabbed item
61 AMA members
62 Pewter component
63 Topeka-to-St. Paul dir.

49
ADD SOME SPACE
By Fred Jackson III

ACROSS
1 Top dog
6 Rick's "Casablanca" flame
10 Word with ran or known as
14 Fortitude
15 Like some tales
16 "Cheerio!"
17 City in Texas
18 Seed covering
19 Bureau closer
20 Part of a musical gig
21 Rehearsal
24 Needle case
25 Preoccupy completely
26 What a skinny-dipper wears
31 Toon light bulbs
32 Listening devices
33 Kind of iron
36 Middle Eastern airline
37 Some are checkered
39 Ringing of bells
40 Homer's neighbor
41 Shore bird
42 Traffic sign
43 Source of many waves?
46 Home of the Norse gods
49 Swampy ground
50 It has feathers and may be airborne
53 Degree that's for filling?
56 Hide
57 River in central Germany
58 That which is expected
60 Spreadsheet unit
61 Get carried away?
62 San Diego athlete
63 Semicircular sanctuary section
64 Dates
65 A radar measurement

DOWN
1 Baseball honorees, briefly
2 Breathing rattle
3 Calf's cry
4 Charged-up atom
5 Warts, tumors, etc.
6 Where Roma is
7 Carefree frolic
8 Skirt feature
9 When some convenience stores are open
10 Sans markup
11 Lash of old westerns
12 Some deer
13 Scouts take them
22 IRS employee (Abbr.)
23 Baseball slugging stats
24 Bibliography abbr.
26 Good, in Grenoble
27 Like some hands
28 Prove one's literacy
29 Kind of question
30 Took a load off
33 Scope or meter attachment
34 Shakespearean schemer
35 Secluded valley
37 Street vendors
38 "Exodus" hero

39 Name used in an exclamation
41 Pucker-producing
42 Price increases
43 Crib plaything
44 Campfire treats
45 Small spasm
46 Humane org.
47 Mindless followers
48 Shore birds
51 Actress Falco
52 Turn over
53 Type of ranch
54 Have the gumption
55 Iditarod need
59 Easy mark

50
VANITY
By Robert H. Wolfe

ACROSS

1 Cut, as a log
5 Peters out
9 Old Nick
14 Melville novel
15 Guard on the deck
16 Feeling of personal worth
17 Start of an egotistical quip
20 Titanic casualty
21 Most unfeeling
22 Heading on Santa's list
25 Sinai number
26 Quip (Part 2)
31 Speaker go-with
34 Top-shelf
35 Environmental sci.
36 Salvaging aid, perhaps
38 Without
39 Shore of song
41 Fifteenth-century caravel
42 Contemptibly familiar
44 Wine-producing region
45 Discharge
46 Word with black or private
47 Quip (Part 3)
50 Security threat
51 Philosopher Zeno of ___
52 Makes like new
57 Floundering
61 End of the quip
64 Go
65 Shallowest Great Lake
66 Wavy lines, in comics
67 Garden tool

68 Pinches
69 Badlands feature

DOWN

1 Sectional, e.g.
2 Book of prophecies
3 Brewer's malt infusion
4 Sort of a guilty plea
5 Transgress
6 Take one's cuts
7 Skewed view
8 Razor cut
9 Small harpsichords
10 Actors Alan or Adam
11 Pea picker
12 Stirs
13 Colorful cold-blooded
   vertebrate
18 He's Idle
19 Reply to the Little Red Hen
23 Kind of softball team, e.g.
24 Live oak of California
26 Fritter away
27 Antediluvian
28 Harold Gray heroine
29 Barbarian of film
30 Go by
31 Jungian life principle
32 Fanatical
33 Brooklyn institute
37 Small depth for a riverboat
40 Praise
43 Capacitate
48 Jane of fiction

49 Cleared of clutter
50 Ben Franklin creation
52 Cause one to get het up
53 Supplemented (with "out")
54 Complication
55 Roulette bet
56 Word in Doris Day's theme song
58 Beef purchase
59 Genesis name
60 Shrine site
62 Tease
63 Word with "I do"

51
FLYING HIGH
By Lynn Lempel

ACROSS
1 Tuck partner
4 Cholesterol watcher's no-no
8 Express forcefully
14 Head opposite
15 Plodding
16 All lined up
17 Graceful descent
19 Done over
20 Java neighbor
21 Shift sharply
23 More likely
24 Self-correcting circuit
27 Vessel from a pump
30 Airplane part
31 Boating platforms
32 Machu Picchu builder
34 500 sheets
38 Buffet pourer
39 Won ton cousin
42 Mailer's subject in "The Fight"
43 Regarding, in memos
45 Birdlike
46 "Peer Gynt" playwright
48 Tropical root
50 Rubber-tree liquid
51 A good press agent, e.g.
57 "Crocodile Rock" singer John
58 Logical
59 Speaker's spot
63 Done for
65 Shoal
67 To no avail
68 Meat piercer

69 Short way to go?
70 Meeting handout
71 Abundance
72 Hanoi Hilton "guest"

DOWN
1 Wreck-checking agcy.
2 It lies between the Mississippi and the Missouri
3 Sound of thunder
4 Trip cause
5 One way to be wanted
6 Succumbed to wanderlust
7 Nerdy guy
8 It can cause inflation
9 Moves stealthily
10 Assortment of chocolates
11 Clio's sister
12 Beverly Hills drive
13 Nerdy guy
18 Swell
22 Ill will
25 Abate
26 Lousy stocking filler
27 Lung attachment?
28 Partly mine
29 Mouth off
32 Nunavut dwellings
33 Org. for straight shooters?
35 It might be Near or Far
36 Away from windward
37 Coquette
40 "Mr. Mom" actress Teri
41 Leslie Caron film

44 Footstool
47 Hotel alternative, familiarly
49 Roman classic
51 Word with circus or blitz
52 Beside
53 It may be wood-burning
54 Admits nothing?

55 Aquarium scavenger
56 Tube pasta
60 Seniors org.
61 Engrossed with
62 Slant unfairly
64 Genome material
66 Nighttime accumulation

52
PICTURE THIS

By Alan Olschwang

ACROSS
1 Sandy substance
5 Cicero's wear
9 Some encs.
14 Importune
15 Galena and mispickel, e.g.
16 Go fishing, in a way
17 Neighbor
18 Castle access
20 Web page access
22 ___ avis
23 Fact follower?
24 Like a couch potato
26 A great quantity are from California
28 Minute quantity
32 Did not pass
33 Formerly, formerly
34 Discontinue, as relations
38 Picture on a PC
40 It's south of the Sahara
43 Peace offering, perhaps
44 Loo sign
46 Certain rapper-turned-actor
48 Electron-deficient atom, e.g.
49 Police department employee
53 Classic role for an actor
56 Andy Taylor's son
57 PFC's address, perhaps
58 Hose color
60 Alpine refrains
64 Heavy-load hauler
67 Matinee follower
68 Casals of tennis

69 Goya's duchess
70 Jamaican fruit export
71 Sign on a gate
72 Russian despot
73 Leave a solid state?

DOWN
1 Island feast
2 Celestial spheres
3 Chills and fever
4 Sort of system
5 Little ones on the go
6 Bruin legend
7 Equipment
8 Teeming
9 Exerts utmost effort
10 Greek tycoon's nickname
11 Words of agreement
12 Illinois city
13 Luges, e.g.
19 Highlands hillside
21 Cannes conception
25 "Born Free" character
27 Word with child or ladder
28 Math offshoot
29 What hearts sometimes do
30 Soon, ere now
31 System of moral values
35 Sundial numeral
36 Poetry collection
37 It's overhead
39 Airline accident investigator (Abbr.)
41 Reverberate

Down (continued)

42 2008, e.g.
45 Picnic pest, in slang
47 Peter, Paul and Mary, e.g.
50 Cut into metal
51 Hemming may clear it
52 Boredom
53 Mexican mountain system, Sierra ___

54 Chef's cover
55 Save fuel
59 Internet identifiers, briefly
61 Head start
62 Take it easy
63 Letter opener's creation
65 Old-time oath
66 Start-up's helper (Abbr.)

53
WHOLE LOT OF NOTHING
By Diane C. Baldwin

ACROSS
1 Laughingstock
5 Ancient
9 Be the life of the party
14 Luck, to some
15 Extremely attractive
16 Domingo, for one
17 On the crest
18 Mennonite decoration
19 Transpire
20 No-nonsense stance
23 Palindromic before
24 Cloud output, sometimes
25 Real scarcity
28 Exercise a certain right
29 Sibling nickname
30 Greek letter
31 Fossil resin
34 Example of scare tactics
35 Enervates
36 Just what we need
40 Personality parts
41 Ivory-tickler's appointment
42 Splendiferous
43 Collection of anecdotes, e.g.
44 Ret. hedge
45 Future branch
47 Bovary's title
49 "Vamoose!"
50 Phrase of commitment
53 What cads often spew
56 Dugout vessel
58 In a drought

59 Republic once known as French Sudan
60 Alter legislation
61 Wash up
62 Tasty paste
63 Fingerprint part
64 Rubbernecked
65 Mark for life?

DOWN
1 Sugarcoat
2 Certain shoot-'em-up
3 "O come let us ___ Him"
4 Keyboard goof
5 Drifting asea
6 Stick-wielding facemask wearer
7 Do very well
8 Unnatural blonde, e.g.
9 Squares things
10 Muslim holy place
11 Iffy
12 Paltry amount
13 Be imperfect
21 Irritant in one's side
22 "Goodbye" somewhere
26 Caught on video
27 Strumpet
28 They are made with two fingers
29 Mayday letters
31 Shipboard direction
32 ___ cum laude
33 Delocalized
34 Panhandle

35 Hunting target, perhaps
37 Plumed wader
38 Spy org.
39 "Going to the dogs," e.g.
44 Stand in the way of
45 Do very well
46 Abounding in trees
48 Included with

49 Ocean phenomenon
50 Father of Esau
51 Fourth Greek letter
52 Willow tree
54 Bulldogs' school
55 Little rascals
56 Elevator unit
57 Parisian pal

54
A KILLER OUTFIT
By B. Venzke & S. Daily

ACROSS
1 Farsighted one?
5 Let fall, as tears
9 Carmarthen citizens, e.g.
14 Like Death's horse
15 Early artist's milieu
16 Name on a range
17 Pinnacle
18 Friendly femme
19 Evenings, in ads
20 Quip (Part 1)
23 Like Mao's book
24 Nick and Nora's terrier
25 Word with light or line
26 Deprive of by deceit
30 Decline
32 Big Ten sch.
33 Flue coat
36 Country singer Steve
40 Quip (Part 2)
44 Emulate a crab
45 Word from Tonto
46 Denier's word
47 A hand for Snoopy
49 Some stuff heroes are made of
52 Respectful Asian address
55 Cassowary relative
58 They've got the vote
59 Quip (Part 3)
65 Plant swelling problem
66 Syllogistic word
67 The Supremes, e.g.
68 Downsizes
69 Corp. heads

70 That little "somethin' somethin'"
71 River to the Humber estuary
72 Class struggle?
73 Swamp thing

DOWN
1 Minor confrontation
2 Every relative?
3 Animated hunter
4 Illicit cigarette
5 Al Capone's identifying feature
6 Meat from the back of thighs
7 Role played by Patti LuPone
8 Is of the opinion
9 Nearly all "American Idol" auditioners
10 Throw off, as light
11 Thin wooden strips
12 Kind of preview
13 Not well thought-out
21 Gilbert & Sullivan's princess
22 Came to a fast stop?
26 Exclamations from Homer
27 Morales of "La Bamba"
28 Today's newspaper letters?
29 Hardly Mr. Cool
31 Part of Ebenezer Scrooge's cry
34 It's found in veins
35 Grant's landmark
37 Sounds like it's right
38 Writer Hubbard
39 Kett of the comics
41 Zugspitze, for one

42 Turkey may be found here
43 Try to win over
48 It's a question of identity
50 "Turandot" slave girl
51 Car safety system brand
52 Made the dust clear, in a way
53 Control-tower device
54 Grenoble's department of France

56 In an upright position
57 Correspond, in grammar
60 Hoover's force, briefly
61 Narcissists' problems
62 Part of a profit calculation
63 Shamrock land
64 Word with kill or hog

55
AN EMBARRASSMENT OF RICHES
By Raymond Hamel

ACROSS

1 Subject of Asimov's three laws
9 Rogue
15 Worthy of copying
16 Like the "Kama Sutra"
17 Expensive subscription?
19 Brawl
20 Capital of Vanuatu
21 Adamson's lioness
22 Away from WSW
24 Calif. setting?
26 Bill showing the Treasury Building
27 Expensive expedition?
33 Lots and lots
34 Became skilled in
38 Type of dancer
39 Place for a future Lt.
40 Classic theater name
41 Willing to comply
44 Kind of hut
46 Expensive sheepskin?
48 Science-funding org.
51 What you stand to lose?
52 Cheer for a toreador
53 Bauxite and stibnite, e.g.
55 Slow run
57 Westphalian wife
61 It could pay for 17-, 27- and 46- Across
65 Valve under the hood
66 Pertaining to women
67 Trojan War sage
68 Took money unscrupulously

DOWN

1 Falling out
2 Melville work
3 Frequent flier?
4 Film director Preminger
5 St. Anthony's cross
6 Son of, in Arabic names
7 Capable of finding a new angle
8 Prefix for automatic
9 Winged horse
10 Rollover subject
11 Friendly chat
12 Slanted
13 Dentist's direction
14 Continental divide?
18 Some males
22 Language suffix, often
23 Neutrino symbols
25 It can make a molehill out of a mountain
27 Costume made from a bed sheet
28 Capacity
29 Move cautiously
30 Word with tag or string
31 Roast host
32 Short and to the point
35 Greeted the judge
36 Company VIP
37 Unit of force
39 Seasoned veteran
42 "You've got mail" letters
43 Screwy talk
44 Paul Tagliabue's org.

45 ___-de-France
47 Pre-owned
48 Type of situation
49 Vernon's dancing partner
50 Increases molecular motion
54 Venetian strip
56 Some switch positions
57 Discovery

58 Make turbid
59 Mrs. Shakespeare
60 Played for a sucker
62 Pugilist's triumph
63 Bon or mon follower
64 Tenth-anniversary gift, traditionally

56
OPPOSITES ATTRACT
By Fred Jackson III

ACROSS
1 Some are broken
5 Shady area
10 Lean and mean
14 Popular succulent
15 French river
16 Big palookas
17 "___ the Explorer" (kids' TV show)
18 Didn't wax
19 Flower with hips
20 Guffaw
21 No set pattern
23 Petitions
25 Bikini blast
26 Alleges
28 Easy basket
30 They follow one in a million?
31 Successful volleyball strikes
32 Support wire
35 Pangolin's diet
36 Where to find John
37 Busy time for ministers
38 Painter Lichtenstein
39 Does a muffler's job
40 Unwanted vegetation
41 Microwave feature
42 Price of redemption
43 The eagle, on a quarter
45 Minor, in law
46 Like some memories
49 Commercially popular
52 Word with guard or hand
53 "___ Gold" (Fonda film)

54 One of Time's Persons of the Year, 2005
55 First name in mysteries
56 Like 007
57 Computer operator
58 Some lab stock
59 "___ to you"
60 First name in slapstick

DOWN
1 Disney dog
2 Felipe, Jesus, Moises or Matty of baseball
3 Crew
4 Overwhelming quantity
5 Eternally
6 Dappled horses
7 Tough spot
8 Ubiquitous crossword cookie
9 Rhode Island's state tree
10 Rabbit's home
11 Mobile music players
12 Type of button
13 Belgian river
21 Some black sheep
22 Mayberry character
24 Grande and de Janeiro
26 Antidrug honcho
27 Late-night laugh maker
28 Rome's river
29 Woes
31 Toy made to be blown up?
32 Job once held by 27-Down
33 Bring to ruin

34 Li'l Abner's "OK" to Mammy Yokum

36 The old heave-ho

37 Stand-up comic Richard

39 One of 26 in a marathon

40 Light bulb measure

41 Earl and duke, e.g.

42 Big name in candy

43 It's fit for a queen

44 Lopsided

45 Bone to pick

46 "Uncle Remus" rabbit

47 Swing around

48 Become frayed

50 High draft rating

51 Unable to decide

54 Urban transport

57
HAIL ME
By Mike VanBlaricom

ACROSS
1 Program part
5 Figures in red
10 Give it up
14 Toss a discus
15 Husband to Bathsheba
16 Locket shape, often
17 Augustus Caesar's boast (Part 1)
20 It's used for a stick-up?
21 Make dots
22 Page of letters?
25 Royal in the 1976 Olympics
26 Japanese title
29 Copycat
31 It joined with Montenegro in 2003
35 Word with faced or fisted
36 Morally acceptable
38 Shore denizens
39 Boast (Part 2)
43 TV's Francis, for one
44 Early photo color
45 Take up space
46 Promise
49 "Revenge of the ___"
50 Make defective
51 Quit, in poker
53 Dash in the kitchen
55 Oceanic osprey, e.g.
58 Tiny things
62 Boast (Part 3)
65 Harplike instrument
66 Calculus pioneer Leonhard
67 Heroic chronicle

68 Provide temporary use
69 Gushes, as a volcano
70 Type of examination

DOWN
1 Model in a bottle
2 Lime spring deposit
3 Greek Cupid
4 Ninth planet
5 You won't get a bang out of it
6 Drop the ball
7 Short personal histories
8 Florida City
9 Charlie and Martin
10 Young rooster
11 Nefarious
12 Go out after a pass?
13 Portrayer of Tarzan
18 Man from Kathmandu
19 Annoying spots
23 On a grand scale
24 Knocks down
26 Old jazz dance
27 Reverential
28 Chemically inert
30 Emulates the sun
32 Carplike fish
33 Prefix with red or structure
34 Daisylike flower
37 Curtain fabric, perhaps
40 Embarrassed
41 Silents star Naldi
42 Showy flower
47 Desert, in Mongolian

48 Type types
52 Desiccate
54 Common sculpture
55 Eyelid problem (Var.)
56 Get, as a reputation
57 1996 presidential candidate

59 Type of ski lift
60 Aquatic organism
61 Notary's tool
62 "___ be back!"
63 Not so many
64 Miniver or Doubtfire, e.g.

58

TOUR DE FRANCE HUMOR

By Elizabeth C. Gorski

ACROSS

- **1** Adam and Eve, e.g.
- **6** Fishhook point
- **10** What chuck is
- **14** Make suitable
- **15** Palliative plant
- **16** Cajun veggie
- **17** Oprah's "The Color Purple" role
- **18** How some like their coffee
- **20** Start of quip
- **22** Gamboling area
- **23** ___ in "able"
- **24** To an exceedingly great extent
- **28** Place of wallowing
- **29** Stay fresh
- **31** Side in a famous case
- **32** Umpire's call, sometimes
- **35** Quip (Part 2)
- **38** Lay claim to
- **40** It's on cable
- **41** "Peachy!"
- **42** Quip (Part 3)
- **45** Pheromone quality
- **46** Like Wonderland's hatter
- **47** Where the worm turns
- **48** Took a powder
- **50** Shoe part
- **52** He's welcome at Thanksgiving?
- **53** Calendar shorthand
- **56** End of the quip
- **60** One who may elicit double takes
- **63** Broadcasting mogul Arledge
- **64** Italian coastal city

- **65** Platte Valley figure (Var.)
- **66** On the ocean blue
- **67** Tomba's transportation
- **68** Trial balloon
- **69** Winslet and Capshaw

DOWN

- **1** Type of tone or passage
- **2** Sun-dried brick
- **3** "GoodFellas" group
- **4** Like some battles
- **5** Patronize, as an inn
- **6** Cries one's eyes out
- **7** "I cannot tell ___"
- **8** Campus mil. group
- **9** Was nice to the babysitter
- **10** Boxing matches
- **11** Ticker tape?
- **12** Period of note
- **13** Partner of away
- **19** Fasten with a pop
- **21** Caribbean getaways
- **25** Three-note chord
- **26** State moneymaker
- **27** "Answer ___ no, please"
- **28** Native of Novi Sad
- **29** Capital of Afghanistan
- **30** Slaughter with a bat
- **32** Finland, to the Finns
- **33** Site of Egyptian dams
- **34** Bankrolls
- **36** Bangkok resident
- **37** Broadway light
- **39** Former coin of Spain

43 Frequent flier
44 Switch suffix
49 Penn Station arrival
51 Polynesian carvings
52 Bird call
53 Pumpkin cover
54 Russell's "Cinderella Man" co-star
55 They may be good, bad or bright

57 Construction zone
58 Ring stoppages, for short
59 Minuscule amount
60 Weigh-in abbr.
61 Tree with a yellow ribbon?
62 ". . . ___ quit!" (ultimatum ending)

59
HUSH
By Fran & Lou Sabin

ACROSS

1 One doing checks and balances?
4 Tough situation
8 Participate in a secret joint venture?
13 Cheese coat, at times
15 Jai ___
16 Caruso, notably
17 Mole
20 Winning or losing follower
21 One of us?
22 Parliamentary response
23 Agricultural tool
24 Game of pursuit
26 Deprive of courage
29 F.H. Burnett's children's classic ("The")
33 Religious offshoot
36 Something that's cut and dried
37 Ham it up
38 Wing-shaped
39 Dame Sitwell
42 Wife in "Finnegans Wake"
43 Edna Ferber novel
45 Fifth day of Kwanzaa
46 Sugar substitute?
47 Sneaky plan
51 "Stop worrying!"
52 Jamaican pop music
53 Mouths, anatomically
56 High-school subj.
58 Cheer opener
60 Stock ticker innovator
62 Furtive mission

66 Alpha opposite
67 Perform in whiteface, perhaps
68 Circular opening?
69 Type of card
70 Collar piercer, perhaps
71 Ham holder, perhaps

DOWN

1 Puppy love
2 Spotted equine
3 First name in tennis
4 Lumbago, e.g.
5 Nobel-winning U.N. agency, 1969
6 Enlistee's choice
7 Cool off, as a fad
8 Aristophanes' H
9 Trek segment
10 Two
11 Small mount
12 Art Deco celebrity
14 River to Solway Firth
18 Offer a critique
19 It offers a step up
25 Type of student or school, briefly
27 West of Hollywood
28 Spain's ill-fated force
29 What some things are taken in?
30 Checking over visually (Var.)
31 Centuries-old Sicilian threat
32 Approach
33 Military band?
34 "The Time Machine" people

35 A meter reader
40 0-0, 50-50, etc.
41 Longed (for)
44 Solidify
48 Boss Tweed caricaturist
49 Self-evident truths
50 Iconoclastic creative movement
53 Wickerworker's willow
54 With plenty of space

55 Feisty fictional orphan
56 William Wallace, for one
57 Insensible condition
59 Polish partner
61 "___ My Party"
63 Adlerian study
64 Untrustworthy sort
65 Bird that's never on the wing

60
TIME TO EAT
By Elizabeth Gorski

ACROSS
1 Informal turndowns
5 Iconic Kate Spade products
9 "Let us know if you're coming"
13 Embossed snack
14 Select group
16 "Would ___ to you?"
17 When early birds exercise
20 Some coffee orders
21 Glitzy hitching post
22 Alpine road shape
23 Beach transport, briefly
25 Turn purple, perhaps
26 Crazy quilts
28 Loser to Sparta
33 K-6 sch. designation
36 Certain insect eggs
38 Apres-ski treat
39 Good time to run errands, for many
42 Glamorous Garbo
43 Indigo-yielding shrub
44 A human bone
45 Army affirmative
47 ___ und Drang
49 Service to be repeated
51 ___-Cat
52 Long-jawed fish
55 Valuable wall hangings
60 Hilo honcho
62 It may follow a big meal
64 Editor's notation, perhaps
65 Besmirch
66 Foil for Garfield

67 Exxon, in Canada
68 Dates
69 Progeny

DOWN
1 Titled peer
2 They may be designated for work or play
3 Lifts with difficulty
4 Sweep's take?
5 Worker-inflicted wound
6 Priestly garb
7 Word with crazy or Friday
8 Home addition?
9 Plethoric
10 Smelting residue
11 It has a stripe on its back
12 They're all adopted
15 Grade made in the shade?
18 Not made up
19 Complain, complain, complain…
24 "There, it's done!"
26 Skips over
27 Shocks
29 Dullsville
30 Earth Day subj.
31 Part of speech
32 "Nobody doesn't like ___ Lee"
33 Tense
34 It may be at the end of the line
35 '70s hit song "___ Tu"
37 Peevish states
40 Carpenter's power tool
41 Junkyard wheels

46 Some wetland flora
48 Big-top sound
50 Salon offerings
52 Sherpa, e.g.
53 Sandy's owner
54 Judged "Dancing With the
   Stars," e.g.

55 Mum's place
56 Young newts
57 USPS delivery patterns
58 "Get ___ the Church on Time"
59 Snick or ___
61 They have plans, for short
63 Rob Roy's "no"

61
NOT SO FAST!

By Fran & Lou Sabin

ACROSS

1 Las Vegas feature
6 Rhyme scheme
10 The 45th of 50
14 Sale item?
15 It's sometimes a drag
16 Charity festivity, perhaps
17 "Not so fast!"
19 Of a similar nature
20 Forked letter
21 Had a little lamb?
22 Type of preview
23 Islamic deity
24 Watercourse channel
25 "Serpico" director Lumet
28 Simulated
32 Soon, to a poet
33 A day's march
34 ___-mo
35 Beginning
38 Auction transactions
40 Trompe l'oeil, e.g.
41 Building addition
43 Budge
44 Camus title character
46 Blotto
48 Letters on a meat stamp
49 Bull Run side
51 Young lady
53 Downhill goof
54 Anonymous litigant
57 Head tail?
58 "Not so fast!"

60 Garnet and jasper, for two
61 1/10th of an ephah
62 Knocked for a loop
63 Roman calendar notation
64 Queen of Carthage, in myth
65 Signs of things to come

DOWN

1 Expel or eject, as lava
2 Kind of table
3 Court order
4 In need of salting
5 Market
6 Place for concessions
7 Run producer, at times
8 Type of rain
9 It may be placed before a window
10 Kampala's country
11 "Not so fast!"
12 Inter ___
13 Coil of rope or yarn
18 Like brilliantine
22 Surfeits
23 Green Gables girl
24 Cleaning cloth
25 Drawn-out accounts
26 Quiescent
27 "Not so fast!"
29 "Duck Soup" name
30 Lycee pupil
31 Did a doctor's job
33 Low-level laborer of old

36 Like beach blankets
37 Swenson of "The Miracle Worker"
39 Word said before a meal, perhaps
42 Blew, as a volcano
45 Determine the costs of
46 Window feature
47 City on Lake Erie
50 Volatile liquid, briefly
51 Yuletide visitors
52 Decorated, as a cake
53 Road hog, at times
54 Have a siesta
55 "The Virginian" author Wister
56 Reaches the coda
58 Nursery offering
59 Dental guard

62
LITTLE OFF THE TOP
By Isaiah Burke

ACROSS
1 Anapest relative
5 Oater sound effects
10 Author Kingsley
14 Oater shout
15 He left his mark
16 Word after Cal or Georgia
17 Curse or vow, e.g.
18 It contains tracks
19 Part of SEATO
20 It's bad to the bone
23 Fanatical
25 Like Ivan
26 Three-match connection
27 Needless bother
30 Calais-to-Paris dir.
31 Ending for pant or road
32 Weight-laden lasso
34 Perturb
36 Well-chosen
38 Slogan for the follicly-impaired?
44 Simile center
45 Require nursing, e.g.
46 Algonquian living in Canada
47 Authority on diamonds, briefly
50 Groovy collection
52 Sot's withdrawal syndrome, briefly
54 Samara bearer
55 Impressions
58 They're guarded at the Olympics
60 Needs to comb less and less, in a way

63 Langston Hughes' "___, Sing America"
64 "___ you!" (challenging words)
65 Launderer's step
68 Trade center
69 Month on the Jewish calendar
70 The Andrews Sisters, e.g.
71 Latin being
72 Breaks one's back, say
73 Arresting word

DOWN
1 "Sands of ___ Jima"
2 Cry of insight
3 Item in the closet, perhaps
4 Religion founded in Iran
5 Kaiser kin
6 Hang loose
7 World revolution?
8 Dried fruits containing vitamin A
9 Gymnast's specialty, perhaps
10 Pong company
11 Range of Minnesota
12 New Year's eave formation?
13 Is visibly frightened
21 Gilbert & Sullivan princess
22 Moved like some reptiles
23 L.B.J. son-in-law Charles
24 Endangered buffalo
28 Let down
29 Spheroid
33 1961 Susan Hayward film
35 Mauna ___ of Hawaii

Down (continued)

37 Nervous reaction
39 Small landmasses
40 Relief
41 Bahamian tourist spot
42 River to the Ubangi
43 Moon-landing transports
47 When computers are working
48 Conductor Zubin and family
49 Abbey bigwigs
51 Universal, for one

53 Matched parts or part of a match
56 Franklin bill, familiarly
57 Former East German secret police
59 Assigned stations
61 River of Russia
62 Desktop items, perhaps
66 Brazilian hot spot, informally
67 Word with dog or dollar

63
FARM FUN
By Fran & Lou Sabin

ACROSS

1 First in a long line?
5 "King of the Elephants"
10 Zippo
14 Kind of monster
15 Pole Position system
16 Yoked pair
17 Knotted
18 Alabama, Georgia, Mississippi, etc.
20 Farm subsidy?
22 Half a comic duo
23 Top-drawer
24 Far from forward
25 Four-chambered organ
28 Type of plug
31 H.S.T. preceder
34 Battle buddies
36 Cheer for a banderillero
37 Medicinal plant
38 They're on many grocery shelves
41 Word with bobby and bowling
42 Three sheets to the wind
43 Type of fence
44 Referendum choice
45 Envelope feature, perhaps
47 Saxes and clarinets, e.g.
48 ... --- ...
49 Wahines' strings, briefly
51 Place for a kiss
54 Lecture around the country
59 Book identifying birds, plants, etc.

61 Hautboy
62 Prefix with American
63 Inordinate
64 Ready for plucking
65 It's a bit controlling?
66 Mill output, perhaps
67 Proofreader's "save"

DOWN

1 They change every year
2 Disreputable place
3 Nautical direction
4 Tangerine-bearing trees
5 It may be saved or served
6 Makes up for
7 Lessen the force of
8 La-di-da
9 Carnival city, briefly
10 In a regal manner
11 Rink leap
12 Franks' place?
13 It may precede a deal
19 Out-of-the-way place
21 Sacred song
24 Advance slowly
25 One of the Seven Dwarfs
26 Andy Taylor's druggist
27 A King and a Shepard
29 Sentry stations
30 Finsteraarhorn, for one
31 Bit of serendipity
32 Showed excessive fondness (with "on")
33 They're found in scores

35 Flies off the shelf
37 Family tree members
39 Drowned valley
40 Buenos ___
45 Extension extension
46 The Boilermakers
48 Beauty parlor
50 Prepare to take a dubbing
51 Way off

52 An "unalienable right"
53 "Tootsie" star Garr
54 Baseball stratagem
55 ___-de-camp
56 Brief memorial column
57 Will Rogers' prop
58 Track-and-field contest
60 Astronaut Grissom

64
WHERE'S BABY?
By Frances Burton

ACROSS

1 Bundle of joy
5 What you often do on the road
9 It's a good thing
14 1/40 of "the back 40"
15 It may be irresistible
16 Wearisome task
17 David Bowie song
19 ___ lily
20 Search for the right word
21 "The Pirates of Penzance" heroine
22 Mandate
23 Mucky earth
24 ___ Gras
26 Toroidal roll
29 Edgar Bergen's Mortimer
31 They're game
34 Parisian palace
36 Yale students
37 "Apollo 13" director Howard
38 Four in a music group
39 Locker room item
41 Soprano-range woodwind
42 Utterances of pain relief
43 Symbol on Vietnam's flag
44 Golf shot
46 "By the way . . ."
47 Hardly talkative
49 Unfathomable cavity, e.g.
50 Hyper
52 Darkens in the light?
54 Exhibited brilliance
56 Humor with a twist, perhaps
58 LAX datum
61 French blueblood
62 Elvis Presley song
64 Split up
65 Hardly helpless
66 Gloss over
67 King of Crete
68 Sine qua non
69 East Indies island

DOWN

1 One of the three B's
2 Joint problem
3 Porkpie part
4 Dough for tempura, perhaps
5 Lumps for the horse
6 Biblical dozen
7 Cruel fellow
8 With undue hurry and confusion
9 Agreements
10 Archaeological fragment
11 Shirelles song
12 Della's creator
13 Word with gas or duct
18 "Walk ___ in my shoes"
23 Event in a hall
25 Sign of the zodiac
26 Failed VCRs
27 "Goodbye, Honolulu"
28 Brian Hyland song
30 Bellies up to
32 Attractiveness
33 You may get weak in them

35 First name in cosmetics
40 Sweater named for an earl
41 Eyeballs, poetically
43 They run around blocks
45 Singer Tucker
48 Rating unit for a Cannes film?
51 Lead-in
53 Fed the kitty

54 Sucker play
55 A Pueblo Indian
57 Hayseed
58 Jane Austen novel
59 Manx cat's lack
60 Opposing prefix
63 Knock over

65
IT'S A PIGSTY
By Lynn Lempel

ACROSS

1 Corner of a diamond
5 Cough up a chip?
9 Glacially carved inlet
14 Distinct time spans
15 Make cloudy
16 Doubled name in a hit song title
17 Load hauler
19 Grocery part
20 Tech giant since 1911
21 Billions of years
22 Lightly colored
23 "Help!"
25 Lively
26 Ripken's nickname
29 It's on the staff
33 Having chutzpah
36 Places for some drums
37 Floating ring
38 Spiny plant
39 Therefore
40 Place to get the big picture
41 Crypt cover
42 Leg up
43 Offer feedback
44 Subway purchase, perhaps
45 Blank first page
47 First person on a ship?
49 Non compos mentis
53 Unsteady
56 Boer foe, once
58 D.C. slugger
59 Disney's little mermaid
60 Binder accessory

62 Out of the past
63 Something to pick?
64 Soggy earth
65 What a rolling stone will not be
66 Country on the Strait of Hormuz
67 British nobleman

DOWN

1 Darken
2 Caribbean cruise stop
3 One of Frank's Rat Pack pals
4 Psychic sense
5 Dry gully
6 Parsing choice
7 Spasms
8 Hunter's trophy, perhaps
9 Knack
10 Some military bigwigs
11 Unseat
12 Arouse resentment
13 Homeowner's document
18 Starting to break down
22 Pluperfect, e.g.
24 Air Force menaces
25 It's a lot for sale
27 Razz
28 Shabby
30 Magical home
31 Middle Eastern flier
32 Like Jimi Hendrix's lady
33 Old automaker
34 Australian supermodel
35 Far more than a snicker

39 Substantial
43 Accumulated, as debt
46 Astronaut Collins
48 Mix of metals
50 Tony-winning musical
51 Mollusk's secretion
52 Old operating-room substance

53 Put in the oven
54 Twistable treat
55 Short comedy routines
56 It brings people closer
57 It's near the radius
60 Cable choice
61 He works on diamonds

66
AIMING HIGH
By Diane C. Baldwin

ACROSS
1 Small deck member
5 Slob's creation
9 Bushes
14 Texas city on the Brazos
15 Archipelago lightweight
16 Sound from a toaster?
17 Like dirty hearths
18 Knock one's socks off
19 Spiny flora
20 Aim high
23 Tailor's challenge
24 Hydrogen's number
25 Lebanon's capital
29 Mongolian abode
31 Bomb that bombs
34 Web site, perhaps?
35 Cribbage markers
36 Jay seen at night
37 There's no ceiling
40 Last word of "The Wizard of Oz"
41 Egyptian goddess
42 Get carried away in Hollywood
43 Start of success?
44 Cat scanners?
45 Does penitence
46 Owner of Alice's restaurant
47 Ostrich-like bird
48 Positive mantra
57 Auburn heads?
58 Overhead contents
59 Arab ruler
60 "Inferno" author

61 Safe sword
62 Madame Bovary
63 Lieu
64 Hog fat
65 It may consist of couplets

DOWN
1 Start of a Christmas classic
2 Impulsive
3 Do likewise
4 Fluctuate repeatedly
5 Maladjusted person
6 Halt, legally speaking
7 Insulting remark
8 E-mail status
9 Emphasis
10 It's seen at the Olympics
11 Affluent, in Acapulco
12 Savvy about
13 Onion covering
21 Convoy member
22 Groom's responsibility
25 One way to come clean
26 Fundamental character of a culture
27 News bits
28 Word from a faith healer, perhaps
29 Abominable snowmen
30 Sounds of disgust
31 Evil spirit
32 Band together
33 Lavishes affection
35 Subtle alert

(Crossword grid)

36 VIP transport
38 Knuckle under
39 Ease
44 Knowledgeable
45 Kept entertained
46 Powerful ray
47 Lawn tool
48 The longer they are, the riskier

49 Undiluted, at the bar
50 Grow smaller
51 The fourth person
52 California wine valley
53 Emulate Niobe
54 Arsenal stash
55 Hoarfrost
56 Avoirdupois unit

67
WEARING SHADES
By Kay Puttnam

ACROSS
1 Customary observance
5 Aircraft representation, at times
9 Twice-baked breads
14 Portent
15 Type of horse
16 Principle of good conduct
17 Shore bird
19 Attraction at St. Peter's
20 Consciousness of one's own identity
21 Residuum
22 Passed, as time
23 Year on campus
25 Small stream
27 Goddess of abundance
28 Windward opposite
29 One cause of absence
32 Discernment
35 Talkative starling
36 One-sidedness
37 Tanks for watching
39 Fine-tunes, e.g.
41 Leaders of the mongrel hordes?
42 Affirmative actions
44 Inhalation anesthetic, once
45 Graceless one
46 Indian garment
47 Blubber
48 Russian pancakes
50 Least incompetent
54 Stir to action
56 Words with jail or pot
58 Bout outcome, in brief

59 Had in mind
60 Certain layabout
62 Blue-haired mom
63 Edvard Munch's home
64 Potato parts
65 Word with tall or short
66 Netherworld river
67 Certain singing voice

DOWN
1 Derby prize
2 Visual representation
3 Mortise insert
4 It may be bitter or loose
5 Masses of prickly plants
6 Where some babies nap
7 Cube holder
8 Each
9 Express discontent
10 Serviceable
11 What some are allergic to
12 Diamond in the sky
13 Large amount
18 Decorous
22 Manipulate dough
24 Some Greek vowels
26 They bear arms?
30 Type of edition
31 SALT signer
32 Word with shell or Bell
33 Marine leader
34 Wave rider
35 A Polynesian language
36 Type of rubber

38 Really silly
40 Leaping rodent
43 Strong revulsion
46 A next of kin
47 Feline convenience
49 Epeeist's attack
51 Kind of alcohol

52 Shooting game
53 Trunk filled with blood
54 Gun shop purchase, often
55 Duff
57 No more than
60 Help wanted notice?
61 Sympathy partner

68
WHAT HENRY WROUGHT
By Raymond Hamel

ACROSS

1 Percussion instrument
5 Stole, perhaps
9 J. Alfred Prufrock's creator
14 Cruising the Pacific, e.g.
15 Alternative to a watering can
16 Hoarse
17 Spanish custard dessert
18 Statement of reassurance
19 Primrose variety
20 Alien in "A Hitchhiker's Guide to the Galaxy"
23 Needle point?
24 Symbol of virtue
25 Threw Molotov cocktails, e.g.
27 It's made off-the-cuff
30 Painter's cover-up
32 Bikini piece
33 "... ___ weepers"
36 Fraudulent activity
40 "The Prairie Capital City"
43 PayPal acquirer
44 '50s nickname
45 [This is not my typo]
46 Emulates Moe
48 Value
50 Full-bodied
53 Ex of Elizabeth Taylor
55 Environmental prefix
56 U.S. coin, 1916-45
62 Guitar attachment
64 Last wife of Charlie Chaplin
65 Become a member
66 Lord or Lady, e.g.
67 Leave out
68 Was in hock
69 Mutual fund outcome
70 Thing to save
71 Makes illegal

DOWN

1 Whaler's hook
2 Ibsen's capital
3 At hand
4 Former Indian Prime Minister Indira
5 Dizzying spin
6 Shakespearean youth
7 Since
8 Lap dog variety, for short
9 Like bedroom eyes
10 Lenient
11 Cay
12 Offer a viewpoint
13 Used a keyboard
21 "Les Demoiselles d'Avignon" painter Picasso
22 First Grammy Lifetime Achievement Award winner
26 Gumbo pod
27 Ready and willing partner
28 Small amount
29 Actress Turner
30 Dispatches
31 Wilbur Post's TV horse
34 Gerontologist's concern
35 Stop, as a winning streak
37 "Back in the ___" (Beatles song)

38 Comedy bit
39 "Into ___ life some rain . . ."
41 Anatomical sac
42 Rambunctious
47 Experienced trouble walking
49 Bond villain
50 Like some barbecue sauce
51 Middle of a play, often
52 Strong suit

53 Toga alternative
54 Make a speech
57 Top of the mouth
58 Whoever's in it is out of it
59 "Field of Dreams" locale
60 Bearing
61 Puts a stop to
63 Every one

69
A GRUFF IDEA
By Joy M. Andrews

ACROSS

1 Like Loesser's boat to China
5 Allegheny plus Monongahela
9 City on the Colorado River
13 Some Asian high priests
15 Place for an egg roll?
16 Heroine of "Because of Winn-Dixie"
17 Prevent
18 Homophone of 1-Across
19 Gusset
20 TRIP
23 Actress Lena
24 Shooter's asset
25 TRAP
33 Soaring, perhaps
34 Member of the household
35 It precedes calc., typically
36 Dirk Nowitzki, briefly
37 Smacked the baseball good and hard
41 A 1950 movie was all about her
42 Not so many
44 He was succeeded by Yusufu
45 Ali's "Rumble in the Jungle" supporters
47 TRIP
51 Toronto-to-Buffalo dir.
52 Where Elian lives
53 TRAP
61 Checklist unit
62 Ringing sound in Adano
63 Utahan chain

64 Elderly member of the household, affectionately
65 He's a Wiesel
66 Studied carefully (with "over")
67 "Following that . . ."
68 Auction actions
69 Its home is 11 Wall St.

DOWN

1 Havel, for one
2 Rock on a roll?
3 Good sign or bad sign
4 Prevent
5 Ashley and Mary-Kate
6 Bursting with health
7 Victor's outburst
8 Minimal food sample
9 Support for an Eastern discipline
10 "___ my word"
11 Winepress residue
12 Out of the storm
14 Needlelike appendages
21 Drink with cassis
22 Slowing, in music
25 Anwar's predecessor
26 Some kingly Norwegian names
27 "'Tis better to have ___ and lost . . ."
28 Type of nerve
29 It's placed at the track
30 Fabric or pancake
31 Inject with energy

32 Opposite of absorb
38 Like an unchallenged receiver
39 Soccer phenom Freddy
40 Little girl's game
43 Solomon, notably
46 Group action at Carnegie Hall
48 Stamp on bad checks
49 Where French students congregate

50 Apply Brylcreem, e.g.
53 Sticky roller's gathering
54 State with a Green River
55 Painter Magritte
56 Move, in realtor-speak
57 "The best-___ plans of mice . . ."
58 '___ 'Iggins
59 Some AAA recommendations
60 The Marquis de ___

70
ENJOY IT WHILE IT LASTS
By Lynn Lempel

ACROSS

1 Springfield kid
5 Current abbr.
9 "House" star Epps
13 Kind of acid
14 Wordsmith Webster
15 Birdbrain
16 Start of a quip
19 Photomuralist Adams
20 Emperor after Claudius
21 Give off
23 New walker and talker
24 Partner of Perrins
26 Open, as shipped goods
28 You look through it
30 Union flouter
32 Wing that won't aid in flying
33 Ma plays with them
35 Sunshine State city
37 End of the quip
40 Millions of Europeans, e.g.
41 Some pole carvings
44 Best-selling female singer of the '90s
47 Space leader?
49 Highlander
50 Supervised
52 It may follow you
54 G-8 summit attendee
55 Caked soy milk
56 Anjou alternative
58 Harmful bacteria
60 Author of the quip
63 The opposite of failed miserably
64 A driver may change one
65 Vogue shelfmate
66 More, in a maxim
67 Not natural
68 Needle apertures

DOWN

1 Maniac
2 Steelmaking need
3 "Stop fidgeting!"
4 Hurt all over
5 King Kong's beloved Darrow
6 French brandy
7 Issue a challenge to
8 Befitting an angel
9 "Intimations of Immortality," e.g.
10 They've broken with the past
11 Tarzan, e.g.
12 Put elsewhere
17 On the sick list
18 Bilk
22 Cowboy Ritter
25 Krupp family home
27 Star's bit part
29 Engineers' gear, once
31 Elicit chuckles from
34 Green-lights
36 Part man?
38 Whale of a park
39 Firmly
42 White wine named for a river
43 Common commodities
44 "M*A*S*H" prop

45 Assertion

46 Restore, as walls

48 City near Milwaukee

51 Writer Burrows

53 Corner key

57 Dance to rock music?

59 "Of ___ I Sing"

61 Six-pt. scores

62 Composer Rorem

71
ON THE KEYBOARD
By Alan Olschwang

ACROSS
1 In __ of (replacing)
5 System of moral values
10 Sing "shooby-doo," e.g.
14 Chop-chop
15 Cold-shoulders
16 Mate's call, perhaps
17 Kind of game
18 Features of some shirts
20 Tropical nut tree
21 Alternative introductions
22 Close by
23 Recipe abbr.
25 Jamaica-based music
26 PC grouping
27 Range, e.g.
33 "Are you a man __ mouse?"
34 Communications system of the past
35 Stun gun
38 Lashing reminder
40 Dark, dull and dirty
42 Race distance, sometimes
43 Water lily
45 Decorative toiletry cases
47 James Bond creator Fleming
48 Come into a person's consciousness
51 Small boy
53 November winners
54 Meadowland
55 He founded the Ottoman dynasty
57 Undecided's abbreviation
59 Harriet Beecher Stowe novel
63 Change suddenly, e.g.
65 Cherish
66 Prehistoric tool
67 Kind of badge
68 "Como __ usted?"
69 Singer/songwriter Paul
70 San Antonio shrine
71 Jack of Tom Clancy novels

DOWN
1 Dearth
2 Aoki of golf
3 Viscount's superior
4 Summary of recent developments
5 Barred legally
6 "__ she blows!"
7 Major airports, e.g.
8 Corporate name ender
9 Larry of the undefeated Dolphins
10 Casa component
11 King of Spain from 1759-88
12 Feeder of the body's organs
13 Jane Pittman portrayer Cicely
19 Inclined, in England
24 Remained unused
25 Oater shootin' iron
27 Caterwaul
28 Two-tone treat
29 Fountain treat
30 Toolbox item
31 Slow, in music

32 Rotating machine part
36 Panache
37 Tear apart
39 Wine cask
41 Allows passing
44 Term of employment, e.g.
46 Chicago-to-Louisville dir.
49 Riddle relative
50 More irate

51 Puccini's "___"
52 Visibly frightened
56 Aqua Velva competitor
57 "Gone With the Wind" mansion
58 Sombrero feature
60 Type of outlook
61 Kett of the comics
62 College bigwig
64 Bioelectric fish

72
LITERAL REACTION
By Ed Early

ACROSS

1 AWOL-hunters
4 Be a night owl
10 To ___ (precisely)
14 Nag's nosh, perhaps
15 Mark a page, in a way
16 Noise from a pride
17 Start of a pun
20 "Cunning hunter" of the Bible
21 Wal-Mart founder Walton
22 Discontinues
23 Mobile-to-Atlanta dir.
25 Prepare jute, e.g.
26 Land starter?
27 Pun (Part 2)
33 Goat-legged mythical creature
34 Sportscaster Dick
35 Teen formal
36 Primate of Madagascar
37 Collagist's need
41 Donahue of "Father Knows Best"
43 Some carpets
44 Pun (Part 3)
46 AC capacity measurement
48 Savvy about (with "to")
49 ___ Lingus (Irish airline)
50 Mandrake's partner in crime-fighting
52 ___ de sac
54 Investigatory aid
58 End of the pun
61 Originate, as a phrase
62 Holy city?

63 Switch to low beam
64 They may be matched
65 Phrase in a kid's argument, perhaps
66 Done with a wink, say

DOWN

1 Small particle
2 Kit's mitts
3 Zeno's promenade
4 Star Wars to R.W.R.
5 Quoits participant
6 Turkish bigwig (Var.)
7 Tom's respectful reply to Aunt Polly
8 Union based in Detroit, Mich.
9 Bargain hunter's delight
10 Te Kanawa specialty
11 It's down in the mouth
12 Faster's opposite?
13 Irregularly notched, as a leaf
18 Seinfeld, Carrey, Rock, collectively
19 Word with heavy or sheet
24 ATM maker
25 Profit made on an investment
27 Hooded menace
28 Part of a train
29 Certain Plains native
30 Tie, as a score
31 Indonesian island
32 Prolific chickens
36 Well-read individuals
38 Counterpart of long.

39 An expression of disdain
40 112.5 degrees
42 "The Merry Widow" composer
43 Pt. of many Quebec place names
44 Win the Home Run Derby, e.g.
45 Choices at some bars
46 Partisan coalitions
47 From head ___

51 Layers in the barnyard
52 CMII divided by II
53 Versatility listings
55 They're sometimes stacked
56 Explore the Seven Seas, e.g.
57 Television award
59 Part of a famous soliloquy
60 "___-hoo!"

73
LIVING WELL?
By B. Venzke & S. Daily

ACROSS
1 Acclaim for Pavarotti
6 Sigma preceder
9 Take as one's own
14 Opponent in business or sports
15 "Rebel Without a Cause" star Mineo
16 Capital of the First State
17 Emotion in defeat, sometimes
18 Engage in rivalry
19 Make accustomed to (Var.)
20 "The Hundred Secret Senses" author
21 Quip (Part 1)
24 Idaho product, slangily
25 Pet for King Solomon
26 Full-bodied, as a woman
29 Former Iranian ruler
31 NAFTA signer
34 Quip (Part 2)
37 Depilatory brand
38 Big ox
39 "On the Waterfront" director Kazan
40 Quip (Part 3)
45 Start of some Californian city names
46 Sneaky laughs
47 Betsy, Diana and others
48 Borrow, as a cigarette
49 Like spoiled meat
50 Quip (Part 4)
55 Pool table success
58 Turn away, as a crisis
59 It's comprised of ages and ages
60 Lulu
62 "Family Circus" cartoonist Bil
63 Woodworker's tool
64 Redheaded orphan
65 Fragrant compound
66 Classic car
67 Brewing agent

DOWN
1 Obnoxious young'un
2 Latvia's largest city
3 Mary Kay competitor
4 Moving vehicle
5 Airline once owned by Onassis
6 Informed the host, in a way
7 Mane makeup
8 Stick in the dairy case?
9 Long Island university
10 Gifted person
11 It may become fertilized
12 Scope starter
13 Uno and dos
22 Butt of many car jokes
23 Jezebel's deity
24 Dele cancellations
26 Whizzing bullet sounds
27 End of "the end of"
28 Certain refrigerant
29 Picket line crossers
30 '50s audiophile's purchase
31 Wrinkly Jamaican fruits
32 Slug, old-style
33 Indian nursemaids

35 Old Testament name
36 Full of the latest info
41 Window attachment or camera part
42 Prefix meaning "half"
43 Streetcar, in Surrey
44 When your prince will come
48 City by the Aare
49 Hook-nosed Muppet

50 Fabricate
51 First name in fashion
52 Orderly
53 Within spitting distance
54 Word with bar or airport
55 Barrett of Hollywood
56 Israeli-made weapons
57 Kremlin negative
61 "A Chorus Line" number?

74
IN THE ARMY
By Lanore Tan

ACROSS
1 They go on and off highways
6 Red played him
10 Bedazzle
14 Nobody's fool
15 Verdi heroine
16 Exclamation of disappointment
17 Good physical health
18 Bootleggers' bane
19 Clark's beloved
20 Trespasser's domain
23 Ablutionary vessels
24 Mi followers
25 Balmoral Castle's river
28 "Every dog ___ its . . ."
29 Piercing tool
30 Serpentine sound
33 Turgenev heroine
35 This org. has a lot of pull
36 Choral category
37 Like a naturalized citizen
41 Involving the ear
42 Cambridgeshire cathedral town
43 Certain citrus fruit
44 Evidence of big foot?
45 Start of Mr. Rogers' song
46 Fa-la linkup
48 Full of tricks
49 They may be classified or personal
50 Narrow groove
52 Lawyer's apparel?
59 Butterfingers' exclamation
60 Sound the tocsin

61 1959 Nobelist Severo
62 Facial part
63 Landed
64 Opposite of everybody
65 Let it stand, to an editor
66 Puppies' plaints
67 Lucy's landlady

DOWN
1 Invitation's request, for short
2 Old song "Abdul Abulbul ___"
3 Yuletide visitors
4 Establish as valid
5 Boater
6 Supplies the victuals
7 Walks lamely
8 Fulda River tributary
9 Warship
10 Parts of tennis shoes
11 Hammer-wielding god
12 The U in BTU
13 Overly curious
21 Herbal brew
22 Close friend
25 Moll Flanders' creator
26 Upper crust
27 Likely to creep you out
29 Stock or block attachment
30 Slenderizes
31 Seat without a back
32 "I Got You Babe" singer
34 Defense advisory grp.
35 "Pick a card, ___ card"
36 Did some noshing

38 Escapes
39 Ernie of the PGA
40 Comprehensive
45 Some may have photos
46 Tenures
47 Guadalajara gold
49 Rainy day need
50 Las Vegas feature
51 English racetrack

52 Bamboozles
53 Swag
54 Domed or vaulted recess
55 Colombian city
56 "Here comes trouble!"
57 "The Last Days of Pompeii" heroine
58 Oriental unit of weight

75
ALL MADE UP
By Carol Lachance

ACROSS
1 Concocted
7 Sometimes it's more
11 Judge made famous in 1995
14 Most earthlings
15 Certain chorister
16 Buster or fella
17 Navigation aids
18 "The Ballad of Reading ___"
19 Barbary beast
20 It can make you shine
23 Form of writing
25 Nuncupative
26 Symbol of virtue
27 One getting by on chicken feed?
28 "O ___ Golden Slippers"
30 Type of patch
32 Sugar substitute?
34 It was once harbored in Boston
36 Bit of baby talk
37 Short-lived success
42 It may be split
43 It may be a bust
44 Words with sit or look
46 Make more substantial, in a way
49 School of thought
51 Certain prayer
52 Toast softener
53 Side by side?
56 Without dissent
58 Gravel Gertie's daughter
61 Amniotic ___
62 Furthermore
63 Rodeo implement

66 Euro forerunner
67 Middle Ages quaff
68 Home of the mountain gorilla
69 Imitate an annoying dog
70 Chamber starter
71 Place for the bottom line

DOWN
1 Jobs result?
2 Wood used for tool handles
3 On the bias
4 Some bluebloods
5 Freed, in a way
6 Relative of "ahem"
7 Keg contents from Milwaukee
8 One of Jupiter's moons
9 Motor vehicle features
10 Band member's moment
11 Nigerian metropolis
12 Elvis' birthplace
13 King of the fairies
21 "My Cousin Vinny" star
22 "Comic Relief" name
23 Coveted degree
24 Ocean obstacle
29 Green Mountain Boys leader
31 Agile deer
33 Meat-eating bird
35 Anecdote collection, e.g.
38 "What did I tell you?"
39 Due process process
40 Pesky
41 Word that's an example of itself
45 Sailing dir.

46 Zoologist Dian
47 Silky wool producer
48 Mad Hatter prop
50 Run
54 Went back into session
55 It has long and short verses

57 Fine violin, for short
59 "___ Sutra"
60 Part of the Jewish calendar
64 Lime drink
65 It may go on a drive

76
AWESOME!
By Ken Twigg

ACROSS

1 Reclusive Garbo
6 Alpine transport, e.g.
10 More than a twinge
14 Turbine part
15 Sound equipment giant
16 "Tom Thumb" composer
17 Awesome!
19 Not in shape?
20 Hebdomad
21 Pub pint
22 Lincoln Center landmark, informally
24 It may be hard to believe
27 Palindromic English river
28 Stonecutters
31 Avoid ignorance
33 It lays eggs out back?
34 Proscribed by society as improper
37 Chain of hills
40 Moment of forgetfulness
42 It's never neutral
43 Poppycock
44 Cowrie cover
45 The ones right here
47 One "A" in Paris
48 Something to rule
50 They get belted regularly
52 Brainsick
54 Collector of foreign stamps
57 Good luck charm
59 Word with drops or canal
60 Horseshoe site

64 Kelly of TV
65 Awesome!
68 Historic assassination date
69 Formal ceremony
70 Battery terminal
71 Desertlike
72 Freedom from financial need
73 Target practice game

DOWN

1 Multiply
2 Dissolute one
3 Conclusion for Ann or Jean
4 Grew fond of
5 Kennel comment
6 Govt. IOU
7 Thesaurus compiler
8 Baseball bat wood
9 Fortitude
10 Kemo ___ ("trusty scout")
11 Awesome!
12 Tack on
13 Midler of stage and screen
18 Dance or sauce
23 Old-style affirmation
25 Animal at home on the range
26 One way to stand
28 Sitcom diner
29 Memsahib's nurse, perhaps
30 Awesome!
32 "Blame it on ___" (Caine film)
35 Posts on a ship's deck
36 Awesome!
38 Squire

39 They may be on the game

41 ___-pitch softball

46 Vowed

49 Lampoon

51 Cogito

52 McGwire broke his record

53 Ammonia compound

55 Splinter groups, sometimes

56 "The Girl From Gay ___" (1927)

58 Emit coherent light

61 Woodwind with a conical bore

62 Ye ___ Curiosity Shoppe

63 They're found in a yard

66 Kwanzaa day

67 "___ Boot" (1981 film)

77
ACTIVE CREATURES
By Gene Newman

ACROSS
1 It may be practical
5 Former central African republic
10 Major river of Spain
14 They're often included in good deals
15 Swashbuckler Flynn
16 Sign of the times
17 Turn and run, e.g.
19 It's sometimes a drag
20 Garden fertilizer brand
21 Not fooled by
22 Bothers
23 Observed
25 A Finger Lake
27 Cool one's heels
29 London and Manhattan districts
32 X, in letters
35 Late PLO head
39 Rap sheet abbr.
40 Exeter-to-London dir.
41 This puzzle's theme includes them
42 It may be in the air
43 Weapons grp.
44 Troubling
45 Laudatory poems
46 Diacritical mark
48 Dinero
50 Arterial trunks
54 Unsettle
58 Go back to square one
60 "Dies ___"
62 Gold measure (Var.)

63 Network signal
64 Tamper
66 History type
67 Organic compound
68 Yearn
69 It's often served with a lemon wedge
70 Helps a child fall to sleep, perhaps
71 Foreteller

DOWN
1 Esau's brother
2 Earthy color
3 Richards of the Rolling Stones
4 Shuns
5 New York's Tappan ___ Bridge
6 Ponte Vecchio river
7 Certain clubs
8 Mail carrier's beat
9 John on the piano
10 Tenor Caruso
11 Help out
12 Plymouth landmark
13 Individuals
18 Beverage nut
24 "Cheers" character
26 Ballpark figs.
28 Cereal for kids
30 "The Grapes of Wrath" figure
31 Enervates
32 County in England
33 Cross initials
34 What a handshake may do

USA TODAY.

78
CD SALE
By Janet Bender

ACROSS

1 Twist's desire
5 El ___, Texas
9 Buckwheat porridge
14 Gas-powered machine gun
15 Steel support beam
16 Word with time or rights
17 Current choice
18 St. Petersburg's river
19 Russian capital
20 Bakery employee
23 Address of St. Patrick's Cathedral?
25 Not of the cloth
26 Word before up, out, off or down
27 Certain plane
30 Boone portrayer Parker
31 Hinny's kin
32 Sumac souvenir, perhaps
33 Mule in a song
35 T, in physics
37 Airline home base
39 Tea serving, in Britain
43 Word sometimes placed between two names
45 Burn protection
47 Place where people twisted
48 Frame part
51 Horse-drawn carriage operators
54 Anglo-Saxon coin
55 Participant in some receptions
56 Emulate Wiley Post
57 Some ranchers
61 Some theater awards
62 Jackie Robinson's alma mater
63 Museum that's called a gallery
66 African peninsula
67 Black shade
68 It may come with intensive care
69 Word with golden or bald
70 Sicilian resort city
71 Inscribe on a trophy, e.g.

DOWN

1 CEO's degree, perhaps
2 Mythical sea creature
3 Relief organization
4 Put down stakes?
5 Pesto ingredient
6 Still under cover
7 Feather one's nest
8 Delphic prophet
9 Irish dairy cattle breed
10 Light blue
11 Insidious
12 Circles in some religious paintings
13 APBs, e.g.
21 Alaskan island
22 Scull propellers
23 Singing style
24 Highland tongue
28 High or elementary (Abbr.)
29 Critic or hitchhiker's need
30 Winter malady
34 Like some volcanoes
36 Chemist's workplace

38 Job estimate
40 Dish served under glass
41 Left onboard?
42 Semicircular room
44 Teen tribulation
46 Singsong syllables
48 Waggish
49 Peninsula near the Red Sea
50 Winning chess matches

52 Bring forward as evidence
53 Moral excellence
55 Borden cow
58 Game bird
59 M.B.A.'s major, perhaps
60 Shepard in space
64 Persistent personal quirk
65 Biblical verb suffix

USA TODAY.

79
BOTTLE OPENERS
By Elizabeth C. Gorski

ACROSS
1 Emulate Gumby
5 Some Surrealist paintings
10 Palpebral swelling
14 Words with equal basis
15 Where Androcles was spared
16 Stereo times two
17 St. Patrick's Day treats
19 Homely citrus fruit
20 LXVII tripled
21 On pins and needles
22 Stud with jewels
23 An Algonquian language
25 It's slapstick material
26 ___ Lingus (Irish airline)
27 Fan fare
32 Music and dance, e.g.
34 Gripes
35 Delight
36 Acceptances
37 Confined
38 Some servings of strong coffee
40 Pandora's boxful
41 They hang around carpenters
42 Santa ___, California
43 El Al's primary destination (Abbr.)
44 When some exams are scheduled
48 ___-Saxon
51 Lamb Chop's manipulator
53 Carte start
54 Request for permission
55 Fried chicken covering, sometimes
57 Irregular French verb
58 Journalist Shriver
59 **** review, e.g.
60 Outback bounders, briefly
61 It's the right alternative
62 Roman passageway

DOWN
1 Bartlett cousins
2 Father of Methuselah
3 First name in gymnastics
4 Modern evidence
5 One who's on the mend?
6 Mountain ridge
7 Grazing places
8 Prof. Jones, familiarly
9 Stockholm-bound flight, perhaps
10 Baseball maneuver
11 Heartstring stimuli
12 Institution founded in 1701
13 Redo a clue
18 Afflictions
22 Dental occlusion
24 Monet subjects
25 Enlivens (with "up")
27 Mexican moolah
28 Short ways to go?
29 Daredevil Knievel
30 See-through item
31 Former J.F.K. lander

32 Likewise
33 Seized vehicle, slangily
34 Bothersome type
35 Understand
36 River of Flanders
39 Exxon, in Canada
40 Forster subject
42 Automotive safety feature
44 Actor Cheech
45 Bother terribly

46 Motrin competitor
47 Less likely to appear
48 Pt. of U.S.A.
49 Cold War side
50 Greek deli order, perhaps
51 Scorch
52 One getting a decoration
55 Yuppie status symbol
56 Prefix with state

80
FIRST FAMILY
By Lynn Lempel

ACROSS

1 "Luncheon on the Grass" painter
6 Some undergrads
11 Cul-de-___
14 Type type
15 Water source
16 Fury
17 Any second now
19 Dejected
20 Bought but not delivered
21 Take in liquids
23 OB partner
24 Beak
26 Eliminates debt
27 At the back of the plane
29 Some electrical plug-in devices
33 Spreadsheet creation, perhaps
36 Phillips-Van Heusen brand
37 Gaelic singer
38 Miss the mark
39 "Anti-art" art movement of WWI
42 Klutz
43 Rampage
45 John and Yoko's son
46 Carried, as by the wind
48 Bengal tiger, for one
50 You do this at home, but not first
51 Round number
52 Witness
54 Spread, as hay
57 Actor Wynn

59 Copied
62 S&L offering
63 Presidential intimates and theme of this puzzle
66 Set of locks
67 It has many rays
68 Give birth in a barn, perhaps
69 Much of Greenland
70 Fraternity letter
71 They have caps

DOWN

1 Note from the boss, perhaps
2 Word with tag or string
3 Vulcan portrayer
4 Never-ending
5 Be inclined
6 Close shave
7 Bruin legend
8 Louvre pyramid architect
9 Rooftop landing sites
10 Stargazer's guide
11 A south-of-the-border assent
12 Al-Jazeera viewer, traditionally
13 Hand over
18 It may be pitched and struck
22 Computer unit
25 Some charity events
28 Put coins in
30 Utterly ruin
31 Film private
32 Box for crackers?
33 Glossary entry
34 Libretto listing

35 Early toolmaking period
36 ___ fixe (obsession)
40 Flabbergast
41 Marketing deg., perhaps
44 Parent's challenge, stereotypically
47 One Constantinople ruler
49 1994 Peace Nobelist
50 Complaint
53 Superfluous

55 Napoleon was one
56 Research deeply
57 Fruit native to China and Taiwan
58 Leif's father
60 Ruin partner
61 They may provide highlights
64 Road with a no.
65 Primed

81
MISER-Y
By Robert H. Wolfe

ACROSS

1 Tour of duty
6 The Crimson Tide, for short
10 Bullets, et al.
14 Ballroom dance
15 They run North-South in N.Y.C.
16 Little hopper
17 Without pause
18 ___ Hashana (Jewish New Year)
19 Type of excuse
20 Start of a quip
23 RPM part
24 Frigid
25 History chapters
26 Under-the-sink item
28 Bucket material, perhaps
31 "Get outta here!"
34 Jackie's ex
35 One way to form a union
37 Middle of the quip
41 Poe's middle name
42 Terre Haute sch.
43 Galley's many
44 Opposite of paleo
45 Indication of very bad things to come
49 Persia, now
50 King's nickname
51 Photo ___ (times for publicity shots)
54 End of the quip
59 Director Kazan
60 Daytime entertainment
61 Meet part

62 Early time for poets
63 Queen before George I
64 Stentorian
65 Edible fat
66 Gams
67 Unpleasant political tactic

DOWN

1 Old punisher
2 Grayish-brown
3 Kind of tube
4 "The Killing Fields" Oscar-winning actor Haing S. ___
5 It sticks in your throat
6 Farm area
7 Swear
8 Interlocks
9 On dry land
10 Mythical one with a heavy burden
11 Castle protection
12 Angela Lansbury role
13 Lyric verses
21 Indian, for one
22 Sultan's pride
26 Club of song
27 Quantity of no importance
28 Chaplin's last wife
29 Imitator
30 Piano pieces?
31 Musial of baseball
32 Financial predicament
33 Storting meeting place
36 Diving bird

38 Madrid month
39 Uranium has many
40 Tally
46 One holding a fief
47 Chant
48 Waters and Barrymore
49 Words from a quitter
51 Weighty

52 One of a famous three vessels
53 Woodland deity
54 They're tailor-made
55 Jesus or Moises
56 Paddock papa
57 Telephoned
58 Female gamete

82
TWINKLE, TWINKLE
By Fred Jackson III

ACROSS
1 Kind of battle
6 Taunt
10 Essential point
14 Video game pioneer
15 The rain in Spain?
16 Nice friend
17 Three-card con
18 Oomph!
19 Dust movers
20 Mom's twins?
21 Understand
24 One of the common folk
25 Hits the snooze button, e.g.
26 Grouper group
31 Survivor, of a sort
32 Is beholden to
33 Meditative school of Buddhism
36 Prefix meaning "flower"
37 Some Islamic people
39 Zap
40 Ore. neighbor
41 Like some inaccurate watches
42 Functions
43 Loses a showdown, e.g.
46 Bright
49 Poetic periods
50 Rooming house offering
53 X ending
56 Students' stats
57 Accelerator particles
58 Ordain
60 Do some arm-twisting
61 Show overaffection

62 Part of a big name in fashion
63 Denials
64 Commercial
65 Guide

DOWN
1 Blow the whistle on
2 Basic bit
3 Movers but not shakers
4 College major
5 Hides out
6 Summerhouse
7 "___ Around" (Beach Boys hit)
8 Australian region
9 Hash houses
10 Loud
11 Word with spitting or public
12 Spectacle
13 Tries out
22 It may be smoked
23 Discounted by
24 Milne creature
26 Symbol of grace
27 It's for public viewing in France
28 Cutting-edge viewing
29 Some are made from snow
30 NBA position
33 A Bantu language
34 Scratches (out)
35 Fit together snugly
37 Long-horned grasshoppers
38 Press into service
39 Silent assents
41 Huckleberry or Mickey

42 Provides with
43 Prejudgments
44 Afternoon service
45 That ship
46 Weapon that isn't deadly to humans
47 Photocopy, for short
48 Traditional truism

51 Betty of toon fame
52 Aware of
53 Stable locks
54 Entr'___
55 Word that could precede the last word in 21, 26, 43 and 50-Across
59 Clear, financially

83
IT'S A WRAP
By Jim Curran

ACROSS
1 Washington follower
6 Finish third
10 Bounders
14 "___ c'est moi"
15 Fashion name
16 Pass over
17 It has true grit
19 Assess
20 Wrap
22 Key contraction
23 Some degrees
24 Beach-goer's catch
27 Duffers' triumphs
30 Gene Vincent's "Be-Bop-___"
34 Important time span
35 Be visibly dispirited
36 1781 discovery
37 Wrap
40 Duty
41 Erstwhile acorns
42 A Nike's perch
43 Untouchables, for one
44 Epitome of grace
45 Parker of "Old Yeller"
46 It doesn't take much?
48 Cry of amused surprise
50 Wrap
57 Panache
58 F, to the Board of Health
59 Perplexing path
60 Name in early TV
61 Brief in speech
62 Earned a warning, in a way

63 Checked out
64 They may be deserted

DOWN
1 Knighted Guinness
2 Singer's sample
3 "Got two fives for ___?"
4 She never got cold feet?
5 Arrange hair
6 Multitude
7 Famous diamond
8 Many many
9 Far from the best
10 Popular side dish
11 Father's word
12 Intentional loss
13 Hog haven
18 Allege
21 Swiss beets
24 Archaeologist's find
25 Wine-taster's consideration
26 Kennel sounds
28 LAPD alert
29 Start a second crop, e.g.
31 Bring together
32 Publishers Henry and Clare
33 Sackcloth partner
35 Capital of Lesotho
36 Anonymous
38 Took a liking (to)
39 Battery type
44 2000 Olympics city
45 Skills
47 Get away from

49 Country on the island of Hispaniola
50 Word with stick
51 "Purple ___" (Hendrix tune)
52 To be, in Roma

53 Sneak attack
54 Earthy deposit
55 Certain Scots
56 Some food grains
57 Ends of a midterm?

84
DON'T DELAY
By Thomas W. Schier

ACROSS
1 Feast of the Unleavened Bread
6 Diamond defect
10 "The Art of Love" poet
14 Earthy pigment
15 Lockheed Martin field
17 Start of a quip about putting things off
19 Big ___, Calif.
20 Wine city
21 Simpleton
22 "See you later"
24 It takes two to do this
27 Socket counterpart
29 Picasso or Neruda
31 Wine region
35 Disney mermaid
37 It splits the Left and Right Banks
39 Bar supply
40 Quip (Part 2)
42 Quip (Part 3)
44 Denver-to-Wichita dir.
45 Syrian sect member (Var.)
47 Stock the party
48 Helen of Troy's mother
50 Grain for the mill
52 More than a miss
53 Beefy bovine
55 Come to a standstill
57 Potato variety
60 Laundry measure
62 Paranormal power, for short
65 End of the quip
69 Initially began

70 Howling winds
71 ". . . __ forgive our debtors"
72 Prefix meaning "billionth"
73 Conquest of Alexander the Great

DOWN
1 Soft drinks or daddies
2 Neutral shade
3 Of limited existence
4 Type of welder
5 Afghan city on the Hari Rud
6 Like lightning
7 The Beatles' last film
8 Mr. Onassis, to friends
9 Prevailed
10 Choice
11 Full of oneself
12 Desktop symbol
13 Claim to be false
16 Warbled
18 Posthaste, briefly
23 Windward's opposite
25 Dresses with flared bottoms
26 Inadvisable action
27 Breakfast item
28 What a question might do
30 Free from doubt
32 In a disturbed manner
33 Suffered from homesickness, e.g.
34 About to explode
36 Dropped hallucinogen
38 All-encompassing abbr.

1	2	3	4	5	■	6	7	8	9	■	10	11	12	13
14					■	15				16				
17				18										
19			■	20				■		21				
■	■	22	23			■	24	25	26			■	■	■
27	28			■	29	30				■	31	32	33	34
35			36	■	37				38	■	39			
40				41		■	42			43				
44			■	45			46		■	47				
48			49	■	50				51	■	52			
■	■	■	53	54				■	55	56			■	■
57	58	59			■	■	60	61			■	62	63	64
65				66	67					68				
69							■	70						
71				■	72				■	73				

41 Advocate
43 Monitor's beat
46 Steak choice
49 Taking liberty
51 Warming of relations
54 Palindromic sound effect
56 Time-honored truism
57 Words with deal or date
58 Children's connectibles

59 What there ought to be
61 Yes ___ (one of two answers)
63 Big feat for baby
64 Racetrack marker
66 Documentary filmer Burns
67 Pharmaceuticals watchdog agcy.
68 Word with doll or mop

85
EASY AS PIE
By Lynn Lempel

ACROSS

1 Attempt at a carnival booth
5 Title role for Jude
10 Scolds ceaselessly
14 Mississippi senator
15 "When We Were Very Young" poet
16 October gem
17 Be very selective
19 Exclusive
20 Cold War figure
21 Cruise ship amenity
22 Marseille miss
23 Portion of the economy
26 Entangle, as traffic
28 Elite bunch
31 Be valetudinarian
32 Colloquial assent
33 Object at the beginning of a hole
34 Mark of omission
36 Bravo or Grande
38 "Como ___ usted?"
42 Persian's cry
45 Casey Jones, for one (Abbr.)
48 Web filmer
49 Person very dear to you
53 Puffed up
54 N.Y.C. sports event
55 Ravel ballet heroine
56 Partner of games
59 CPR giver
60 Acne-prone
61 Beat around the bush, in a way

65 Turn tail
66 Opera highlights
67 Greek pantheon leader
68 ___ for oneself
69 "She loves me" unit
70 First-ever winner of 54-Across

DOWN

1 Compassionate letters
2 Sound of amazement
3 Controversial research focus
4 Rock layers
5 Jimmy and Rosalynn's daughter
6 They might be sealed
7 Gymnastic feat
8 How some pay
9 Cry of surprise
10 "Of course not!"
11 God of poetry
12 Public opinion expert
13 New parent's lack?
18 Commodious
22 Cliff surface
23 Whole lot
24 Large freshwater lake
25 Beluga delicacy
27 Invoice item, perhaps
29 Wide partner
30 Fence supplier
35 Working
37 "Double Fantasy" performer
39 Sovereignties, in Britain
40 "Rent" actor Diggs
41 "Lilies of the Field" song

43 Glamour competitor
44 Teensy
46 Brindled beast
47 Stitch up a torn seam, e.g.
49 Some time
50 Allergy trigger
51 Blazing
52 Former Nicaraguan dictator

53 Laugh at mockingly
57 Military division
58 Sports org.
61 Cartographer's creation
62 Subj. for green card holders, perhaps
63 Sarcastic retort
64 Nottingham-to-Brighton dir.

86
I'M READY
By David Sullivan

ACROSS

1 "You're soaking in it" spokeswoman
6 Compartment
10 Poise
14 Hold 'em alternative
15 "I, ___," rock autobiography
16 In the thick of
17 Moves, realtor-style
18 Declare positively
19 They keep a close eye on figures
20 Astronaut's "I'm ready!"
23 "South Pacific" ingenue
24 Dulles Airport designer Saarinen
25 Song of David
29 Kodak founder
31 Org. that might help fund an exhibit
33 Darius, to Alexander
34 Cereal grain
35 "The Real World" network
36 Word with cut or neck
37 Performer's "I'm ready!"
41 Encumbrance
42 Creighton Chaney, professionally
43 Soissons street
44 Shade of blond
45 Perfect score, perhaps
46 Threatening sorts
50 Citizen competitor
52 Sloan entrance requirement
54 Scholarly volume
55 Skydiver's "I'm ready!"
58 St. Petersburg museum
61 Be hopping mad
62 "It's ___!" (meeting confirmation)
63 Word often said while kneeling
64 Memo opener
65 Alpine warble
66 Unit of computer storage
67 "Yikes!"
68 Traffic jam, e.g.

DOWN

1 Esprit de corps
2 First name in aviation
3 Neighbor of Irving
4 Western tourist attraction
5 How some things come and go?
6 Island over the Verrazano-Narrows Bridge
7 It may be served with fried onions
8 Length of a lunar cycle, roughly
9 Cigarette substances
10 Folded entrees
11 Electrical measure
12 KGB counterpart
13 Cowboys' aims?
21 "Frasier" setting
22 Magna cum laude determiner
26 Natural do
27 MGM name, once
28 It may be heard after littering

Page 177 of 448

30 ___ tai
32 Puget Sound port
35 Rockies abbr.
36 Was unfaithful to
37 Seine tributary
38 Radar's refreshment
39 Region at the mouth of the Pearl River
40 Baltimore newspaper
41 Vegas opener?
45 Overly

46 Attacked by a lion, e.g.
47 Pineapple cocktail, for one
48 Ham
49 "Black Beauty" author
51 "The Pink Panther" actor (2006)
53 Shearer of ballet
56 Off-Broadway award
57 Howls, as a wolf
58 Tiny bit, as of cream
59 Vanderbilt or Irving
60 Tennis do-over

USA TODAY.

87
JEWELRY DEPARTMENT
By Fran & Lou Sabin

ACROSS

1 Kiddie pool user, perhaps
6 Take in
10 Numbskull
14 Isolated
15 Crude come-on
16 Holly
17 Prospecting woman?
19 Million finish
20 "Get my meaning?"
21 Certain celebration times
22 Celebrated
24 Duke or earl, e.g.
25 Super-heavyweight's sport
26 Family emblems
29 Plains tribesman
33 Polonius' hiding place
34 Emulate an attacking bull
35 Unpromising outlook
36 Poker holding, perhaps
37 Corporate hotshots, slangily
38 In fine shape
39 Footnote abbreviation
40 Coffee containers, often
41 Fictional rabbit
42 Some men and women
44 Mermanesque
45 It traveled past sirens
46 God's handy work, according to God
47 "Go get 'em!"
50 Unfortunate motor sound
51 Welcome sign for a producer

54 Chef's secret ingredient, sometimes
55 Military award
58 Creamy nibble
59 Pennsylvania city
60 Trixie's sitcom pal
61 Still-life object
62 Suffix for four
63 Mushroom type

DOWN

1 Turns tail?
2 Soap additive, often
3 He ran beside a Ford
4 Word with bitter or tail
5 Turns in coupons
6 Wilco preceder
7 Many were hidden on April 16, 2006
8 It may be drawn
9 Air sweeteners
10 Oahu landmark
11 Hodgepodge
12 Where the Ucayali flows
13 Some signatures
18 Currier's partner
23 Ob-gyn's org.
24 Inlet near 10-Down
25 Puts into piles, e.g.
26 Come to a head?
27 Valedictorians do it
28 Three of a kind
29 Invents, as a word

30 Checked items
31 Greenskeeper's concern
32 Kind of board or cloth
34 Painter Reni
37 Play scenery
41 Something to get with (with "the")
43 Work unit, in physics
44 Meat holder
46 Established fact

47 Rough seas feature
48 Pointer's word
49 Kind of rug
50 Barre movement
51 Budge
52 Word with human or foot
53 Oka River city
56 Choler
57 ___-mo special effect

88
DON'T BRING ME DOWN
By Damon J. Gulczynski

ACROSS

1 It's not a good thing in pink
5 "___ like old times"
10 Sandwich alternative
14 "Swan Lake" garb
15 Paella pots, perhaps
16 Shakespearean character
17 Descended
18 Type of fire
19 "Go away!"
20 Tips of the cap, hitches of the belt, perhaps
22 Jury constituents
23 Participates in a hunt
24 Cilium
25 Exculpate
28 Portions between radii
31 Word with in, out or up
32 J. Crew customer, perhaps
35 Antique car
36 They might be false
38 Worthless coin
39 Portia de ___ of "Arrested Development"
41 Klondike find
42 Industrial results
45 Nautical centerpiece
46 If they look like you they may be dead
48 Casts out
50 Kind of curve, in math
51 Steel-driver John
53 Batting crown winner his first two seasons

55 Possible theme, but not a description of this puzzle
59 Pass the time idly
60 Product in FedEx Kinko's inventory
61 Union joiner of 1803
62 "You said it!"
63 Domain of one of the Muses
64 Distance letters
65 ___ up (tell all)
66 Box score data
67 Comfort

DOWN

1 Run through
2 Lollapalooza
3 Pack ___ (quit trying)
4 Type of golf
5 Beau monde
6 Plaintive poem
7 Panaches
8 Type of production
9 Kathmandu-to-Calcutta dir.
10 Most like Solomon
11 They have purses on them
12 Gel in biology class, perhaps
13 They may be made of chips or pennies
21 ___ Lanka
22 Conseco Fieldhouse player
24 Welcome garland
25 Titanic casualty
26 Comedic actress Oteri
27 Some mattresses

28 Tater
29 Trip meter button
30 Garden mixes
33 Employs
34 Ward heeler, e.g.
37 Mirthful carnivore
40 "You betcha"
43 Umbrage
44 Spanish letter opener?
47 Presumed truths

49 Watchdog warning
51 Barbera's partner
52 Oust by force
53 Scandinavian name
54 Quite uncool
55 Castle protector
56 Ostrich relative
57 Puts on the small screen
58 Neither here nor there
60 Some one-yd. runs

89
GO FOR BROKE
By Fran & Lou Sabin

ACROSS

1 Type of tube
5 Seeks a pardon?
9 Bad thing to be out of
14 Discourteous
15 War of 1812 lake
16 Likely Dubrovnik resident
17 Car battery component
18 Great deal
19 Grow less
20 Gambler's credo, perhaps
23 Lacking in vitality
24 Spiker's barrier
25 Cutting remark
27 Made tracks competitively
30 More than due
33 See the light
35 Long-jawed fish
36 Gunsel, e.g.
37 Gambler's credo, perhaps
40 Cause of painter's colic
41 Barely manage (with "out")
42 Skins' foe
43 On the wagon, perhaps
44 Places to have dates?
46 Wraps up
47 Elm and Maple, briefly
48 Merry prank
50 Gambler's credo, perhaps
58 Love like mad
59 Panhandler's desire
60 Candidate's desire
61 Jewish observance
62 It may precede old age

63 Zero-zero or 30-30, e.g.
64 Word in "The Shadow" intro
65 Ambassadorship, e.g.
66 Some SWAT team equipment

DOWN

1 Teacher's pest?
2 Hurt expression
3 "Garfield" pup
4 Night cover?
5 Emerald or aquamarine, e.g.
6 Classroom tool
7 Rare talent
8 Clockmeister Thomas
9 Like a lizard or Mt. Everest
10 It's a round trip
11 Peregrinate
12 "Mon Oncle" star
13 Dele negator
21 Afghanistan's capital
22 Jalisco year starters
25 Word with nail or back
26 Evaluate
28 Share an opinion
29 Corn unit, perhaps
30 Bronze position
31 Pipsqueaks
32 Diner staple
33 Woolly partner
34 Pretty follower?
36 Give consideration
38 Brief green lights
39 Consoling word, when said twice

44 Not these or those folks
45 Hard times for batters
47 Throw here and there
49 Cash or property, e.g.
50 Enjoy the limelight
51 Our starting place?

52 Workman's list
53 Type of seal
54 Gallimaufry
55 Variety of smoked salmon
56 Thing, in an express checkout
57 Math class column

90
CHILD PSYCHOLOGY?

By Lynn Lempel

ACROSS

1 Object of aversion
5 Cause of some bellyaching
9 Filch
14 City with 40 islands
15 Clod
16 "Only the Lonely" actress Maureen
17 Start of a quip for parents
20 Meeting room prop
21 Heroic chronicle
22 It may precede a crash
23 Pampering, briefly
25 Daytime refresher
27 Quip (Part 2)
35 Parcheesi goal
36 Spanish-speaking quarter
37 Small float
39 Some Middle Eastern statesmen
41 Play about robots
42 Athens philosopher
44 Came across
45 Declined a bid
48 1970s tyrant
49 Quip (Part 3)
52 Mel, baseball All-Star 1934-45
53 Take the plunge
54 Prominent do
57 Enjoy profits, e.g.
61 Painter's coverall
65 End of the quip
68 "The Taming of the Shrew" setting
69 Scant

70 Mottled horse
71 Was dead to the world
72 Dazzled
73 Maintained

DOWN

1 Carry-on
2 Protector of U.S. workers
3 Some pub brews
4 Improve
5 Exercise focus, perhaps
6 Barracks staples
7 Herbert Hoover's birthplace
8 Wind resistance
9 Lush
10 First name in the "Sister Act" cast
11 Enemy of the Moor
12 Make ready
13 Refreshments
18 Some housing add-ons
19 New Age instrumentalist from Greece
24 It gives you a lift
26 Resting on
27 Pause filler
28 Oscar winner Marisa
29 Neglects to include
30 Ankle bones
31 Kind of fund
32 Got it wrong
33 Illinois junior senator
34 Away
38 No foe

40 Tough position
43 Historical turning point
46 2005 World Series player
47 Big name in chemicals
50 Started, as a hobby
51 America and its allies, popularly
54 Turin Olympic venue
55 Stable newcomer
56 Teased

58 Austen's Miss Woodhouse
59 Words on some Marine posters
60 Skin feature
62 Wind up on stage?
63 Sound of thunder
64 "Mild-mannered reporter"
66 Dick Whittington's companion
67 Kind of tape

91
PICNIC IN THE PARK
By Diane C. Baldwin

ACROSS
1 Place for la familia
5 Cries of delight
8 Reach the top
14 Constantly
15 First name in bombshells
16 "Twelfth Night" character
17 Kind of cod
18 School of thought
19 Bad place to be hanging
20 "Nothing to it!"
23 Slalom trail, perhaps
24 Moonshiners' devices
25 Legumes used in soup
29 Sculpted, as muscles
30 Monogamy quorum
32 Eye feature
33 Unit of force
34 Casting requirement
36 Overrun, in a troublesome way
38 Toss out
40 You may have seen them before
43 Large number
44 Egg ___ yong
47 Grp. with crude intentions?
48 Stat equivalent
50 Do parquetry
52 Rooney and Spillane
54 Matrimonial hopefuls
55 Egyptian viper
56 A romp
59 Awkward fellow
62 Hand holder
63 High point

64 Hint at
65 Kind of party
66 Go at a gallop
67 Showed one's shock
68 Mother ptarmigan
69 Sea eagles

DOWN
1 First name in the "All About Eve" cast
2 Flyboy
3 Somehow being aware of
4 Fancy sock
5 Off target
6 Barn door hardware
7 Trucker's rig
8 Addressee of many requests
9 Extraterrestrial
10 Child's play
11 Deliberately vague
12 Sundial number
13 Old salt
21 U.S. astronaut Buzz
22 Yalie
26 Some native New Yorkers
27 "___ Miserables"
28 Was left idle
30 Vitality
31 Tower in Honolulu
35 Literary composition
37 Fanciful idea
38 A breeze
39 Conciliatory offering
40 CD follower

41 Start for center or tome
42 Thinks back on
44 Scam artist
45 Crew member
46 Settings for pearls
49 Common ID
51 Write down

53 Lyric poem
54 Testatrix or aviatrix, e.g.
57 Solemn promise
58 Certain Manitoba Indian
59 Curtail one's freedom of speech
60 Carte words
61 Kennedy in Congress

92
HURRY!
By Fran & Lou Sabin

ACROSS
1 Conspire with
5 Great dog?
9 Disappear slowly, in a way
14 Dullsville denizen
15 "Family Ties" character
16 Four-lobed organ
17 Create, linguistically
18 Glass maven Lalique
19 Chooser's choice
20 What a well-wisher may wish for
23 Cheese concoction
24 Foil East-West, perhaps
25 Leader of the Green Mountain Boys
28 Certain sheet material
31 It may be acquired in a booth
34 Made independent
36 Needlefish
37 Swiss Alps river
38 Roger Clemens, notably
41 Applications
42 First name in slapstick
43 Corner of a diamond
44 Was a bellwether
45 Phony gem
47 Ruth Lilly Prize winners
48 It may burn on the range
49 Old or trick ending
51 Ready to retaliate, e.g.
58 Parabola
59 Sugar substitute?
60 Hawkeye State

61 Champing at the bit
62 Go with
63 Type of rack
64 Paradisiacal places
65 Mulligan, e.g.
66 Termitarium, e.g.

DOWN
1 Basics training?
2 Girl of old comics
3 HOMES member
4 Run-down digs
5 Hall of fame in music
6 Advisories
7 Big Island bird
8 CEO or CFO, e.g.
9 Tween age
10 One way to fix firmly
11 At an end
12 Fail to allow
13 Stammerer's syllables
21 Star in Cygnus
22 Egyptian king of the dead
25 Beyond bad
26 Realty document
27 Treated with light, in a way
29 Shoelace tip
30 Spigot
31 U.S. lake
32 Isn't for you?
33 Uncool ones
35 Reversible fabric
37 Squeezebox
39 ___ Gatos, Calif.

40 Conical shelter
45 Indiana five
46 Executorial concern
48 Donated
50 Lost intentionally
51 Court on campus
52 Driving force

53 Handicapping factor
54 Pinlike, metaphorically
55 Travel randomly
56 Impresses deeply
57 Covet
58 So-so average

93
FUN WITH DICK AND JANE
By Pamela Peterson

ACROSS
1 It's drawn with an eye
5 Mud dauber, e.g.
9 On way to remove a paper trail
14 Tolstoy's Madame Karenina
15 Chills and fever
16 Temblor
17 Dick and Jane
20 Operatic highlights
21 Men showing devotion to ideals
22 Hide
25 Land to which Cain fled
26 Wash out with solvent
28 Goes on and on and on
32 Ski resort's wish
37 Tony's song in "West Side Story"
38 Dick and Jane
41 "God bless us ___ one"
42 Wrights got it right
43 Use hip boots
44 Mule's cousin
46 Questionnaire answer
47 It's written in stone
53 Knickknack cabinets
58 Cowboy circus
59 Dick and Jane
62 Sluggish
63 Miss Scarlett's home
64 More than a snack
65 Ticks off
66 One-time word in a marriage vow
67 Holiday log

DOWN
1 Rum-laced cakes
2 Become accustomed to (Var.)
3 Prank
4 Senegal's capital
5 "Who ___ that masked man?"
6 Khan III or IV
7 Has done choral work
8 Intellectual show-off
9 Type of car
10 It can fall over a crowd
11 Pro ___
12 ___ out a living
13 Cubby holes?
18 Put into service
19 Cosmetics additive, often
23 Shade of blue
24 First lady of scat
27 Relating to a forearm bone
28 Small sailing vessel
29 Length X width
30 Potter's oven
31 Word with garage or holiday
32 Gush
33 Suddenly bright star
34 Had outstanding debts
35 "___ number one!"
36 Zipper opening
37 Janitor's implement
39 Like some circumstances
40 Theatrical object
44 Switzerland's capital
45 Familiar with

46 "The Second Coming" poet
48 A Gershwin
49 1975 rock opera
50 Goodbye, in Grenoble
51 "She loves me" unit
52 Card-game authority Edmond
53 Bahrain bigwig

54 Tennille of Captain and Tennille
55 Genesis shepherd
56 Circular course
57 Indication of healing
60 "Butterflies ___ Free"
61 Word with about or away

94
AFTER EXPENSES
By Fred Jackson III

ACROSS
1 Daffy trademark
5 Shed
9 Rising star
14 Way back when
15 Melville novel
16 Nautical warning
17 Pull down
18 Without delay, in poetry
19 Gives in
20 Typical Vincent Price film, e.g.
23 Ireland's patron, for short
24 Swift's specialties
28 Fenland
32 Small hot rod
33 Tweaked
37 Sicilian resort
38 Ranch add-on
39 They have flights between them
42 Crowd commotion
43 "Why don't we?"
45 Spent
47 A way to pay
50 Hawaiian geese
51 Bright-colored blooms
53 Environmentalist's urge
57 Answering machine game
61 Celestial point
64 Change course suddenly
65 Top baccarat score
66 Presbyter, e.g.
67 Peer of Dashiell
68 Auto pioneer

69 Colorful aquarium fish
70 Tach readings
71 Type of wind

DOWN
1 Gardener's soil, perhaps
2 Not relevant
3 Makeshift money
4 Mark Twain or Saki, e.g.
5 Medieval defense
6 Present opener?
7 Bird on a Canadian dollar
8 Hinged implement
9 Regained consciousness
10 Not neat
11 Start to function?
12 Wild ending
13 They may be civil, briefly
21 Les ___-Unis
22 Jet effect
25 Purpose of many vacations, informally
26 Comical Kovacs
27 Honor Your Honor
29 Travel channel?
30 Highfalutin type
31 Everglades wader
33 Belonging to the cat family
34 "The Faerie Queene" character
35 Mark with a cut
36 Wine companion
40 Poetic time
41 Like some warnings
44 More saline

46 "That clarifies it!"
48 Lead-in for Madre or Leone
49 Kubrick's computer
52 Cut off
54 Handy
55 "___ of Iwo Jima"
56 Pass off, as perspiration

58 Alleged suspect, to the law
59 Big wheel
60 Metal-bearing minerals
61 Word found within 20, 33, 45 and 57-Across
62 Inn order, perhaps
63 Banned insecticide

95
GETTING EVEN
By B. Venzke & S. Daily

ACROSS

1 Swiftly
6 Dice toss
10 Mountain climber?
14 Like a three-dollar bill
15 S-shaped molding
16 Truckee resort town
17 Date
18 Ash cans?
19 Deplaned, e.g.
20 First part of a proverb
23 Slangy affirmative
24 Beginners
25 Massive ref. work
28 ___ Lisa
30 Negative function word
31 Visionary flower?
33 Army chow hall
35 Clever
39 Middle of the proverb
42 Social embarrassment
43 Fictional reporter
44 A way to drink whiskey
45 Avarice, e.g.
47 It may shine or fall
49 Title in India
50 Made use of
54 Hustles
56 Last part of proverb
60 Prefix with knock or lock
61 Hair salon stock
62 "Going to the dogs," e.g.
64 Canal to the Red Sea
65 Mandolin's ancestor

66 National Zoo creature
67 There companion
68 Poetry collection
69 To prevent by legal means

DOWN

1 Disney owns it
2 "___ Richard's Almanac"
3 A malarial fever
4 Winding, as a road
5 Regard highly
6 Hooligan
7 Folklore fiend
8 Soviet revolutionary
9 Unit of instruction
10 It's handed down
11 Historical object
12 Licorice-flavored herb
13 Naphthalene repels them
21 Ruth's mother-in-law
22 Declares openly
25 Certain paintings
26 Clapton
27 Dutch river sight
29 Word before and after "to"
32 To make emotionally receptive
34 Deductive reasonings
36 Loserless outcomes
37 Nicholas II was the last
38 Abominable snowman
40 Conceals
41 Prim and reserved
46 Tease
48 Back-of-the-package item, often

50 Embarrass
51 Legal location
52 Rayed flower
53 Evaporate
55 Soft drinks

57 Presidential thumbs-down
58 It may get the brush-off
59 Long-gone bird
63 It shows the way

96
GOOD FOR A LAUGH
By Lynn Lempel

ACROSS

1 Town with a witch museum
6 Bus leader?
10 Reason to backspace, perhaps
14 It may be humble
15 Belly filler
16 Band around a barrel
17 Oil alternative
19 A famous one is golden
20 Schedule abbr.
21 United Nations agcy.
22 Sometime thereafter
24 Car named for its maker's monogram
25 Spanish boy
27 Jeepers!
28 Be indifferent
32 Toys with tails
35 Soprano who toured with Barnum
36 Shooters' org.
37 Jeepers!
38 Proofreading symbol
40 Boggy expanse
41 Cured salmon
42 Mongolian hot spot
43 Everglades resident
44 Therapeutic outburst
48 Liquidate
49 Shut down
50 Compass pt.
53 Uncomfortable spot
56 Marseille Mrs.
57 "Harper Valley ___"

58 Shakespearean "Bummer!"
59 Result of cell division?
62 Trait transmitter
63 Forefather
64 Tom or Sam
65 Adds to one's turf
66 Long-distance kisses
67 Score settler

DOWN

1 Less loony
2 Demean
3 State revenue booster
4 Part of some Web addresses
5 Sheep with fine wool
6 Like a circle stretched in one direction
7 "Kate & Leopold" star Ryan
8 Oscar winner for "Hud"
9 One concerned with how much money you make
10 Beat, as grain
11 Courtroom address
12 Sport of princes
13 Word from a dentist
18 Dismounted
23 Kenneth Grahame character
26 Like Saudi Arabia, e.g.
28 Animated Flanders
29 Engage in rivalry
30 Double-reed instrument
31 Bakery pastry
32 Seaweed variety
33 Borodin's prince

34 Where to go to be taken for a ride
38 Topple
39 Washboard components
40 Famed movie studio
42 Burst of laughter
43 Consumed completely
45 Cans of worms
46 Name of 11 pharaohs
47 Red monster with an orange nose

50 Word on Chinese menus
51 Embezzled
52 Kind of rat or snake
53 Shrews
54 Toast spread
55 Cereal for kids
60 Choler
61 Retrovirus material

97
BIG EATS
By Victor Fleming

ACROSS

1 Soup bean
5 Satisfy, in a way
10 Having a row, maybe?
14 "Not returnable"
15 Quotes
16 Chrysler Corporation car
17 Treat one's adversary shabbily?
20 Ice, in Innsbruck
21 "___ Rappaport"
22 U.S. radio service
23 Corner fixture
25 Refuses drugs?
28 Ream component
29 Tie-score word
30 "In what way?"
31 "Let's toast the end of hostilities!"
35 Rob of "About Last Night . . ."
36 Tell what one has heard
39 Film rating org.
40 Fastened, in a way
41 Apt. coolers
42 Film locale, often
43 Installs a bathroom floor, perhaps
47 Machine loads
49 Something that may be better left alone
52 Geisha's accessory
53 One of the Chekhov's "Three Sisters"
54 Snoopy, in his fantasies
55 Take a gander at
59 Leave out
60 City between Gainesville and Orlando
61 Saarinen of Finland
62 Word with mob or slide
63 Practiced deception
64 D-Day craft

DOWN

1 Mailing supplies
2 Old Testament prophet
3 "Did you notice I was gone?"
4 Andiron residue
5 Blockhead
6 Property securities
7 On ___ (doing some heavy drinking)
8 Fulfilled, as a promise
9 Disputed psych. phenomenon
10 Be a bother to
11 One thing to do in New York City
12 Unit of time
13 Industrious carpenter, e.g.
18 Walk on eggshells, e.g.
19 Like some mirrors
24 Ancient ruined city of Edom
25 Winter fall
26 "___ as good a time as any"
27 Be encumbered to
29 Have a sore spot
32 Skins
33 Tinker with the text
34 Off-road transport, briefly

35 Escorted to the living room, e.g.
36 Stray home, briefly
37 Basic grading system
38 Take-home amount
39 Breadbasket
42 Posted
44 Flat contracts
45 One of the Fords
46 Dictation pros

48 It makes waste
49 Verb with havoc
50 Seating request, perhaps
51 Links legend Sam
53 Peruvian of old
55 In favor of
56 Australian coat-of-arms bird
57 Punch-in-the-gut sound
58 Sushi option

98
FIRST COMES LOVE
By S. Daily & B. Venzke

ACROSS
1 Many an outdoor restaurant
5 Brilliant success
10 Manicurists' locales
14 Like the Sahara
15 Flies like an eagle
16 Diamond number
17 First comes love, then these three
20 Part of China
21 Eye-bending pictures
22 Lunched, e.g.
23 Den fixtures
25 Placekicker's prop
26 First comes love, then these four
32 Admittance
33 Place for a spare tire?
34 Redheaded sitcom legend
35 According to
36 What means may justify
40 Stand for the arts?
43 One doing clerical work
45 First comes love, then comes these two
49 Before, in verse
50 Giants Hall-of-Famer
51 Einstein's birthplace
52 Pet restraint
54 Eats to excess
59 First comes love, then comes these three
62 Bar on the table
63 Egypt's Mubarak
64 Pro's opposite
65 Native of Novi Sad
66 Bottomless pit
67 Soothsayer

DOWN
1 Storm preceder
2 "Don Giovanni" highlight
3 Poodle name, sometimes
4 Idyllic locale
5 Dead giveaways?
6 Membrane of the eye
7 Give praise to
8 Jeanne d'___
9 "Shame on you!"
10 Barbershop sound
11 Steel City pro
12 Tuscan tenor Bocelli
13 Part of a sonnet, perhaps
18 Marble units
19 Ship petty officers, for short
23 Russian ruler of old
24 Sundial's seven
26 Erie Canal mule
27 Hospital area, briefly
28 XXX x X
29 Tense (with "up")
30 Resided
31 Oktoberfest vessel
35 Brat or bug, e.g.
37 Not pos.
38 Alternative to dial-up, briefly
39 Sault ___ Marie
41 Parting word in one of 50

42 Filming area, often
43 Mayflower passenger
44 Philippine president Fidel
45 Greeting words
46 Nipple ring (Var.)
47 Closer
48 Clashes, as with the law
53 Arrogant one

54 Not very challenging
55 Transfer and messenger materials
56 Chromosome part
57 Noble Italian name
58 Prison, slangily
60 Agcy. for homeowners
61 Certain pocket-watch retainer

99
IDYLL THOUGHTS
By Joy M. Andrews

ACROSS

1 Casey of radio
6 Underway, to Sherlock Holmes
11 Inventor's cry
14 The personification of peace
15 To-the-max prefix
16 Delta-shaped sail
17 Piece of land
18 Daytime TV talker, once
20 Freight car hopper, stereotypically
21 Thun's river
22 Unit of resolution
23 Work against the current
27 Paddock papa
28 Hemingway and Shackleton
32 Type of rechargeable battery
34 It features "Memory"
36 Kind of steward
37 Tigers' sch.
38 In a difficult situation
41 Special room in a Muslim palace
42 London essayist
44 One way to stand by
45 The voices of Oberon, Rinaldo and Erda
47 Daily grind
49 Word with field or guilt
50 Retired, metaphorically
55 G sharp equivalent
58 Sound of an electronic bug lure in action
59 Anatomical canal

60 Something immune to criticism
63 Drive-through sign
64 Newman role
65 Coll. with a husky mascot
66 Allen or Martin
67 Funnel center?
68 Taxi trips
69 Prepared apples for dumplings, e.g.

DOWN

1 Endogamous cultures
2 It's guided by a mouse
3 2003 sports biopic
4 Glowing tributes
5 Encountered
6 Subjective atmospheres
7 Bat eyelashes, etc.
8 Like some stocks, for short
9 Mork's sitcom planet
10 Large snake or James Clavell best seller
11 Trojan War hero
12 Mountainous walk
13 Famous fratricide victim
19 They're picked green
21 Monkey's uncle?
24 Pakistani tongue
25 Hear again
26 British Isles tongue
29 Certain track-and-field participant
30 Pother
31 Places that pamper

32	One without a DH in his league
33	Cuba, to a Cuban
34	Midshipman's counterpart
35	E. Coast ocean
39	Early Briton
40	Prominent donkey features
43	Supporting the home team, e.g.
46	Assailed
48	Filmmaker with total creative control
49	Pub fixture
51	Layer with a hole in it
52	Chess row
53	"Superman" star
54	Committed a faux pas
55	Tennis legend Arthur
56	Certain denizen of Narnia
57	Calculator displays, briefly
61	601, in old Rome
62	Boston fish
63	PC key

100
FURNITURE STORE
By Fred Jackson III

ACROSS
1 Coffee hour requirements, perhaps
5 Midwife's action
9 Tropical fruit
14 Saddle, e.g.
15 Water or land sport
16 Teen tag
17 Statistics
18 Items often bruised
19 Adam and Eve, for two
20 DAVENPORT
23 Dog show org.
24 Politician in D.C.
25 Newspaper section
29 Exalt
31 Lawyers' grp.
34 "Sesame Street" quintet
35 German auto pioneer
36 On
37 TABLE part
40 Tot's spot, sometimes
41 Antonym for out of
42 Dress shape or style
43 Neighbor of Isr.
44 Legal postponement
45 They may be made during tantrums
46 Word with second, hour or day
47 Recital rebuke
48 CABINET
57 Tropical vine
58 100 cents, perhaps
59 Daughter of Ming the Merciless

60 Kind of buddy
61 Settled down
62 Those in favor
63 Sharp, narrow ridge
64 Apollo vehicles, briefly
65 In ecstasy

DOWN
1 Letters on a certain stamp
2 Gather, as the rewards of labor
3 Kosovo peacekeeping group
4 Critic's bestowal
5 Itty-bitty spots
6 Common sense
7 Scads
8 Nosegay
9 Like some space flights
10 One way you can say that
11 Fictional submarine skipper
12 Snowballed
13 Olympus Mountains peak
21 First name among the "Paper Moon" cast
22 Mazda competitor
25 Flour holders
26 Flashy flower
27 Gulf ship
28 Philandering fellow
29 Southpaw
30 365 days in old Rome
31 Had a traditional dinner
32 Lifted by the wind, e.g.
33 Architectural recesses
35 ___ fide

36 Up to it
38 Volatile liquid, for short
39 ___ Picchu
44 Seed or Street
45 Fashion photo sessions
46 Burgundy grape
47 Curtain fabric
48 Goya's "The Duchess of ___"

49 Big name in fashion
50 Ming artifact
51 Heartfelt
52 Holiday time
53 Cats take them
54 Put in the smokehouse, e.g.
55 Hemoglobin component
56 Hang in there

101
NATURE CALLS
By Eugene Newman

ACROSS

1 Jack's proverbial need
5 Remain
10 Like one who cannot bear you?
14 Longest Swiss waterway
15 Baffler
16 Dyeing plant
17 Conspiring conifers?
20 Shooters' grp.
21 "Time's Arrow" novelist
22 Kind of hole or layer
23 Actress Drescher
24 Made like a dove
26 Bellowing billows?
30 URL suffix
33 Runs in neutral
34 Veep's superior
35 Wingless extinct bird
36 Numskull
37 Clodhoppers, e.g.
39 Tilt
40 Prior to, in verse
41 Refrigerated bar
42 Choosing word
43 Important ID
44 Ghoulish gale?
47 Victor over Tilden
49 Hereditary peer
50 Former Standard Oil of Indiana
52 Lily kin
53 School grp.
56 Reticent runnel?
60 Ancient serf
61 First name in cosmetics

62 Florence is on it
63 Untouchables leader
64 They're secret for some
65 Certain scent

DOWN

1 Patsy
2 Trio completer with Bolger and Haley
3 Bocelli delivery, perhaps
4 "Indubitably"
5 Tarzan, for one
6 Tedious
7 Goddess pictured in Egyptian tombs
8 Place for thieves
9 Metric work unit
10 Pilgrim provender
11 It's initially on some buildings
12 Legal claim
13 Word with who, what or where
18 Helen's captor
19 Sounds of magical disappearances
23 Relieve from
24 Lasting treatment
25 Smeltery needs
26 Needles
27 Osmics focuses
28 High altitude instruments?
29 Sewing kit item
31 For pitchers, it's in the bag
32 Type of community
37 Type of gin

38 Axes
39 Obscene
41 "___ Beautiful Doll"
42 Crane kin
45 Words with "by" or "back to you"
46 Hangmen's needs
48 High points
50 Church corner

51 Source of inspiration
52 Army and others
53 Callao location
54 Gets less and less pale
55 In a frenzy
57 Bench press unit
58 Words separating this test?
59 Golden Fleece source

102
HEY IN THERE!
By Lynn Lempel

ACROSS

1 Dove's domain
5 Ongoing squabble
9 Watery tract
14 Sulfur attribute
15 Implore
16 Silver-mining state
17 Explorer of Polynesia
19 Type of blockade
20 Handy gambling, briefly
21 Ref's mark-offs
22 Special favorite
24 Curling inning
25 Fancy wrap
27 Fighters at Custer's Last Stand
29 Go down the runway
30 Sluggish sort?
32 Jordanian queen
33 Former Israeli Prime Minister
35 Astounds
36 Some chocolaty indulgences
39 Worship
41 Work of art
42 All ears
43 Condition
45 Jungfrau locale
49 Gold Rush destination
51 Early arcade game supplier
52 Advised leader?
53 Uncle of note
54 Safety org.
56 Mighty small
57 Wartime tactic
59 Smilers of song

62 Nonlethal weapon brand
63 Between-meal bite
64 It may be hammered out
65 Leaders of Sesame Street?
66 Oxcart hookup
67 Starry beast

DOWN

1 Help run, as a party
2 Singer given a 1999 National Medal of Arts
3 Kids' catchall
4 Before, before
5 Hunter of Bugs
6 Noteworthy times
7 "Ick!"
8 Oracle's place
9 Like many breath fresheners
10 Oral surgeon's org.
11 Famished
12 Ireland's longest river
13 You can't kick field goals without them
18 Flour-making grain
23 Nocturnal swimmer
26 Word on a dime
27 Kitchen item used near your birthday
28 Implore
30 AARP concerns
31 "Uh-uh"
34 Were up to date?
35 Marsupial pocket
36 Futile

37 Pup's plaint
38 Waggle dance performer
39 Montmartre frequenter
40 Flowers named for a Swedish botanist
43 Reggae relative
44 Corn product for grits
46 One skilled in defense
47 Lingers at the mirror, say
48 Afternoon snooze

50 Patronizing ones?
51 Patient reply, sometimes
54 Catcher Carlton
55 Tennis legend Arthur
58 Beaver's word
60 Pooh playmate
61 Part of a campus e-mail address

103
MBA CLASSES?
By Randall J. Hartman

ACROSS

1 Feathered projectile
5 Wedels, e.g.
9 Florida's cigar city
14 Gallimaufry
15 El ___, California
16 French farewell
17 Carry on
18 Soon, poetically
19 Allen of "Animal House"
20 Sandler/Nicholson movie
23 Where X marks the spot
24 Official whistle blower, briefly
25 Music genre
28 Guys' companions
31 Jim Ryun and Marty Liquori, e.g.
36 Presley's middle name
38 Quote
40 Estimated worth
41 Contents of lots of mail
44 Minute Maid Park player
45 Jai ___
46 Part of Caesar's last sentence
47 Vacation destination, perhaps
49 Erupter of 2002
51 Part of a needle
52 Mom's mate
54 Type of evidence
56 Supply-side slander
65 Former Egyptian president Sadat
66 ___ Beauty (apple variety)
67 Rabbit, to David Copperfield

68 Yellowhammer State city
69 Fleur-de-lis
70 Refrain syllables
71 Stand for Renoir
72 "Why don't we ..."
73 Tom Brady targets

DOWN

1 "Dumb ___" (old comic strip)
2 Alda of "The West Wing"
3 Tinkle in a phone booth
4 Clan symbol
5 Tax bill imposed on the American colonies
6 Hawaiian wind
7 Word with hand or fist
8 Bass boat feature, sometimes
9 "Relax!"
10 Garden of Eden evictee
11 Bog
12 Certain hammerhead
13 Esther, to Lamont Sanford
21 Music from "The Sting," e.g.
22 Tourmaline or amethyst, e.g.
25 Scientific breakthrough of the '30s
26 Respond to reveille
27 New York City and Los Angeles, e.g.
29 Capital of Peru
30 Flat, like beer
32 Well into the night
33 Type type
34 Hardly the pick of the litter

Crossword Grid

	1	2	3	4		5	6	7	8		9	10	11	12	13
14						15					16				
17						18					19				
20				21					22						
			23				24								
25	26	27		28		29	30		31		32	33	34	35	
36			37		38			39		40					
41				42					43						
44						45					46				
47				48		49			50		51				
			52		53			54		55					
56	57	58	59				60	61				62	63	64	
65						66					67				
68						69					70				
71						72					73				

35 Follow without interruption

37 Emperor after Claudius

39 Part of QED

42 Type of punishment

43 Benevolence

48 Likewise

50 Year, in the Yucatan

53 Grave risk

55 More than enough

56 Ming artifact

57 Draft status

58 Some may be spotted

59 Agatha Christie or Margot Fonteyn, e.g.

60 Uneaten part of an apple

61 Leave out

62 Home of ancient Persepolis

63 Like Antarctica

64 Luxury hotel features

104
HAVE A CLUE?
By George Shayler

ACROSS
1 Sprint
5 Ententes
10 Computer keyboard key
13 Carmela portrayer on HBO
14 Up to this point
15 XIII x IV
16 Answer: Aloe
19 Abroad broadcaster, briefly
20 Verizon, once
21 Church doctrine
22 Valiant's son
23 1947 Oscar winner Celeste
25 Super thin
26 Group with a lot of bills
28 Cultural introduction?
30 Buffalo-to-Chesapeake Bay dir.
31 City on the Nile
32 Sport with schussing
34 Words with "a kind" or "many"
35 Violin part
36 Beat the pants off
40 Coat ___ (family insignia)
42 Human resources person, at times
43 Good thing to give your child
46 "Dragonwyck" author Seton
47 Go on a pension
48 Discord
50 Pull your weapon
52 Platoon members or "Platoon" extras
53 Full of chutzpah
54 Clean Air Act org.

55 Good serves, but not necessarily aces
56 Answer: Reno
61 My ___, Vietnam
62 Greek nymph
63 Jacob's twin
64 They loop the Loop
65 Smartly dressed
66 Actor's desire

DOWN
1 1980s auto with gull-wing doors
2 "Oklahoma!" character
3 Pose for an artist
4 Answer: Hem
5 Discussion group
6 White-sheet connector
7 Dancer Charisse
8 Spread grass for drying
9 Answer: Oar
10 Border patrol concerns
11 Perks (up)
12 Hippie coloring method
17 Platte River Sioux
18 Prefix meaning "three"
19 Explorer Balboa
24 Answer: Incense
25 Lanka lead-in
27 Buck's finish
29 Bookings
32 Lively
33 "True ___" (John Wayne movie)
37 Not a fake

38 Pie topping
39 Fourth estate
41 Tiny symbol of industriousness
43 Telescope name
44 Artificial
45 Free of charge
47 Engrossed

49 Guinness suffix
51 Tall and thin
57 Gun owner's org.
58 Understand
59 Gathered dust
60 Prefix with metrics

105

ZOOGENIC

By Leonard Williams

ACROSS

1 Org. since 1909
6 Early Mexican inhabitant
11 More than inquire
14 Tank covering
15 Tropical fruit
16 Slangy affirmative
17 Early medico
19 It may hold feathers in place
20 Part of le tricolore
21 TV Cunningham
23 Hardhearted
27 The over-60 set
28 French satellite launcher
29 The Gipper
30 River into Utah Lake
31 "Mr. ___ Goes to Town"
32 Terrestrial amphibian
35 Billions of years
36 Uninviting to a vegan, e.g.
37 Nicholas, for one
38 Elec. meter unit
39 Producer Ponti
40 Provoke, as interest
41 Marshall Mathers, familiarly
43 Do the wrong thing with
44 Felix Unger, for one
46 Official seals
47 Dark red
48 Grammy winner Turner
49 Public hangings?
50 Bit of high jinks
56 ___ de la Cite
57 Despise

58 Gent from Argentina
59 Major ref. work
60 Spicy condiment
61 Rust is one

DOWN

1 Slangy negative
2 Ex-spokesman Fleischer
3 Current unit
4 Take surreptitiously
5 Gratis, for a lawyer
6 Shrek and Fiona, for two
7 Oahu party
8 Place for a table setting
9 Duracell competitor
10 Shell discards
11 Humorously surrealistic
12 Broadcast a second time
13 WWI battle site
18 Mustard is in this game
22 OSS successor
23 "RUR" author
24 Directing sign
25 King Richard I, they say
26 UK bathrooms
27 Tend
29 Domain
31 10 of "10"
33 Goethe's masterpiece
34 Apple and orange, for two
36 Provincial neighbor of North Dakota
37 Nickname for Mrs. Addams
39 Mall features, often

40 Famous cubist
42 High pt. in an atlas
43 More than several
44 Mystery author Marsh
45 Bogart's role in "High Sierra"
46 Olds model

48 Boxer's stat
51 Mighty Ducks' org.
52 Put a spell on
53 Common pasta suffix
54 Affirmative signal
55 Poetic adverb

106
COLOR WHEEL
By Amy Greene

ACROSS

1 Toothed device
5 Footwear of yore
10 Morse symbols
14 Slim margin of victory
15 Take one's time
16 Once again
17 Germany's von Bismarck
18 Peculiar speech form
19 Defaulter's loss, briefly
20 Sound of relief
21 Intellect, informally
23 Norton Sound city
25 Reverberated
26 Type of oil
29 Small speck
31 Viva voce
32 Reason for a family gathering, perhaps
37 Yard holder
38 Irritable and impatient, e.g.
39 Word with act or gear
40 Keeps alive, e.g.
42 Succubus, e.g.
43 They're often caught lying down
44 Daily ritual, below the border
45 Unwanted twist
49 Trumpeting bird
50 Bechamel, e.g.
53 Ballet finale
57 Freedom from hardship
58 Bicycle and then some
59 Jai ___

60 Off the coast, e.g.
61 ___ ear and out the other
62 Small brook
63 Glossary entry
64 Bivouac quarters
65 Some forest creatures

DOWN

1 Rough seas feature
2 President's pledge
3 Tiny arachnid
4 Power company problems
5 Mark of infamy
6 Military chaplain
7 "Si, Mi Chiamano Mimi," e.g.
8 City to which Helen was abducted
9 Crossword grid feature
10 Honorific for Luke's father
11 ___ a customer
12 Wickiup relative
13 Scimitar, e.g.
22 More than passed
24 Outmoded, e.g.
26 Tent city
27 Winglike
28 Investigatory aid
29 Grandma of art
30 Cereal of the frisky?
32 Group of quail
33 Immigrant's document
34 Intentions
35 Subject to debate
36 Sicilian peak

38 Send over the airwaves
41 Pennsylvania port city
42 Day in Durango
44 Subjects of Gustavus I
45 Blood and tears partner
46 Aspect
47 Stair part

48 Mr. T's gang
49 Olfactory perception
51 First-class
52 On top of
54 Spicy stew
55 Hill companion
56 Is unwell

107
TAKE TO THE CLEANERS
By Lynn Lempel

ACROSS
1 "'Cause I ___ me spinach"
5 Some farm critters
9 Part of "Titanic," e.g.
14 ___ gin fizz
15 Canal to Buffalo
16 Took enough guff
17 Unparalleled
18 Moneyed
20 It has electric organs
21 Siddhartha Gautama
22 Dental woe
23 Stuff up
25 Speak indistinctly
27 Church adornment, perhaps
32 Cut evenly
33 June star?
34 Pat and Pete, among others
37 Unctuous
38 Words with tear or good day
39 De novo
40 Some railway systems
41 Part of Great Britain since 1536
43 "The Nutcracker" heroine
44 Part of NBA practices
46 In it together
49 Temple outcast, perhaps
50 Straight up or straightened up
51 Not susceptible
55 Place to find a legend, often
58 Dubious tactic
60 Holiday lure, often
61 More than booed
62 Fashionable reading

63 It has a stripe on its back
64 Gets fur all over the rug, e.g.
65 Kind of duck
66 Red herring

DOWN
1 Existence
2 Burn soother
3 Long-distance chats
4 Diocese
5 Safe place
6 Desiccated
7 Temperate
8 Third son
9 Diffident
10 Gemologist's concern
11 Order from on high
12 Cubbyhole
13 Chloroform substitute
19 PLO rival
21 Sacrum or parietal, e.g.
24 Roman who wrote about the history of Rome
26 Put into service
27 Nursery rhyme domicile
28 Word with pig or pony
29 Whimsically funny
30 Parents' legacies
31 Dog walker's need
34 Nonelectronic correspondence
35 Bird on the beach, perhaps
36 Pirate's booty
39 Word on a Mexican stop sign
41 Handwringer's feeling

42 Embezzler's worry
43 Word with bar or area
44 Like some sheets
45 Emulated a pig
46 Inca Trail site
47 O'Hara's portrayer
48 Sizable

52 Comical equine
53 Bannister distance
54 Arthur Ashe's alma mater
56 Not only that
57 Latitude
59 Fabric amts., often
60 Sports VIP

108
POSITIONING
By Alice Walker

ACROSS
1 Place for sweaters?
4 Chicago suburb
9 Mortify
14 Pronominal contraction
15 Who might be to blame
16 Bomb fins
17 Matchless, e.g.
18 Fuel receptacles
19 "Maids a-milking" group, e.g.
20 Help for the lame, perhaps
23 Postal creed obstacle
24 Morena, Leone and Madre
28 Letter before beth
32 Addison's collaborator
33 Symbol of solidity
36 "Middlemarch" author
38 March through mud, e.g.
39 Performer's thrill
43 Cuba libre ingredient
44 Fleshy-snouted beast
45 Nos. head
46 Member of a kingdom
49 Snow clouds, perhaps
51 One who cries foul?
53 Nostalgic tune
57 Parlors
61 Some "Monday, Monday" singers
64 Find irresistible
65 Increases
66 Up and at it
67 Put forward
68 Dead expanse

69 Gives up
70 Daughter of King Juan Carlos
71 England's Isle of ___

DOWN
1 Finishes third
2 Treadle
3 Make muddled
4 Qualified for by right
5 Advance, e.g.
6 Sound that ends some acts
7 They're in pens
8 Homes in the sticks?
9 Long-legged shorebird
10 Support you can lean on
11 Hill inhabitant
12 Match in chips
13 Buffalo hrs.
21 Mauna ___
22 "___ for Innocent" (Grafton)
25 Piece of history?
26 Emotionally detached
27 Musical repeat sign
29 Hebrew priest
30 Half quart
31 Golf great Ben
33 "Crash" prize
34 Send a note of apology, e.g.
35 Muslim religious leader (Var.)
37 Pith helmet
40 Junior, for one
41 Potency
42 Where trees may be cultivated
47 Comes to mind

48 Book end?
50 United Nations agency (Abbr.)
52 Military march
54 Pour water on
55 Drive
56 "Civil Disobedience," e.g.
58 Golden calf, e.g.

59 Race-winning margin, sometimes
60 Jack-o'-lantern feature, perhaps
61 "Big" burger
62 Veneration
63 Satirical magazine

109
OLDIES
By Diane C. Baldwin

ACROSS

1 Quick punches
5 Aid partner
9 Absence of stress
14 Poet Pound
15 File fillers
16 "The ___ Incident" (Henry Fonda oater)
17 Siren's call
18 Force
19 Beetle Bailey's boss
20 Seasoned government advisor
23 Buy alternative
24 Letterless phone button
25 Nursery offering
27 "Do the Right Thing" character
28 Honky-tonk sights
32 Play charades, e.g.
33 Newscaster Couric
34 Ray Lewis, e.g.
35 Golden ager
39 Car feature
40 Bowie's weapon
41 Zenith
42 Fez adornment
44 Blubber
47 Mess up
48 One way to level the playing field?
49 Bolt then hitch
51 Coleridge's seafaring subject
56 Subatomic particle with a negative charge
57 Mineral supplement

58 Mouth-puckering
59 Gambling game
60 Shipshape
61 The 45th of 50
62 So far
63 Heredity determinant
64 While away

DOWN

1 Word with crown or precious
2 Fragrant shrub
3 Shower type
4 They may be gross, white or for one day only
5 Tacks on
6 Can of worms, perhaps
7 Sicilian spouter
8 Bugle call
9 Sheriff's band
10 Final, perhaps
11 Scratchy
12 Nickname, formally
13 Certain bleater
21 Put in working order
22 Annapolis grad
26 Cozy hideaway
29 Figure skater Midori
30 Express openly
31 Makes out
32 Rodent's ordeal
33 First secretary of war
34 Robber, e.g.
35 Fictional crime family
36 Timelessness

37 Election winners
38 Deadlock
39 West in old films
42 Word with hold or nail
43 Window canopy
44 Classical music composition
45 Some dramas set to music
46 Moorages

48 North Dakota city
50 Started on a Havana, e.g.
52 Pigeon shelter
53 Arboretum sight
54 Mournful utterance
55 Deal prelude, often
56 In the manner of

≡USA TODAY.

110
1-2-3 SHOOT!
By Jim Curran

ACROSS
1 Engine and caboose, e.g.
5 Sen. Thurmond
10 It might be presidential
14 Persia, now
15 Sao ___
16 Spiraling current
17 Turner or Louise
18 Encrypt?
19 Word with bar or zip
20 Pretend mount
23 Program offerer
24 They may follow midday meals
28 Jack of "Barney Miller"
29 Space beginner
33 Street for children
34 Coxswain's command
36 Mill material
37 Summer vacation requirement, for some
41 Retro art style
42 From Damascus, e.g.
43 Become overcast
46 Forced under water
47 Novel by Nabokov
50 "Rock-a-Bye Baby" locale
52 Ruhr valley city
54 Sidestroke component
58 Group of draft animals
61 Ignominy
62 Word with false or teen
63 Coloratura's piece
64 Word with flop or dog
65 Word with formality or pittance

66 It has a broad side
67 Certain Tchaikovsky ballet characters
68 "Hey, over here!"

DOWN
1 Kind of grove
2 Melodic
3 Vaquero's place
4 Weave in and out
5 Joyride
6 Piquancy
7 Babe that's famous
8 Common spreads
9 Commercial cat
10 Movement led by South Carolina
11 Tokyo of old
12 Work with a calculator, in a way
13 Caustic chemical
21 More than peeved
22 Wait partner
25 Tropical tuber
26 One way to run?
27 Rep. counterpart
30 Drop an easy one, e.g.
31 Knocks over, so to speak
32 Gives a thumbs-up
34 Employee of a major bicycle manufacturing company?
35 Pale tan
37 Common still life subject
38 Decent lot
39 Aunts and uncles, e.g.

40 Tans too long
41 Banned insecticide
44 Yadda-yadda-yadda, briefly
45 Squeaks and squeals, e.g.
47 Comments from the stage
48 Decorating styles
49 Knee-high alternative
51 "Nonsense!"

53 Be stingy with
55 First name in cakes
56 Black cat, to some
57 Wine store section
58 Keyboard word
59 Historic period
60 Travel mode

111
LONG, LONG AGO
By Alice Walker

ACROSS
1 Kind of ID
6 Literary snippets, e.g.
10 Priggish
14 Pollster Elmo
15 Trooper start
16 Sackcloth material
17 Pitched in for a hand
18 Experiencing jitters
19 Word after a faux pas, perhaps
20 Old info
23 Time scale section
24 Where many are relieved in London?
25 Type of witness
28 "... the violet-embroidered ___" (Milton)
31 Note notation
35 Pull with perspiration?
36 "I lack iniquity" speaker
37 Fear
38 Relic, e.g.
41 Point of view
42 Contemptible person
43 Look or must adjunct
44 Studier of the Upanishads
45 Rhodamine and eosin, for two
46 Nonflowering plant
47 Altar word, sometimes
49 Seventh Greek letter
51 It may be studied in school
58 Certain East Asian
59 One of nine Siamese kings
60 Not docked

61 Loam, e.g.
62 Muslim chief
63 Further shorten, as a board
64 Mayberry denizen
65 Untold centuries
66 Clothes closers

DOWN
1 What many do in church
2 Improve, as skills
3 Comes to a decision
4 Show instability
5 It's taken at the diner
6 Flattered most sincerely
7 Bubkes
8 Having a diamond-shaped pattern
9 Authority to decide
10 What women do at the mall, stereotypically
11 Maltese comment
12 Masked men at home
13 HMO listing
21 Do ruinous damage
22 Had a snack
25 Reduce drastically, as prices
26 Word in a Little Richard song title
27 Ninth month of the Hindu calendar
29 "Long, Long ___"
30 Like some goals
32 Insult badly
33 Stair step part

34 Chalice partner
36 Some male demons
37 Start of a master plan, perhaps
39 Ungovernable
40 Big or little digit
45 Superenergetic one
46 Make more substantial
48 Like some premonitions
50 Peter and Alexander, notably

51 "___ there, matey!"
52 It may be covered with polish
53 U.S. Treasury agent
54 Lovers of the stage
55 Mountain of Greek legend
56 Take in
57 Swerves, at sea
58 Cookbook abbreviation

112
PAY ATTENTION
By Clark Forsham

ACROSS

1 It's immeasurably deep
6 On ___ (as a gamble)
10 Menhaden kin
14 Expressed with a pen
15 Tibetan teacher
16 Fashionable first name
17 Type of cake
18 Actor Baldwin
19 Certain deer
20 Makeshift solution
23 Word with hour or mile
24 What buffalo do
25 Having the necessary power
28 Sushi servings
31 Some domestics
35 Excessively
36 "Nay!" sayer
37 Poem of 14 lines
38 Classic John Osborne play
41 Determine how much damage was done, e.g.
42 Leprechauns' land
43 Contents of a lode-bearing wall?
44 Cubic meter
45 Cereal elf
46 Hobo concoction
47 Twice removed from thrice
49 It may appear before long
51 Be wise, in a way
58 Wee parasite
59 Pig product
60 English topic
61 Hit from The Impressions
62 Holder of combs, perfumes, etc.
63 More angry
64 Rotunda feature
65 "___ there, done that"
66 Broke off

DOWN

1 Belt-makers' tools
2 Baby sitter's handful
3 Need for "walking the dog"
4 Grassland
5 Amalgamate
6 It may cause indignation
7 Conceal, as a magician
8 Arab nobles (Var.)
9 Chocolate source
10 German composer Robert
11 Ground covering on some mornings
12 Plot part, perhaps
13 Point to be made in a sentence?
21 Madison Square Garden and others
22 Certain islander
25 Book with inlets and insets
26 Hoist
27 Baggy
29 And the like (Abbr.)
30 Compare
32 Metal shaped by casting, perhaps
33 Big name in plows
34 Throw around

36 Not in attendance
37 Sneaky marksman
39 Early Rockefeller product
40 Bit of financial planning, for short
45 Andrew Johnson served there
46 Kind of tickets
48 Show-biz biggie
50 Environmentalist's urge

51 It can move stars
52 Checklist unit
53 Definitely the case
54 Ruler of the Aesir
55 Reddish-brown chalcedony
56 S-shaped molding
57 Uncool fellow, stereotypically
58 Like King George III

113
HEAD START
By Lynn Lempel

ACROSS

1 Helpless?
6 Assist in the weight room, e.g.
10 Culmination
14 Suitors
15 Daughter of Laban
16 Later
17 It could be catastrophic
19 Ukraine's capital
20 QB's most successful passes
21 "Travels With My ___"
22 Stony toward tender feelings
24 Verbal abuse
25 Obsolete coin
26 Gave a recital, e.g.
29 Apollo undertaking
32 Abu Dhabi leaders
33 Vocal limits
34 Rocks in a bar?
35 Marathoner's destination
36 Electrical units
37 Odd circus performer
38 Start of a form?
39 Holds out
40 Kind of energy
41 Cheesy restaurant?
43 Newest NFLers
44 "Yikes!"
45 Scam
46 Country between Lakes Victoria and Albert
48 Quotes the raven
49 Topsy's playmate
52 Kind of top
53 Dessert-to-be
56 "A Death in the Family" writer
57 Lie in wait
58 Singer portrayed in "Sweet Dreams"
59 Hardly a no-brainer
60 Completes the coda, e.g.
61 They come with strings attached

DOWN

1 Be a bad helper?
2 Pb
3 Boathouse gear
4 Brazil, for one
5 Completes a respiration
6 Moved furtively
7 Earthy fertilizer
8 Timber tree
9 Aristophanes comedy
10 Diet guru
11 Furry Andes dweller
12 Swim competition
13 A deadly sin
18 Campus courtyard
23 Drury, for one
24 Driver's shout
25 Print choices
26 Sting's relative?
27 Arabian Peninsula native, perhaps
28 Equine performer
29 Sicily's neighbor
30 Place to have a sub?

31 Eyedrops?
33 One-time TV host O'Donnell
36 X or Y, in algebra
37 Best Actor for "Ray"
39 Licentious
40 Affected by the waves
42 Spaced out
43 Chicago, in a song
45 Doves' antitheses

46 Site of five national parks
47 Totally smitten
48 Extension extension
49 Give off
50 Hollywood cross street
51 Cans
54 Emulate a coward
55 Gin maker Whitney

114
THE YELLOW PAGES
By Robert H. Wolfe

ACROSS
1 Yale benefactor
6 Researcher's quest
11 Golf score, sometimes
14 Squelch
15 Entomb
16 Huxley's "___ and Essence"
17 Listing for behaviorists?
19 CD tag
20 Gets busy
21 FHA concern
22 Decadent
25 Crop dusted, e.g.
27 ". . . good for what ___ you"
28 Pass
31 Buddy Holly player
32 Commercial charge
33 Chad's cont.
34 River deposits
35 Land's end, perhaps
36 Involves
38 Celestial body
41 FYI circular
43 Nouvelle Caledonie, e.g.
44 Spiritedness
45 Foghorn, e.g.
47 Like some hands
48 Geological time
49 Some Europeans
51 Spot that's hardly spotless
53 Paul of song
54 "Give My Regards to Broadway" ending
57 Holy Fr. female

58 Listing for lawyers?
62 Rigidify
63 "A Passage to India" woman
64 Checks figures?
65 Employed pols
66 10th president
67 Oxen units

DOWN
1 Medium skill?
2 Golf position
3 Tag antagonists
4 Most popular
5 Not abridged
6 Raft traveler
7 Little industrialists?
8 Bend respectfully
9 Scout group
10 NBC long-running hit, initially
11 Listing for politicos?
12 Orbital point
13 Cure
18 Marjoram
21 Mangle
22 Truck stop offering
23 Bad thing to be under
24 Listing for entomologists?
26 Clutch hitters' fortes
29 Frequently
30 Hair feature, perhaps
34 Not judge hastily, e.g.
36 Aurora Greenway's daughter
37 Not well
39 Laugh-a-minute

40 Without much meat or fat
42 Writer Bombeck
44 Kind of handler
45 Court star
46 Suitable for Ash Wednesday
47 Land with a blue and white flag
50 Strapped

52 Metal bar
55 First name in crime fiction
56 Unreliable source
58 Millinery sale
59 Waterfront org.
60 GOP foe
61 Sound of escaping air

115
COUNT TO TEN
By Norm Guggenbiller

ACROSS
1 Theater extension?
5 Part of Lake Titicaca is in it
9 Mexican bread
14 Peter Fonda role
15 "Clue" variable
16 Southern side
17 "Relax!"
19 Chain mail
20 Impersonate
21 Appointments for duffers
23 John's follower
25 Monotonous sound
26 Some pro football players
30 Toddler
33 Stop, off land
34 "I am just ___ boy . . ."
36 Aberdeen's river
37 Womanizer, e.g.
38 "Relax!"
39 Local knowledge
40 No-win situation
41 Prepared cotton for shipment
42 Greeted and seated
43 Goof
45 Some restaurant freebies
47 Spud
49 Pippin
50 They have to face the music
53 Traffic tie-ups
57 Rub together harshly
58 "Relax!"
60 Stage platform
61 "The Morning Watch" author

62 "Fernando" group
63 In a crafty way
64 Inquisitive
65 River crossing France's Nord
department

DOWN
1 Swallowing sound
2 Bit of this and a bit of that
3 Brain tests, for short
4 Run through lines, e.g.
5 In a fast tempo
6 Long time, geologically
7 Win in a walk
8 Worked behind the plate
9 Place for great drivers?
10 Displaying one's humanity?
11 "Relax!"
12 Missouri Valley tribesman
13 Some Eur. nations, not long ago
18 Not spoken
22 Robin portrayer
24 "60 Minutes" reporter
26 Labor cohort?
27 Be of use to
28 "Relax!"
29 Operatives
31 Eagle's home
32 Some freezing temperatures
35 Words with Methuselah or the
hills
38 Shenanigan
39 Stored pending payment
41 Storeroom for foods or wines

42 Dictator's assistant
44 Soft hue
46 First name of 24-Down
48 Eternal City dweller
50 Some dept. heads
51 Seed covering

52 Utah lily
54 Holds up
55 Mechanic's grease job
56 Rating unit
59 Arles article

116
YOURS TRULY
By Isaiah Burke

ACROSS
1 Childhood illness
6 Memory route
10 Some marbled breads
14 Separated
15 Target of fawning
16 Disney prefix
17 Record groove, e.g.
18 Due follower
19 "Oh, me!"
20 "Easy!"
23 Mentalist's claim
24 Nephew of Cain
25 Some are tops
28 Look after
31 Kind of cow
35 Suffix with correct or collect
36 He is not one to speak?
37 Oriental temple
38 "Be polite!"
41 Detain during wartime
42 High-level denial
43 Something given to pacify
44 Bought and sold, e.g.
45 Pool component?
46 Poli sci subjects
47 Or follower
49 Winter quaff
51 "Hush!"
58 Type of cam or bus
59 Split violently
60 Diamond center
61 Nobelist Hahn

62 "It seemed like a good ___ at the time!"
63 Talk on and on
64 Mexican slave, e.g.
65 Acronym used in many offices
66 Leggy wader

DOWN
1 Radar's unit
2 As many as
3 Earthy deposit
4 They hang around in dens
5 Grandma's corset
6 In ___ of (replacing)
7 Month before Nisan
8 Had some munchies
9 Pop's John
10 Redeploy, e.g.
11 Holiday time
12 Mesozoic and Cenozoic
13 Palindromic plea
21 Extra-cost item
22 Type of cheese
25 Cautious and fearful
26 Sheeplike
27 Gossipy gal
29 Tall, flightless bird
30 Word with gas or cell
32 Loamy deposit
33 Kind of drive
34 Some door fasteners
36 Flowering tree
37 Unconcealed

39 Removal of text, e.g.
40 Most senators
45 Equipotential surfaces of the Earth
46 Give the cold shoulder
48 UAR component
50 Vitality
51 Dental occlusion

52 Avid about
53 It contains the ciliary body and choroid
54 Cradle grain, e.g.
55 Gum-producing plant
56 "Lamp ___ My Feet"
57 Jack London sailor
58 Unruly hairdo

117
EYE CANDY
By Lynn Lempel

ACROSS
1 NASCAR figure
4 Economic surge
8 Kindergarten supply
13 "The Stepford Wives" author Levin
14 Soft and lustrous
15 Some painted vessels
16 It goes on some at night
18 Start a drive
19 Be able to buy
20 Burning heap
22 Stimpy's sidekick
23 Talmud scholar
25 Parts of eons
27 Like a mama's boy?
30 Passover remembrance
32 Industrial-strength cleaners
33 Deflect
35 They may be odd in a drawer
37 Liquor type
38 Phrase of disappointment
40 Campground letters
41 Blacksmith's need
43 Unattached
44 Classic sneakers brand
45 Hollow rocks
47 Some rabbits
49 Artifice
50 Tested out
51 Turntable extension
53 Winglike
55 Lacking the skill, e.g.
59 Put in the fridge, say

61 Romantic milestone
63 Principle
64 Fencing pieces
65 Percussive dance style
66 Appeases hunger
67 Ends an engagement, in a way
68 It's fit for a pig

DOWN
1 Sparkly mineral
2 Tenured instr.
3 Equal part
4 Backyard attraction
5 Shout to the torero
6 Animal with stripes
7 "What have we here?"
8 Baseball's 1963 Rookie of the Year
9 Stupefaction
10 Crinkly fabric
11 Authentic
12 Disney acquisition
14 Type of metal
17 Day of song
21 Part of a dinosaur's name
24 Some poker ploys
26 Unproductive commotion
27 Olympian Korbut
28 Checking out, in a way (Var.)
29 Moneymaker out West?
30 Make lovable
31 Czech auto
34 Karel Capek drama
36 Backtalk

38 Veteran seamen
39 Typical Mensa members
42 Payer's promise
44 George Eastman started it
46 Long-bodied swimmer
48 Chivalrous chaps
50 Worthless writing, e.g.
51 Play makers?
52 It has wings but can't take wing
54 Not very many
56 Fragments
57 Test of reasoning skills
58 Observe
60 Light-Horse Harry
62 Kind of onion or cabbage

118
POST OFFICE VISIT
By Avery Rice

ACROSS
1 Bestial hideaway
5 "Victory ___" (Rodgers score)
10 "Aeneid," e.g.
14 "Let's not forget . . ."
15 Slacken off or allow to surface
16 Can't help but
17 Adorn, in a way
18 Cultured gem
19 Atlas dot
20 Hard to climb, perhaps
22 Certain rocket launching
24 Even chance
27 Mayflower pole
28 Too rehearsed
30 Could be better
31 "A German Requiem" composer
34 Grandpa Simpson
35 Unclean, by Jewish law
36 Rural swimming spot
37 Contented sound
39 Old crowned heads?
42 Monster of the Himalayas
43 On the say-so of
45 Color-deficient
47 Neither companion
48 Transuded
50 Speak up?
51 Remote control button
52 Punjabi royal
53 Look up to
55 Like sidewalk dining
58 Displays displeasure, in a way
61 Operatic love scene, usually

62 Yielded to pressure
65 First name in famous models
66 Whenever
67 Application
68 Accessible to everyone
69 Fill till full
70 Drawing room
71 Cattail, e.g.

DOWN
1 Straggles
2 Quit flying, e.g.
3 Is correct to the last detail
4 Copland composition
5 Gran Paradiso, e.g.
6 Athletic supporter?
7 Endorsement
8 Bond or market start
9 Unshaken nerve
10 Ambassador, e.g.
11 Exceed normal boundaries
12 Kon-Tiki Museum site
13 "Don't expunge that," e.g.
21 Surreptitious sound
23 Pusher's bane
25 Ilk
26 Purposes
28 Two of a '60s vocal quartet
29 Mistreatment
32 "Same here"
33 Bagpipe sound
38 Banter
40 Nearly extinct
41 Balkan native

44 First Cartesian
46 They may be painful if black
49 Olympic saucer
54 It could be spread human-to-human
55 Ructions

56 Russian spacecraft series
57 What Castro calls home?
59 It's easy to skin
60 Beach blanket?
63 Teamwork disrupter
64 Bookcase locale, often

119
MEASURE UP
By Elizabeth C. Gorski

ACROSS
1 Word with panel or power
6 Place to unwind
9 Essences
14 State a point of view
15 Tell's home canton
16 Tenantless
17 One way to land
19 Noted composition?
20 Clause connector
21 Arm bones
22 Erne's territory
23 For fear that
24 Train component
26 Bright blue
30 Sci-fi creatures
31 Reunion attendees
32 Lofty structure?
34 Slightly
38 Life partner?
39 Poet T.S.
40 "Fiesque" composer
41 Majesty lead-in
42 Jellifies
43 Majority of Oprah's audience
44 Genetic letters
46 Lack of variety
48 In theaters, e.g.
52 "Turandot" role
53 Sachet scent, perhaps
54 Separated
56 Goddess of plenty
59 Raring to go
60 Lila Crane portrayer

62 Requisites
63 "A mouse!"
64 Emotional heat
65 Painter Max
66 They were spun
67 Good buys

DOWN
1 "Nude Lying on a ___" (Francois Boucher painting)
2 Dentist's word
3 Invited a perjury charge
4 Insect that may be covered in chocolate
5 Does some airplane maintenance
6 Place for 66-Across
7 Celestial bear
8 Emulates Dracula
9 Garment insert
10 Moves like a slug
11 Single-master
12 ___ Haute, Indiana
13 Take the reins
18 Pianist von Alpenheim
23 Carpenters visit them
25 Fat Tuesday follower
26 Word with curtain or cattle
27 Author Wiesel
28 Pirate quaffs
29 Things to be filed
33 Civil rights movement figure
35 Domesticated
36 Draft selections

37 Family figures?
39 Cardinal O'Connor's successor
43 Lost one's marbles
45 Most sweet and kind
47 Oscar winner Sorvino
48 It takes off a lot
49 He's in for good
50 UFO pilot

51 It makes noise in the courtroom
55 Slightest sound
56 Olympian Korbut
57 Banana's cover
58 Lat. and Ukr., once
61 Tchaikovsky's Symphony No. 5 ___ minor

120
COVER UP!
By Fred Jackson III

ACROSS

1 Some Pontiacs of yore
5 Color of linen, sometimes
9 Gangster film character, perhaps
14 Spew fire and brimstone
15 They may twinkle
16 See 11-Down
17 Lover of Irish Rose
18 Stuff
19 Trifled (with)
20 Expose, in a way
23 More lucid
24 Negative link
25 Thing, in legalese
28 Expose, in a way
33 Hairstyle with a man's name
36 Sweat site
37 Muralist Rivera
38 Decoy
40 Kind of personality
43 Bank deposit?
44 Vintage video game name
46 Trounce
48 "The Lost Weekend" subject
49 Expose, in a way
53 Brunei coin
54 First name in the "Pulp Fiction" cast
55 Sister of Calliope
59 Expose, in a way
64 Radiance
66 Hoop site
67 Honey holders
68 City in Oklahoma
69 Eastern tribe
70 Catalog used by Wile E. Coyote
71 Hits again and again
72 Li'l Abner's affirmative
73 Arboreal abode

DOWN

1 Seizes, as a brass ring
2 Indian drum
3 Soubise base
4 Like some tomatoes
5 Impress into memory
6 Heart
7 Kind of time or world
8 It always has a lot of money
9 Drove
10 Mouth part
11 Alley Oop to 16-Across
12 Project's end?
13 Travel (about)
21 Type of wire
22 Homer's cry
26 Cereal fungus
27 Packs away
29 Sentimental stuff
30 Mantel piece, perhaps
31 Wisdom unit
32 Sass, street-style
33 Sings, so to speak
34 Bizarre
35 Piece of mind?
39 It follows any direction
41 "___ Dalmatians"

42 Toupee, in slang
45 Arboreal lizards
47 Fare-well link
50 HBO alternative
51 "Annie Get Your Gun" protagonist
52 USC athlete
56 Lickety-split

57 Serving times
58 Start
60 Doctor's advice, often
61 Modeled
62 Sacred bird
63 Consider
64 Big name at Indy
65 Tone

121
PULL AWAY
By Kenneth Drury

ACROSS

1 "___ mia!"
6 "Goodnight, ___" (1950 hit)
11 Cardinals' cap insignia
14 On one's toes
15 Denison denizen
16 State or sect starter
17 Paper holder, perhaps
19 Displayed fear, in a way
20 North Carolina college town
21 Potential heiress
23 Construction worker's craft, perhaps
26 Linger aimlessly
27 Strudel fruit, sometimes
28 Radio woe
30 Currency in Rome, once
31 Sharp or severe
32 Shaker ___, OH
35 Mai ___ cocktail
36 Subjects of some jury deliberations
38 Partner of order
39 Raggedy doll
40 Les ___-Unis
41 Polynesian idol
42 Urchins
44 London river
46 Bring under control
48 Stone and Gless
49 Like a raucous stadium crowd
50 One way to give the cook a break

52 Many a CEO
53 Gawks
58 It's needed for a stroke
59 Gay over Hiroshima
60 Bygone leaders
61 "The significance being . . . ?"
62 Went to Spago, e.g.
63 Horse stall bedding, often

DOWN

1 West, of films
2 Last word of the Pledge of Allegiance
3 "Cry ___ River"
4 One-time presidential candidate Elizabeth, politely
5 Make harmonious
6 Like some trigger fingers
7 Country queen McEntire
8 Course climax, often
9 Palindromic literary twin
10 Chapter explanation, e.g.
11 Ritzy ride
12 Vestige
13 Large ocean vessel
18 Like some discount clothes, briefly
22 Certain grandson
23 Island south of Sicily
24 Pertaining to bees
25 Jumping-off place?
26 Not at the expected time
28 Sings like Torme

29 Tots' attention-getters, perhaps
31 "___ for All Seasons" (1966 film)
33 Like a saved seat
34 Type of cheese
36 Took exception to
37 Two silkworms raced and ended in ___
41 Most likely to elicit a pucker
43 Tooth pullers' grp.
44 Mythical god of thunder
45 Frequented spots
46 One place to see a lavalava
47 Part of HUD
48 Bed or home ending
50 Dark, poetically
51 With the wherewithal
54 Cycle starter
55 Word with pool or port
56 Malay Peninsula's Isthmus of ___
57 Philadelphia-to-Norfolk dir.

122
CLASSIC SILENT G
By Ruth Keller

ACROSS

1 Some car-related injuries
11 "Beowulf" or "Iliad," e.g.
15 Some powerful storms
16 Nod neighbor
17 Dylan classic
19 Gremlins, Pacers, etc.
20 Pilate's "Behold!"
21 Sandy's human
22 Reacts to the alarm
23 Strategems
24 March VIP
27 Uncommon sense
28 Sought the favor of
29 Window section
32 The Chiffons' "___ So Fine"
35 Rolling Stones classic
39 One's wife (with "the")
40 Exxon predecessor
41 Major heart vessel
42 Took a load off
44 Pianist's exercise
45 Land of the Rising Sun
48 Emulates a trucker
51 Roughly
52 Flat plinth
53 One of the utils.
57 Irving Berlin classic
60 Novel ending?
61 Popular vacation spot
62 Frightening sound for a balloonist
63 Terrestrial amphibian

DOWN

1 New York Liberty's org.
2 Oscar winner Celeste
3 High-performance Camaro ___-Z
4 Worshippers' seats
5 My ___, Vietnam
6 Start of a pin simile
7 Cinnamon unit
8 From this time
9 Some Art Deco collectibles
10 Command in a library
11 Concluded or tailored successfully
12 Tennis server's scores after deuce
13 Magical wish granter
14 Chile's main ingredient?
18 Missing pencils may be found behind these
22 Dry streambed
24 Whiskey drink
25 ___ River, N.J.
26 Kind of talk or rally
27 Scream in a balloon?
28 Ted Baxter's station
29 Beddy-bye wear
30 ___ in Able
31 Cpl. or sgt., e.g.
32 How you may find this puzzle
33 Villa d'___ (Italian landmark)
34 Na Na lead-in
36 Center court fixture
37 They might be saturated

38 Bud's bud
42 Fries in a bit of butter, e.g.
43 "Nay!" sayer
44 God in the Hebrew Scriptures
45 Mocks
46 Is next to
47 "Designing Women" co-star
48 Uproar
49 Synthetic fiber brand

50 Extreme
53 "___ go bragh"
54 Told fibs
55 Raison d'___
56 Ivan the Terrible, e.g.
58 P.M. times
59 One of the Gabors

123
VICE SQUADS
By Eugene Newman

ACROSS
1 Bad reviews
5 It could be great or snowy
10 Pilate's "Behold!"
14 Have an edge against
15 Duplicity
16 Word with canal or beer
17 Puerto ___
18 Ruhr city
19 Aquatic organism
20 The 23rd
23 Maiden name preceder
24 R.M.N.'s vice president
25 Part of a car's steering system
27 Part of a Charlie Brown catchphrase
29 Puzzle theme, briefly
32 Hyde Park conveyances
33 Gout target, often
35 Feel under par
37 "___ gratias!"
38 The fourth
43 Anti-fray border
44 Tree of the beech family
45 "The Sleeper" poet
46 ___ Gay
49 Dos Passos trilogy
51 Diamond covers
55 Freshen the salad
57 "I, Claudius" network
59 Before, in poesy
60 The ninth
64 Word with phone or comic
65 Any "Seinfeld" episode

66 Consumes
67 Mystic character
68 Revere
69 Gin type
70 Rt.-hand person
71 They're high on opening day
72 Incline

DOWN
1 Malaysian machete
2 Enduring one
3 Atom centers
4 Greek portico
5 Discharge
6 One of six Swedish kings
7 Swell, as a river
8 Ft. above sea level
9 Belief
10 It clears the boards
11 Grand Canyon river
12 Nickname
13 Timetable abbreviation
21 "'M' ___ the many . . ." (song lyric)
22 Tuck partner
26 U.K. military award
28 Ike's WWII domain
30 Fills a portmanteau, e.g.
31 The "S" of R.S.V.P.
34 Type of trip
36 Sass
38 Magnanimous
39 Feelings
40 Mer content

41 Tally mark
42 Beverage for a genteel affair, e.g.
43 That miss
47 Memento receptacle
48 Volcanic discharge
50 Recant officially
52 Secondhand deal
53 Positive particle

54 Felt
56 Jazz singer Vaughan
58 Tibiae and others
61 Go back to square one
62 Small dose
63 Arboreal home
64 Lingerie item

124
ALL OF ME
By Mark Milhet

ACROSS
1 Judy's daughter
5 Weightlifter's maneuver
9 Dizzying genre
14 One of the Osmonds
15 Atlas datum
16 "Walk Away ___" (1966 hit)
17 Behave
20 Treating
21 Praise highly
22 Personal items?
23 Bioelectric critters, perhaps
25 Old radio feature
27 Govt. property overseer
30 There's no "I" in it
32 Solicit, as business
36 Acquired kin
38 It may be for the birds
40 Father on the farm
41 Group of learned individuals
44 Transvaal settler
45 Starting from
46 Eponym indicating failure
47 Bolt stripped?
49 Entranced
51 Six-pt. plays
52 Bernadette and Genevieve (Abbr.)
54 Root words?
56 Cyberspace initials
59 It's in the bridal shower, traditionally
61 "Deck the Halls" syllables
65 Smithsonian exhibit

68 Reeves of "Feeling Minnesota"
69 Get the show on the road?
70 Links hazard
71 Impolite dismissal
72 Middling domino
73 Overactors

DOWN
1 Genie's home
2 Pelvic bones
3 Kooky
4 Actress MacDowell
5 Sound of keys, e.g.
6 Palindromist's preposition
7 Word with bed or head
8 Sleeping bag stuffing, perhaps
9 Expert in elocution
10 It may be felt
11 Wing-prayer link
12 Not opt.
13 Hardy's "Pure Woman"
18 Punch combo
19 Fly-eating swamp plant
24 Gives the gate
26 Transported, in a way
27 The Bee Gees family
28 High-hatter
29 Birch kin
31 Estate home
33 In the ___ of (among)
34 Gave encouragement to
35 Strips away
37 Dr. Kildare portrayer
39 Make it

42 Put on an act
43 Deadly
48 Open center in a structure
50 Insultingly small
53 Key's middle name
55 One of seven deadly sins
56 Responds in "Jeopardy!"
57 Crude bunch?
58 Untrustworthy one
60 ___ effort
62 Angelic quality, perhaps
63 Neeson of "Nell"
64 Venomous varmints
66 Geneticist's concern
67 Word of lawyerly advice, perhaps

125
DECISIONS, DECISIONS
By Fran & Lou Sabin

ACROSS
1 Rigging holder
5 Badger State, briefly
9 Barely beat
14 Chorus member
15 Code word?
16 Preset path
17 Daters' decision
20 "My, my!"
21 Orly flier, once
22 Water holder?
23 Sea skate, e.g.
24 Throw the shot
26 Shopper's path
29 Buyer's decision
33 Former empire abbr.
35 Labyrinth locale
36 Shopper's mecca, once
37 Letter from Greece
38 Plunge like an eagle
41 Gelatin substitute
42 Verbose
44 Scot's "nope"
45 Mao follower?
46 Espresso drinker's decision
50 Calyx leaf
51 Moscow-to-Volgograd dir.
52 Baby food
55 Kaa's sound in "The Jungle Book"
57 Playground game
59 Upsweep, e.g.
61 Flier's decision
65 West Indies getaway

66 Word with field or guilt
67 Caen companion
68 Like prank birthday candles
69 Undulating swimmers
70 Half a Melville title

DOWN
1 Ossie Davis role in "Do The Right Thing"
2 "Welcome to the islands!"
3 Reading room
4 Made tracks
5 Seals' kin
6 Sr. investment, perhaps
7 Moments, informally
8 Guy who had a lot of Gaul?
9 Blow it
10 ___ Perignon
11 Helpers of the handicapped
12 It held down the giant Enceladus, in myth
13 Consider
18 Family man
19 Referring to 35-Across
25 Microwave option
27 Lady of Linares, briefly
28 Smooth and flowing, musically
29 Handset holder
30 Home of Maine's Black Bears
31 Hymn "Dies ___"
32 Surfacing stuff
33 Procrastinator's promise
34 Hard to bear
37 ___ Jima

39 Bireme pullers
40 Fish vendors, in a way
43 Nope counterpart
47 Buddy, Down Under
48 Missouri River feeder
49 Tear companion
52 First-class, in slang
53 Improvise
54 Hoosegow

55 Old battle line?
56 Feeling yesterday's exercise, perhaps
58 "Pretty Woman" star
60 Mosque official
62 Org. with many agents
63 Refuel oneself
64 Have something to complain about

126
LONGING FOR LOVE
By Randall J. Hartman

ACROSS

1 Stare, in wonder
5 Some geometric findings
10 Where all bids are silent
14 Nutritive mineral
15 Brouhaha
16 Tinkerbell prop
17 Deli orders, briefly
18 Wyoming mountain range
19 Yale students
20 Start of a quip
23 "Knock, knock" response
24 It was dropped before trips
25 Jumping jacks unit
27 Classic Royale, of automotive fame
28 Mariner in a classic literary tale
32 Composer Joplin
34 Computer attachments
37 They're often on the back burner
38 Middle of the quip
42 Give in
43 Policeman's assignment
44 Lipton of "The Mod Squad"
46 Belgrade resident
47 Mary's sitcom boss
50 Stand buy?
51 Driving-exam curve
54 Shaped like an avocado
56 End of the quip
61 Organic necklaces
62 Mad as a wet hen
63 Gin Rickey ingredient
64 Pt. of the NBA
65 Like some forces
66 Winter Palace resident
67 Proofer's never-mind
68 Relieve temporarily
69 ___ souci (carefree)

DOWN

1 Prattle away
2 "What's My Line?" panelist Francis
3 Word with hot or sweet
4 Come after
5 Piedmont wine city
6 Snorkeling destination, perhaps
7 Question to Brutus
8 6-Down is part of it
9 They may be called numbers
10 Wide-mouthed jug
11 Dancing style
12 Licorice-flavored liqueur
13 PGA measurements
21 Delineate
22 Asks for a driver's license, briefly
26 NFL score units, e.g.
29 Heavenly instrument
30 Palindromic pop group
31 Dirty blemishes
33 Something administered by an EMT
35 Raison d'___
36 Restaurateur Toots
38 Most indigent

39 One way to get a word in
40 ___ out (do nothing, in slang)
41 Pipe bend
42 IRS return expert
45 Possible answer
47 Creator of Meg, Jo, Beth and Amy
48 J. Paul Getty, e.g.
49 They provide milk

52 They may be kicked in a soccer match
53 Part of a camisole
55 Power units
57 That special leader?
58 Possess
59 Footnote finish, perhaps
60 Part of a cheerleader's routine
61 ___ Vegas

127
BELLY LAUGH
By Lynn Lempel

ACROSS

1 Muffler
6 Bricklayer's trough
9 Ruling Romanovs
14 Knights-in-training
15 Meiji constitution drafter
16 Carpenter's tool
17 Start of an expansive definition
19 One's own ism, e.g.
20 Choose badly, e.g.
21 Medieval Spanish hero
23 Witch's concoction
24 Broadway opening?
26 Follow relentlessly
28 Formal assent
29 Definition (Part 2)
34 Khmer Rouge leader Pot
35 Climactic start?
36 "Night" author Wiesel
37 Jew's-harp sound
39 Each one begins at love
41 It's sometimes between your teeth
44 "Wozzeck" composer
46 Playbill listing
48 Queen Lili'uokalani's instrument, briefly
49 Definition (Part 3)
53 Paddle alternative
54 Yeah opposite
55 Remus rabbit
56 Elliptical shape
58 ___ cotta
60 Promising letters?

63 Scheduling needs
65 End of the definition
68 Starlet's hiree
69 It's for two, in song
70 Relinquished
71 See 32-Down
72 Material for wine barrels, perhaps
73 Swiss trio?

DOWN

1 Facial spot?
2 Chaplin prop
3 Petri dish contents, perhaps
4 Change, as boundaries
5 Home of the Seminoles
6 Mob compilations
7 Ear-related
8 Call to a bunch of squares
9 Motherly ministering, for short
10 Belgrade native
11 Find a happy medium
12 Late plane ride
13 Adagio, vis-a-vis andante
18 Disclose
22 Loser to Clinton
25 Dismay
27 Driver's support?
29 Choose
30 Without further delay
31 Added details
32 Eleanor Roosevelt, to 71-Across
33 Zero
38 Fresh

40 Help come April 15
42 Glider used with a pole
43 Sun Yat-___ of China
45 Flying pest
47 "Get lost!"
49 Skilled in
50 Wreak havoc on
51 Warsaw uprising site

52 Lion families
57 Extend credit
59 Cassowary kin
61 Risks at the races
62 Beekeeper role for Peter
64 Porker's pen
66 Injury soother
67 Some People readers, briefly

128
IN THE DARK?
By Joy M. Andrews

ACROSS
1 Unexciting
5 Herding dog's name, perhaps
9 Asset purportedly found among thieves
14 Make over
15 Misty condition
16 Countryman near the Arabian Sea
17 Place of excess
19 Distributed proportionally
20 It involves "sill-y" plantings?
22 Fangorn figure
23 Santa's soil
24 Parnassian tribute
25 Unbuttered toast at Christmas
29 Prep school youth, usually
31 Letters for an atty.
32 "You've Made ___ Very Happy"
35 Audio equipment brand
37 MacMurray/Stanwyck film
42 Trip charge
43 Emulate a Mr. Universe contestant
44 Mother of Flopsy, Mopsy and Cottontail, e.g.
45 "Love's Labour's ___"
47 More than disgusts
50 Unfeathered wing
52 Pyramid of Cheops, for one
55 ___ chi (meditative exercise)
56 Technology introduced in the U.S. in '50s
62 "A Dog of Flanders" author

63 Purchaser's agreement to buy a second product
64 Like some paper or a sleeping bag
65 Teens always have them
66 Pop-Tarts alternative
67 Rhone tributary
68 Classical theaters
69 Speckled horse

DOWN
1 Place to see big bangs?
2 Strauss of denim fame
3 Gulf between Somalia and Yemen
4 Hun groups
5 When the reels start to roll
6 Dutch name of the Hague
7 Pound and Cornell
8 "Don Quixote" role
9 Who to root for
10 Sign of things to come
11 From sea to shining sea
12 Uninterruptedly
13 Fingerprint part
18 ___ fide (authentic)
21 Initial follower
25 Make two become one
26 Dating from
27 Edge of the storm
28 Eric the Red's son
30 German article
33 Eddie Murphy's old show, for short

34 Some poetic works
36 Like ___ of bricks
38 Sis's counterpart
39 Doyle's Scotland Yard inspector
40 Requirement for leaving some countries
41 Response solicited by a salesman
46 Likely "Sesame Street" devotee
48 Biblical villain
49 Mug

50 One cause of food poisoning
51 Boxing's Joe
53 Including yours truly
54 Word that can follow the first word of 20, 37 or 56-Across
57 Part of the Germany/Poland border
58 Size for a big foot?
59 Shakespearean villain
60 Belarusian gymnast Korbut
61 Periodic table's no. 10

129
MAKE A STAND
By Fred Jackson III

ACROSS
1 Pinochle play
5 Some Pennsylvania people
10 First name in humorous writing
14 "Dies ___"
15 Former Ford
16 Sugar substitute?
17 STAND
19 Family hand-me-down?
20 Type of tray
21 Benevolent and protective order
22 Microscopic media
24 Informal
26 Big foot
27 STAND
34 Troutlike fish
37 What SASEs are
38 Carnival site, for short
39 Luck was this to Sky Masterson
40 Like some mouthwashes
41 Poet
42 Put away
43 Indian princess (Var.)
44 Coaches
45 STAND
48 Co. famous for "You've got mail"
49 Short stars
53 Enhances
56 Brief moments, in brief
58 Script ending?
59 Part of a Beatles refrain
60 STAND
63 Women's magazine

64 Small cases
65 Goddess of victory
66 Crop starter
67 E-mails
68 Wine sediment

DOWN
1 Chameleonic comedian
2 Novelist Jong
3 There are five great ones in North America
4 Low grade
5 Armstrong's program
6 Grocery list item, often
7 Neither Dems. nor Reps.
8 Sault ___ Marie
9 Pony pest
10 More jittery
11 Symbol of slimness
12 Stable locks
13 War god
18 Courage
23 Permits
25 Unpleasant to view
28 Blood lines
29 Feminine suffixes
30 Chamber group, perhaps
31 Specific times in history
32 Cork's place
33 Does some lawn work
34 Serb or Croat, e.g.
35 Pal, Down Under
36 First place
40 Philip and Christopher

41 Unwanted china shop visitor?
43 Tooth part
44 "God ___ America"
46 Sprinted
47 Admittance
50 Jazz pianist Blake
51 Without dough
52 Famous battle participants
53 They carry motions
54 Take out, editorially
55 Chip's partner
56 Knock for a loop
57 Wife of Geraint
61 Follower of Israel?
62 "Not Ready for Prime Time Players" show

130
NEAT IDEA
By Elizabeth C. Gorski

ACROSS

1 Biblical father
5 "Star Wars" character
10 Take this for that
14 Certain textile worker
15 Distinctive glows
16 Helicopter's sound
17 Start of an office quip
19 Dynamic starter
20 One to hang with
21 Segments
22 Wilbur Post's horse
23 "The Sound of Music" family (with "von")
25 The latest thing in lists?
26 Bow, for one
27 Like a lawn at dawn
29 P.O. box item
31 Jokester
34 One of many by Beethoven
37 Tacna's country
38 Hard-rock middle
39 Middle of the quip
42 Kentucky legend
43 A lot of pizzazz?
44 Pixie
45 Actress Gretchen
46 Medium ability
47 What you used to be
48 Growing season, briefly
50 Start of Cain's query
52 Sounds of time passing
56 Green variety

58 Port St. ___, Florida
60 Lennon's lady
61 Mercury or Saturn vehicles?
62 End of the quip
64 Lizard look-alike
65 First name in cosmetics
66 First name in modeling
67 Possesses
68 Homes in the sticks
69 One-time J.F.K. arrivals

DOWN

1 Conform
2 How some get about
3 Lovely, as a signorina
4 Common verb
5 Tennis pro Novotna
6 Jackie's co-star in "The Honeymooners"
7 Quarterback Favre
8 Notation on most piano music
9 Pop the question, e.g.
10 Recipient of many questions
11 "My mind wandered . . ."
12 Frigid suffix?
13 Egg on
18 Shrimp cocktail, often
24 Pocket PCs and the like
26 Al Hirt or Dizzy Gillespie, notably
28 They were frozen on August 15, 1971
30 Place for non-recyclables

32 Aide to the DA
33 "What's Goin' On?" singer Marvin
34 Thailand, once
35 Norway's most populous city
36 Settles once and for all
37 Letters on a battery terminal
40 From Kathmandu, e.g.
41 ". . . ___ saw Elba"
47 Word with meal or pawn

49 They're a nuisance
51 Essentials
53 Draped necklines
54 Used a prayer cushion, e.g.
55 They're often tender
56 Jupiter's sister
57 Not many
59 Roman calendar notation
62 Study at home?
63 Monogram in '50s politics

131
CALLING MR. FIX-IT
By Fran & Lou Sabin

ACROSS

1 Pitcher's place
6 Balzac's "Le ___ Goriot"
10 Traveler's stretch
14 Pansy's young'un
15 Candid
16 Word of exclusivity
17 Needing repair
19 Sioux speaker
20 Virtual hero?
21 Wooden king, e.g.
22 Heavens, poetically
23 Many an Indian worshipper
24 Aweather's opposite
25 In decline
28 Bottom feeder's sphere, perhaps
32 Bog down
33 Army doc
34 Hilo neckwear
35 Occlusion
38 Nimble Fred
40 Deer friend?
41 Permeates slowly
43 Foul mood
44 Canines
46 Some volleyball shots
48 Inept individual, stereotypically
49 Antiquing applications
51 Ball park quaffs
53 Mexicali month
54 Newt wannabe
57 Ruckuses
58 Needing repair

60 Brat Pack member Rob
61 Slogged along
62 Musical composition
63 Shore fliers
64 Heavy reading
65 Like a fleabag

DOWN

1 "Buddenbrooks" author
2 Reed under Muti
3 "For ___ us a child is born"
4 Spanking follower
5 Pay an unexpected visit to
6 Gave the elbow
7 Diner extraordinaire
8 Artist Magritte
9 Chang's twin
10 Noisy fan or truffle-hunting hog, e.g.
11 Needing repair
12 Lotion base, perhaps
13 Salon specialist
18 Arboreal age indicator
22 Word on a campaign button
23 Rushes along
24 Hertz alternative
25 Nitery host
26 Keystone Kop's club
27 Needing repair
29 Lupino and Cantor
30 Shiver-causing
31 Practices girth control, e.g.
33 Comply with
36 Product requirements?

37 Sax object
39 Deal conditions, sometimes
42 Opera interrupter of note
45 Makes fun of
46 Peasant of yore
47 Reads for errors
50 Crystal-lined stone
51 Holiday event

52 Barbecue factor
53 It gets more bang than the buck
54 Nose out
55 Montague vs. Capulet, e.g.
56 Low card
58 Giant of a Giant
59 Wish otherwise

132
GETTING YOUR KICKS
By Lynn Lempel

ACROSS
1 Cruise ship accesses
6 Part of 6-Down
10 COINTELPRO overseer
13 Districts
14 Breathy utterance
15 It's a ball for teens
16 It depends on a digit's position
18 Kennel sound
19 Creator of Sula and Sethe
20 Belief system
21 Oscar-winning film for Beatty
22 Company
24 Overindulges
26 Soother of the savage beast
29 Super Bowl stats
31 Olympic Stadium team of old
34 Worldwide children's advocate
36 Co. interested in zip codes
38 Rockies roamer
39 Tom Sawyer's brother
40 Quitter of a sort
42 Tony winner Wallach
43 Summer on the Seine
44 Ancient Phoenician seaport
45 George's funny wife
47 Steel plow maker
49 Tally
51 Wedding participant
52 Sumptuous spread
54 Angry bombast
56 It may hide a bed
58 Wee bits
60 Memo prodding

64 Org. based in Vienna
65 Fairy-tale suitor
67 Religious group
68 Post-WWII Communist leader
69 It excites a sense
70 Pantry invader
71 In short order
72 Crown adornment

DOWN
1 Enthralled
2 Guthrie with a guitar
3 Malicious
4 Sight from a Malibu beach
5 Beirut-to-Mecca dir.
6 Concern for Sec. Rumsfeld
7 It's more than 4,000 miles long
8 Reluctant assent
9 Bara, "The Vamp"
10 Basic right
11 Fearless and daring
12 Little hellions
15 Ovenware brand
17 Entertainment system component, perhaps
23 Drink popularized at the 1904 World's Fair
25 Tryout
26 Pondered
27 Band together
28 Unintended consequence
30 Hoodwinked
32 1950s TV puppet
33 One on the run?

35 Word with small or stir
37 Short-snouted pooch
41 "Messiah," e.g.
46 Star born Frederick Austerlitz
48 Respond
50 32-Down, for one
53 Puts through a sieve
55 Pharaoh's symbol of royalty
56 He was a Ranger before he was a Cub

57 Forthright
59 Four-footed adventurer from Kansas
61 April or November surprise
62 Summit
63 Resound
66 Colonial rule until 1947

133
RUEFUL WORDS
By Victor Fleming

ACROSS

1 Sound before the crash of dishes
5 Tickled Muppet
9 Some jacket attachments
14 Large quantity
15 Dappled horse
16 Golf's "Army" leader
17 Word with for or white
18 Author Wiesel
19 Singer Frankie
20 Utters rueful words
23 New walker
24 Rwy. stop
25 Gaelic pop star
26 Car in Disney comedies
30 Supporters' agreements
32 Bread maker
33 Words of likelihood
35 Go head to head
38 Utters rueful words
42 It may have periods
43 Palindromic title
44 Welshman, e.g.
45 Latin I word
46 One who's sprung the coop
49 Southwestern land formation
52 Place to lay over
54 Drink with crumpets
55 Utters rueful words
61 Chanel No. 5, e.g.
62 Opposite of flushed
63 Words of self pity
64 Printer need

65 Mayberry sot
66 Lo ___ (Chinese noodle dish)
67 "My Dinner with ___"
68 Male cats
69 They may pop in flight

DOWN

1 ___ buco
2 Norwegian royal name
3 Booty
4 Adds, as to the pot
5 Spanish pop tune of the '70s
6 "Damn Yankees" role
7 Some underground pipes
8 Individually
9 Angelic accoutrement
10 Papal capes
11 It may cause tearing
12 Dark and dreary
13 "I'm history!"
21 Swindle
22 One place to catch a movie
26 Occipital ___
27 Concluded
28 Old Chevy
29 Place fit for a green thumb
31 Classified letters, perhaps
34 Links grp.
35 L.B.J. or R.M.N., once
36 Molokai, for one
37 Italian noble surname
39 Some radio stations
40 Mirage subject
41 March Madness event

45 Potential taxpayer
47 Emphasize
48 Mark of mediocrity
49 "Call Me Madam" inspiration
50 One with a complete sentence
51 Go on a shopping spree
53 "Gee, that's swell!"

56 Basic French verb
57 Like a long shot's chances
58 Bird whose male hatches the eggs
59 Kuwaiti VIP
60 Perfect scores, perhaps

134
FOR LOSERS ONLY
By Verna Suit

ACROSS

1 Back-up sounds
6 Vast expanse
9 Extended narratives
14 Wool substitute
15 Cousin of the speaker?
16 Old heartthrob Flynn
17 Beginning of a quip for losers
19 Actor Reeves
20 SASE, e.g.
21 Like stadium seats
23 Bud holder
24 Cosmetic procedure
26 Judge
28 Quip (Part 2)
33 Heaps
34 Where the congregation sits
35 Journalist Joseph or Stewart
40 West Pointer
42 Place for a nap, maybe
43 One-time Swedish statesman
44 Oglers
45 Cuzco people
47 Clancy hero
48 Quip (Part 3)
51 You can take it to the bank
55 Velvety ground cover
56 Genesis brother
57 Brennan of "Private Benjamin"
61 "Hulk" director Lee
64 Handy sort
66 End of the quip
68 It's in the bucket
69 Stage of history

70 Maine college town
71 Army shelters
72 Rendezvoused
73 Famous battle participants

DOWN

1 Portend
2 "___ go bragh"
3 Battery part
4 Place to lay down bets
5 Jailhouse fink
6 Mint plant
7 Arab prince
8 Vaulted recess
9 Mouse's reception
10 Media
11 Seething
12 Traffic diverters
13 Some tenements
18 Canon rival
22 Dit alternative
25 Total
27 It comes in cakes
28 Confront
29 Oil of ___
30 Sexy lady of a Beatles song
31 Word with main or blessed
32 Shakespearean barmaid
36 Escapades
37 Very cunning
38 A sultanate
39 Await action
41 Romanov title
46 Anouk of "La Dolce Vita"

49 Grain in a Salinger title
50 Complex units, perhaps
51 Camp David Accords participant
52 Home
53 Acquire mentally
54 Apportion

58 Agenda entry
59 Old capital of Italy
60 QED middle
62 Number of cat lives
63 Sporty Pontiacs
65 CD predecessors
67 Lode load

USA TODAY.

135
BLOWING IN THE WIND
By Diane C. Baldwin

ACROSS
1 Keep for oneself
6 Small ruckuses
10 First name in slapstick
14 Faux pas, e.g.
15 Trunk cover
16 Porter of note
17 Lacking gumption
19 Lhasa ___ (small dog)
20 Like some grins
21 Brussels export
22 Purple plum
24 On the clammy side
25 Commune member, maybe (Var.)
26 Tailor's specialty
29 Party hearty
32 Gave one's best shot
33 Cooks in the kitchen, in a way
34 Wear and tear
35 Right on the map?
36 Like one Pliny
37 Honest-to-goodness
38 Eruption particle
39 Smile of contempt
40 Fellow contestant
41 Gives the main speech
43 Some mineral gems
44 Strikingly odd
45 Get going
46 How some things are denied
48 Right-hand man
49 Dickensian interjection
52 Required consolation, perhaps

53 Without choice
56 Workout memento
57 Topmost spot
58 Prepare
59 Hopalong Cassidy's portrayer
60 Revolutionary period?
61 Gobbled-up

DOWN
1 Lobster moms
2 Spoken
3 Their mascot is a mule
4 Pull a heist
5 Welcome sight to Columbus
6 Taken ___ (caught by surprise)
7 Agatha Christie title
8 Poetic peeper
9 Parachutist
10 Shrimp dish
11 Head over heels
12 Likewise
13 Sign enhancement
18 Twinge of distress
23 Mimics
24 One may cheat on it
25 Path finder
26 Something rarely served?
27 Totally eliminate, in a way
28 Without much of a backbone
29 Fills the hull, e.g.
30 Everyday
31 Items in a compost heap, perhaps
33 Extort money from, e.g.

36 Portal
37 Run out of steam
39 Agronomist's concern
40 Crime motive, sometimes
42 Made after taxes
43 Main part of a letter
45 Certain distance runner
46 Blubber

47 Wacky as can be
48 "Summer and Smoke" heroine
49 Soak up liquid
50 Medicinal plant
51 Song for the masses?
54 Diamonds, slangily
55 Roth acct., e.g.

136
WAY TO GO!
By Jay Sullivan

ACROSS

1 Kid stuff
5 A step up
10 Warrior princess of TV
14 James Brown's bag
15 Lacking resonance
16 Jr. high preceder
17 Early TV Western hero
20 Men and boys
21 Sgt. Bilko, for one
22 Internet user's concern
26 One of the great five
30 In the vicinity
31 Biome border
33 Jockey strap
34 Inuit's abode
36 "Imagine that!"
37 Traditional camp song
41 Self-proclaimed "Greatest"
43 Pork portions
44 Write up, e.g.
47 Fir coats?
49 Last reliever called
51 Chess master Kasparov
52 Stewing
55 ___-win situation
57 Fragrant resin
58 Springboard?
65 "That makes sense"
66 "Shaddup!"
67 One not to be trusted
68 Convalesce
69 A lot of sissies?
70 Morning line

DOWN

1 Gray matter
2 Poor reception
3 NHL trophy type
4 Piece of cake
5 Impassive
6 Possessing prongs
7 Acute feeling of anxiety
8 Company name tag?
9 Winner of 324 baseball games
10 Crosses off, in a way
11 Dubya classmate
12 Beatty or Flanders
13 White House kid of the '70s
18 Suburban spread
19 Classy spot?
22 Tender spot?
23 It may be following you?
24 More raucous
25 Longtime North Carolina senator
27 Rascally
28 Number for the books?
29 Genealogy word
32 Playing hard-to-get
34 "Who goes there?" response, perhaps
35 Suffix with hexa- or deca-
38 Big Ten team
39 "The Cask of Amontillado" author
40 Shrub of the southwestern desert
41 Director Lee

42 Meadow land
45 Start of a giggle
46 Make a mistake
48 Hung loosely
49 Indentations, as in chins
50 It will shed light on things
53 Some city lights
54 Michael Caine title role (1966)

56 Not again
58 Carrey or Croce
59 ___ as directed
60 Chess pieces
61 Word with tank or range
62 Help out
63 Contemptible fellow
64 Conversation fillers

137
COINING A PHRASE
By Fran & Lou Sabin

ACROSS
1 Chicken or egg preparation
6 Common dog's name
10 Oliver's request
14 It fell March 6, 1836
15 "Magical Mystery ___" (Beatles)
16 Wall St. listing
17 Puffer's pleasure, perhaps
18 Rock star's faithful
20 Scrooge, famously
22 Deli choice
25 It's in the center of Jerusalem
26 Formicary resident
27 Gabor or Peron
28 Shoreline indentation
31 Overcomes
33 Carbonated beverage
35 Absorb the cost of
36 Bar tab item
37 Small-time con artists
43 Word with "day now" or "other questions"
44 Syllables of uncertainty
45 Put away
46 Kind of jaw
49 Characteristic
51 In the way of
52 British river isle
53 Medium for temporary statues
55 Become lessor while lessee
57 Successfully brakes suddenly
61 See 17-Across
62 Terse
66 Noun-forming suffix
67 Snookums
68 Sierra ___
69 Tannery employee
70 Last word of a holiday song title
71 Piano piece

DOWN
1 Natural pouch
2 Husband of Fatima
3 Drop behind
4 Macapa is its capital
5 Green stuff
6 WWII weapon
7 Chincoteague equine
8 Production manager's concern
9 Les Mousquetaires, par exemple
10 Artist Chagall
11 1935 Triple Crown winner and a Nebraska city
12 King's stand-in
13 Puts forth with effort
19 Not capable
21 Like some nonagenarians
22 Clan group
23 Acknowledge
24 "Fiesque" composer
29 Resinous deposit
30 Antiknock additive
32 Scaleless wonders
34 Desert garments
36 Birthplace of St. Francis
38 Stand firm
39 Lyricist Gershwin
40 List wrap-up, perhaps

41 Juliet is a common one
42 ___ team
46 Showed surprise, in a way
47 Extended tirade
48 "Now!"
49 Two-time world skating champ Albright
50 Take a fall

54 Campus figures
56 Toulouse topper
58 Source of pressure, often
59 A.A. Milne's first name
60 Have the gumption
63 Debtor's onus
64 Close down
65 Professional charge

138
LAY OF THE LAND
By Gail Grabowski

ACROSS

1 Booty
5 Some sloped surfaces
10 Tatum's father
14 Fictional ship
15 Banish
16 Soothe
17 Fashionable New York City street
19 In need of water
20 Great bargain
21 Refuse to admit
22 Vitamin bottle letters
23 A relative of mine?
24 Passes through a fence?
26 Thus far
30 In first place, e.g.
33 Guys who cry foul?
36 Show fallibility
37 Salad vegetable, perhaps
38 Kentucky legend
39 Some notices from Detroit
41 Copyright symbol
42 Moors, as a boat
44 Acapulco ayes
45 Johnny Fever's station
46 Landlubbers' opposites
47 Swiss or American
49 "Same here!"
51 Try not to be taken by surprise
54 Abbr. spotted in the mailroom
56 "Born Free" feline
59 Some choir members
61 Rudely brief
62 Dry breakfast item
64 Toledo's lake
65 Patriotic symbol
66 Without commitments
67 Frisco's finest
68 Clear data, in a way
69 Punch ingredient

DOWN

1 Robs of energy
2 Vindictive anger
3 Acquiesce
4 Some recreational vehicles
5 Prepare to drag
6 Involuntarily out of a job
7 Destroyer destroyer, perhaps
8 What some necklines do
9 "I'm outta here!"
10 Hit from behind
11 Comparison standard
12 "The Travels of Marco Polo" subject
13 Beatty and Sparks
18 It may precede an extra point
25 Heavy weights
27 Hard to fathom
28 Fogbow's shape
29 Can type
31 Of higher rank than
32 Look like Tom?
33 Brown exclamation
34 Lamb's pen name
35 Educational excursion
37 "You're something ___!"

39 Fall shade
40 Conceal the truth
43 Pinched pennies
45 Prosperous
47 Shirt feature
48 Young oyster
50 Conical dwelling
52 Nintendo precursor

53 They smell
54 Ones in suits?
55 Gang territory
57 Epic tale
58 Isn't up to snuff
60 Editor's note, perhaps
63 Maiden name preceder

139
CARROT-TOPS
By Verna Suit

ACROSS

1 No big shot?
4 Like some sheepdogs
10 H.H. Munro pen name
14 Caviar, e.g.
15 "McTeague" novelist Frank
16 "___ helpless as a kitten up a tree"
17 Colonial insect
18 Redheaded comedian
20 Mythical haunter of the Himalayas
22 Sleep stage
23 Actress Blakley of "Nashville"
24 Redheaded restaurant figure
28 Whichever
29 "___ Miserables"
30 Kind of plug
33 Director Kazan
35 Its tail flaps in the wind
39 Redheaded president
42 Has the flu, e.g.
43 Kind of wave
44 Union member since 1820
45 Game name start
46 Mighty tree
47 Redheaded impressionist painter
55 Squirrel snack
56 Avian source of red meat
57 Travails
59 Redheaded CBS star
63 Brainiac school
64 Hot tempers

65 Group within a group
66 College e-mail address part
67 Blanc and Brooks
68 Judge
69 Adam's contribution

DOWN

1 Barnyard cry
2 Big goof
3 Heated conflict
4 NBC show since 1975
5 Like some pay rates
6 Jumped between electrodes
7 Fairy tale teller
8 Artist Scott-Heron
9 Fashion monogram
10 "C'est ___" Eartha Kitt song
11 Range maker
12 Superman's birth name
13 Placed on Capri, e.g.
19 God of love
21 Up ___ (extremely upset)
25 "My Way" songwriter Paul
26 "From Here to Eternity" actor Montgomery
27 Not hearing
30 RR stop
31 Greek F
32 Popular ISP
33 VCR button
34 Meadow
35 Former Polish capital
36 "... it ___" (Book of Matthew)
37 Weigh station unit, perhaps

38 Vane direction, sometimes
40 Guarded leg part
41 Webzine
45 Man the bar
46 Unwelcome obligations
47 Husband of Bardot and Fonda
48 Words of sympathy
49 Work of fiction
50 Cross leader

51 Words denoting action
52 Be the life of the party
53 Private Pyle
54 Alpine classic
58 Ticket end
60 R.E. Lee's org.
61 Ger. neighbor
62 NFL tiebreaker periods

140
INITIALLY SHORTENED
By Lane Gutz

ACROSS
1 "I ___ it!"
5 Snow shovel or shovel snow
10 Crossed the Channel, a la Ederle
14 Best of the best
15 See 6-Down
16 Nut variety
17 Initial lawyer
19 Flatten flannel
20 Capital of Uganda
21 Steps to the side
23 No matter which
24 Optical aid
26 Higher power
27 Initial FBI director
32 Long prose narratives
35 The last stand?
36 Choler
37 Prepare for tomorrow
38 Snail mail cubbyhole
40 First name in philosophy
41 Grown elver
42 "Jaws" ship
43 It may be precious and
   mounted
44 Initial surgeon general
48 Cenozoic, for one
49 Undeleted expletive
50 Barnyard bleat
53 Second vending
56 Not on the windy side
58 Play parts
59 Initial name in fashion
62 Horse tail?

63 Boy Wonder
64 Timotheus or Phrynichus, e.g.
65 Tadpole territory
66 Arkin and Hale
67 Partners of odds

DOWN
1 "The Trial" novelist Franz
2 Ex-Ranger Ryan
3 Kind of aircraft
4 Do more than tear up
5 Like a lizard or Mt. Everest
6 Kai-shek, former leader of
   15-Across
7 Wildcatter's find
8 "___ singular sensation . . ."
9 Reduces debt
10 Word with 23
11 Collection of beliefs about life
12 Shower gel ingredient, perhaps
13 Takes control of
18 Makes hay, in a way
22 Stravinsky or Sikorsky
25 Lord's day
27 Brady Bunch member
28 Carnival location, for short
29 Nut variety
30 Lough Gowna's river
31 Fail the sobriety test, in a way
32 What some things are built on
33 Not on the windy side
34 Texas island city
38 Start to soak?
39 10th mo.

40 Bench press unit
42 From the pie hole
43 One of two sans suit
45 Wiped out
46 Temperature unit
47 Eleven or Twelve, in film
50 Fillet wrapper, sometimes
51 Jumped between electrodes

52 Mine entrances
53 Carpenter's tool
54 Sound rebound
55 Poet Pound
57 Help with the dishes
60 Army VIP
61 Atty. resume letters

141
FARM TEAM
By Jay Sullivan

ACROSS

1 Nimble
6 Raised, as rabbits
10 Online room
14 Lake Nasser dam
15 Suction introduction?
16 It's often plastered
17 Hand holder
18 Opposed to, to Pappy Yokum
19 Fascinated by
20 Naif
23 CD return, briefly
25 Company title letters, perhaps
26 Expressing amazement, in a way
27 Chick watcher
31 Food and water, for two
32 Melodic composition
33 A colon has two
35 Marvel superheroes
36 Imitative
38 Future CEOs, perhaps
42 Ready for printing
43 List ending, perhaps
45 It shows the way
49 Big eater
51 Occur to
53 ___ Beta Kappa
54 August in Paris
55 Faux candidate
59 "Curses!"
60 Andean land
61 Doctor's instruction
64 The scarlet letter

65 Uzbekistan lake
66 Difficult expeditions
67 Muffin stuffin', sometimes
68 Kiddie litter?
69 Mubarak predecessor

DOWN

1 Partner of order
2 Mt. Carmel site, briefly
3 Trash bag securer
4 Latch
5 They're found in a log
6 Grow pale
7 "The Avengers" actress
8 Colossal
9 Hawaiian singing legend
10 Overworked phrase
11 Monogram bearer
12 Be there
13 Some beachwear
21 Damaging encroachment
22 They're from Saturn
23 Film format for tall tales?
24 Group standard
28 Wooer's word, especially in Baltimore
29 Meathead's mother-in-law
30 Turndowns
34 "Tommy" group
37 Snapshot, for short
38 Famous chairman
39 Like Sinatra
40 Word that makes grammarians cringe

41 "Smooth Operator" chanteuse
42 Fuzzy member of Skywalker's army
44 Lacks proper hydration
45 Gather on a surface, in chemistry
46 Alternative word
47 Where Kigali is

48 Lent
50 Classic film director Max
52 Attack, as a puppy
56 Successor to Claudius
57 Color associated with aging
58 "Two Mules for Sister ___"
62 Police blotter word, often
63 F.D.R.'s veep

142
OCEAN ACTION
By Fred Jackson III

ACROSS
1 Rise ominously
5 Kind of whale
10 They may be stacked
14 Spat mate
15 Free-for-all
16 Corn or beans, e.g.
17 One-time rank for seaman at 56-Across
19 Cantina tidbit
20 Refrigerator reminders
21 Degrees
23 CBS logo
24 Diet guru Jenny
26 Incantation opener
28 Debate side
29 A yoga position
33 Deuce topper
34 One-time rank for seaman at 56-Across
36 Help-wanted abbr.
37 Rocker Pat
38 Palter
39 Creator of seaman at 56-Across
41 Small fry
42 "Siddhartha" author
43 Multivolume ref.
44 Staffs
45 Affluence
47 Trim a limb, e.g.
48 Repairs the green, e.g.
51 Most unctuous
55 Uniform

56 Fictional seaman and theme of puzzle
59 Word with tired or heat
60 Draw out
61 Unresponsive state
62 Grounded fliers, briefly
63 Type of prize
64 Actor Tamiroff

DOWN
1 It may have a gooseneck
2 A mixed bag
3 Auto pioneer
4 Christie product
5 Strike
6 ___ up (invigorates)
7 Colonnade tree, perhaps
8 "The Crying Game" actor
9 Bright bunch
10 Stop-sign shape
11 Air resistance
12 Dumbbell
13 Restful resorts
18 "Wassup!"
22 Bathroom floor installer
24 Causes to exist
25 Defeated handily
26 Popped up
27 Complaints, in slang
28 Attaches, as a carnation
30 Kite's claw
31 Course sections
32 Fr. holy women

33 Kind of support
34 Spider-Man creator
35 Two-lane topper, often
37 Raise, as cattle
40 Singing family
41 Popular pudding
44 Gangland gal
46 Anemic-looking
47 Slander counterpart

48 1990 World Series champs
49 Nights before
50 Show to a chair
51 Some years back
52 "Return of the Jedi" critter
53 Rig
54 Coal car
57 Prefix with meter
58 Hamlet's catch

143
LET THERE BE LIGHT
By Robert H. Wolfe

ACROSS

1 Disney's "___ of the South"
5 "On the double!"
9 Type of pad
14 Concluded
15 Flower holder
16 Cried softly
17 Lee known for desserts
18 Victor Laszlo's wife
19 Homer epic
20 Girlfriend from the past, e.g.
22 Jurists
23 Special educator
24 Alley-___
25 Uncompromising law
28 Concentrate
30 Waited or tarried
34 You can count on these
36 Flier out of Stockholm
37 Gone (with "up")
38 At an unspecified future time
41 Searching through someone's stuff
43 Flash of brilliance, perhaps
44 Weep convulsively
46 In need of a diet
47 Not more
48 Would-be spouse
51 Possible wine order
52 Direction to a capt.
54 Type of dynamics
56 Fish out of water
59 Hollywood VIP
63 Remove, as a badge

64 Kappa's preceder
65 Singer Guthrie
66 Give a start to
67 Like Arthur Fonzarelli
68 Take charge on the dance floor
69 Long-snouted mammal
70 Sicilian volcano
71 Kind of room

DOWN

1 Hardly thrilling
2 Shaped like a face
3 Square, updated
4 Chicanery
5 Fly a plane
6 Chinook, e.g.
7 Puts forth
8 Tine target
9 Agnew who resigned
10 Nursery buy, perhaps
11 Nobelist Wiesel
12 Close by
13 Vegas numbers
21 Crystal clear
22 Body trunks
25 Aromatic herb
26 Legal residence
27 A-list items
29 Toreador's trophy
31 Willow tree
32 Very thick
33 Won by a nose
35 Official truce
39 Useful quality

40 Thee, now
42 Discussion medium
45 Mythical humanoid
49 Sea god
50 "C'est magnifique!"
53 Connective tissue
55 One of many written by David

56 Make untidy
57 Kind of worm
58 Fight verbally, perhaps
60 Tall growth
61 Alda of "The West Wing"
62 Retinal cells
64 Word with cap or cream

144

SOLD!

By Lynn Lempel

ACROSS

1 Scatter
6 Head honcho
10 Mower's bane
14 Piano key material
15 What a player may risk first
16 French spread
17 Beginning of an auction definition
19 Dump, so to speak
20 Shakespeare's Puck, for one
21 Eunice, to Ted
22 Some pancake-like fish
23 "Spaghetti" poet Silverstein
25 Joe, to Ted
27 Animated brat
30 Popular brew
32 Obtain underhandedly
36 Stir
37 Bumpy-skinned critters
39 Young haddock, e.g.
40 Middle of the definition
43 Bean on Broadway
44 Familiar refrain
45 Vegetable that rolls
46 Disquiet
48 Medium talent?
49 Fraulein's catch
50 Flowery keepsakes
52 Able-bodied
54 Rugged vehicle
57 Fed. mortgage insurer
59 Montenegro's former partner
63 Large fair

64 End of the definition
66 Inconclusive results
67 Lake named for an Indian tribe
68 Artistic style
69 Text preserver, to an editor
70 Helen of Troy's mythic mother
71 Outer limits

DOWN

1 Seven wet ones
2 Recipe amt., perhaps
3 Blast furnace sound
4 Sign up
5 Family name in American art
6 "Nonsense!"
7 "Annuit coeptis" is written on them
8 Las Vegas feature
9 Recreation for two
10 Stonewall, Texas landmark
11 It's sung solo
12 Cunning
13 Meadowlands celebs
18 Kiddie
24 Slightest
26 Entree category
27 Marshy tributary, e.g.
28 Embellish
29 Shake awake
31 Be smitten with
33 Moan and groan
34 Recluse
35 Bergen who spoke for Charlie
37 Uptight

38 Boffo hit
41 Gridiron marker
42 Juarez's border twin
47 Namesake tower designer
49 Punched cattle
51 End of the road, for sure
53 Cliff protrusion
54 Tony's buddies in "West Side Story"

55 Withdrawal
56 Rapier descendant
58 Bone-dry
60 Bob's road films co-star
61 Concerning
62 Month of Sundays
65 Educator's org.

145
TIVO ALERT
By Joy M. Andrews

ACROSS
1 Sharecrop
5 Paddle boat?
10 Horse's halter
14 Mexican water
15 Place to shop for togas
16 Couple's pronoun
17 TiVo alert
20 Psalms pause
21 Where beauty is, to the beholder
22 Business card abbr.
23 Emulate a cat
26 City on the Meuse
28 TiVo alert
32 "___ Fire" (Springsteen hit)
33 Convened to consider legislation
34 Cheerleader's asset
35 Important cribbage card
36 Impanels
38 Let the bug have it
41 Express
42 Classic car
43 It may settle the score?
44 TiVo alert
49 Bruin, e.g.
50 Get new under wear?
51 Uris hero
52 Serve well done?
54 A to Z
57 TiVo alert
62 Essayist's pseudonym
63 Pataki's predecessor

64 Aspersion, e.g.
65 Make one roll in the aisles
66 Arctic
67 In neat order

DOWN
1 Passing fancy
2 Innocence and others
3 Country bumpkin
4 Cartoonist noted for his drawings of soldiers in battle
5 Liquid resources
6 PR person
7 Japanese theater (Var.)
8 Get one's bearings
9 Kind of chair or street
10 Ply with posies and sweets, e.g.
11 Didn't gather?
12 Sandinista's Daniel
13 Judd sister
18 Small glacial lake
19 Rhubarbs
24 Something sought by 49-Across
25 Student teacher or medical apprentice (Var.)
27 AOL or EarthLink, e.g.
28 Recycling container
29 Comedian Philips
30 Tar
31 Planning mischief
36 Hindu aphorisms
37 Co. honchos
38 Place for not-so-wild animals
39 Soccer's Freddy

40 Equity in value
41 Prefix with teen
43 Druggist, in London
44 Racers and rattlers
45 Type of ride
46 Keys with a diary album
47 Full of anger, e.g.
48 Distinctive and stylish elegance

53 "Your Show of Shows" co-star
55 Wrinkly tangelo
56 None-too-gentle landing
58 Beauty queen Mary
59 Mirror blurrer
60 Pa. newsmaker of 1979
61 Test, as patience

146
RECKLESS DRIVER
By Bonnie L. Gentry

ACROSS
1 First name in hoteliers
6 Journalist Stewart or Joseph
11 Eeyore's bookmate
14 One with parts
15 Place for a grilling
16 Psych. research topic
17 John Daly commenting on his golf game
19 Bodybuilder's concern, among others
20 Clown feature
21 Roman god of love
22 Kon-___ (Heyerdahl's raft)
23 Comment (Part 2)
27 Black or white drink
30 Post-workout symptom
31 Is a good dog
32 Type of computer cable
36 Put bucks on the Bulls, say
37 Musk producer
39 Percent suffix
40 Queensland's capital
43 "When ___ said and done . . ."
45 Opera solo
46 Most likely to cause goose flesh
48 Comment (Part 3)
52 Propane holder
53 Oppositionist
54 Submarine sandwich
58 Calypso cousin
59 End of the comment
62 Hr. fragment
63 Palindromist's dogma

64 "All That Jazz" director
65 Browning's before
66 Contest submission
67 Preppy's fabric, e.g.

DOWN
1 Form of lie
2 Kind of chamber
3 "Miss ___ Regrets" (Porter tune)
4 Tough
5 Life imitator
6 Tarzan, for one
7 Part of a repair bill
8 It's not measured in traditional years
9 Black gold
10 Washington fig.
11 Museum piece
12 Japanese site of Expo '70
13 Decide to join, e.g.
18 Punchline response
22 Shea section
24 Familial moniker
25 Zwei cubed
26 Any ship at sea
27 L.B.J. son-in-law
28 ". . . Deutschland ___ alles"
29 Outer space probers, briefly
32 Wife who had no in-laws
33 Locale in a Christie title
34 Connecticut Ivy Leaguers
35 Microphone word
37 It's raised during a ruckus
38 Swooning, e.g.

41 Potatoes purchase, perhaps
42 Bikini part
43 Jackie's second mate
44 "3rd Rock From the Sun" star
46 Independent being
47 Get to work on Time?
48 Answer to "Who's there?"
49 Bed of nails user
50 Lacking any point
51 ___ alia (among other things)
55 Smooth the way of
56 Swell, as a river
57 Linear, for short
59 Suffix with Israel
60 She lays around the farm
61 Back on the briny

147
UP A TREE
By Jay Sullivan

ACROSS

1 Home of Italian bubbly
5 A dancing Astaire
10 Dare into doing
14 Frost
15 Ryan with the fastball
16 "Rats!"
17 Start to mate?
18 Language of Sri Lanka
19 Visitor to Oz
20 It's up in the air?
23 Flag down
24 Auto shaft attachment
25 Gross out
28 Step over the line, perhaps
33 Major transportation routes
35 Entrance requirement?
36 Current events?
37 Alley-___
38 One who gives a hoot
40 Do not delay
41 Spot for a nest?
43 Comeback
46 Gives the slip
47 Stammering syllables
48 Start a triathlon
49 Eve's offering
56 Hairwear
57 Incline
58 Less than rarely
59 Home of the Kon-Tiki Museum
60 "Papa Bear"
61 Concert halls
62 Reply to a bartender

63 Some siblings
64 One thing to do with a coin

DOWN

1 Ishmael's skipper
2 Type of grapes
3 Bye words
4 Something to rule with
5 Aardvark's target
6 Factotum
7 Salt's saint
8 Like members of the flock
9 Ties up
10 Relax completely
11 River or state
12 Soon, to a bard
13 Head of a syndicate
21 Horseshoe parts
22 ___ in turkey
25 In conflict
26 Haggling point
27 Some kicks
28 Gov't security
29 Tow-truck attachment, perhaps
30 Having a sharp taste
31 "Guys and Dolls" tune
32 Kostunica followers
34 Letters of credit?
38 Nev. neighbor
39 Plant used as an astringent
41 At first glance
42 Neophobe's fear
44 Man or woman
45 Symbol of sovereignty

48 Assembly line item
49 Sea things
50 Give the once-over
51 Western command
52 Miro contemporary

53 Word processing command
54 Finishes the cupcakes, e.g.
55 Drinks from a bag, often
56 "Holy smoke!"

148
IN FORE TROUBLE
By Randall J. Hartman

ACROSS
1 U.S. election mo.
4 Policeman's badge
10 Mountain route
14 Boxer known as the "Louisville Lip"
15 White-flag discussion
16 Diva's big moment
17 Oil well drilling gear
18 Start of a quip
20 Beehive, for one
22 Black fly, e.g.
23 Yosemite photographer Adams
24 Luke Skywalker's sister
26 Church nooks
27 Quip (Part 2)
32 Seven-time Tour de France winner Armstrong
33 Like a good Bordeaux
34 Online nuisance
38 ___ Park, Colorado
39 Genetic inits.
40 Observe Yom Kippur
41 Give off, as light
42 Crude cartel
43 Shapes and forms
44 Quip (Part 3)
46 Zagreb resident
49 ___-friendly
50 Film a scene
51 Campaigner's skill
54 Shaving injury
57 End of the quip

60 Where to see lions and tigers and bears
61 Skin cream ingredient
62 Polo club
63 "Turn to Stone" rockers, briefly
64 Geek
65 Cute as a button
66 Actor Benicio ___ Toro

DOWN
1 DEA agent, e.g.
2 Hodgepodge
3 Self-appointed lawman
4 Mineral spring
5 Old Testament book
6 Word with hand or fist
7 Fitzgerald of scat fame
8 Outfield position for Barry Bonds
9 Color Easter eggs
10 Chessboard pieces
11 Respond to a rooster, perhaps
12 Positions
13 Satirist Mort
19 Vocalizes like Nelly
21 Enclosed, like a backyard
25 Roman date
26 Lend a hand
27 Microbrewery offerings
28 Discuss (with "over")
29 ___ diem
30 Vice president who resigned in 1973

31 Juicy fruit
34 Hot, in a sense
35 Sharply divided
36 Raggedy doll
37 Many a teenager's room
40 They're for The Byrds
42 Home of Sault Ste. Marie
44 Words from one on the stand
45 Start
46 South American nation
47 Turbine part
48 Exclaimed surprise
50 Graceful dive
51 Former Russian despot
52 Up to the task
53 Young zebra
55 Singer Nat King ___
56 Singer with The Gang
58 Little demon
59 Pigpen

149
BOOK END?
By Ed Early

ACROSS
1 Patio activities, for short
5 Polecat's trademark
9 Disney deer
14 Landslide
15 ___ colada
16 Completely unfamiliar
17 To ___ (exactly)
18 What one isn't?
19 End of the line for cable?
20 Start of a quip
23 He was fired by Godfrey on the air
24 Salon item
25 Ending for Caesar
28 "West Side Story" faction
30 Texas city on the Mexican border
33 Beach vehicle, for short
36 Give a hand
39 "The ___ Incident" (1943 film)
40 Middle of the quip
44 Free from
45 Bean curd
46 Doughboys
47 "Romanian Rhapsody" composer
49 They give people big heads
52 "O Sole ___"
53 Bud's funny buddy
56 Football's "Galloping Ghost"
60 End of the quip
64 Fad
66 General ___ Chicken

67 Word describing Abby?
68 Fictional Uncle
69 Longtime Broadway hit
70 Land unit
71 Open
72 Greek letters
73 Become liquid

DOWN
1 More than a scuffle
2 South Africa's first prime minister
3 Strange
4 Court worker, for short
5 Modus follower
6 Plunge into the water
7 First year after B.C.
8 First name among the "American Idol" judges
9 Shower alternative
10 Thomas ___ Edison
11 Stereotypical gangster film character
12 Royal jelly producer
13 Bank earnings (Abbr.)
21 "This ___ recording"
22 Lou Grant's anchorman
26 Garlicky fish garnish
27 "___ not the time!"
29 Chap
31 Classified ad letters
32 Half of CXXX
33 Pertinent, as a remark
34 "Lemon Tree" singer Lopez

1	2	3	4		5	6	7	8		9	10	11	12	13
14					15					16				
17					18					19				
20				21					22					
23							24					25	26	27
			28			29			30	31	32			
33	34	35			36		37	38		39				
40			41	42					43					
44					45						46			
47					48			49		50	51			
52					53	54	55		56			57	58	59
	60	61	62				63							
64	65					66				67				
68					69					70				
71					72					73				

35 Ms. Pac-Man, famously
37 In the past
38 Kind of insurance
41 Turndowns
42 Col. Sanders' outfit
43 Drops a hint
48 Grand ___ Opry
50 "... man ___ mouse?"
51 Former Iraqi ruler Hussein
54 Unconventional

55 Favorite's defeat
57 Family member
58 Knot on a tree
59 Wading bird
61 The Riviera's Cote d'___
62 It may cover a shirt
63 Novelist Jaffe
64 ___-Magnon
65 Gun, as an engine

150
PAIRING UP
By Robert H. Wolfe

ACROSS
1 Former Indian leader
6 Request for Fido
11 "___ Miserables"
14 Useful plants
15 "Little House" daughter
16 Man-mouse filler
17 Pair for Hood
19 Early second-century date
20 Window part
21 Disgraced VP
22 Related
23 Tenets
25 Sweepstakes hopeful
27 Fen
30 Lady lobster
32 Dearie
33 Having a strong fragrance
35 Recipient of mail
38 X-ray unit
39 Answer back
41 Mary ___ Place
42 Holds tightly
44 Certain Himalayan native
46 Scottish negative
47 Felonious "artist"
48 "When I Need You" singer Leo
49 North Atlantic delicacy
52 Certain Asian holidays
54 Fishing attachment
55 Frontier dwelling
57 The Taj Mahal, e.g.
61 Did some noshing
62 Pair for a sheriff

64 Strong emotion
65 Graff of "Mr. Belvedere"
66 Composure and coolness
67 Harris or Torme
68 Trike part
69 Aerobics result

DOWN
1 Catches in the act
2 "The Time Machine" people
3 Plaintive sound
4 Winslow Homer's painting style
5 Annapolis inits.
6 The USS Enterprise, e.g.
7 Work hard for
8 Serving dish
9 Tooth covering, perhaps
10 Hem companion
11 Pair for a certain smith
12 Senator of Watergate fame
13 Sanctified one
18 Sire's mate
22 Presley's middle name
24 Wrinkled dog
26 Orient, familiarly
27 Artist Chagall
28 Sea that's a lake
29 Pair for a fisherman
31 "Low-budget," in brand names
34 It is, that is
35 Indy sponsor
36 Relaxation
37 Rubbernecker
40 Orlando newspaper

43 Place for valuables

45 Where it may be hardest to see the stage

47 Chewed without swallowing

49 It may be staked

50 Bizarre

51 Make it to the top

53 Word with run or result

56 Eric of "Munich"

58 Garfield's foil

59 Flat formation

60 Author Harte

62 It's right under your nose

63 Photo ___ (media events)

151
TRESS TEST
By Elizabeth C. Gorski

ACROSS
1 People in Xings
5 Messy sound effect
10 Film star Grant
14 1997 Peter Fonda role
15 ___ straight face (don't crack up)
16 ___ facto
17 Athlete Archibald
18 Tehran native
19 Many NYC living quarters
20 Having fixed opinions
23 Working together perfectly
24 Bern's river (Var.)
25 Cezanne's summer
28 Winter celebration in Vietnam
29 Magma on the move
32 Snoozed
34 Tennis star Williams
36 Helps
37 Anti-glare eyewear
41 Retro skirt style
42 Sounds the alarm, e.g.
43 Mobile bride?
46 Italian noble family
47 Gave the go-ahead to
50 Furry visitor in a 1980s sitcom
51 Old Microsoft product
53 Words of consent
55 Morning bowlful, perhaps
59 Cincinnati's river
61 ___ cotta
62 Sicilian province or its capital
63 Pay stub acronym, often

64 Archeologist's quest
65 Type of balloon
66 Began a golf game
67 Proficient
68 "Auld Lang ___"

DOWN
1 Learned one
2 Comedian Boosler
3 More than dislike
4 Hardly posh
5 Estee Lauder's business
6 Impertinent
7 Genesis figure
8 Sleep problem
9 The Tropic of Cancer runs through it
10 Tuscany ta-ta
11 Pastry cart item
12 Alphabetic run
13 Casual greetings
21 Cove
22 "Are you a man ___ mouse?"
26 Danson and Koppel
27 Bradley and Sullivan
30 Sacred Hindu writings
31 What a protractor measures
33 Bridge declaration
34 Hair salon sound
35 Pub drinks
37 Cultivate land, in a way
38 Politician's place
39 Dig discovery, perhaps
40 Exceptional deal

41 ___ culpa
44 Tokyo's former name
45 Spots for speakers
47 Island group off Scotland
48 Character actor Wynn
49 Infamous Marquis
52 Knight's horse

54 Isle of Man residents
56 It has shoulders but no head
57 ___ Stanley Gardner
58 Sound from a coffee maker
59 Frequently, poetically
60 Rush along

152
ART FOR ART'S SAKE
By Fred Jackson III

ACROSS
1 Nullified tennis serves
5 Kind of test or rain
9 Mormon title
14 Gossip unit
15 "The Sweetest Taboo" singer
16 Dangerous loop
17 Continental prefix
18 Branch location?
19 Grammy winner Eydie
20 ART
23 Infantile syllable
24 Capp and Hirt
25 Bee batteries
29 Fair share?
31 Piece of cheesecake?
34 Chocolate source
35 Intrepid
36 Inside information, in slang
37 ART
40 Decant
41 "___ & Janis" (comic strip)
42 Equip again
43 More than intuition
44 Saskatchewan tribe
45 Emeralds, for example
46 Steak go-with, sometimes
47 Dude kin
48 ART
57 Studio sign
58 Bring home the bacon
59 Gray-headed
60 Adhered
61 Awestruck

62 Traditional lab item
63 Tannery inventory
64 Brooding bunch?
65 Palindromic address

DOWN
1 Tells tales
2 Sundries case
3 Shore bird
4 Unhealthy visibility reducer
5 Some Houston athletes
6 Hold contents
7 Genesis of an invention
8 Bucks
9 Cover completely
10 Some diving birds
11 Social misfit, to some
12 Salinger heroine
13 A line winds out of it
21 Incite
22 Three-time Masters winner
25 Dream or moon attachment
26 Tropical tubers
27 Become dangerous, as roads
28 Depilatory brand
29 Card game authority Edmond
30 What's more
31 Disney star
32 "___ in Paris"
33 Boy-girl link
35 Reveal
36 Salon specialist
38 Person chanting "I bet you can't"

39 Certain refrigerant
44 Some office workers
45 Takes here
46 Roosevelt's daughter
47 British peer
48 "Gee willikers!"
49 Pro foe
50 Exalt

51 Part of a Beatles refrain, when tripled
52 Web site unit
53 Joyce Carol Oates novel
54 Itty bitty bit
55 "Peter Pan" dog
56 About 15 grains

153
MALE LEADS
By Randall J. Hartman

ACROSS

1 Helmet attachment, perhaps
6 Li'l Abner creator
10 Word with duck or cash
14 Very busy American airport
15 "A Death in the Family" novelist James
16 Award given by The Village Voice
17 Sci-fi strip
19 Insensible condition
20 Israel-to-Yemen dir.
21 Split the scene
22 Hire
24 Tractor-trailers
25 Ward of "The Fugitive"
26 Certain Tokyo temple
29 Old salts
33 Stainless steel or brass, e.g.
34 Glowing review
35 They do it often in Vegas
36 New Mexico art community
37 Spoke in jest
38 Soft cheese
39 Harness race pace
40 Secondhand
41 Medieval band of merchants
42 Places under a liquid, e.g.
44 Every bit
45 Nine-to-five grinds, e.g.
46 Strings member
47 Om, for one
50 Tell all
51 Deeply regret

54 Diva's big moment
55 Gin drink
58 West African nation
59 Length X width
60 Weird Al's first Top 40 hit
61 Victim of Genesis
62 Bambi and kin
63 Sudden outpouring

DOWN

1 Boo-hoos
2 "___ Spoke Zarathustra"
3 Run for the money
4 Ham's craft
5 Breach of faith
6 Elevator cars
7 Long in the tooth
8 ___ capita
9 Made a nuisance of oneself
10 Absurd type of story
11 Woodwind instrument
12 Ride to the prom, perhaps
13 Person with a list
18 Gymnast Korbut
23 Thrilla in Manila winner
24 Wake behind a speedboat
25 Economized
26 Country crooner Page
27 Sound a Klaxon
28 Low spirits
29 Mercury and Saturn, e.g.
30 Creepy
31 Complains
32 Seasonal transports

1	2	3	4	5		6	7	8	9		10	11	12	13
14						15					16			
17				18							19			
20				21					22	23				
		24					25							
26	27	28				29					30	31	32
33					34				35			
36				37				38			
39			40				41			
42			43				44			
		45				46			
47	48	49			50				51	52	53
54			55	56				57			
58			59				60			
61			62				63			

34 Thorny bunch
37 Smidgen
41 Does a certain online search
43 Play by Karel Capek
44 El ___
46 Parish priest
47 Nursery cry
48 Bahrain resident, usually

49 Longest river in the world
50 Hook's toady
51 A lovely meter maid
52 Soldier's group
53 Renaissance family name
56 Vein glory?
57 Place for a cat, often

154
THE GRAPEVINE
By Diane C. Baldwin

ACROSS

1 Kid's flier
5 Deep-six
10 Sudden impact
14 Race anagram
15 Sharp-crested ridge
16 "Peter and the Wolf" duck
17 Gossiper's opening remark, perhaps
20 Hydrogen's number
21 Pindar works
22 Plus on the ledger
23 Make ready
24 Horse leads
26 Loathing
29 Water sources
30 Hodgepodge
31 Perform a certain driving maneuver
32 Aspiration
35 Last words of ho-hum gossip, perhaps
39 Unmeasured amount
40 Hinged implement
41 It creates division in the home
42 Brouhaha
43 Tooth protection
45 Brief runs
48 Small deck member
49 Doctorate hurdles
50 Pretensions
51 Musician's engagement
54 Response to unwanted gossip, perhaps

58 Nautical direction
59 Do some tailoring
60 Army outfit
61 It moves tirelessly
62 Rows placed one above the other
63 Private dinner?

DOWN

1 Bout rout
2 Graphics image
3 Bona fide
4 Elusive one
5 Smoothed wood
6 Pussyfoot
7 Prepares to drag
8 Made a fast stop?
9 For each
10 Tilting matches
11 Like Falstaff
12 He may be sore
13 They'll question you
18 Old wives' tales, e.g.
19 Ship's kitchen
23 Spur on
24 Elephant groups
25 Pond scum component
26 Georgetown player
27 Actor Rickman
28 Type of profit
29 It can split wood
31 Leonine ruffs
32 Sixth-day creation
33 Gathering dust

34 Symbol of suburbia
36 Relaxed
37 Hollandaise sauce ingredient
38 Far partner
42 Dissolved
43 Causes of unearned runs
44 Biddy's bailiwick
45 They may be behind bars
46 Billy goat's nemesis

47 Indian princess (Var.)
48 Type of lily
50 Kick in on a deal
51 Heredity carrier
52 Eye part
53 Picks up on
55 Dye container
56 Inventor Whitney
57 Sing wordlessly

155
SAME OLD, SAME OLD
By Allan E. Parrish

ACROSS

1 Actor Dillon
5 Unkempt state
9 Wordsworth creations
14 Shower gel ingredient, sometimes
15 Utah ski resort
16 Conclude by
17 "The Lion King" character
18 Stir up
19 Famous children's Dr.
20 Regular way of doing things
23 Fallopian tube travelers
24 Minute
25 Boring individual
27 It fits into a mortise
29 Movie music
31 Mai ___ cocktail
32 Espoused
34 Actress Ullmann
35 Elbow benders
36 NBC owner
41 Numbered musical work
42 Sea, si?
43 Oil can letters
44 Lower the lights
45 Volleyball maneuver
47 Grumpy is one
51 Precipitated in winter, in a way
53 Car nut?
55 Paste eaten in Polynesia
56 Film directed by Robert Redford
59 One more time
60 Stinging insect
61 Peddle
62 Acquire by fraud
63 "A Death in the Family" novelist James
64 Mentioned before
65 Nuisances
66 Belgian waterway
67 Tram loads, often

DOWN

1 Tiger at Princeton, e.g.
2 Breakfast nook, e.g.
3 Without exception
4 Tenure
5 1914 battle river
6 Eschews nuptial formalities
7 Cookbook verb
8 Dressing ingredient
9 Mortar go-with
10 Baseball legend Buck
11 College professor, e.g.
12 Quattroporte maker
13 N. Dakota or S. Dakota, for two
21 Not just a franchisee
22 Some pitches
26 Type of jockey
28 Is in the red
30 Uriah Heep, for one
33 Lessen in effect
35 Bouillabaisse or burgoo, e.g.
36 Pantheon figures
37 Afterword
38 Mathematical figures
39 Stowed for future use

40 Mooch
45 Tours of duty
46 French president's residence
48 Seem to be
49 Fingers of Cooperstown
50 Branches of knowledge

52 Public decree
54 Hand type
57 Cleaning cloths
58 ___ buco
59 Sound booster

156
P.S., I LOVE YOU
By Lynn Lempel

ACROSS

1 Rooms for contemplative leisure
5 Largest artery
10 Lotion base, perhaps
14 Discharge, as light
15 Thick mass
16 Monster of a lizard
17 He inspired a 2006 Springsteen album
19 Eternity, seemingly
20 Gear components, often
21 Musher's footwear
23 Abbreviation in an Eddie Murphy film title
24 Subside
27 Days of yore
28 Best Actor winner of 1966
33 Luau entertainment
36 Like a cat's tongue
37 Bill-killing vote
38 Cousin of salmonella
40 Event from 1914-1918
41 Numbered highway
43 Realtor's abbr.
44 Dangerous insect
47 Imitated
48 Pol who called Reagan the Teflon President
51 Sounds of mirth
52 What it all adds up to
53 Whammy
56 1960s folk rock band
60 Silly

62 Junior, e.g.
63 Record-setting doubles champ
66 Trim
67 Practice piece
68 2003 Pixar star
69 Chooses
70 Mayor in the Katrina spotlight
71 Quartz used in jewelry

DOWN

1 Distance down
2 Islamic prince (Var.)
3 Evenings, in adspeak
4 Cancel a dele
5 Impeccable service
6 "Bravo!" relative
7 Navajo weavings
8 U.S. investigators
9 Fitting
10 Winner of all four Grand Slam titles
11 "Don't be so serious!"
12 Oil-rich spread
13 Assuage
18 Subway Series locale
22 Thin cookie
25 Super Bowl XXXVII celebrant, briefly
26 Word with leaf or snow
28 Buddy
29 Was responsible for
30 Critical situations
31 Accommodating to night owls
32 Like Easter eggs

33 Rope-making fiber
34 Pauley Pavilion locale
35 Became discouraged
39 Affected by poison ivy, e.g.
42 Galley mover
45 Whet
46 Part of some e-mail addresses
49 Cavalry swords (Var.)
50 Islamic prince
53 Refuge

54 Antagonist
55 Copy of a trade name?
56 Manuscript blunder
57 Junker of a car
58 Research results
59 Cocky
61 El ___ (weather problem)
64 Reagan mil. plan
65 Egg protector

157
ARCTIC CHILL
By Carol Lachance

ACROSS

1 Owner of the Millennium Falcon
5 Pet received on Christmas, for many
9 Checks for prints
14 Joyce's motherland
15 Some are over it
16 Feeling of boredom
17 An ice cream treat
19 Well-clipped
20 Lively little tune
21 Some municipalities
22 Three-match link
23 Stratego piece
24 Pulsate
26 Where stars shine
27 Mattel bean-bag baby
30 Insect stages
33 Minute
34 MOMA locale
35 Perched on
36 Practical worker?
37 ___ Eleanor Roosevelt
38 Mule of "The Erie Canal"
39 Frost's "___ Major"
40 William Jennings ___
41 Poe classic
43 Louisville Slugger, e.g.
44 Exercises a certain right
45 Playfully shy
46 Egyptian biter
49 Bridge player's "no bid"
51 Australian seaport

54 Itinerary
55 Hotel room staple
56 Space between buildings
57 Certain Asian cuisine
58 Euros replaced them
59 "The Hunchback of ___ Dame"
60 Warning device
61 "No ifs, ___ or buts!"

DOWN

1 Handle the arrangements for
2 Welles of "Citizen Kane"
3 Simile phrase
4 Words with sit or step
5 Like turbulent waves
6 Pear-shaped, as a human
7 Court foe of Bjorn
8 Sentry's attribute
9 Cream
10 Loose a bra
11 Certain skier
12 Reason for signaling
13 Confessional topics
18 Disguises
25 Sharpen
26 Vermont harvest
27 Small finch
28 Chatty starling
29 Glance over
30 Kind of tense
31 Brigham Young's destination
32 Track-and-field event
33 Songwriter, poetically
36 Apse neighbor

37 Louvre exhibits, collectively
39 Certain marble
40 Arm or outlet of a lake
42 Personnel list
43 Thread supplier
45 Spelled out
46 Alan of "Wait Until Dark"

47 Last name in famous dummies
48 "For ___ sake!"
49 Middle Eastern country
50 Royal sport
52 It may be off the wall
53 West Coast school

158
THAT'S ODD
By Fran & Lou Sabin

ACROSS
1 Pitch in at a crime scene?
5 Specimen collector
9 Question closely
14 Icy coat
15 Clipper's target
16 Man mentioned in Exodus
17 Southwest Asian airline
18 Vinick portrayer in "The West Wing"
19 Sammy of links renown
20 Destinations of the USS Enterprise
23 Poet Plath
24 Pool strategies
27 Prefix with mural or galactic
30 Cinco de Mayo treat
32 Magnum follower
35 Relevant
37 Wahine's giveaway
38 Secretary of state
42 Calendar abbr.
43 Microwaved, slangily
44 First-aid kit item
45 Fan locale
47 Chutzpah
50 Word with bed and scandal
52 Exposure to public view
56 Gypsy Rose Lee, famously
59 Parenthetical script comment
62 Jai ___
63 Possible roof repair site
64 Artist known to etch a sketch?
65 Hit alternative

66 "Peter Pan" baddie
67 Some Monopoly cards
68 Garden access
69 Marine bird

DOWN
1 Room measurements, e.g.
2 Keystone Kop's club
3 Modern communique
4 Air, in a way
5 Speak irritably to
6 Privacy insurer
7 Famous opera
8 Mont ___
9 Deli listing
10 Kidnap demand
11 Tram contents
12 Flapper accessory
13 Closing
21 Author Anais
22 Packed away
25 Island below Sicily
26 Hypnotist's command
28 File partner
29 They create spots
31 Democracy since 1937
32 Murders, mob-style
33 Computer access points
34 Dickens' Heep
36 It's a fair feature
39 Certain Simon & Schuster employees
40 Lively enjoyment
41 Most unforgiving

46 More than wanted
48 Edible root
49 Airline ticket word, sometimes
51 It's stuck in the corner
53 Veni, to Caesar
54 "When donkeys fly!"

55 Color for the inexperienced
57 Hipbones
58 Playgroup?
59 Tack on
60 Legal advice, at times
61 Furious reaction

159
CAPISCE?
By Carol Lachance

ACROSS
1 "That's a lie!"
6 Imam's faith
11 One with a beat
14 Groovy phrase
15 ___ apso
16 Alias letters
17 Wake up!
19 Determine judicially
20 National song, e.g.
21 Spice Islands, today
23 CIA relative
24 Reason to serve again
26 Fergie, formally
27 Issued walking papers
29 Beats back
32 Held one's temper
36 "Wake Up, Little ___"
37 Irish Rose's beau
38 Rabbit fur
40 Studio site, perhaps
41 Strongly advocated
43 Anti-war campaigns, e.g.
45 Gaudier
47 Rembrandt's "___ and Anna With a Kid"
48 Lover of Shakespeare?
50 Prom attire, briefly
51 Something I cannot use, but you can?
54 Some lab workers
57 Raise dough
59 Rock's ___ Speedwagon
60 Understand, in slang

62 Indonesian island group
63 Old concert hall
64 Unmitigated
65 Bon ___ (witticism)
66 Stitches over holes
67 Arctic explorer

DOWN
1 Passover month
2 Harbingers
3 Eighth letter in a series
4 They were wiped out by the Jedi
5 Hamlet's love interest
6 Prepared introduction?
7 Gap-filling wedge
8 Nigerian port
9 Rectangular building stone
10 Ripens
11 Gets it
12 Gumbo pods
13 Antes up, e.g.
18 TV chef
22 Montague's enemy
25 Time for late risers, perhaps
27 Bill of Rights word
28 Bus stop?
30 Hitchhiker's ride
31 Cupboard groupings
32 Actor Julia
33 Zaragoza's river
34 Put two and two together, e.g.
35 Hole made by a golfer
39 Little cloud

42 Deified mortal
44 Confused
46 Source of yellow dye
49 Endangered sea mammal
51 Acne treatment
52 Consult the dictionary, e.g.
53 Ledger notation

54 Burn the midnight oil
55 Apt lunch for Superman?
56 ___ gun
58 "Verrrrry interesting" comedian Johnson
61 "___ Pinafore"

160
OH, PLEASE!

By Fran & Lou Sabin

ACROSS

1 Word with road and weather
5 Moved quietly
10 Frisbee, e.g.
14 First Dominican major-league manager
15 Come to a point
16 Mimic
17 "Oh, please!"
20 Some parking places
21 Hotel listing
22 Church calendar
23 Word with dive or Lake
25 "Oh, please!"
30 Hangs in there
32 Five after four?
33 New prefix
34 Fraternal group
35 Pickling agent
37 It grows on you
38 Took in
39 USNA mascot
40 Virile
41 "Oh, please!"
45 Clears
46 Pig product
47 City near Los Angeles
50 Crushing defeat
54 "Oh, please!"
57 What George couldn't tell
58 Parlor piece, perhaps
59 Social note
60 Coarse file
61 Treat a wound
62 Bottom of the barrel, perhaps

DOWN

1 Gender abbr.
2 Utah sports area
3 Impecunious
4 Backs
5 Strongly built
6 Figure on one's figure
7 Stops wavering
8 Hula hoop?
9 South end
10 Insist upon
11 "Law & Order: SVU" player
12 Blackjack table item
13 Some pen pals?
18 Sweat sites
19 A or D, e.g.
23 Surface layer
24 Port or gooseberry
25 Off-center
26 Bring together
27 Senseless
28 Playwright, Simon
29 Like some horror flicks
30 Be inclined
31 Certain sax
35 It may come from out of the blue
36 Opposite of "Yippee!"
37 Banister
39 Flash of light

40 Edible mushroom
42 Marching with the group
43 Incan transports
44 Makes tardy
47 Month before Nisan
48 "J'accuse" penner
49 Les Etats ___

50 "___ Only Just Begun"
51 Guitar's kin
52 Curved molding
53 Electrical units of resistance
55 Speak further
56 White wine cocktail

161
YOU COWARD!
By Gordon Seaberg

ACROSS

1 First name in jeans
5 Nursemaids in India
10 Blizzard feature
14 Power-serving whiz
15 Close to home
16 Roll-call reply
17 Call it quits
20 Hang out
21 It's under pressure
22 Like autumn air, sometimes
25 Colorful carp
26 Type of proprietor
28 He's a real turkey
30 Up to such time as
34 Humane org.
35 Vietnamese port
37 Bill in a till, perhaps
38 Cut and run
41 On sick leave
42 Roundup rope
43 In good order
44 Finish second
46 Puzo's Tessio
47 What results may do
48 ___ ipsa loquitur
50 Sheepish shelters
52 Lawyer's case?
56 Fanatic soldiers
60 Walk out on
63 Dorothy of Kansas
64 Tot's taboos
65 Quote a source
66 Revival meeting cry
67 Operatic Simon
68 Robbin' Robin

DOWN

1 Base for plaster
2 Chamber sound
3 Predicate part
4 Unbreakable, as a contract
5 Defense mechanism
6 Not hither
7 End up in a cast?
8 Sounds of mirth
9 Trim and graceful
10 Sure thing
11 Start for worthy or paper
12 Nabisco treat
13 Wishing place
18 Became frayed
19 Pig feeder
23 Bart and Ringo
24 Bonneville maker
26 Bit of witchcraft
27 City in Florida
29 Island thanks
31 Charlie Chan portrayer Sidney
32 Cavity filler
33 Just in case
34 Send via freighter
35 Morgue acronym
36 It can be a lifesaver
39 Take to the cleaners
40 Seeing that
45 Lacking courage
47 Osso buco meat

49 Rise partner
51 Long lock
52 Part of a pond problem
53 Pair of horses or oxen
54 Imaginary narrative
55 A chimpanzee astronaut

57 Vivaldi's vivacity
58 Arachnid-appropriate prefix
59 Threw off
61 Explosive stuff
62 Gardening tool

162
TAKING STOCK
By Lynn Lempel

ACROSS

1 Spreader of news from 71-Across
5 Shelter grp.
9 Decorative scarf
14 Rubs the wrong way
15 Country renamed in 1935
16 Advisory group
17 Description of the stock market (Part 1)
19 An arm and a leg?
20 Sashimilike
21 Matador's boost
22 Novi Sad native
23 Succinct saying
25 Starting point
30 Jazzy woodwinds, briefly
31 Surf partner
32 Locale of a historic fall
33 "Deal or No Deal" airer
35 Roman date
37 End of a sequel's sequel
38 Description (Part 2)
43 Hoping for passage
44 Paint amateurishly
45 Kennel cry
46 Tightly stretched
48 Kennel cry
50 Some wild cats
54 Longest of long odds
56 Chilling?
57 Pinto or lima, e.g.
58 Debtor's letters
60 Trinity member

61 Dentist's advice
63 Description (Part 3)
66 It's often glazed, informally
67 First name in daredevilry
68 James Bond classic
69 Scraping tools
70 Tuber used for poi
71 See 1-Across

DOWN

1 Royal coronets
2 Fighting fleet
3 Slick coat for the slopes
4 IRS requirement
5 Plant shelf, maybe
6 Miter wearer
7 Food drive collectible
8 2005 Best Director Lee
9 More competent
10 Evening gala
11 Angkor Wat locale
12 The sun, for one
13 Brief causes of some Bear hugs?
18 Rots
22 Without danger
24 Sometimes-spliced item
26 Petty complaint
27 Language similar to Hindi
28 Deutsch denial
29 "Idylls of the King" lady
34 Chalk alternative
36 Leave unobtrusively
38 Decides
39 Mrs. Katzenjammer, e.g.

40 French Revolution targets
41 Hires an ambulance chaser, e.g.
42 Created a web site?
47 Prepares for a drive
49 First coat of paint, sometimes
51 Cheapskates
52 Squirrel's stash
53 Gauge of heat or light, e.g.

55 Stays to the conclusion
59 Home to the Munch Museum
61 Creator of the SEC
62 Mauna ___
63 It may be placed before a window
64 Duke rival, for short
65 Dot follower, in some addresses

163
RIGHT HERE
By Alice Walker

ACROSS

1 Stop bleeding
5 Short summation
10 Wine sediment
14 "___ & Stitch"
15 Tongue neighbor
16 Inscribe
17 Qatari ruler
18 Tracts of swampy ground
19 Ambiance
20 Patriots hit the ground here
23 Mighty beeches
24 Postal abbr.
25 Pre-Apollo project
28 You may feed and house them
33 Expression of unhappiness
34 Well-seasoned stew
35 Bush once headed it
36 Pirates have a ball here
40 Polo Grounds legend Mel
41 Call forth
42 Sitcom legend Alan
43 Takes paint off again
45 Least cluttered
47 Schnozz ender
48 Word with fat or funny
49 Bobcats jump for you here
57 "Legally Blonde" character
58 Dragon puppet
59 Blackthorn
60 Short type of jacket
61 Generic dog name
62 Organic compound
63 Decomposes

64 Doesn't support
65 Not racy

DOWN

1 It's on the staff
2 It can be a stretch
3 Miscellany
4 Winner in a fabled upset
5 Chicken liver appetizer
6 Pandora's releases
7 Bicep exercise
8 Draft selections
9 Ham alternative
10 Like some glass or old gas
11 Small ornamental case
12 Fashion shade
13 Bedding item
21 Forbiddance
22 Heart chambers
25 Famous actress from Hungary
26 Opposite of deject
27 Ketch's pair
28 Refuses to obey
29 Word after "Ye," perhaps
30 Parisian school
31 Orange covers
32 Nobelist at Camp David
34 Pig fare
37 Early TV legend
38 Some American employees
39 Small monkey
44 Mementos
45 They make bundles
46 Dart's path

48 Advertisement delivered by hand
49 Part of a boilermaker
50 Voice below soprano
51 Part of a jukebox

52 Remove with absorbent material
53 Part of T.A.E.
54 Part of a skeleton
55 Study, for one
56 Phone or port attachment

164
DOUGH, BOY!
By Kelly Johnson

ACROSS
1 Neighbor of Hong Kong
6 Joule fractions
10 Music genre
14 Bee-fitting description?
15 Acidulous
16 Blunted blade
17 Rolling in dough
19 Occident
20 Family tree word
21 It makes for a moving experience
22 Calgary's province
24 Not just given
26 Regular's order
27 Rolling in dough
32 Wooden-soled shoe
35 Infamous Ugandan
36 Serpent with nine heads
37 Backboard attachment
38 Apologetic ones
41 Entertainer's job
42 Hoard
44 Make a little ___ long way
45 Brood overseers
46 Rolling in dough
50 Gun an engine
51 Written in verse, in a way
55 Certain anterior
58 Ballpark fig.
59 Words with roll or diet
60 Snug corner
61 Rolling in dough
64 Do a slow burn

65 Diner sign
66 Stretch of turf
67 Sawbuck's 10
68 Surfer's sobriquet, sometimes
69 In a peeved mood

DOWN
1 Home to a well-known King
2 Suspension of breathing
3 One who quotes, e.g.
4 Physical sound?
5 Not on the level?
6 College that spawned a jacket
7 Displayed cowardice
8 Type of spoon
9 Victrola part
10 Bijouterie
11 Copycat
12 Gusto
13 Epsilon follower
18 Succeeded
23 Spa features
25 Peg
26 Consuming rapidly
28 Unproductive commotion
29 Head start, e.g.
30 Start of a slogan heard in March
31 Plates in motion?
32 Crop of a bird
33 Wheels for a wheel
34 Poet Khayyam
38 What comes from the bottom of my hearth
39 Billion-year stretch

40 Mustard relative
43 X's in an alley
45 Equivocate
47 Openly declared
48 Article of furniture
49 Up-to-the-minute
52 Gauchos' weapons
53 Sluggish by nature

54 Tea holder
55 Scuttlebutt
56 Something in writing?
57 Inviting word
58 Word in an ultimatum
62 Bygone Ford
63 Shepherd's charge

165
REALITY CHECK
By Fran & Lou Sabin

ACROSS

1 Easy to handle
5 Bell-shaped blossom, often
9 Half of TV's "The Odd Couple"
14 On sabbatical, e.g.
15 "Dies ___"
16 Regional life forms
17 Word with back or knuckle
18 Phony report
20 Curb
22 Muscat's partner, once
23 It's for two, in song
24 Passing word?
25 Part of REO
27 Rival of Sparta and Athens
29 Symbol of phoniness
33 Pop group, forward or backward
36 Affirmation of a sort
37 Word of coming and going
38 Guernsey's grasslands
39 First American to orbit Earth
42 Passe preposition
43 It's a sensation
44 Dundee brush-off
45 Future attorney's exam, briefly
46 Phony ID
51 Thin soup
52 Emulate a peeping Tom
53 Trip starter
56 Don't just seem
58 Word with there or lively
60 God's domain
62 Some phony press output

65 Chromosome occupant
66 Make sense
67 Jousting blow
68 Leprechaun land
69 Some come between notes
70 Lid problem
71 Unnatural, as hair

DOWN

1 Meow maker
2 Alerted to
3 Memorable Von Trapp
4 Checked out, in a way
5 Like some friends
6 First name in lyrics
7 "Fiesque" composer
8 Hardly the assertive type
9 River to the Congo
10 Zip
11 Leather wine holders
12 Raison d'___
13 Hindu deity
19 Take in
21 Virgo's neighbor
26 Word with teen or American
28 Mystical science
29 Appliance purchase
30 Ideal locations
31 "I could ___ horse!"
32 Stolen goods
33 It comes before ba
34 Loser to VHS
35 Some acrobatic feats
40 Drifts off

41 Greenhorn
47 Tentacled sea creatures
48 Split bit
49 Takes pictures, e.g.
50 Ingredient in an old fashioned
53 One and all
54 Lamp resident
55 Without letup
56 Many miles away
57 Ungentlemanly
59 Wrinkle one's brow
61 Like many cheeses
63 Violin part
64 English cathedral town

166
PROMOTE FROM WITHIN
By Norm Guggenbiller

ACROSS

1 Dirk
5 Is indiscreet
10 Proofer's retraction
14 Rodentlike mammal
15 Bowling alley button
16 Part of MSG
17 Seaweed, e.g.
18 Informed
19 Stay to the finish
20 Like some computer peripherals
23 Directly, directionally
24 Shadow area
25 Gone by
27 Some Arab leaders
30 Flue accumulation
31 Walk all over
34 Words with crow flies
36 Like some causes
39 Test limits
43 Grp. concerned with lab safety?
44 The Trojans, for short
45 Soap-making need
46 October baseball letters since 1969
49 Hosiery brand
51 Modern business equipment
54 Having many branches
58 Rathskeller fare
59 What some decide to do to Barry Bonds
62 Exhaust, for one
64 Joan of Arc died here in 1431

65 He helped raise people to higher levels
66 Environmental sci.
67 Fully conscious
68 It may turn
69 Some watch displays
70 Turkish currency
71 Pump part

DOWN

1 Mold
2 Score
3 Have words
4 Snoopy, for one
5 Wave, as a sword
6 Salacious
7 Quickly, on memos
8 "Mr. Television"
9 Swipes
10 What uniforms are, initially?
11 Deadly mushroom
12 Follow as a result
13 Schlepped
21 Draw a bead on
22 Rockets center
26 Random sampling
28 Traveler's options, briefly
29 Abode of the dead
31 Augments
32 Dine
33 Last resort, in some sci-fi films
35 Suffix with infer
37 Man of intelligence?

38 Something to drive off of
40 Come to a standstill
41 Wanderers
42 British composer Edward
47 Bobby's relative
48 Kind of notebook
50 ___ over (mitigate)
51 Microphone's spot, often

52 Queen of Hearts irritator
53 Vodka brand, familiarly
55 Navel phenomenon
56 Nasty, as a remark
57 '50s flop
60 Line provider
61 Zeus' jealous wife
63 Chicago trains

167
ZERO
By Fred Jackson III

ACROSS
1 One way to run
5 Ancient portico
9 All in
14 Get by somehow
15 Mia of soccer
16 Unmentionable
17 Where some Sargents are seen
18 Dermal dilemma
19 Real cards
20 ZERO
23 Possibly pleasing figure?
24 Kind of meal
25 They make a great sauce
29 Stare stupidly
31 Some NFL stats
34 "West Side Story" song
35 Lacquered metalware
36 Jackrabbit, e.g.
37 ZERO
40 Use a surgical beam
41 Spellbound
42 Sudden increase
43 Printing widths
44 Kind of bet or thing
45 Makes right
46 A squat, e.g.
47 ___-cone
48 ZERO
57 Attacked vigorously
58 Missing from Camp Swampy, e.g.
59 Mideast airline
60 Pontificate

61 Farm dam
62 Mild oath
63 Hafez al-___, Syrian president
64 They're all in your head
65 Series of programs seeking ETs

DOWN
1 It may follow an overture
2 Tower of London feature
3 Stops wavering
4 Keeping an even one is recommended
5 Some tonsorial touchups
6 Be silent, in music
7 Old Dodge
8 Word said before looking up, sometimes
9 Unbroken string
10 House coat?
11 Black, in some poems
12 "Don't look at me!"
13 Turn partner
21 Shaq's surname
22 Beach staple
25 Mosey
26 Hymn of thanksgiving
27 Automated telephone menu command
28 Word losers look for?
29 Blow a gasket
30 Settled down
31 Easy golf stroke
32 Globe circumnavigator
33 Palindromic tennis champ

35 Way up a mountain
36 Shot shooter, for short
38 Hit the roof
39 Block, legally
44 Ready to be served
45 Low-down joints?
46 Lasso
47 Step on the plate, e.g.
48 "Hold it!"

49 Arms are raised for these
50 Lupino and Tarbell
51 Far from shocking
52 Far partner
53 Chicken choices
54 Burn balm
55 Political cartoonist Thomas
56 K-12 appropriate

168
GOING UP
By Fran & Lou Sabin

ACROSS
1 Sedates
6 Contemptible one
11 Gran Paradiso, e.g.
14 Cause of some tears
15 Sea duck
16 Easter preceder
17 Happy beyond words
19 It gets under your collar
20 Assume, as responsibility
21 Homesteaders
23 Australian summer mo.
25 Eats away
26 Star witnesses?
30 Morocco neighbor
33 Megastar
34 Sweep's collection
35 "Beauty is only skin deep," e.g.
39 Optimist's belief
42 Mysteriously spooky
43 Dulles stats
44 NASA failure
45 Positively charged particles
47 Put on a happy face
48 In flames
51 Brain-wave test, briefly
53 Turin was its capital
56 Chewy sampler sample
61 Busy activity
62 "My word!"
64 Reunion members
65 Nobelist Sadat
66 ___ hand (assist)
67 It may be hung

68 Closes in on
69 Dionysian reveler

DOWN
1 Crotchety oldster
2 Noted tutor
3 Beat soundly
4 Double agent
5 Hairnet
6 Hall-of-Famer Williams
7 Standings column
8 Carmela on "The Sopranos"
9 Blockbuster patron
10 Kind of hearing
11 Fed the poker pot
12 France's longest river
13 Publicity
18 Feeling restless
22 Getting ready to shoot
24 Home for some skeletons
26 Wee thing
27 Need an ice bag, perhaps
28 Theater or party attachment
29 Dull as dishwater
31 Succeeded in annoying
32 Component of natural gas
36 Roman god of love
37 Oscar song, 1958
38 College town on the Thames
40 Olympic figure skater Nancy
41 Certain ancient Jew
46 Paris jilted her for Helen of Troy
48 Honshu city
49 Depth of despair, e.g.

50 "All Quiet on the Western ___"
52 Hockey scores
54 Presidential caucus state
55 Month after Shevat
57 Pupil's setting

58 Leman's leader
59 Griffith or Kaufman
60 Despot of old
63 Daily segs.

169
SECRET SPOTS
By Joy C. Frank

ACROSS
1 Cause of discouraging marks
5 "Kiss From ___"
10 What an umpire makes
14 Some deer
15 Libya's neighbor
16 Toast-topping spread
17 Underground deposits
18 Undercover operation
19 Tallies
20 One places for bribes
23 Perceive
24 Of a previous time
25 Cereal-box info
28 Dig in
29 McEntire of country
33 Tooth part
35 Censure severely
37 Calendar quarter
38 Where strings may be pulled
43 Landed
44 Recreation for two
45 California coastal region
48 Narrow cut
49 Brief author's submissions
52 Affirmative in "Fargo"
53 Eeyore's bookmate
55 Choose, as a nonrequired course
57 One place to fly
62 Juno's Greek counterpart
64 One-masted sailboat
65 Ditty
66 A month of Sundays

67 Short and to-the-point
68 Social conclusions
69 Statistical calculation
70 Union member
71 Some floor votes

DOWN
1 Pique, as suspicion
2 Window of an eye
3 Contraction between you and bother
4 A lot of sass?
5 Type of coach, briefly
6 Baseball legend
7 Jim Davis pup
8 List recipient
9 Mesh
10 Barbecue material
11 Council member
12 Took by the hand
13 Article for Alamos
21 Familiar episode
22 Word with voyage
26 X out
27 "___ Well That Ends Well"
30 Abolish
31 Tiny particles
32 Sackcloth partner
34 Start of a Tom Cruise film title
35 Holes in the ground
36 It might be said to a dog
38 One who may need to be pacified?
39 Lamb by another name

40 Born of superior stock
41 Certain fed. funds
42 Supply party food
46 Address for a browser (Abbr.)
47 Fowl poles
49 Mythological woman with unruly hair
50 Meager
51 Word with test or fracture
54 Forest fledgling
56 Tiberius' tongue
58 Freedom from financial need
59 Part of a Japanese war cry
60 Graft recipient
61 Sport played on a strip
62 It's often cured
63 It might get in the way of an apology

170
CAN ONLY GO UP
By Irma Afram

ACROSS

1 Punic Wars soldier, perhaps
6 Foggy image
10 Practice with a palooka
14 Without substance
15 "Goodbye, Columbus" author
16 Letter from Greece
17 Giacomo della ___ (St. Peter's architect)
18 "And lead us not ___ . . ."
19 Builder's units
20 "Song of the South" song
23 "And how!"
25 Madrid Mrs.
26 Sound at the door
27 A white one is little
28 Noted wine center
30 K through 12
32 Most college freshman
34 1993 accord signer
36 Like some canned tuna
38 Incentive of some finance deals
41 Make an allocution
42 Make possible
45 Wren's Beau
48 States under Stalin (Abbr.)
50 Everybody down South?
51 Draft pick?
52 RR stop
54 Bailout key on a PC
56 Giant sixes, briefly?
57 Disciplinarian's decision
61 At any time
62 Bequeath

63 Bixby's "My Favorite Martian" role
66 The "B" of NB
67 Nike rival
68 Math table
69 Math column
70 Provide capital for
71 Some bridge seats

DOWN

1 Mr. Van Winkle
2 "Double Fantasy" artist
3 Almond paste, sugar and egg whites
4 "Nay!" sayer
5 Weak tides
6 Type of veil
7 Solitary
8 Verbalizing
9 Classic TV sitcom neighbor
10 Grain storage locale
11 Rich woman's pooch, stereotypically
12 Apt rhyme for gain
13 Diaper wearers' woes
21 First name in soul
22 Auto extra
23 Kind of testing, briefly
24 Skiff tool
29 Under way, as a game
31 Gregory of tap and "Tap"
33 Legendary quarterback John
35 Like a body in Newton's first law

37 Sight from the Black Sea
39 Horror flick cry
40 Wizards and Kings, e.g.
43 Bar degree
44 Level ends?
45 Elegant garden feature
46 One after another?
47 Tranquil

49 Scan again
53 Roman wraps
55 100 smackers
58 Smeltery material
59 "A Letter for ___" (1945)
60 Pet name?
64 Drench, as flax or hemp
65 Balaam's beast

171
KNOTTY, KNOTTY
By Carol Lachance

ACROSS
1 Gave a bad imitation of King Kong?
5 Actor's study
11 Keogh kin
14 Sly stratagem
15 Aftershock
16 Senor Quixote
17 Lunch box item, sometimes
19 Calendar col.
20 Paper-folding art
21 Talks big
23 Ice skating pattern
27 Fidelis starter
31 Finds a spot
32 Terra ___
33 Nick Charles' barker
34 Part of a sweepstakes' fine print
38 Biblical patsy
39 March fliers
40 Word with rat or mouse
41 Word with taught or employed
42 "___ helpless as a kitten . . ."
43 Reporter for The Flash
44 Manicurist, at times
46 Noted TV engineer
47 It's supposed to be circulated
51 February 1945 conference site
52 Piano keys
57 Caesar's 151
58 Hoedown
62 "My Name Is Asher ___" (Potok novel)
63 One-time Disney bigwig
64 Type of formality
65 It's sometimes winkin' or blinkin', but doesn't nod
66 Certain music holder
67 Cote d'___

DOWN
1 Mythical ship
2 Run like a charm, as an engine
3 Morales of TV and film
4 Chinese statesman ___ Xiaoping
5 Throw up a stumbling block
6 Last name in diets
7 It's earned on the street, briefly
8 Scalawag
9 Vote seeker, briefly
10 Game-show host Alex
11 Every dog should have one
12 Unpolished
13 ". . . ___ of robins in her hair"
18 Gore-Perot debate topic
22 Rice dish, in Rome
24 One suddenly raised to importance
25 Lending figures
26 Timeline divisions
27 Hold 'em holdings, sometimes
28 Sickroom serving
29 Catchall Latin citation
30 How do you shut up a turkey?
33 Evangelist McPherson
35 "Oh, darn!"
36 Blowgun insert
37 Agile

39 "Thou shalt not ___"
43 Young haddock
45 Momentarily, informally
46 Like some weather
47 Ride a two-wheeler
48 "Roots" author
49 Kicking partner
50 Spare things

53 "___ Lama Ding Dong"
54 "Mockingbird" singer Foxx
55 Neutral hue
56 Oracle
59 Prescription abbr.
60 Los Angeles campus
61 Collection of Will Rogers quips, e.g.

172
SHELLING OUT
By Steven Ginzburg

ACROSS
1 Contractor's detail, briefly
5 Handle roughly
10 Ran, as dyes
14 Like paraffin
15 Skip the big ceremony
16 All you need, according to a 1967 hit
17 Envelope or memo abbr., perhaps
18 Flax cousin
19 Jidda resident
20 Moses' sister
22 Infamous Arnold
24 Caught illicitly
26 French film
27 Fried quickly
29 Query
32 Woman, to a waiter
36 Infamous nuclear site, for short
37 Dwight's opponent in 1952
39 22, 24, 52 and 57-Across
43 Wipe out
44 Legal matter
45 Untouchable name
46 Cigarette substance
47 Purge, as of sins
51 Subatomic particle
52 Vexed
57 Words stated with some breakfast orders
61 Lacking marbles?
62 Mint or sage, e.g.
63 Sonny and Cher songs, e.g.

65 Display happiness, in a way
66 Noted Christmas visitors
67 Sesame Street character
68 Query from Caesar
69 Wade knee-deep
70 Lay down more green?
71 Active type

DOWN
1 Overwhelm, as with work
2 Kind of furniture
3 Newsboy's cry
4 Negative sort
5 Soak in
6 In the style of
7 Place to get a life?
8 For each
9 ". . . yellow polka dot bikini" word
10 Ice skate part
11 Actress Petty
12 Take to a MASH, briefly
13 Obligation
21 Sounds of contentment
23 Finish by
25 Landfill
28 Homecoming queen item
29 Lotion base, perhaps
30 Lacking
31 Affectionate smack
32 Track follower?
33 Taj Mahal locale
34 Cultural medium?
35 AWOL apprehenders

38 Racket
40 Prompt an actor again
41 Rip apart
42 Took stock of
48 Dump truck kin
49 Remove all doubt
50 Day before
51 Chris Noth on "Sex and the City"
53 Retired for the night

54 Be dishonest with, in a way
55 Tickle pink
56 Raise objections
57 Measures of resistance
58 Scaloppini ingredient, traditionally
59 Cogito-sum connector
60 Strong desires
64 Madre's brother

173
LET'S PLAY
By Fran & Lou Sabin

ACROSS
1 Financial limit
4 Jussi Bjorling, notably
9 No longer novel
14 Thurman of "Kill Bill"
15 Crockett's last stand
16 Eucharist offering
17 Truly dependable person
20 Finals preceders
21 Just right
22 Abba of Israel
23 They're held for questioning
25 ___ Grande
28 Playground feature
30 Popeye's energizer
33 Like old mattresses, perhaps
35 Hingis opponent
36 Feature of some cathedrals
40 Binge
41 Broccoli unit
42 Kept to oneself?
45 Workers' compensations
49 They cover a lot of space?
50 First name among Motown legends
52 Spelling of TV
53 Some are difficult to break
56 Benny in "Benny & Joon"
57 Flimsy apology
61 Coronation wear
62 Roman magistrate (Var.)
63 Archer of fiction
64 Append

65 Paper units
66 Start start

DOWN
1 Bad spells?
2 Changeable life form
3 Video game classic
4 New Mexico art colony
5 Diminutive creature of folklore
6 Pick, pick, pick
7 Passes over
8 Cheap factory workers
9 Hard-hitting team?
10 Campfire entertainment
11 Finally
12 Herd's hangout
13 Show fallibility
18 More benevolent
19 Speak like a tough guy
23 ___ River, N.J.
24 World's fair
26 "Law & Order: SVU" star
27 Raised-eyebrow exclamations
29 Took to school, in a way
31 Jacob's father
32 Needing a shrink, perhaps
34 2000 B.C. and A.D., e.g.
36 Help a weightlifter
37 Passenger protection
38 Kind of doctor?
39 ___ cava
40 H. Rider Haggard classic
43 Work on proofs

44 State of excitement
46 Spacecraft segment
47 Makes an error on tape?
48 Iron-pumpers' displays
51 Parenthetical script comment
54 Dynamics lead-in

55 Cereal ingredient, sometimes
56 Fire truck gear
57 Kids' support grp.
58 Helping hand
59 Fifth day of Kwanzaa
60 Street in a horror film

174
GO FLY A . . .
By Fred Jackson III

ACROSS

1 Play a big part?
5 Part of an Irish funeral, traditionally
9 Thing in a subway
14 Shield border
15 Bad to the bone
16 Word with basin or wave
17 Bug
18 River City's state
19 Smart guy?
20 KITE
23 Spots
24 Preschoolers?
25 It can be too hot for some
29 Hoover was one
31 Tach reading
34 Word with patrol or leave
35 Bibliophile's unit
36 Like a certain ethnic cuisine
37 KITE
40 Lover of Aphrodite
41 Hitchcock thriller
42 Puts in order
43 Joined
44 String instrument
45 Most difficult to find
46 Leave a little extra
47 Total
48 KITE
57 For all to see
58 Kuwaiti bigwig
59 Thereabouts
60 Photo finish
61 Columbian ship
62 Garden annoyance
63 Run in water
64 Margin notation
65 Network terminal

DOWN

1 Put into pigeonholes
2 Group of three
3 Party to a defense pact
4 Great Barrier, e.g.
5 Eccentric
6 Admits frankly
7 Fuzzy fruit
8 Pizzazz
9 Extend one's visit
10 It adorns Senor's middle
11 It precedes an invention
12 Like some lingerie
13 Antlered animals
21 Film with guns
22 16th-century circumnavigator
25 "Nonsense!"
26 Midwestern hub
27 Pulled along
28 Some ancient chests
29 Flip out
30 Particle
31 River starting in Switzerland
32 Uses a lot?
33 In the ___ of (among)
35 Smudge
36 Skiers' transport
38 Burst out

39 Acting major
44 Stole
45 Toddler
46 Rich dessert
47 Place for many a title
48 Pyramid, essentially
49 One of Clinton's old offices

50 Allot
51 Brooding bunch?
52 Discharge
53 Some people paint it red
54 Popular cookie
55 Secondhand
56 Harassed

175
MATERIAL WORLD
By Elizabeth Babikan

ACROSS

1 It needs a good paddling
6 Topmost cervical vertebra
11 Certain body of water
14 For all to hear
15 Early morning sound
16 Push to the limit
17 Carnival treat
19 Language suffix
20 Once more
21 Surpass any expectations
22 Super Bowl III winner
23 Complex character?
25 "Harry Potter" owl
27 Plaid
29 Small salamanders
32 Cry uncontrollably
35 Hilarious person
36 Wild West hangout
37 Psychology topics
39 Nobody's fool
41 Lounger's locale, perhaps
42 Passover
44 Coral ridge
46 Clumsy guy
47 Inventor Nikola
48 Ade ingredient, perhaps
50 The Lone Ranger's sidekick
52 Carousel site
56 Up partner
58 In an excited state
60 Morales of "NYPD Blue"
61 Madison or Park (Abbr.)
62 Breakfast item
64 Remick of film
65 Soft and sweet, in music
66 Harley rider
67 Word with split or tail
68 Paid to play
69 Windy City tower

DOWN

1 Chocolate source
2 Unescorted
3 Made mention of
4 One of the goals of a "Survivor"
5 Tokyo, formerly
6 Familiarize
7 Just one of those things?
8 Hal of "Barney Miller"
9 Great enthusiasm
10 Operative
11 Abrasive polishing aid
12 Point in the right direction?
13 Fires
18 Nutrify
22 Coen and Grey
24 Something to shoot for in golf
26 Genetic material
28 Video game pioneer
30 Bean curd
31 Damage nylons
32 Mo. when some Virgos are born
33 S-shaped molding
34 Notorious New York politician
36 Germfree
38 Beauty shop
40 Kept in possession

43 Is able to
45 Expensive wrap
48 Georg Brandt's discovery
49 Coins, collectively
51 Vulture's weapon
53 Honshu city
54 Autumn toiler

55 Levels
56 Broad valley
57 Convection follower
59 As soon as
62 Gov. agency
63 Barbell letters

176
THE MASTERS
By Alan Olschwang

ACROSS
1 Fatigued
6 College cheer
9 Tibetan monks
14 He has his own army
15 Author Umberto
16 Sort of model
17 Sauna
19 Poisonous substance
20 A really good place to sit?
21 Not cook
23 First name in country music
24 Vegas staple that has a degree?
26 Rouse
29 They're administered in ERs
30 Small ornamental case
31 Notorious bacteria
34 Knight's address
37 Reagan's secretary of commerce who has a degree?
41 Be inquisitive
42 Perform in a tournament of yore
43 Big name in shirts
44 ___ Paulo, Brazil
45 Sunflower relatives
47 Insult that contains a degree?
53 Farm measure
54 Most played parts of LPs, you'd think
55 Guileful
58 Swine enclosures
60 Thurston Howell III portrayer with a degree?

62 Pet ___ (grievance)
63 Alley-___ (basketball pass)
64 Ship sunk in 1898
65 Scatter
66 Wartime entertainer group
67 Bush senior, e.g.

DOWN
1 Insect with a slender waist
2 Art deco designer
3 Fresh
4 Spanish estuary
5 Sana citizen
6 The ranch in "Giant"
7 All the stage is his world
8 Mundane
9 WWII craft
10 Things to squirrel away
11 Used all available credit (with "out")
12 Defense's focal point
13 French legislature
18 "The Beverly Hillbillies" cast member
22 Fed offering
24 Involving the ear
25 Dyed-in-the-wool
26 Church platform
27 Info about touchdowns
28 Mope
31 Cassowary cousin
32 A major network
33 Stable morsel
34 Pipsqueak's problem

35 Composer Stravinsky
36 Fire engine and beet, e.g.
38 Resort town near Santa Barbara
39 Weaving equipment
40 Ceremony
44 Record jacket
45 Speedy steed
46 Seed or Street
47 Shocked responses
48 Two quartets combined

49 Town employee of yore
50 Old movie theater name
51 "So long, amigo"
52 Musical speed
55 Fishtail on ice, e.g.
56 Moon over my ami?
57 Flanders river
59 Follow a pattern?
61 Ripken, Jr. or Sr.

177
THE END
By Matthew J. Koceich

ACROSS

1 Just this time
5 Caper
10 Festive party
14 Bering and Tasman
15 Largest city in Africa
16 French friends
17 Historic meal
19 Scallion relative
20 Controls
21 Type of monkey
23 Homophone for eau
24 King Carlos
25 Doctor's interruption
27 "60 Minutes" feature
32 Bogged down
33 Treaties
34 Chinese dynasty
35 Nerve fiber
36 Some stretches
37 Alluvial deposit
38 Flange
39 Fills a spot
40 Convinces
41 Truce
43 Symbol of virtue
44 One joule/second
45 Bit of ointment
46 Bob on "VeggieTales"
49 North and South, for example
54 "I'll get right ___!"
55 Completed manuscript, e.g.
57 Traditional story
58 Jack or Robert

59 Horse cart
60 Tic-tac-toe side
61 Fe antecedent
62 Withered

DOWN

1 Edvard Munch's home
2 Tide type
3 Grammatical category
4 Female steroid
5 Less than 90 degrees
6 Back of the neck
7 Rewards for waiting?
8 Anger
9 Succeeds in bribing
10 Blue-gray mineral
11 Iowa town
12 In ___ of
13 Sets a price
18 Worked in a lumber mill
22 Partners of hems
24 Humorous
25 Imp
26 Fragrance
27 Team morale
28 Less exciting
29 Trouser material, perhaps
30 Stringed instrument
31 They can bring you home safely
32 Singer Anthony
36 NASA specialties
37 Petrels and pelicans
39 2006 NBA champs
40 Fragment

42 Scythe creations
45 United competitor
46 Hefty volume
47 Type of chalcedony
48 Speck
49 At another time

50 Sail supporter
51 Kind of package
52 At a great distance
53 Eye infection
56 Author Levin

178
HAIR-RAISERS
By Lynn Lempel

ACROSS

1 Latino media award
5 Word with maker or box
10 Look radiant
14 It's what's on one's mind sometimes
15 One-time part of the Oregon Territory
16 Public art show, e.g.
17 Second human on the moon
19 Fair maid
20 Large duck
21 Baby's perch
22 Depravities
23 Spanish 101 pronoun
24 Name in a Sally Field film title
26 Postal creed obstacle
28 Rather short-term follower?
32 Sanctions
35 Rips off
36 Terminate
37 Bewailed
38 Wax theatrical
40 Small songbird
41 Sitcom alien
42 Some bills
43 Least plentiful
45 Robber of film fame
48 Ancient Mexican
49 "The $64,000 Question" host March
50 Trial org.
53 Spelunking sites
55 Poison Ivy portrayer
57 Record-setter chased by Bonds
59 Patron
60 Geraldine of classic TV
62 Arctic floater
63 Transient cessation of respiration
64 Bag style
65 Promiscuous
66 Oliver Warbucks, notably
67 Banded gemstone

DOWN

1 "The Sandbox" dramatist
2 Name of several French kings
3 Hiroshima-based automaker
4 Woodworking tool
5 Cool number?
6 Confuses
7 O'Hara home
8 One way onto the green
9 Sweetie
10 Any cognitive content held as true
11 Public transportation requirement, often
12 Part of a church
13 Rootless plant
18 Heart-piercer of myth
22 Some peace signs
25 Total lack
27 Oldest republic in Africa
28 Place for pecs and abs
29 In a snit
30 Past partners

31 Flat payment?
32 League that includes Qatar
33 Remarkable person, object or idea
34 Tomorrow's dinner, maybe
39 Words of guilt
40 Mocking
42 Resistance units
44 Former presidential-hopeful Stevenson
46 Service providers?

47 Contoured
50 Burning passion?
51 Subject of many a rap song
52 Architectural wing
53 It has six faces
54 Enjoying a cruise
56 Heed
58 Like Charlie Parker's sax
60 It's here today, gone tomorrow
61 Route

179
THE FIGHT GAME
By Fran & Lou Sabin

ACROSS

1 Megalomaniac's desire
6 Pirates or Buccaneers, e.g.
10 Regarding
14 Santa ___
15 Comfort
16 Do the deck
17 Hitting the time clock
19 Round Table address
20 Propose marriage, e.g.
21 Pink wines
22 Happy as a lark
23 Wickerwork specialist
24 Town
25 Scrolls read at bar mitzvahs
28 Philanthropy
32 Nero's bird
33 Nation abutting Jordan
34 Replacement for that guy
35 Mosque tower
38 Unwelcome houseguest
40 Chang's twin
41 Obliterate
43 Off in the distance
44 Apropos
46 Guardian at the gate
48 Some signatures
49 Word with level or form
51 Goal of a certain quest
53 Cousin of 50-Down
54 ___-mo replay
57 Rhode Island fowls
58 Oblong vegetable
60 Sanction misdeeds

61 Avid about
62 A criminal may be caught in one
63 Word with monkey or parallel
64 Author Noel or Aphra
65 Moth-eaten

DOWN

1 Famous bear
2 Worrisome thing
3 Playful signal
4 And so on, briefly
5 Gung-ho
6 Pluperfect, e.g.
7 With anticipation
8 With defects and all
9 Woman's exasperated comment?
10 Give one's backing
11 Factory work assignment
12 Mountain lake
13 Follow instructions
18 Charged particles
22 Monroe in "Some Like It Hot"
23 Hidalgo's house
24 Soft, white cheese
25 Lion follower
26 Sheeplike
27 Chief instigator
29 Commedia dell'___
30 It's played with a plectrum
31 Manicurist's board
33 First name in slapstick
36 Have a ball

37 Memorable periods
39 Gobs and gobs
42 Burglar's forte
45 Isn't imaginary
46 "Enough, already!"
47 Jim Varney role
50 Hose fabric
51 Seize forcibly

52 Country singer McEntire
53 Court legend Lacoste
54 Barbecue rod
55 Advanced, as cash
56 Bacchanalian event
58 Lobster catcher?
59 "Harper Valley ___"

180
GO FISH
By Matthew J. Koceich

ACROSS

1 Two diamonds and others
5 Mathematical column
9 Realities
14 Beige hue
15 Certain skating jump
16 Antiquity
17 Go from place to place
18 Angler's attraction
19 Subject for a wine connoisseur
20 Three fish
23 Caught stealing
24 Employ
25 Showman Phineas Taylor
29 Society newcomer, briefly
31 Coastal fish
35 Now partner
36 Jewish holy day
38 Turk's title, perhaps
39 Three fish
42 Tag antagonists
43 Virtually pointless weapons
44 Wavy-patterned fabric
45 Spike and Bruce
47 Consumer bait
48 Cardiologists' concerns
49 Right angle shape
51 Many home computers
52 Four "fish"
61 Non-earthling
62 Shelterward
63 Pride noise
64 Mel of cartoon-voice fame
65 Some deer

66 Addendum conjunction
67 Wife of Abraham
68 Twilights, poetically
69 Voyeur's look-see

DOWN

1 Word with blocker or carotene
2 It may open Windows
3 Regulated item
4 Certain
5 Powder type
6 Express great joy
7 Burner of Rome, in legend
8 Great deal
9 Brief chapters?
10 High habitations
11 Backup cause
12 Fourth dimension
13 Blemish
21 Waiting area, often
22 Region of ancient Africa
25 Spaghetti sauce seasoning, sometimes
26 Certain chalcedony
27 You may do this with a full house
28 Zero
29 Vacationers on a ranch
30 Barks up the wrong tree
32 Convent wear
33 Shopping hub of Athens
34 Thirtieth vice president
36 Emulated an attorney
37 Champagne cocktail

40 Some gemstones
41 "___ gloom of night . . ."
46 Singer played by Jennifer Lopez
48 Admittance
50 Type of mob
51 Comb and comb and comb
52 Some boxing punches
53 A famous Fitzgerald

54 Baloney peddler
55 Weight allowance
56 Medicinal plant
57 Word with fly or clap
58 Part
59 Simplicity
60 Tear or rain ender

181
STEALTH FOOD
By Joy M. Andrews

ACROSS

1 Patriot's target in the Gulf War
5 Genesis of many great inventions
9 Like some alluring stockings
13 It may be found in Greek bars
14 Solar system's comet-intensive cloud
15 Words said with a nod
16 Beginning of a pun
20 Frank's pal
21 Concurs
22 Part of a perp's record
25 Etiquette authority
27 Night stalker
28 Mia of soccer fame
29 Doting letters
30 Mexican border state
33 Rapscallion
34 Top and over, for two
36 One administering corporal punishment
37 Middle of the pun (part 2)
40 Pope remembered on Nov. 10
42 Secretly watches
43 Type of maniac
46 Chess piece
48 Versatile truck, informally
49 Attraction
50 Rue Morgue killer
51 Passport adjunct
53 If conditions permit
54 Maliciously misrepresented
57 Ivan IV was Russia's first

59 End of the pun
64 Dermatologist's removal, perhaps
65 Meat type
66 Quaker State port
67 In the matter of
68 Employs a Singer
69 Baggage checker's call

DOWN

1 Shoat's mom
2 It's about five feet long in some halls
3 Israeli-designed weapon
4 Canine world
5 Minuscule amount
6 Diminishes in importance
7 "___ tu che macchiavi"
8 Famous muscle man
9 Lonelyhearts' title
10 Ancient serf
11 Bond, once
12 2.471 acres
17 Part of HRH
18 D-Day transports
19 Orange-to-red star, as Aldebaran
22 21st Greek letter
23 It's followed by a bull in some circles
24 Spur-of-the-moment purchases
26 Relative of a nautilus
29 Quantity of bricks
31 '60s protest singer Phil

32 "... we fear ___ evil" (Burns)
34 "___ Hand Luke"
35 Litigation
38 It may be housebroken
39 Microscopic
40 Like a lizard's skin
41 Pudding choice
44 Talker's gift?
45 Have creditors
47 "___ Cowgirls Get the Blues"
49 Become overcast
52 Barrino and Hicks
53 High-collared type of jacket
55 Formerly, formerly
56 Mother of Apollo and Artemis
58 My boys or your boys
60 It must be crossed to become more than one
61 Anger
62 Say no to
63 Garner

182
DRINK UP
By Tracey Snyder

ACROSS

1 Tavern servings
6 Tends to the lawn
10 Roadies' equipment
14 Send payment
15 Related
16 Territory discovered by Magellan
17 Indirectly suggest
18 Actress Gershon
19 Stare at
20 Some traffic tie-ups
23 Costa del ___, Spain
24 Damaging, in a way
25 Optical range
27 A hole in the head?
28 Egyptian goddess
30 R&B's Sam
31 Take downtown
33 This gently weeps, in song
34 "Moulin Rouge!" dancers, e.g.
36 Point of origin
38 Shoemaker's staff
39 Send packing
40 It might require surgery
41 Rambouillet remark
44 Minute life form
46 Some glass artists
49 Actress Lupino
50 Bad places for stone throwers
52 Director's shoot
54 1952 Winter Olympics site
55 Organic compound containing nitrogen

56 New couple
57 Goal oriented group
58 Jerks make them
59 ___ la vie
60 Eye annoyance
61 Part of a chignon

DOWN

1 Graft recipient
2 Sucking fish
3 Caveat follower
4 Goes limp
5 Engraving pens
6 Antacid substance
7 Tom Joad, e.g.
8 Reacts to a sudden pain
9 Serpentine or twisty
10 In the past
11 Police may ask you to look at them
12 Second-rate fighter
13 Where ores are melted
21 Show expression
22 Free from danger
26 Dirties
29 Type of circle
31 More desirable to collectors
32 What a plumber does often
33 Biblical verb
34 Birthday party fare, perhaps
35 Elated
36 Arabic or Hebrew
37 Add Oxygen
40 Wedding present possibility

41 Next to
42 Sporting event sites
43 Determine
45 Uses a paper towel, in a way

47 Water's edge
48 Drollery
51 Dispatch, as a dragon
53 CPR administrant

183
HELP IN THE KITCHEN
By Alice Walker

ACROSS
1 Evidence of healing
5 Donne, for one
9 "Hit the road!"
14 Neck feature
15 St. Patrick's section
16 Limerick starter, often
17 ". . . ___, up the chimney he rose"
18 Like some ground chuck
19 Change, chemically
20 Kitchen utensil
23 Parts of typeset characters
24 Forcible ejection
28 "Stand and Deliver" star
32 Iago's spouse
33 Kitchen utensil
37 It may be in your pocket right now
38 "Dear" one
39 Words after "take a"
42 Birthday figure
43 Three, somewhere in the world
45 Kitchen utensil
47 Fills with high hopes
50 Kind of cartridge
51 Monticello and Mount Vernon, e.g.
53 "Midnight Cowboy" name
57 Kitchen utensil
61 It's hot stuff in Texas
64 Valleyspeak word
65 Some coffee containers
66 Wooden pin

67 Verdi's "D'amor sull'ali rosee," e.g.
68 Give a fresh look to
69 Book ending?
70 Title evidence
71 McGregor of "Trainspotting"

DOWN
1 After-school nosh
2 It needs a good paddling
3 "I am just ___ boy . . ."
4 Object in a 1971 Disney title
5 Opposite of flushed
6 Bloc with barrels, briefly
7 Son of Isaac
8 Common fraction
9 Water source
10 Parsley relative
11 "The Crying Game" actor Stephen
12 Three-point line, e.g.
13 Yankee hater
21 Bahamas, e.g.
22 Palmer's peg
25 Boy in 2000 headlines
26 Door device
27 "Stagecoach," for one
29 ___-jongg
30 Of the ear
31 Group of Parisian lawmakers
33 Lipstick maker Lauder
34 One-third of an Elvis song title
35 Like Alexander
36 Place of many deals

40 Coal unit
41 "Billy Budd" for one
44 Office item
46 Expungement
48 Loire star
49 Kitchen canisters, e.g.
52 Type of bar
54 Lost intentionally
55 Words with telegram or message

56 Welles of film fame
58 Makeshift tree swing
59 "The Grapes of Wrath" migrant
60 "Coming of Age in Samoa" author
61 Music lovers' stacks
62 In
63 ___ Jima

USA TODAY.

184
FORMAL DINNER
By Irma Afram

ACROSS
1 Rub off
6 Dorm denizen
10 Winter blanket
14 Pack again, as groceries
15 He sang about Alice
16 Brazilian soccer hero
17 Tropical tree
18 Scott of "Happy Days"
19 Blown away
20 Woman's garment
23 Santa ___ winds
24 Yankee homecoming?
25 Comic Philips
26 Where the N.Y. Knicks play
29 Suffix like -like
30 Bassett of film
32 Snap-brimmed lid
38 Some works from Wordsworth
39 Sills selections
40 Word with soccer or "Hi"
41 Supporting stalk
42 Knee-high to a grasshopper
43 Seemingly makes more pleasant
45 50-50 chance
47 Positive or negative item
48 It makes Paul feminine
49 Button on 51-Across
51 Entertainment system component
52 Helm heading, sometimes
55 Thurston Howell had several

59 College hero, briefly
61 Blockhead
62 City of Afghanistan
63 Longest sentence
64 Feline female of film
65 Oligarchy, e.g.
66 27th U.S. president
67 Full of promise, as one's future
68 Head of a ranch?

DOWN
1 "All My Children" regular
2 Scouting job, briefly
3 Philippine banana tree
4 Plunder
5 What the vain may go on
6 Log lodging
7 Word-of-mouth
8 Say "somethin'"
9 Habitually humiliated human
10 Healthy resorts
11 They inform
12 Good boy's heart?
13 Tie the knot
21 German wheels
22 Billion-year stretch
27 It comes between Washington and here
28 Krypton and oxygen, e.g.
29 Green lights
31 Mounted
32 Page of music?
33 Stellar hunter
34 Removed soap and dirt, e.g.

35 Flightless fowl
36 Monopolize
37 Van Druten's "I ___ Camera"
41 Burns superficially
43 Princess Diana's family name
44 Costa ___
46 Java vessel
50 Ma plays it in front of people
51 Aug. 15, 1945

52 Able to creep you out
53 A star represents it
54 Banana oil, e.g.
56 Rapper-actor
57 Monica's brother on TV
58 A salmon that has spawned
59 Initial serving at lunch?
60 Soon-Yi's mom

185
SURROUNDED BY COPS
By Randall J. Hartman

ACROSS
1 He may coach Little League
4 Sand castle building aids
9 Eager and excited, to an arsonist?
14 Stage actress Hagen
15 Any Time?
16 A to Z, e.g.
17 Fritos, e.g.
19 Jimmy of the Daily Planet
20 Negatively charged atom, e.g.
21 Go lickety-split
23 Orange or cream, e.g.
24 Roger Federer's sport
26 Perth pals
28 Places with a latte going for them?
33 Use the flat part of the shovel
37 Couple's adjective
38 Where to eat Seoul food
39 Race car driver Luyendyk
40 True companion
43 Rock groups?
44 South American plain
46 Cosell's longtime foil
47 Unit of force
48 "Dilbert" and "Doonesbury," e.g.
52 Active beginning?
53 It has 100 seats
58 Cheerleader's output
60 Cushiness
63 Buenos ___, Argentina
64 Get the better of

66 Winter phenomena
68 Having lost effervescence
69 Like forbidden fruit
70 This may sting a little
71 Indian stringed instrument
72 Give birth to
73 Birth certificate datum

DOWN
1 Gold coin of old
2 Redress a wrong
3 "Mack the Knife" vocalist
4 Pulitzer Prize-winning play by William Inge
5 Result of an eruption, perhaps
6 Start of a "Superman" query
7 "Mexican Spitfire" star Velez
8 Seed or Street
9 In the past
10 Lie
11 "A thousand pardons!"
12 Regretted
13 Vesuvius relative
18 Persona ___ grata
22 "Norma ___"
25 Lampblack
27 "You should be ashamed of yourself!"
29 Garment no longer politically correct
30 Man with a mission
31 Shape with a hammer
32 R.S.V.P. enclosure
33 Baby powder component

34 "Alice's Restaurant" chronicler Guthrie
35 A 2006 champion team
36 Cape Cod, notably
41 Bulldog of the Ivy League
42 Ballroom dance maneuvers
45 National Dessert Mo.
49 "Get the picture?"
50 Land parcels
51 Kind of tickets
54 "Seduction of the Minotaur" author Anais

55 Al Jazeera viewing audience, mostly
56 One-time home of the brave
57 Roaring Twenties auto
58 "Friends" role
59 Not behind
61 It's sold in bars
62 Napoleon's isle of exile
65 A pop
67 Wall Street index, briefly

186
THREW'S COMPANY
By Joy M. Andrews

ACROSS
1 Specialized vocabulary
6 Film brand
10 Alfred E. Neuman's smile feature
13 Noted Helmsley
14 Emulated a hen
15 Top-drawer
16 It may be loaded
17 Noted nickname in hoops
19 Cast aspersions
21 Make lovable
22 Gallivant
25 Mr. Bumble's metaphor for the law
26 Don't waste words
29 Aptitude for note-worthy creations?
30 Blows before the derby
31 Like rough-cut logs
32 Course with good greens?
35 Tingling with excitement
37 Word in a Nicole Kidman film title
38 Coxswain's order
39 Certain African inhabitant
41 Short mornings?
44 Things people do to get their kicks?
46 Make untidy, e.g.
48 Intense fighting at close range
51 Engagement ring choice
53 Cheese town near Rotterdam
54 Famous movie river

55 Condescender
56 Key key on the keyboard
57 Koizumi's cash
58 Troublemakers at meetings
59 Oracles

DOWN
1 International Tennis Hall of Fame's Gibson
2 Classic TV enthusiast's delight
3 Decorations seen with cornstalks
4 "Mon ___" (Tati film)
5 Go by Greyhound, e.g.
6 Kyrgyzstan range
7 Make up ground
8 Philatelist's collectible
9 Make a solemn request
10 "Have a safe journey!"
11 Literary collection, e.g.
12 Sword trumper
15 A freshman humanities course
18 Scandinavian saint
20 Bottom-of-the-barrel stuff
23 Observed
24 Eagle surmounting a wave
27 Causing flaws in
28 French painter Odilon
30 Quagmire
31 Solo on film
32 Municipal development guideline
33 What March may go out like
34 Pedigrees

35 Certain eyebrow shape
36 Indian area formerly annexed with Daman and Diu
39 Intl. commerce pact
40 Take from the crate
41 Sharp as a tack
42 Fox on "The X-Files"

43 Some primitive weapons
45 103, in old Rome
47 Fourteen pounds, in Brighton
49 Switch or buck add-on
50 They come out at balls
51 Optimist's limit
52 Have an outstanding liability

187
DUKES
By Tracey Snyder

ACROSS

1 Homer's progeny
5 Cain's brother
9 Miss Universe wear
13 Bread spread
14 Roman emperor
15 Pocket bread
16 DUKE
19 Rights
20 Geological span
21 Lethargic, perhaps
22 Zsa Zsa's sister
23 Feather partner
24 Leaves the union
26 DUKE
29 City 25 miles west of Dayton
30 Force onward
31 Spike or Ang
34 Once more
35 Lions' dos, e.g.
37 Adidas rival
38 Rocky hill
39 "The King of Queens" character
40 Some "Sesame Street" dolls
41 DUKE
44 Lift-off followers
47 Mine find
48 Building extension
49 Lavender flower
50 Pitcher's concern
51 Actor Kristofferson
52 DUKE
56 Auntie of the theater
57 White knight, stereotypically

58 Enthusiasm
59 Some blood relatives, for short
60 Meany of literature
61 Word with oxygen or pup

DOWN

1 La Paz currency
2 Sculptor's medium, perhaps
3 Nine start in Ohio
4 As well
5 Sweater material
6 "I've ___ robbed!"
7 Commit a faux pas, e.g.
8 Word with Lobos or Alamos
9 It's less than a grand
10 Helped out
11 Cubic meter
12 Some deer
17 College appointment
18 Small concavity
19 Overpower
23 Like the heartless man
24 Title of respect
25 You may have two before noon
27 Bring back to the shop, in a way
28 Mold and mushrooms, e.g.
31 Paul Bunyan, e.g.
32 Soothing agent
33 Painters' needs
35 ___ Blanc
36 Diving sea birds
37 Arafat's group
39 Terpsichore's forte
40 Chemical ending

ACROSS

41 Pillages
42 Kramden's neighbor
43 Type of matter
44 School grads
45 Moses' Mount
46 Don't just see Everest
50 Ireland, romantically
51 Cabbage variety
53 Greek letter
54 Stitch up
55 Earn after taxes

188
CONFUSION REIGNS
By James E. Buell

ACROSS
1 Pound sound
4 Says it's so
9 Like fall air
14 First word of Dante's "Inferno"
15 "There's no I in team," for one
16 Divulge
17 Confused response
20 Coleridge's was ancient
21 Small antelope
22 Burrows and Vigoda
23 Famous uncle
25 Big name in dolls
26 Rubber-stamps
28 Pet for King Solomon
30 Kind of lift
34 Confused response (with 45-Across)
39 "The Name of the Rose" penner
40 Surrealist Max
41 Green peg
42 Countess complements
44 Spearheaded
45 See 34-Across
48 Sneak a peek
50 Watchdog feds
51 Ebenezer's outburst
52 In the style of
54 "You rang?"
56 Regarding
60 Keep from keeping
64 Business, in a retort to the nosy
66 Confused response
68 Vigorous vitality

69 Do some waiting
70 "The Bridge of San Luis ___" (Wilder)
71 Web destinations
72 Hall's singing partner
73 Taiwan or Peking addition

DOWN
1 Inner personality, to Jung
2 Purpose of The Betty Ford Center
3 Motorist's aid
4 "My sentiments exactly!"
5 One of the Huxtables
6 Actor in a crowd
7 Manipulate fraudulently
8 Big city problem
9 Five-alarmer, e.g.
10 Not long past
11 "___ do" (resigned acceptance)
12 The "Motown sound," e.g.
13 Where a dummy sits
18 Sun shields
19 No longer available
24 "Move aside!"
27 Etta of old comics
29 Docking platform
31 Arctic Ocean sighting
32 Org. co-founded by Jane Addams
33 Cheeky shade?
34 One way to get someone's attention
35 Popular cookie

36 Bring to ruin
37 Dance unit
38 Rowlands of film
43 Filled with fright
46 Film villain
47 Watch
49 Kind of chop
53 Wheels for big wheels
55 Noted film reviewer

57 Crossed one's heart, e.g.
58 Emulates a horse whisperer
59 Type of daisy
60 Sarcastic remarks
61 Decorative toiletry case
62 "Hey, over here!"
63 Humble Oil brand
65 They are protected by lids
67 Genteel affair

189
HIDDEN HUNTERS
By Alan Olschwang

ACROSS

1 Tour de France division
6 Michigan city (with 14-Across)
9 First position
14 See 6-Across
15 Barcelona uncle
16 Ham it up
17 TV program today, almost certainly
19 Place atop
20 Unkempt abode
21 They may ring through bullrings
22 Way the wind blows
23 Many yacht owners, e.g.
26 Came to terms
29 Pipe with a quarter bend, e.g.
30 Knack
31 California wine area
34 Affirmative vote
37 It's used to carry perishables
41 Toronto's prov.
42 Deal with, as a challenge
43 Pixie and Dixie's nemesis, in the cartoons
44 Org. that features driving
46 Least threatening
47 Chip component
53 Wedding acquisition
54 Nothing more than specified
55 Forty-niner's tool
58 "And hast thou ___ the Jabberwock?"
59 Sort of sauce

62 To-the-point
63 The Trojans
64 Word in a Willie Nelson hit title
65 Proud mount
66 Mouse-spotter's cry
67 Faux pas

DOWN

1 Animal pouches
2 Race pace, perhaps
3 In a proficient manner
4 Mawkish drivel
5 Make a mistake
6 In the least bit
7 American of Japanese heritage
8 Words of denial
9 Fit for a holiday
10 First name in cooking
11 Schlepper
12 Offer reparation
13 Imparts
18 Word with cuts or War
23 Golda of Israel
24 Yesterday, in Italy
25 Straight up or straightened up
26 "Natural" hairstyle
27 Rustic setting
28 It may be blown up
31 Born as
32 Is for many?
33 Too rehearsed
34 Benzoyl peroxide target
35 Ties up the phone, e.g.
36 Prefix with while

38 Auto finance co.
39 City near Santa Barbara
40 Severance
44 Acclaim
45 Dressed for a ball
46 Person bringing a case
47 Fine rains
48 Estuary
49 ___ Boothe Luce

50 Suffuse with color
51 Witherspoon of "Walk the Line"
52 Succumb to pressure
55 Chanteuse Edith
56 "Like I'd ever do that!"
57 Hawaiian state bird
60 Pester
61 Turkish title

190
TIP-TOP
By Tracey Snyder

ACROSS
1 Plankton components
6 Cleopatra is a big one
10 It may have a soft shell
14 Elementary school door sign
15 Soothing lotion
16 Gather from the fields
17 In tip-top shape
20 Common conjunctions
21 A dog's age
22 UFO passenger
23 Gang's concern
25 Feral cats' haunts
26 In tip-top shape
31 Love intensely
32 Agree, in a way
33 Tranquil exercise
37 Wear
38 Ask for
42 Everyone has one
43 Narrow opening
45 Junkyard canine, perhaps
46 Lift up
48 In tip-top shape
52 Rich cake
55 Pretentious
56 Nitrogen, once
57 Fit the sound to the action
59 On the Caribbean, e.g.
63 Is in tip-top shape
66 House for kids?
67 Bring up
68 "Key ___" (Bogart film)
69 His mate

70 Askew
71 Austin Powers portrayer

DOWN
1 Turkish leader
2 Property encumbrance
3 Kind of student
4 Sports honorary title
5 Suffix denoting extremeness
6 Bribe
7 Funny King
8 Joey's friend
9 Leaves for a drink?
10 San Francisco transportation
11 Home with an awesome view
12 Famous man at the bat
13 Unclogs
18 Wife of Zeus
19 Corridor
24 Computer operator
25 Sums it up
26 Passing fancies
27 Baal, e.g.
28 Author Morrison
29 Entomb
30 Woodland denizen
34 Land east of Saudi Arabia
35 First words on a certain Monopoly card
36 NYSE colleague
39 Light brown
40 Quid pro ___
41 Word with pattern or drive
44 African flies

47 Purchasing option
49 Asian weight
50 Sinclair Lewis' Elmer
51 St. Louis landmark
52 Singer Brooks
53 Color of the sky
54 Printer need

57 Distort
58 Time it takes for our revolution?
60 Father
61 NASA employee
62 Ruckuses
64 Roth plan, for one
65 Popular street name

191
ROW 1, SEAT 1?
By Alice Walker

ACROSS

1 Acquires through effort
6 Wind indicator
10 They may set up haymakers
14 Eavesdrop or eavesdropper
15 Prerequisite for gain?
16 Label on the first of two file drawers, often
17 Potbelly, e.g.
18 Sgt. Snorkel's dog
19 Novelist Jaffe
20 Start of a thought-provoking question
23 Plenty
24 Rarebit description
25 Type of TV
29 Pinochle declaration
31 Provide bearings
32 Hell, to Sherman
33 La-la lead-in
36 Thought-provoking question (Part 2)
40 Do followers
41 Actor Alejandro
42 Certain graduate
43 Ottoman officials
45 Impaled
46 Insects in motion
49 Quarter deck?
50 Thought-provoking question (Part 3)
56 Show of wealth
57 Sciences' partner
58 Private Ryan portrayer
60 Boleyn, for one
61 Brief message
62 Andean wool provider
63 First name in the Rat Pack
64 Granny or square follower
65 Aden locale

DOWN

1 Lion add-on
2 "Nay!" sayer
3 It's over your head
4 Astronomer's sighting, sometimes
5 Putting letters in the right order
6 Erratic
7 Court rituals
8 Give as a reference, e.g.
9 Have memorized
10 Jolted
11 Ringlike coral island
12 Adheres
13 Break into smithereens
21 Ticket that could bring wealth
22 It prefers the nightlife?
25 Jungle warning
26 Scots Gaelic, e.g.
27 Small islands, to Brits
28 Grazing place
29 Screen vamp West
30 Inconsistent
32 Toddler's frequent query
33 Where's mummy?
34 French jeweler Lalique
35 Words before "state of affairs"

37 Thriller director Craven
38 With joy
39 Add sound effects, e.g.
43 Audacious
44 Australian with three toes
45 Strip in Hollywood
46 Valuable violin, briefly
47 Caterwaul
48 Insurance giant
49 Brief fight
51 Like some old basements
52 Resolve (with "out")
53 Merchandise-mover
54 Islamic leader
55 Thick reference book, e.g.
59 Bert Bobbsey's sis

192
TO AND FRO
By Amy Grossman

ACROSS

1 By the same token
5 It may be gray
9 Keep from drying out
14 "She Loves You" word
15 Equipment
16 San Antonio tourist destination
17 Fervent
18 Have coming
19 Noted pardon recipient
20 Childhood game
23 Supped
24 Justice Dept. worker
25 Wrote
27 Emulate Paul Revere
30 Turned something into somethin'
32 Shelley's fairy queen
33 Kind of clock or number
36 Ballet bird
39 Lettuce variety
41 Donizetti heroine
42 Hardly racy
43 Kind of surgeon
44 Some Monopoly pieces
46 Part of a famous soliloquy
47 Low points
49 Onion and garlic relatives
51 Part of a Shriner's attire
53 Sting operators?
55 Polar worker
56 Good-natured exchange
62 Solzhenitsyn's "The ___ Archipelago"

64 River in New York
65 Opera highlight
66 Brick dried in the sun
67 For, how or what ending
68 Items in a London pantry
69 Comparatively modern
70 Be dependent (on)
71 Country singer Arnold

DOWN

1 Nursemaid in India
2 First name in denim
3 Mentioned before
4 "Goodness gracious!"
5 Word with secret or press
6 Good to go
7 They may pop or wiggle
8 English composer Thomas
9 Listed by ability, e.g.
10 One attending Yale
11 Lunar actions
12 Behave theatrically
13 Not flabby
21 Lead-in to "boy!" or "girl!"
22 Of historic proportions
26 Bunting's home
27 Early church pulpit
28 Dingo's den
29 Emulate a tide
30 Gives off
31 It may be overheard in a bar
34 A Society Island
35 Olfactory perception
37 In a crazed frenzy

38 Clears, on a pay stub
40 Dull
45 Inuit conveyance
48 Cloak partner
50 Typical Beverly Hills home
51 One of King Lear's daughters
52 Give the slip to
53 Divided Swiss canton

54 Journal item
57 One way to avoid a collision
58 Roof part
59 Sunbaked
60 Good-hearted
61 Word with chair or street
63 Honest Lincoln

193
I'M A GOOD BOY
By George Keller

ACROSS

1 Like slightly tainted meat
6 Movie locations
10 Storm preceder
14 Admiral Byrd's book
15 Owl feature
16 Mutt of Garfield's jokes
17 Be a good boy
20 Mate of a famous gardener
21 Miser's pronoun
22 Doglike scavengers
23 Follow a previous path
25 Up to, colloquially
26 It goes on the dotted line
27 Enormous
32 Penal institution of a sort
35 Be a good boy
37 Number of sides on stop signs
39 Anger or wrath
40 Corporate department
41 Be a good boy
44 Things sometimes exchanged
45 Suspect's right
46 Start of Cain's query
48 Current powers-that-be
49 Suffered humiliation, informally
53 Rainier's land
57 "Be that ___ may . . ."
58 Common contraction
59 Be a good boy
62 Lotto variant
63 Type of edition
64 Not reactive
65 They may be probing or private
66 Earthbound avians
67 An arm and a leg, maybe

DOWN

1 More courageous
2 One way to look
3 Water lily painter
4 Abolish
5 Beefeater, e.g.
6 Ugly public encounter
7 Alternative word
8 Highlands hat
9 Bantu language
10 Great place for a dip
11 Gulf southeast of the Sinai
12 Old Italian bread
13 Unkempt state
18 Styptic pencil targets
19 You may buy them nude
24 Brit's confirmation
25 Tinkerer
27 Hall-of-Fame announcer Harry
28 Serbo-Croatian, e.g.
29 Tower by the barn, often
30 From square one
31 More alternative
32 Phi-Kappa connector
33 Word with act or gear
34 "Is this all the thanks ___?"
36 Math term
38 Again and again?
42 Raise to high status
43 Couric of TV
47 Measurement system

49 Powdery remains
50 Infuriates
51 Difficult to miss
52 AL and NL divisions
53 Model companion
54 Be a good boy

55 Supreme Court complement
56 Teapot tempests
57 Westernmost Aleutian Island
60 Starchy tuber
61 Family card game

194
ALL IN THE FAMILY
By Gordon Seaberg

ACROSS

1 Pad type
6 Aired "Leave It to Beaver"
11 Produce duds
14 ___ Penh
15 Noted exercise?
16 Flowery ring
17 Drew Barrymore to Steven Spielberg
19 Spot on a spud
20 Tidal bore
21 Brainstorm
23 Miss the mark
25 Makes, as a putt
28 Scary character
29 Put ammo into
31 Joseph to Jesus
34 Like Mozart's flute
36 Artful deception
37 Arrestee's privilege
40 You'll travel if you don't do this enough
44 True partner
46 Gogol's "___ Bulba"
47 Lord Mountbatten to Prince Charles
52 Inhale in astonishment
53 Spew fire and brimstone
54 Snail trail
56 Far from forward
57 Exit, to P.T. Barnum
60 Grade diminisher
62 It goes before the carte
63 David to Keith Carradine

68 Lose firmness
69 Mentally acute
70 Landlord's contract
71 D.C.-to-Dover dir.
72 Boat or cycle attachment
73 With competence

DOWN

1 Car sticker stat
2 "What have we here?!"
3 Not old enough
4 Scotch go-with
5 Online reads, briefly
6 King's sub
7 Biblical verb suffix
8 This can be monotonous
9 Port on its own gulf
10 Great-great grandson of Augustus
11 Seasonal vehicle?
12 Milne pessimist
13 Ballpark fare
18 "Topaz" author
22 Shopper's aid
23 Big Bird cohort
24 Sprinkled with gray or white
26 Beer bust delivery, perhaps
27 Carb source
30 Issue commands
32 Spruce cousin
33 Hit terra firma
35 It may get pushed around
38 Lucy of "Kill Bill"
39 Loupe, essentially

41 High military muck-a-muck
42 Shipboard punishment
43 Lay eyes on
45 650, on a slab
47 Travolta film
48 Sleeve style
49 Infuriate
50 Flexible
51 Abu Dhabi leader

55 Part of a B-29 bomber name
58 False pretense
59 Pudding starch
61 Lone Star State sch.
64 Set aflame
65 "Alice" character
66 Immigrant's study, often (Abbr.)
67 "The Bridge of San Luis ___"

195
ON HAND
By Matthew J. Koceich

ACROSS

1 Rice dish
6 Quick letters?
10 Lash
14 Gilgamesh goddess
15 Mail recipient's bane
16 Smidgen
17 Celebration of Christ's triumphal entry into Jerusalem
19 Meshuga
20 Darkroom prod.
21 Word with family or shoe
22 There's much fun under it
24 More speculative
26 Carryall
27 Equine vote?
28 Four-line stanza
32 Certain Southern cuisine
35 Aaron or Raymond
36 French father
37 Petroleum org.
38 African antelope
39 La Citta Eterna
40 What many drink before noon
41 Some computers
42 Important test
43 Like some figures
45 Automobile ID
46 Marine bird
47 Some linemen
51 Spanish explorer
54 Gourmand's wish, perhaps
55 Unit of force
56 Cantatrice's offering

57 Instrument of torture
60 Spool
61 Relaxation
62 It's used in straining
63 Christian missionary
64 Manuscript marking, perhaps
65 Smorgasbord fan

DOWN

1 Communication medium
2 He may come from Qom
3 Deceives into trustfulness
4 It's connected to this puzzle's theme
5 Grandiloquence
6 Li'l one of the comics
7 Beef unit
8 ___ carte
9 Laminate
10 Its arch might be plain or tented
11 Klutz
12 ___ von Bismarck
13 Fight for air
18 U.S. chemist who discovered deuterium
23 Addams family cousin
25 Tricky delivery at 43-Across
26 They're taken in chess
28 Dubious doctor
29 Long period of time
30 "___ La Douce"
31 Patricia of film
32 Search thoroughly
33 Capital of Samoa

34 ___-O
35 Sound of trumpets, e.g.
38 Gives forth
42 Skill plus delicacy
44 In favor of
45 Action word
47 Halley's namesake
48 Wading bird

49 Christopher of Superman fame
50 Underground system
51 They may be parallel or uneven
52 Length x width
53 In ___ of
54 Calliope, for one
58 Toque, for one
59 Govt. agency

196
IT'S ALL RELATIVE
By Gloria & Larry Hanigofsky

ACROSS
1 Bestowed titles
5 Word with box or maker
10 Word sometimes said with a tear
14 Certain bra size
15 Notorious bacteria
16 Prepare apples for baking
17 Mother of Pollux
18 "Homage to Clio" poet W.H.
19 Savoir-faire
20 Bathing suit try-on, for some?
23 Singer Torme
24 Sodium hydroxide
25 Snack for a ladybug
27 Red or structure attachment
29 Goblet feature
32 It climbs the walls
33 In writing
36 It can be replaced
37 His pants are too short?
40 A Great Lake
41 CD of an old LP, e.g.
42 Poetic contraction
43 Examine by touch
44 Grind one's teeth
48 Skewer tidbit (Var.)
50 Chicago-to-Miami dir.
52 Averse to first moves, e.g.
53 One who has his work done by Friday?
58 Fraught with danger
59 On the bounding main
60 Kind of signal

61 Rooms for contemplative leisure
62 More wan
63 Kind of code used every day
64 Genealogical diagram
65 Part of some chains
66 Shell competitor

DOWN
1 Stromboli meat, perhaps
2 Old-time vendors
3 Ballet's Nureyev
4 E-mail deleted quickly
5 Slang for nasty person
6 Type of angle
7 Kind of list
8 Musical character
9 Teacher's aid?
10 Misbehave
11 Repugnance
12 Storage place for records
13 Game-match connection
21 Large antelope
22 Dodge vehicle
26 Redhead maker
28 Badgered
29 Curdle
30 Hamilton's notes
31 Energy units
34 Funeral pile
35 Away from the wind
36 Sharp-witted
37 More cheerless
38 Floating, as dust

39 Semiautomatic pistol
40 "A mouse!"
43 CIA ally
45 Guarantee
46 Coastlines
47 Carrion-eating animals
49 Scale-busting

50 Unwelcome look
51 Terrify
54 Cats take them
55 ASAP equivalent
56 Where many kroner are spent
57 Beehive State
58 Banned chemical

197
BE GONE!
By Lynn Lempel

ACROSS

1 Word with truth or blood
6 "By ___!" (mild oath)
10 Unhurried gait
14 Make amends
15 "Trinity" novelist
16 Celestial point
17 Toss dice for money, in slang
19 Being nothing more than specified
20 All the rage
21 Stir up
22 Tilts a plane
23 Launches an attack
25 Auto rolled out in 1954
27 Absentminded type
31 When to open the curtain
34 Eye membrane
35 Likewise
36 Funds for the golden yrs.
37 Curriculum ___ (resume)
39 Does some mending
40 Brine-cured salmon
41 Horizontal window piece
42 "Verily, ___ unto you"
43 Short-order order
48 Fencing choices
49 Jail feature
53 Dramatist with three Pulitzers
55 Bad to the bone
56 Words with whim or roll
57 Good soil
58 Leading
61 Schlep

62 Yemen neighbor
63 Like some premonitions
64 Bodement
65 First American executed for spying
66 Valentine's Day gifts, often

DOWN

1 Cohen on ice
2 Set of beliefs
3 Miniseries that won nine Emmys
4 One across the border?
5 Type of measuring system
6 Legal expert
7 Like some vaccines
8 Red-carpet treader
9 Thick dictionary section
10 "Tortilla Flat" actress of 1942
11 Unfilled calendar squares
12 Job benefit
13 Some past dates?
18 Fountain fare
22 Things to drool over
24 Seller's warning
25 Prefix meaning "trillion"
26 French cheese
28 Lord or Lady, e.g.
29 A soybean state
30 Meddlesome
31 Needs a doctor
32 Hook's nemesis, briefly
33 Reason for a government check, perhaps

37 Unspoken feeling
38 Troubles or woes
39 Indication
41 Hook's assistant
44 Knuckle-dragging sorts
45 Godly
46 Poetic name for Ireland
47 One who could be a Sunday driver

50 Yokels
51 Sandy's human
52 Fixed prices
53 Countertenor
54 Hover menacingly
55 Etc. cousin
58 Sound of delight
59 "Kill Bill" star Thurman
60 Vintage vehicle

198
LOST IN THE SHUFFLE
By Robert H. Wolfe

ACROSS

1 Big wheel?
7 It's been said before
11 Adipose tissue component
14 Pindar's country
15 42, once
16 Tie consequences, briefly
17 A little assistance
19 66 is a famous one (Abbr.)
20 How to serve Welsh rabbit
21 Pinhead
22 Button on a camcorder
25 Aggregation
26 Burns the surface of
27 Big name in Norway
29 Gridiron meas.
30 Yes follower
31 Stan's partner
33 Moved a bit
35 Is defeated by
37 Noisy insects
40 Generous offer
42 Fred's dancing sister
43 One-dimensional
45 TV plugs
47 Tug follower
48 Like Sidney Lumet's 12 men
49 Those against
51 Range of knowledge
52 Anatomical pouches
53 It can be social or natural, e.g.
55 Lady of Sp.
56 Offering of numerous items

60 ". . . night of ___ dear Savior's birth"
61 Cultural heading?
62 Part of E=mc^2
63 Pt. of EST
64 Specification to a butcher, perhaps
65 Upper house

DOWN

1 Alphabet trio
2 Blake's "before"
3 Parochial sch. subject
4 Defaulted auto
5 It's on the cake
6 One on guard
7 Use up
8 Envelope feature
9 Give a clue
10 Human or fact ending
11 Part of a ship
12 Garb
13 Dangerous fly
18 Todman's game show partner
21 Clothes, slangily
22 Fiddler's spot?
23 Jazz great Fitzgerald
24 The Lone Ranger's silver bullet, e.g.
26 About the time of
28 Some cigarettes have them
30 Mr., abroad
32 "Civil Disobedience," e.g.

34 Summer drink
36 Rocky ridge
38 Useful plant
39 Stitched
41 Well-dressed dummy?
43 Thrown ropes
44 Stuck and not going anywhere
46 Burns the edges of

49 Ghana's capital
50 Public display
53 Aromatic seasoning
54 First place
56 Sidekick
57 Stage of history
58 T-man, e.g.
59 Soapmaker's solution

199
HANDYMAN'S SPECIAL
By Joy C. Frank

ACROSS

1 Pizza perimeter
6 "Brian's Song" star
10 Vent sound
14 Alfred Hitchcock in the background, e.g.
15 Name on a pump
16 Lumbago, e.g.
17 Dashed dream
20 Friendly intro?
21 Moderate paces
22 Duel prelude
25 Eliminate as excessive
27 Hindu social group
28 Animated Petunia, for one
29 Will bequest, perhaps
32 ___ in Tango
33 Menotti's shepherd boy
35 Hirsute ones
38 Unfulfilled vow
43 Lauder of perfumes
44 Dramatic device
46 "The Real World" network
49 Not in motion
52 Famous plaintiff
53 Bold, impatient type, astrologically
56 Conned one
57 Exterminator's quarry
58 Three-dimensional scene
61 Trident part
63 Grammatical gaffe
68 Joie de vivre
69 Cause to be immobile

70 Downsizes
71 Nitti's bane
72 Community hootenanny
73 Blind strips

DOWN

1 IV measures
2 Short cheer
3 Thurman of films
4 Assemble the components
5 They hold sippy cups
6 Symbolic incentive
7 Something I can't use, but you can
8 Current description
9 Pacific salmon
10 "___ la vista, baby"
11 Most dispassionate
12 Feature of "fat" but not "fate"
13 Physiological pentad
18 Sushi servings
19 Business letter abbr., perhaps
22 Curative locale
23 Precarious perch
24 Petri dish gel
26 Babies
29 Some forest rangers
30 Petroleum residue
31 "Turn to Stone" rock grp.
34 Weeding implement
36 Give off
37 Word with "yes" or "dear"
39 Greek letter
40 It's in the center of center court

41 Word with thumb or loser
42 Genesis son
45 "The best is ___ to come!"
46 Actress Virginia
47 Rare hit
48 Some chamber music instruments
50 Gourmand's pastime
51 Short drive
54 TV's Gray and Moran
55 Remained unused
57 "She loves me" unit
59 It's as good as a mile
60 Climax beginning
62 Beats by a nose
64 Partner of games
65 Keogh plan relative
66 Old pro
67 Snaky shape

200
FOOT FAULT
By Alice Walker

ACROSS

1 Extends across
6 Verdi's "Caro nome," e.g.
10 "Uh-oh!"
14 Donnybrook
15 Fourth of July sound
16 Oaf
17 Start of a suburbanite's lament
20 TV producers?
21 March celeb
22 Thoroughly unpleasant, as weather
23 "Defense of Fort M'Henry" author
24 Scoundrel
25 Waikiki wear
27 Suburbanite's lament (Part 2)
33 Caviar on toast, e.g.
36 Symbol of industriousness
37 Enveloping atmosphere
38 Ralph's wife
39 Win at musical chairs
40 Timer sounds
41 Nessie's waterway
42 Roadside sign
43 Student's second chance
44 Suburbanite's lament (Part 3)
47 Outback creature
48 Furthermore
49 "I do," for one
52 Mirage subject
56 Less plentiful
58 One-time wife of Mickey
59 Suburbanite's lament (Part 4)

62 Entertainer Falana
63 Emulate a banshee
64 Heckle
65 Augury
66 Word with green or googly
67 Weapons that are hardly cutting edge

DOWN

1 Smile of the smug
2 Tranquility partner
3 Quench
4 Word with spanking or brand
5 View from a beach house
6 Ludicrous
7 Charlie Brown exclamation
8 Asthma spray, e.g.
9 Kingsley novel "Two Years ___"
10 Gymnast Korbut
11 Outcries of amazement
12 It may lead to a birdie
13 Don't take another card
18 "___ No Good" (Ronstadt hit)
19 Curriculum section
26 Suffix with great
27 America's Cup entry
28 The middle number of 36-24-36
29 Nation on Hispaniola
30 Ancient alphabetic symbol
31 Work units
32 Geographic area
33 Dogie
34 Burn reliever

35 Congenial
39 The seventh of seven on a calendar
40 Nerve fiber
42 Word with chewing or bubble
43 Avoid cancellation
45 Brightest cohort
46 Maude's movie mate
49 Hazy
50 Like 60-Down

51 Electrical power units
52 Today's Christiania
53 Physicist's subject
54 Retailer's lure
55 Country on the Caspian
57 Girlfriend, in French 101
60 Farm female
61 Something you may get caught taking

1

E	S	T	E			I	C	E	S			F	E	A	S	T
L	E	A	P			R	A	C	E			O	L	L	I	E
M	E	X	I	C	A	N	H	A	I	R	L	E	S	S	
		M	I	L	A	N			O	R	R			F	I	T
			O	L	I	O			C	A	L	M				
B	E	L	G	I	A	N	S	H	E	E	P	D	O	G	
E	T	A	S			N	E	W				O	H	A	R	A
A	H	S			A	S	S	I	S	T	S			L	A	M
R	I	S	E	N			S	I	R			T	A	T	E	
S	C	O	T	T	I	S	H	T	E	R	R	I	E	R	
			C	E	N	T			E	S	A	I				
R	O	M			C	A	T			T	R	U	C	E	
A	L	A	S	K	A	N	M	A	L	A	M	U	T	E	
T	E	P	E	E			C	A	N	E			P	R	O	D
E	S	S	A	Y			E	N	D	S			H	E	N	S

2

L	I	P			L	E	M	M	E			S	C	R	U	B
A	L	L			I	D	E	A	L			C	H	U	R	L
M	I	A			Q	U	I	C	K	C	H	A	N	G	E	
B	A	Y	O	U			N	E	E	R			L	I	E	S
			A	R	I	A				U	P	E	N	D	S	
R	A	P	I	D	T	R	A	N	S	I	T					
A	R	A	B			L	E	G	A	T	E			S	O	B
P	E	R	I	S			B	O	A			S	T	O	M	A
S	A	T			P	A	U	N	C	H			U	L	A	N
			H	A	S	T	Y	P	U	D	D	I	N	G		
S	E	C	A	N	T					T	O	O	T			
A	R	A	L			R	E	S	T			O	R	A	T	E
F	A	S	T	F	O	R	W	A	R	D			I	O	N	
E	S	T	E	R			L	I	B	E	L			R	I	D
R	E	E	D	Y			E	T	U	D	E			E	L	S

3

A	M	O	C	O			C	E	L	L	O			S	A	T
R	A	N	D	S			A	B	O	I	L			T	S	E
M	U	S	C	L	E	B	O	U	N	D			A	H	A	
A	L	T			O	N	E	L			I	O	T	A		
D	I	A	S			T	R	I	P	L	E	J	U	M	P	
A	N	G	L	E	R	S			L	E	S	S	E	E	S	
	G	E	A	R			P	I	E			S	D	S		
		G	E	T	O	V	E	R	I	T						
H	U	G			H	U	T			C	O	D	A			
A	M	A	D	E	U	S			E	L	E	G	A	N	T	
S	P	R	I	N	G	T	I	M	E			A	N	N	E	
	T	R	I	B			M	B	A	S			D	E	E	
C	E	O			L	E	A	P	O	F	F	A	I	T	H	
R	E	T			O	G	L	E	S			C	R	E	T	E
O	N	E			C	O	A	L	S			S	P	R	E	E

4

C	O	D	E	R			P	R	E	P			S	O	Y	A
O	P	E	R	A			E	A	V	E			A	B	E	T
V	A	C	A	N	T	A	P	A	R	T	M	E	N	T		
E	L	K			S	O	R	T			S	I	E	S	T	A
			R	A	F				T	I	E			E	A	R
B	A	R	E	C	U	P	B	O	A	R	D					
A	L	E	C	K			L	I	E	N			R	A	U	L
L	A	N	E	S			A	T	C			P	E	N	T	A
K	I	D	D			A	T	T	A			R	A	T	E	D
			E	M	P	T	Y	P	R	O	M	I	S	E		
R	I	O			E	T	E				O	P	T			
U	N	S	E	E	N			S	O	L	O			A	L	I
B	L	A	N	K	E	X	P	R	E	S	S	I	O	N		
L	A	G	O			S	V	E	N			A	P	R	O	N
E	Y	E	S			S	I	D	E			L	A	S	T	S

5

S	C	A	M	P			A	N	T	I			S	I	P	S
P	U	R	E	E			L	A	I	N			U	N	I	T
A	R	E	A	S			L	I	N	T			A	S	T	A
C	E	N	T	E	R	O	F	G	R	A	V	I	T	Y		
E	S	T			T	O	T				O	D	E	D		
			J	A	G			I	L	S	A			E	L	K
S	E	A	U			U	T	N	E			G	I	J	O	E
M	I	D	D	L	E	O	F	T	H	E	R	O	A	D		
E	N	J	O	Y			M	E	S	A			I	B	M	S
E	E	O			R	E	A	R			I	T	S			
			U	T	I	L			S	T	U			L	I	S
C	O	R	E	C	O	N	S	T	I	T	U	E	N	T		
L	A	N	E			P	U	N	Y			T	R	I	T	E
A	H	E	M			E	D	I	E			U	N	L	E	T
D	U	D	S			R	E	P	S			T	S	A	R	S

6

L	A	U	G	H	■	S	L	A	P	■	K	U	D	O
A	L	L	E	Y	■	H	I	R	E	■	A	S	I	A
D	O	N	T	B	E	I	M	P	A	T	I	E	N	T
Y	E	A	■	R	E	N	O	■	■	E	S	S	E	S
■	■	A	I	N	T	■	T	O	N	E	■	■	■	■
■	H	O	L	D	Y	O	U	R	H	O	R	S	E	S
P	E	R	P	S	■	■	P	A	I	R	■	W	Y	E
L	A	O	S	■	H	I	P	P	O	■	P	A	R	R
U	R	N	■	C	O	N	E	■	■	S	E	R	I	F
S	T	O	P	H	U	R	R	Y	I	N	G	M	E	■
■	■	■	L	U	R	E	■	O	N	U	S	■	■	■
A	T	E	A	M	■	■	B	U	R	G	■	M	A	C
W	H	A	T	S	T	H	E	B	I	G	R	U	S	H
R	A	R	E	■	S	O	R	E	■	L	A	T	H	E
Y	I	P	S	■	K	E	N	T	■	E	N	T	E	R

7

C	A	R	O	B	■	S	H	A	M	■	T	O	G	A
A	L	O	H	A	■	H	O	P	E	■	I	V	A	N
S	E	C	O	N	D	A	M	E	N	D	M	E	N	T
T	S	K	■	D	A	Z	E	■	■	M	E	R	G	E
■	■	P	I	T	A	■	P	E	A	S	■	■	■	■
M	I	N	U	T	E	M	A	I	D	J	U	I	C	E
O	D	E	T	S	■	■	P	E	G	■	P	L	U	M
N	A	H	■	■	K	E	R	R	Y	■	■	U	R	I
T	H	R	O	■	I	R	E	■	■	N	A	V	E	L
H	O	U	R	G	L	A	S	S	F	I	G	U	R	E
■	■	■	E	O	N	S	■	P	A	N	E	■	■	■
A	D	L	I	B	■	■	E	A	V	E	■	S	O	U
D	A	Y	L	I	G	H	T	S	A	V	I	N	G	S
I	D	O	L	■	S	E	A	M	■	E	V	I	L	S
T	O	N	Y	■	A	W	L	S	■	H	Y	P	E	R

8

A	I	M	E	D	■	E	T	A	T	S	■	F	A	D
B	R	O	A	D	■	C	I	G	A	R	■	A	P	R
B	A	S	S	E	T	H	O	R	N	S	■	N	E	E
E	T	U	I	■	R	O	S	E	N	■	M	L	X	I
S	E	L	E	N	A	■	■	E	E	R	I	E	■	■
■	■	R	E	C	O	R	D	S	E	T	T	E	R	■
L	O	S	■	B	E	L	A	■	T	A	T	T	L	E
O	A	T	S	■	■	E	B	B	■	■	S	E	L	A
S	T	I	N	G	S	■	B	A	S	H	■	R	E	D
■	T	H	R	E	E	P	O	I	N	T	E	R	■	■
■	■	R	E	R	U	N	■	■	A	M	E	B	A	S
U	S	E	R	■	M	Y	W	A	Y	■	S	O	F	A
R	O	D	■	B	O	X	E	R	S	H	O	R	T	S
A	S	U	■	I	N	E	P	T	■	A	L	O	E	S
L	O	P	■	G	I	S	T	S	■	H	E	N	R	Y

9

G	E	L	■	C	R	O	W	D	■	B	A	M	B	I
A	M	I	■	H	O	W	I	E	■	E	X	A	L	T
M	U	G	G	I	N	E	S	S	■	E	L	V	E	S
■	■	H	E	C	A	N	C	O	M	P	R	E	S	S
A	L	T	O	■	■	■	T	I	E	O	N	T	O	■
T	H	E	M	O	S	T	W	O	R	D	S	■	■	■
P	A	N	■	N	O	A	H	■	■	E	S	P	N	■
A	S	U	■	I	N	T	O	T	H	E	■	H	O	O
R	A	P	T	■	■	R	E	A	D	■	A	W	W	■
■	■	■	S	M	A	L	L	E	S	T	I	D	E	A
S	A	G	U	A	R	O	■	■	D	O	R	Y	■	■
O	F	A	N	Y	M	A	N	I	K	N	O	W	■	■
N	O	T	A	T	■	V	A	L	U	E	L	E	S	S
A	R	O	M	A	■	E	M	I	R	S	■	R	A	P
R	E	R	I	G	■	S	E	A	T	S	■	S	T	Y

10

N	A	B	O	B	■	A	B	E	T	■	B	A	N	K
A	L	O	H	A	■	M	E	M	O	■	E	L	A	N
Y	O	Y	O	S	■	M	A	I	M	■	F	I	D	E
S	E	W	■	S	M	A	R	T	C	O	O	K	I	E
■	■	O	C	E	A	N	■	■	A	U	G	E	R	S
S	A	N	E	S	T	■	H	U	T	S	■	■	■	■
A	I	D	A	■	C	R	O	P	■	T	A	K	E	S
I	D	E	S	■	H	E	R	O	N	■	S	N	I	P
D	E	R	E	K	■	E	D	N	A	■	T	O	R	E
■	■	■	I	D	L	E	■	C	H	E	W	E	D	■
A	L	U	M	N	A	■	S	H	A	R	I	■	■	■
N	O	B	O	D	Y	S	F	O	O	L	■	T	U	G
I	D	O	L	■	B	O	I	L	■	L	E	A	S	E
T	E	A	L	■	E	L	S	E	■	O	W	L	E	T
A	N	T	S	■	D	O	T	S	■	W	E	L	D	S

11

```
T U T O R   O P E N   B A B A
A N I T A   F A C E   O V I D
M O P T H E F L O O R W I T H
  P O S S E   N O T A T E
A M Y   P R A M   D O T E R
L E T F L Y   B E D   E R E
M O O L A   A S L E E P
S W E E P S E C O N D H A N D
  E P H R O N   G E N O A
G M C   Y I N   P E W T E R
R A R E R   E D D A   E L K
U N I S O N   I C I E R
D U S T B E M Y D E S T I N Y
G A P E   W R E N   A T O N E
E L S E   T I N T   W A R E S
```

12

```
L O R D   A R R O W   P O L A
O B O E   L A U R A   A X E L
B E D C L O T H E S   J E E P
E Y E L I N E R   Y A N K S
    A V E   P O E M
S C A R E   C A R D T A B L E
L A T E R   H E I D I   L A D
O N E S   H A D E S   C A R E
S T U   S A L E S   S U D A N
H O P E C H E S T   T R E S S
  C O A T   F R A
S I G H T   B L E A T E R S
H A L O   C H A I R W O M A N
O G E E   S O B E R   R I G A
P O N D   T E E N Y   S T E P
```

13

```
C O M M A   M A Y S   S L O W
A R I A L   O M A N   N O V A
C R A C K A J O K E   A B E T
H I T   A V O N   E X P E R T
E N A B L E   G I Z M O
    R I N D   R E A U M U R
G A M E   G E E K   S T A R E
E L I A   E M A I L   O L G A
T A N K S   A R N O   F L E D
S I X T E E N   G O B I
    H A N D S   K I T B A G
A S C E N D   A L A S   A G E
M A L I   S P L I T H A I R S
E R I C   U R S A   O G L E S
N A P E   P E A R   P A S E O
```

14

```
M U S T   D A F T   V I S O R
O P E R   E R I E   I N T R O
U K R A I N I A N   C A R E T
S E E I N   A T T N   S A L E
S E N N A S   H O S N I
E P E E   C C R   R A I N E R
    E T A P E S   U T E R O
M O D   B R A I N E D   R E D
P A R D O   S T A S I S
G R A I N S   S P A   H I R E
    I C E U P   I S O B A R
R E N T   M A S T   O W E T O
O N A I R   S C A T T E R E D
L O G O N   T A R E   R I D E
E L E N A   A N T E   S A G S
```

15

```
R A S P S   S U L U   C A I N
E X T R A   A G I N   I N D O
F L Y O F F T H E H A N D L E
S E X   E L I   N E M E S E S
    S T U N S   A I M
B O O T Y   S C A R   A R T S
U N R I P E   O D D S   H U E
T E A R I N T O S O M E O N E
T U T   N E A T   F E N D E R
E P E E   R U E D   L O A D S
    L A G   R E E L S
T H I N N E R   A V A   O A K
R U N I N T E R F E R E N C E
E G A N   I D O L   A G I N G
K E N O   C O D Y   T O T E S
```

16

```
YOUR  CANS  BRAVO
APSE  OLEO  RECAP
KEEPALOWPROFILE
SCRUPLE  HOW  DEN
   TEE  PIANISTS
STEERCLEAROF
TODD  TEN  USAGE
EGG  BSA  TNT  GOA
PAYEE  OHO  LOSS
   THESPOTLIGHT
BACCARAT  HAN
ERA  VIV  GAZETTE
REMAINANONYMOUS
MARCO  GOOK  ERRS
SLYER  ENDS  NONO
```

17

```
ERAS  COAL  AMOR
DAME  SONIA  MILO
GREENTHUMB  ENDS
YEN  IRAS  ONRUSH
   SCAN  FRUIT
RAFTED  PRINCESS
ERIES  RAN  AHEM
EGG  TAPINGS  ATE
LOUD  RIO  PINTA
STRUMMER  CANDOR
   EBERT  SARK
ETHANE  HERS  VIA
LEER  SQUAREFOOT
BEAR  TUMMY  OTTO
ANDY  SOPS  BEAM
```

18

```
LIBRA  CPOS  PSIS
UBOAT  LORI  ETNA
REMIT  OOZE  ARON
CABLETVHOSTKING
HMS  NEE  TASK
   PDA  STAG  EEL
ACME  CIAO  UPONE
FRENCHFRYOPTION
RATSO  SASS  ALSO
OWE  ANON  HAS
   RATE  OED  BYA
SIMPSONSBARKEEP
ASAP  COPE  IOTAS
SAIL  ONUS  ABASE
HYDE  NONE  NESTS
```

19

```
GRAF  DUHS  ARIAL
OHIO  ETUI  LANCE
GENX  FIST  LITHE
HATTRICKS  USHER
   RELAY  ODIE
ALCOVE  SPENCER
VIRTU  SALE  SHEA
ILE  POTLUCK  IRK
ALDO  PIER  EPPIE
NEITHER  PLUSES
   THUD  SAULT
PACED  PENNYANTE
URALS  ENID  WOOD
MARLO  ASTI  AGOG
ADDON  SEAT  YOKE
```

20

```
LILAC  WHY  CRABS
ARENA  EAU  HENRI
BEETS  ARK  EDGED
   ITUSESAWHEEL
ASK  ATE  ISOLDE
THATSELDOM  TASS
MORRIS  RUSH
SOLID  GUT  UMASS
   ESPN  PLAQUE
IVES  TAKESATURN
NINETY  NAH  AFT
FORTHEBETTOR
ELITE  OBI  OOMPH
RICER  MAR  PIOUS
SNORE  BYE  SLEPT
```

21

P	A	U	L	█	S	U	B	S	█	A	T	T	A	R
O	L	G	A	█	O	T	O	E	█	G	R	E	B	E
M	A	L	T	█	F	L	O	E	█	A	U	R	A	L
P	R	I	V	A	T	E	P	R	O	P	E	R	T	Y
█	█	I	T	S	Y	█	█	L	E	G	█	█	█	█
C	D	R	A	T	E	█	A	M	A	█	R	A	P	T
O	R	A	█	I	L	L	B	E	█	M	I	L	L	I
M	A	J	O	R	L	E	A	G	U	E	T	E	A	M
I	N	A	N	E	█	S	C	A	N	T	█	R	T	E
C	O	S	T	█	E	E	K	█	C	R	A	T	E	R
█	█	█	H	O	P	█	█	F	L	I	T	█	█	█
G	E	N	E	R	A	L	E	L	E	C	T	I	O	N
E	R	O	S	E	█	E	G	O	S	█	I	D	L	E
M	A	R	L	O	█	A	G	U	A	█	C	O	L	A
S	T	A	Y	S	█	D	O	R	M	█	S	L	A	P

22

O	G	L	E	█	S	A	L	T	█	M	A	D	A	M
T	R	U	E	█	C	L	A	W	█	A	R	E	N	A
T	A	B	L	E	O	F	C	O	N	T	E	N	T	S
O	D	E	█	X	R	A	Y	█	O	U	T	S	E	T
█	█	█	A	P	E	S	█	S	O	R	E	█	█	█
B	O	O	M	E	D	█	L	O	D	E	█	G	A	D
U	L	N	A	R	█	D	I	A	L	█	A	L	S	O
L	E	S	S	T	H	A	N	P	E	R	F	E	C	T
G	O	E	S	█	A	R	T	S	█	E	R	N	I	E
E	S	T	█	P	R	E	Y	█	A	D	O	N	I	S
█	█	█	H	O	D	S	█	A	R	C	S	█	█	█
S	H	R	I	N	E	█	E	D	D	A	█	B	A	N
K	E	E	P	I	N	G	T	H	E	P	E	A	C	E
I	R	A	T	E	█	A	N	O	N	█	L	I	N	E
P	O	L	O	S	█	P	A	C	T	█	F	L	E	D

23

O	A	T	H	█	S	P	E	R	M	█	D	A	T	A
P	L	E	A	█	A	T	R	I	A	█	E	L	A	N
S	P	A	R	E	P	A	R	T	S	█	W	I	L	T
█	█	P	E	P	█	S	E	T	B	A	C	K	S	█
C	A	B	█	L	E	G	█	H	E	R	E	S	Y	█
H	O	O	D	█	D	I	P	P	E	R	█	█	█	█
A	R	E	A	█	R	E	L	A	Y	R	A	C	E	█
S	T	R	I	K	E	D	E	A	D	L	I	N	E	S
M	A	S	S	I	V	E	L	Y	█	█	S	E	A	S
█	█	█	T	A	R	S	U	S	█	E	A	S	E	█
B	A	L	E	E	N	█	P	E	A	█	R	E	X	█
O	D	Y	S	S	E	U	S	█	T	S	E	█	█	█
O	M	I	T	█	S	P	L	I	T	H	A	I	R	S
N	I	N	E	█	C	O	O	K	E	█	R	I	O	T
E	N	G	R	█	E	N	T	E	R	█	L	I	E	U

24

A	D	I	T	█	C	A	V	S	█	P	A	S	H	A
B	E	T	E	█	O	P	E	C	█	A	B	H	O	R
A	V	E	R	█	R	E	N	O	█	C	O	A	S	T
C	O	M	M	O	N	S	T	O	C	K	█	D	E	S
I	N	S	I	D	E	█	█	T	A	E	B	O	█	█
█	█	█	T	O	A	S	T	█	C	R	A	W	L	S
H	A	T	E	R	█	A	S	C	H	█	A	B	U	T
A	S	H	█	S	W	I	L	L	E	D	█	O	L	E
J	E	E	P	█	A	L	O	E	█	W	A	X	U	P
J	A	P	E	R	Y	█	T	O	W	E	L	█	█	█
█	█	O	Z	O	N	E	█	█	E	L	E	C	T	S
G	A	L	█	D	E	L	L	A	S	T	R	E	E	T
A	M	I	C	E	█	Z	A	G	S	█	T	A	R	O
P	E	C	A	N	█	I	M	H	O	█	E	S	S	O
E	X	E	R	T	█	E	B	A	N	█	D	E	E	P

25

P	I	G	█	S	A	L	A	D	S	█	H	A	L	E
A	N	O	█	O	C	E	L	O	T	█	O	L	A	V
P	U	S	H	B	U	T	T	O	N	█	O	O	Z	E
A	I	W	A	█	M	O	O	R	█	P	R	E	E	N
█	T	I	L	D	E	█	█	A	A	A	█	█	█	█
█	M	O	U	N	T	A	I	N	C	H	A	I	N	█
H	O	M	E	D	█	A	S	C	O	T	█	N	R	A
A	M	I	S	█	A	R	K	I	N	█	O	T	I	S
I	N	N	█	E	O	S	I	N	█	M	O	I	S	T
L	I	G	H	T	N	I	N	G	B	O	L	T	█	█
█	█	O	R	E	█	█	A	M	A	H	S	█	█	█
A	D	O	B	E	█	C	O	S	T	█	L	E	E	J
V	E	R	B	█	T	O	O	T	H	P	A	S	T	E
E	L	S	E	█	A	P	P	L	E	S	█	I	T	T
R	E	O	S	█	R	E	S	O	D	S	█	S	O	S

26

C	H	I	M	P		G	A	V	E		P	R	O	S
A	E	R	I	E		O	T	I	S		L	I	R	A
P	R	O	D	S		L	O	O	P		A	V	I	D
E	R	N	I	E	L	L	L	L		K	N	E	E	L
			S	T	A	Y	L	A	T	E		S	L	Y
M	G	M		A	U	G		S	H	O	P			
E	R	A	S		G	E	S		E	G	I	S	E	S
S	A	I	L	T	H	E	H	I	G	H	C	C	C	C
A	F	L	O	A	T		U	N	O		K	A	R	O
		P	R	E	P		A	R	A		T	U	T	
A	D	Z		P	R	O	P	J	E	T	S			
B	O	Z	O	S		I	R	I	S	H	I	I	I	I
A	L	T	O		A	S	I	F		A	T	O	M	S
S	L	O	B		R	E	E	F		N	A	T	A	L
E	S	P	Y		E	D	D	Y		D	R	A	M	A

27

M	U	M	P	S		T	A	C	O		K	H	A	N
A	T	T	I	C		R	Y	A	N		H	A	R	E
T	H	E	E	A	S	I	E	S	T	W	A	Y	T	O
H	A	T		L	U	X		H	O	O	K	S		
I	N	N		P	R	I	S	S		N	I	E	C	E
S	T	A	Y		N	E	P	A	L		S	E	E	P
			A	M	A		O	L	A	F		D	N	A
	M	A	K	E	M	O	N	E	Y	L	A	S	T	
J	O	N		L	E	N	S		A	U	G			
R	A	C	E		S	L	O	O	P		E	A	S	E
S	T	E	N	O		O	R	A	L	S		L	A	X
		S	C	H	M	O		R	O	O		D	Y	E
I	S	T	O	M	A	K	E	I	T	F	I	R	S	T
M	O	O	D		D	E	A	N		A	L	I	N	E
P	U	R	E		D	R	U	G		S	E	N	O	R

28

U	M	P	S		P	R	O	S	Y		G	L	O	B
N	A	I	L		L	A	D	L	E		R	I	P	E
I	D	E	A		O	N	I	O	N		A	N	T	E
C	A	R	V	E	D	I	N	S	T	O	N	E		
E	M	C	E	E			H	A	N	D	S	A	W	
F	E	E		L	I	S	A			M	A	M	B	A
		S	C	U	L	P	T	E	D	A	B	S		
E	L	S	A		E	D	G	A	R		S	N	A	P
M	O	L	D	E	D	S	A	L	A	D				
I	B	O	O	K			E	M	M	A		P	C	S
R	E	T	R	E	A	D			I	S	L	A	M	
	C	A	S	T	I	R	O	N	S	T	O	V	E	
S	C	A	B		T	R	I	B	E		E	V	I	L
C	U	R	L		A	G	L	O	W		V	E	A	L
I	P	S	E		R	E	L	E	T		E	R	R	S

29

W	O	L	F		T	E	S	S		S	P	E	N	T
H	A	I	R		U	T	A	H		C	O	C	O	A
O	K	R	A		N	U	K	E		H	I	R	E	D
A	S	A	N	A	D	D	E	D	B	O	N	U	S	
			C	U	R	E			R	O	T			
A	P	T		G	A	S	O	H	O	L		C	B	S
T	R	A	S	H		C	O	O		B	E	E	T	
L	I	M	I	T	E	D	T	I	M	E	O	N	L	Y
A	M	E	N		C	U	E			U	N	T	I	L
S	A	D		B	L	O	T	T	E	R		S	E	E
		P	E	A			A	L	O	E				
	W	A	I	T	T	H	E	R	E	S	M	O	R	E
M	O	L	A	R		E	R	I	C		P	L	E	A
A	R	E	N	A		R	I	F	T		T	E	E	S
D	E	C	O	Y		R	E	F	S		Y	O	K	E

30

M	O	N	K		L	A	W	S			T	R	I	B
I	T	O	R		A	L	O	H	A		H	O	N	E
L	O	D	I		G	O	M	A	D		R	O	A	D
D	O	E	S	D	O	U	B	L	E	D	U	T	Y	
E	L	A	T	E	S			L	E	D		B	E	A
R	E	L	I	C		P	L	O		T	R	E	A	D
			O	U	R	O	W	N		H	E	R	O	
	W	O	R	D	O	F	H	O	N	O	R			
A	S	E	A		O	N	T	A	P	E				
C	H	E	F	S		O	Y	L		H	B	O	M	B
H	U	H		E	A	U			T	R	A	C	E	R
	T	O	W	N	A	N	D	C	O	U	N	T	R	Y
T	O	U	R		A	C	R	I	D		G	A	G	A
A	U	R	A		S	E	A	T	O		O	V	E	N
I	T	S	Y			S	T	E	S		R	E	S	T

31

A	S	H	E	N		M	R	S		G	I	F	T	S
G	H	A	N	A		Y	O	U		I	S	L	E	T
L	O	V	E	B	I	R	D	S		G	O	O	E	Y
E	V	A		S	O	R	E		B	O	B			
T	E	N	S		C	H	O	C	O	L	A	T	E	S
S	L	A	I	N				A	M	O	R	O	S	O
			L	E	I		F	E	B			G	P	S
	V	A	L	E	N	T	I	N	E	S	D	A	Y	
L	E	T			S	O	T		D	O	E			
S	T	O	R	I	E	D				N	A	S	A	L
D	O	Z	E	N	R	O	S	E	S		F	E	T	A
	O	F	T		C	L	U	E		R	O	B		
T	A	M	P	A		C	H	A	M	P	A	G	N	E
A	L	I	E	N		O	U	T		I	D	E	A	L
D	I	D	N	T		O	L	E		C	O	I	L	S

32

U	N	M	E	T		O	C	T	E	T		R	A	M
P	A	B	L	O		T	H	I	G	H		I	D	O
S	M	A	L	L	C	H	A	N	G	E		S	E	W
		A	D	H	E	R	E		A	N	K	L	E	
O	W	L		A	I	R		S	P	I	C	E	D	
S	H	E	L	L	S		S	H	E	E	N	A		
S	E	G	A	L		T	H	A	T		E	P	I	C
I	R	A	N		S	A	I	L	S		M	I	M	E
E	E	L	Y		T	R	E	E		P	E	T	A	L
		T	A	I	L	O	R		L	I	N	A	G	E
S	T	E	R	N	O		F	E	E			L	O	B
P	A	N	D	A		T	O	R	E	R	O			
A	N	D		R	U	B	B	E	R	C	H	E	C	K
D	Y	E		U	S	A	I	R		E	N	N	U	I
E	A	R		T	E	R	S	E		D	O	S	E	D

33

A	M	F	M		S	E	P	T	A		S	L	A	P
G	A	L	A		A	D	H	O	C		E	E	R	O
I	C	O	N		P	O	I	N	T	B	L	A	N	K
L	O	O	T	S			G	R	I	F	F	E	Y	
E	N	D	R	U	N		I	S	E	E				
		L	A	S	E	R	S		S	N	O	C	A	T
A	L	I		A	T	E	A	M	S		L	A	R	A
L	O	G	O	N		A	D	E		F	A	R	G	O
A	G	H	A		F	L	O	R	A	L		D	O	S
S	E	T	T	E	E		R	E	M	A	N	D		
			A	A	A	A		A	S	L	E	E	P	
I	N	S	E	R	T	S		H	E	A	R	A		
B	A	C	K	N	U	M	B	E	R		A	L	A	N
A	L	A	E		R	A	I	S	E		S	E	T	S
R	A	T	S		E	D	G	E	D		T	R	O	Y

34

T	A	N	G	O		S	L	I	T		H	I	Y	A
A	L	O	O	F		C	A	S	A		A	C	E	S
C	A	N	O	F	W	O	R	M	S		Z	E	T	A
O	R	E		K	I	W	I		H	A	M			
			B	E	L	L		T	R	A	C	E	D	
B	I	G	E	Y	E		T	H	E	S	T	A	G	E
E	N	Y	A			F	U	E	G	O		M	O	I
B	A	R	R	E	L	O	F	M	O	N	K	E	Y	S
O	R	A		S	O	R	T	S			A	R	A	T
P	O	T	A	T	O	E	S		G	R	O	A	N	S
S	W	E	D	E	N			G	R	A	S			
		H	E	Y		A	H	A	B		A	B	E	
S	A	K	E		B	A	G	O	F	B	O	N	E	S
I	G	O	R		I	V	E	S		L	I	K	E	S
N	O	P	E		N	E	S	T		E	L	A	T	E

35

S	W	E	E	P		P	L	A	Y		S	T	A	R
H	I	D	E	S		R	A	C	E		E	U	R	O
A	N	D	R	E		I	R	M	A		A	N	E	W
D	O	Y	O	U	U	N	D	E	R	S	T	A	N	D
			D	S	T				E	S	S	A	Y	
W	A	L	T	O	N		W	H	A	T				
A	S	I	A			S	H	I	N	T	O	I	S	M
T	H	E	G	R	A	V	I	T	Y	O	F	T	H	E
T	E	N	S	E	N	E	S	S			F	O	O	L
			A	I	N	T		H	A	S	N	O	T	
U	N	A	P	T			O	U	T					
S	I	T	U	A	T	I	O	N	A	T	H	A	N	D
A	G	A	R		A	N	K	A		A	I	L	E	Y
G	E	R	E		U	G	L	I		C	L	O	W	N
E	R	I	E		T	E	A	R		K	L	U	T	E

36

```
E L S E   T A M E D   S H O E
S O L D   S M I L E   T O O K
C O U G H H A C K W H E E Z E
  P R E M I S E   E A S E S
      O R S   C L A D
A G H A S T   S L A V   M I A
T O A D   B L A S E   I N N
B U Z Z W H O O S H S P L A T
A D E   A U N T S   A L P S
T A D   D E U S   S A N I T Y
    M I S S   H E R
A L L I N   C O N C E A L
B O I N G S P L A S H G L U B
B O N E   O H A R E   G E N E
A M E S   W I N D S   S C A D
```

37

```
U S U R P   I N T R O   N E T
T A P E R   A E I O U   I N A
A G O V E R N M E N T   M T V
H E N   P E S O S   S P I R E
    M A E       T E E T E R
R E G A R D S A C I T I Z E N
A G A T E   A S H E S
P O L E   A L T A R   A R C H
    E L V I S   S H A P E
A S S O M E O N E W H O H A S
C H I R P S     H E Y
R O D E O   C A M E L   S L O
O W N   W H A T I T T A K E S
S U E   E U R O S   E M A I L
S P Y   R E A M S   R A T S O
```

38

```
  E S S A   M E A T   A F R O
  S E L F   A O N E   D R A B
  K N O C K K N O C K J O K E
R I D E   I E S     Y O D E L
U M A   A T M   A P R I O R I
D O W N T H E D R A I N
O P I N E   I O N E   L S D
L I R E   B E E N E   H I T E
F E E   B E R G   R E V E L
  D R A G O N E S F E E T
H O N E Y D O   A N A   S L A
O C A L A   A N U   S A Y S
O U T I N L E F T F I E L D
C L A M   B R A E   L E I A
H O L E   J A R S   O P E N
```

39

```
M A C H O   L O C O   A C E D
A C E R B   I D E A   M A X I
T H E H O U N D O F M U S I C
H E S   I N N S   E L A T E
    E S T E   J A N E
B A C K T O T H E S U T U R E
E M A G S   E S P   S T I R
F I N   S W A T S   E P A
O N O R   K I T   F A R E S
G O N E W I T H T H E W I N E
  V A N S   H E A L
G I B E D   S E A T   A D S
M A R R I E D T O T H E M O P
A G E S   B O A R   E L I Z A
N O D E   B A B Y   R I D E R
```

40

```
L O B B Y   E D G E   B Y R D
O H A R E   U R S A   R O A R
F I N I S H C O A T   E U R O
T O G S   E L L   P E R E S
    T R A I L B L A Z E R S
I N B O A R D   R A V E
B A L L E T   N A M E S A K E
I T O   C A N     M E G
S E C O N D L Y   A I L I N G
    B E A U   I N V E S T S
Y E L L O W J A C K E T
A M A I N   T I L   T R E E
R A N G   S P A C E S U I T S
D I C E   T E L L   I C O N S
S L E D   Y A L E   S E T A E
```

41

```
H E M   R E V A M P   A B B A
I T O   A M E L I A   M E A L
G H O S T S T O R Y   E L L A
H A L E     S E E S   R I M S
S N A R E S       U N I T
    A R L E N S P E C T E R
C O G   S A D A T   W A L D O
O K R A   W I D E N   N E E R
E L A N D   T I R E D   S N Y
D A N N Y P H A N T O M
    D U E L     S H A D O W
E V I L   A U R A   R E A R
W O O L   S P I R I T L A K E
E L S E   M O N I C A   T U N
R E E D   A N G L E D   H M S
```

42

```
C O S M O   E L E C   C P O S
H U N A N   R O L L   A O N E
A G E R S   I O W A   S W A T
T H E T I M E T O M A K E
S T R A T A   S O O T   R E D
    E N D   D R S   T A I
R U S H   O A F   E M O T E
U P Y O U R M I N D A B O U T
N O N E T   N E E   A L P S
I N C   E L F   G A S
N E O   R A I D   L A T E S T
    P E O P L E I S N E V E R
B E A D   T I L T   D E E R E
M A T E   O A T S   R U N G S
W R E N   P L A Y   A P S E S
```

43

```
O L E G   D O W S E   H A W K
D E A R   O N E A L   A S A N
D I R E   L O R N E   L I K E
  F L A V O R E D C O F F E E
    S I R       T N T
V I P E R   F A R   A I M A T
I R E   G A I N E D   M O D E
S E A S O N E D V E T E R A N
I N C A   T R O U G H   A G O
T E E T H   O R E   O W N E R
    S U E   O N E
S P I C E D T H I N G S U P
N O G O   G R A C E   L V I I
I N O R   E A T O N   E E L S
P Y R E   S P E N D   Y A L E
```

44

```
M A R S   D E C A L   C O A T
A V O N   A M O N G   A M M O
R E D O   P O W D E R R O O M
C R E W   H T S     A W O K E
    O P I N E   R O C A
R E C E D E   S A L E S M A N
H U L A S   A M I D   H A L E
I L O   C L A S S   S I R
N E W S   H I R E   R A T E D
O R N A M E N T   P A T E N S
    B A R E   S O W E R
A D O R N   S A L   I W I N
D I V I N G B E L L   N O S E
E V E N   E R A S E   T R E E
N A N A   L O M A N   O K E D
```

45

```
S H A G   F A C T S   T A S S
L O C I   I L L A T   O G L E
I H A V E N O I D E A W H A T
T O R E I N T O   M E A T S
    A G E   R O I L
A P A T H Y M E A N S   M I V
B L U R T   O A T E S   E V A
B O G Y   L U T E S   I D O L
E T H   S Y N O D   S N A R L
S S T   A N D F R A N K L Y I
    A W N S   L A W
S W O R E   S H A K E S U P
C O U L D N T C A R E L E S S
A R T E   S W A R M   L E T S
M E S S   F O N T S   S P A T
```

46

P	E	A	R	S		G	N	P		S	C	E	N	E
I	N	L	E	T		L	I	E		A	L	T	E	R
T	O	M	M	Y	T	U	N	E	S	T	U	N	E	S
A	L	S	O		H	E	A	V	E		B	A	D	E
		V	I	A			E	T	E	S				
T	I	G	E	R	W	O	O	D	S	W	O	O	D	S
A	S	L		R	E	B	A			E	D	W	I	N
S	L	A	P		D	I	T	T	O		A	N	N	A
T	E	S	L	A			E	E	L	S		E	E	G
E	D	S	E	L	F	O	R	D	S	F	O	R	D	S
		A	I	L	S			E	C	O				
A	M	O	S		A	G	A	I	N		L	I	I	I
J	A	M	E	S	B	O	N	D	S	B	O	N	D	S
A	D	A	G	E		O	N	E		A	N	T	I	S
X	E	N	O	N		D	O	A		A	G	O	G	O

47

S	H	A	G	S		S	L	A	B		G	R	O	W
A	I	S	L	E		H	O	B	O		A	I	D	A
S	K	I	I	N	G	I	S	A	W	I	N	T	E	R
H	E	A	T	S	U	P		S	T	A	G	E	S	
			Z	E	N		R	E	I	N	S			
N	A	V	Y		S	W	E	D	E		T	W	I	T
A	M	I		S	H	O	P			H	E	I	D	I
S	P	O	R	T	Y	O	U	L	E	A	R	N	I	N
A	L	L	E	Y			T	E	X	T		C	O	T
L	E	A	D		S	C	E	N	E		B	E	T	S
		A	C	T	E	D		M	A	O				
	S	A	L	A	R	Y		O	P	E	N	S	E	A
S	E	V	E	R	A	L	S	I	T	T	I	N	G	S
I	G	O	R		F	O	U	L		N	E	I	G	H
P	A	N	T		E	N	V	Y		A	R	T	S	Y

48

S	E	A	L		F	O	N	D	U	E		D	S	T
I	L	L	E		O	R	I	E	N	T		A	W	E
G	I	F	T	W	R	A	P	P	E	D		L	O	M
H	A	I	T	I			A	T	V		A	A	R	P
T	S	E		C	L	O	T	H	E	S	L	I	N	E
		A	C	A	T		S	N	A	I	L			
L	A	M	B	A	S	T	E			O	M	A	H	A
O	D	E	R		H	O	R	S	E		O	M	I	T
B	O	S	U	N			R	U	M	I	N	A	T	E
	C	Z	A	R	S		C	I	T	Y				
C	R	A	Z	Y	E	I	G	H	T	S		Q	B	S
H	E	L	I		G	L	O			S	Q	U	A	T
U	N	I		D	R	A	F	T	N	O	T	I	C	E
T	A	N		R	E	G	A	I	N		I	R	O	N
E	L	E		S	T	E	R	N	E		P	E	N	S

49

M	R	B	I	G			I	L	S	A		A	L	S	O
V	A	L	O	R		T	A	L	L		T	A	T	A	
P	L	A	N	O		A	R	I	L		C	R	A	T	
S	E	T		W	A	L	K	T	H	R	O	U	G	H	
			E	T	U	I			O	B	S	E	S	S	
B	I	R	T	H	D	A	Y	S	U	I	T				
I	D	E	A	S			E	A	R	S		P	I	G	
E	L	A	L		P	A	S	T	S		P	E	A	L	
N	E	D		T	E	R	N			M	E	R	G	E	
		R	A	D	I	O	S	T	A	T	I	O	N		
A	S	G	A	R	D			M	I	R	E				
S	H	U	T	T	L	E	C	O	C	K		D	D	S	
P	E	L	T		E	D	E	R		U	S	U	A	L	
C	E	L	L		R	I	D	E		P	A	D	R	E	
A	P	S	E		S	E	E	S		S	P	E	E	D	

50

S	A	W	N		E	B	B	S		S	A	T	A	N
O	M	O	O		R	A	I	L		P	R	I	D	E
F	O	R	C	E	R	T	A	I	N	I	K	N	O	W
A	S	T	O	R			S	T	O	N	I	E	S	T
			N	I	C	E			T	E	N			
W	H	A	T	C	O	N	C	E	I	T		A	M	P
A	O	N	E		E	C	O	L		S	O	N	A	R
S	A	N	S		D	I	N	A	H		N	I	N	A
T	R	I	T	E		N	A	P	A		E	M	I	T
E	Y	E		M	E	A	N	S	I	N	F	A	C	T
		S	P	Y			E	L	E	A				
R	E	S	T	O	R	E	S			A	T	S	E	A
I	K	N	O	W	E	V	E	R	Y	T	H	I	N	G
L	E	A	V	E		E	R	I	E		O	D	O	R
E	D	G	E	R		N	A	B	S		M	E	S	A

51

```
N I P   . L A R D . A S S E R T
T O E   . S L O W . I N A R O W
S W A N D I V E . R E M A D E .
B A L I . V E E R . A P T E R .
.   F E E D B A C K L O O P .
A O R T A .   N O S E .   .
Q U A Y S . I N C A . R E A M
U R N . E G G R O L L . A L I
A S T O . A L A R . I B S E N
.   T A R O .   L A T E X
M A S T E R O F S P I N .
E L T O N . S A N E . D A I S
D O O M E D . S A N D B A N K
I N V A I N . T I N E . R T E
A G E N D A . S L E W . P O W
```

52

```
L O A M . T O G A . S A S E S
U R G E . O R E S . T R O L L
A B U T . D R A W B R I D G E
U S E R I D . R A R A . O I D
.   I D L E . R A I S I N S
T R A C E E L E M E N T .
R A N . E R S T .   S E V E R
I C O N . S A H E L . P I P E
G E N T S .   I C E T . I O N
.   S K E T C H A R T I S T
M A C B E T H . O P I E .
A P O . E C R U . Y O D E L S
D R A F T H O R S E . I D O L
R O S I E . A L B A . U G L I
E N T E R . T S A R . M E L T
```

53

```
G O A T . A G E D . A M U S E
L A D Y . F O X Y . T E N O R
A T O P . L A C E . O C C U R
Z E R O T O L E R A N C E .
E R E . H A I L . D E A R T H
.   V O T E . S I S . T A U
A M B E R .   B O O . S A P S
B A R E N E C E S S I T I E S
E G O S . G I G .   D A N D Y
A N A . I R A . T W I G .
M A D A M E . S H O O . I D O
.   E M P T Y P R O M I S E S
C A N O E . A R I D . M A L I
A M E N D . L A V E . P A T E
R I D G E . E Y E D . S C A R
```

54

```
S E E R . S H E D . W E L S H
P A L E . C A V E . A M A N A
A C M E . A M I E . N I T E S
T H E F I R S T M A N T H A T
.   R E D .   A S T A . S K Y
D E F R A U D .   E B B .
O S U . S O O T . E A R L E
H A D A N A R R O W S H I R T
S I D L E . K E M O . N O T
.   P A W .   B O L O G N A
S R I . R H E A .   I N S .
W A S G E O R G E C U S T E R
E D E M A . E R G O . T R I O
P A R E S . C E O S . A U R A
T R E N T . T E S T . R E E D
```

55

```
R O B O T I C S . P I C A R O
I M I T A B L E . E R O T I C
F O R T U N E M A G A Z I N E
T O D O .   V I L A . E L S A
.   E N E . P S T . T E N .
T R E A S U R E H U N T .
O O D L E S . M A S T E R E D
G O G O .   O C S .   R O X Y
A M E N A B L E . N I S S E N
.   G O L D E N F L E E C E
N I H . L A P . O L E .
O R E S . T R O T . F R A U
W E A L T H O F N A T I O N S
I N T A K E . F E M I N I N E
N E S T O R . S W I N D L E D
```

56

L	A	W	S		A	R	B	O	R		W	I	R	Y
A	L	O	E		L	O	I	R	E		A	P	E	S
D	O	R	A		W	A	N	E	D		R	O	S	E
Y	U	K		R	A	N	D	O	M	O	R	D	E	R
		P	R	A	Y	S		A	T	E	S	T		
C	L	A	I	M	S		T	I	P	I	N			
Z	E	R	O	S		K	I	L	L	S		G	U	Y
A	N	T	S		B	I	B	L	E		J	U	N	E
R	O	Y		M	U	T	E	S		W	E	E	D	S
		T	I	M	E	R		R	A	N	S	O	M	
	T	A	I	L	S		P	E	T	I	T			
B	I	T	T	E	R	S	W	E	E	T		H	O	T
R	A	I	L		U	L	E	E	S		B	O	N	O
E	R	L	E		S	U	A	V	E		U	S	E	R
R	A	T	S		H	E	R	E	S		S	T	A	N

57

S	T	E	P		D	E	B	T	S		C	E	D	E
H	U	R	L		U	R	I	A	H		O	V	A	L
I	F	O	U	N	D	R	O	M	E	A	C	I	T	Y
P	A	S	T	E			S	P	E	C	K	L	E	
		O	P	E	D		A	N	N	E				
S	A	N		A	P	E	R		S	E	R	B	I	A
T	W	O		L	I	C	I	T		E	R	N	S	
O	F	B	R	I	C	K	S	A	N	D	L	E	F	T
M	U	L	E		S	E	P	I	A		A	R	E	
P	L	E	D	G	E		S	I	T	H		M	A	R
	F	O	L	D		S	A	L	T					
	S	E	A	B	I	R	D		I	O	T	A	S	
I	T	A	C	I	T	Y	O	F	M	A	R	B	L	E
L	Y	R	E		E	U	L	E	R		S	A	G	A
L	E	N	D		S	P	E	W	S		O	R	A	L

58

N	A	M	E	S		B	A	R	B		B	E	E	F
A	D	A	P	T		A	L	O	E		O	K	R	A
S	O	F	I	A		W	I	T	H	S	U	G	A	R
A	B	I	C	Y	C	L	E	C	A	N	T			
L	E	A		A	A	S		V	A	S	T	L	Y	
		S	T	Y		K	E	E	P		R	O	E	
S	A	F	E		S	T	A	N	D	O	N	I	T	S
U	S	U	R	P		H	B	O		N	E	A	T	O
O	W	N	B	E	C	A	U	S	E		O	D	O	R
M	A	D		S	O	I	L		R	A	N			
I	N	S	T	E	P		T	O	M		F	R	I	
		I	T	I	S	T	W	O	T	I	R	E	D	
L	O	O	K	A	L	I	K	E		R	O	O	N	E
B	A	R	I		O	T	O	E		A	T	S	E	A
S	K	I	S		T	E	S	T		K	A	T	E	S

59

C	P	A		B	I	N	D		E	L	O	P	E	
R	I	N	D		A	L	A	I		T	E	N	O	R
U	N	D	E	R	C	O	V	E	R	A	G	E	N	T
S	T	R	E	A	K		Y	O	U		A	Y	E	
H	O	E		T	A	G		U	N	M	A	N		
		S	E	C	R	E	T	G	A	R	D	E	N	
S	E	C	T		H	A	Y		E	M	O	T	E	
A	L	A	R		E	D	I	T	H		A	N	N	A
S	O	B	I	G		N	I	A		D	E	A	R	
H	I	D	D	E	N	A	G	E	N	D	A			
	R	E	L	A	X		S	K	A		O	R	A	
S	C	I		S	I	S		E	D	I	S	O	N	
C	O	V	E	R	T	O	P	E	R	A	T	I	O	N
O	M	E	G	A		M	I	M	E		S	E	M	I
T	A	R	O	T		S	T	U	D		R	Y	E	

60

N	A	H	S		B	A	G	S		R	S	V	P	
O	R	E	O		E	L	I	T	E		I	L	I	E
B	E	F	O	R	E	B	R	E	A	K	F	A	S	T
L	A	T	T	E	S		L	A	S	V	E	G	A	S
E	S	S		A	T	V		D	Y	E				
		O	L	I	O	S		A	T	H	E	N	S	
E	L	E	M		N	I	T	S		C	O	C	O	A
D	U	R	I	N	G	L	U	N	C	H	H	O	U	R
G	R	E	T	A		A	N	I	L		U	L	N	A
Y	E	S	S	I	R		S	T	U	R	M			
		L	E	T		S	N	O		G	A	R		
V	E	R	M	E	E	R	S		K	A	H	U	N	A
A	F	T	E	R	D	I	N	N	E	R	M	I	N	T
S	T	E	T		S	M	E	A	R		O	D	I	E
E	S	S	O		S	E	E	S		S	E	E	D	

61

S	T	R	I	P		A	B	A	B		U	T	A	H
P	R	I	C	E		R	A	C	E		G	A	L	A
E	A	S	Y	D	O	E	S	I	T		A	K	I	N
W	Y	E		D	I	N	E	D		S	N	E	A	K
		A	L	L	A	H		W	A	D	I			
S	I	D	N	E	Y		I	M	I	T	A	T	E	D
A	N	O	N		E	T	A	P	E		S	L	O	
G	E	N	E	S	I	S		R	E	S	A	L	E	S
A	R	T		A	N	N	E	X		M	O	V	E	
S	T	R	A	N	G	E	R		S	T	E	W	E	D
	U	S	D	A		U	N	I	O	N				
M	I	S	S	Y		S	P	I	L	L		D	O	E
A	C	H	E		S	E	T	T	L	E	D	O	W	N
G	E	M	S		O	M	E	R		D	A	Z	E	D
I	D	E	S		D	I	D	O		O	M	E	N	S

62

I	A	M	B		C	L	O	P	S		A	M	I	S
W	H	O	A		Z	O	R	R	O		T	E	C	H
O	A	T	H		A	L	B	U	M		A	S	I	A
	H	A	I	R	L	I	N	E	C	R	A	C	K	
R	A	B	I	D			T	E	R	R	I	B	L	E
O	N	A		A	D	O		S	S	E		I	E	S
B	O	L	A		I	R	K		A	P	T			
B	A	L	D	I	S	B	E	A	U	T	I	F	U	L
		A	S	A		A	I	L		C	R	E	E	
U	M	P		L	P	S		D	T	S		E	L	M
P	E	R	C	E	P	T	S		E	P	E	E	S	
T	H	I	N	S	O	U	T	U	P	T	O	P		
I	T	O	O		I	D	A	R	E		S	O	R	T
M	A	R	T		N	I	S	A	N		T	R	I	O
E	S	S	E		T	O	I	L	S		S	T	O	P

63

A	D	A	M		B	A	B	A	R		N	A	D	A
G	I	L	A		A	T	A	R	I		O	X	E	N
E	V	E	N		C	O	T	T	O	N	B	E	L	T
S	E	E	D	M	O	N	E	Y		O	L	L	I	E
		A	O	N	E		C	O	Y					
H	E	A	R	T		S	P	A	R	K		F	D	R
A	L	L	I	E	S		O	L	E		A	L	O	E
P	L	A	N	T	E	R	S	P	E	A	N	U	T	S
P	I	N	S		L	I	T		P	I	C	K	E	T
Y	E	S		C	L	A	S	P		R	E	E	D	S
		S	O	S		U	K	E	S					
A	L	T	A	R		B	A	R	N	S	T	O	R	M
F	I	E	L	D	G	U	I	D	E		O	B	O	E
A	F	R	O		U	N	D	U	E		R	I	P	E
R	E	I	N		S	T	E	E	L		S	T	E	T

64

B	A	B	Y		S	T	O	P		A	S	S	E	T
A	C	R	E		U	R	G	E		C	H	O	R	E
C	H	I	N	A	G	I	R	L		C	A	L	L	A
H	E	M		M	A	B	E	L		O	R	D	E	R
		M	I	R	E		M	A	R	D	I			
B	A	G	E	L		S	N	E	R	D		E	L	K
E	L	Y	S	E	E		E	L	I	S		R	O	N
T	O	P	S		S	C	A	L	E		O	B	O	E
A	H	S		S	T	A	R		S	T	R	O	K	E
S	A	Y		T	E	R	S	E		A	B	Y	S	S
	W	I	R	E	D		T	A	N	S				
S	H	O	N	E		I	R	O	N	Y		E	T	A
C	O	M	T	E		G	U	I	T	A	R	M	A	N
A	P	A	R	T		A	B	L	E		O	M	I	T
M	I	N	O	S		N	E	E	D		B	A	L	I

65

B	A	S	E		A	N	T	E		F	J	O	R	D
E	R	A	S		R	O	I	L		L	O	U	I	E
D	U	M	P	T	R	U	C	K		A	I	S	L	E
I	B	M		E	O	N	S		T	I	N	T	E	D
M	A	Y	D	A	Y			P	E	R	T			
		I	R	O	N	M	A	N		C	L	E	F	
N	E	R	V	Y		E	A	R	S		H	A	L	O
A	L	O	E		H	E	N	C	E		I	M	A	X
S	L	A	B		E	D	G	E		R	E	P	L	Y
H	E	R	O		F	L	Y	L	E	A	F			
		M	A	T	E			I	N	S	A	N	E	
W	O	B	B	L	Y		Z	U	L	U		N	A	T
A	R	I	E	L		H	O	L	E	P	U	N	C	H
R	E	T	R	O		B	O	N	E		M	I	R	E
M	O	S	S	Y		O	M	A	N		P	E	E	R

66

T	R	E	Y	■	M	E	S	S	■	A	F	R	O	S
W	A	C	O	■	I	S	L	E	■	C	L	I	N	K
A	S	H	Y	■	S	T	U	N	■	C	A	C	T	I
S	H	O	O	T	F	O	R	T	H	E	M	O	O	N
■	■	■	R	I	P	■	■	O	N	E	■	■	■	■
B	E	I	R	U	T	■	Y	U	R	T	■	D	U	D
A	T	T	I	C	■	P	E	G	S	■	L	E	N	O
T	H	E	S	K	Y	S	T	H	E	L	I	M	I	T
H	O	M	E	■	I	S	I	S	■	E	M	O	T	E
E	S	S	■	V	E	T	S	■	A	T	O	N	E	S
■	■	■	M	E	L	■	E	M	U	■	■	■	■	■
O	N	W	A	R	D	A	N	D	U	P	W	A	R	D
D	E	A	N	S	■	B	A	G	S	■	E	M	I	R
D	A	N	T	E	■	E	P	E	E	■	E	M	M	A
S	T	E	A	D	■	L	A	R	D	■	P	O	E	M

67

R	I	T	E	■	B	L	I	P	■	R	U	S	K	S
O	M	E	N	■	R	A	C	E	■	E	T	H	I	C
S	A	N	D	P	I	P	E	R	■	P	I	E	T	A
E	G	O	■	R	E	S	T	■	K	I	L	L	E	D
S	E	N	I	O	R	■	R	U	N	N	E	L	■	■
■	■	O	P	S	■	A	L	E	E	■	F	L	U	■
T	A	S	T	E	■	M	Y	N	A	■	B	I	A	S
A	Q	U	A	R	I	A	■	A	D	J	U	S	T	S
C	U	R	S	■	N	O	D	S	■	E	T	H	E	R
O	A	F	■	S	A	R	I	■	C	R	Y	■	■	■
■	■	B	L	I	N	I	S	■	A	B	L	E	S	T
A	R	O	U	S	E	■	G	O	T	O	■	T	K	O
M	E	A	N	T	■	S	U	N	B	A	T	H	E	R
M	A	R	G	E	■	O	S	L	O	■	E	Y	E	S
O	R	D	E	R	■	S	T	Y	X	■	A	L	T	O

68

G	O	N	G	■	W	R	A	P	■	E	L	I	O	T
A	S	E	A	■	H	O	S	E	■	R	A	S	P	Y
F	L	A	N	■	I	M	O	K	■	O	X	L	I	P
F	O	R	D	P	R	E	F	E	C	T	■	E	N	E
■	■	H	A	L	O	■	■	R	I	O	T	E	D	■
A	D	L	I	B	■	■	S	M	O	C	K	■	■	■
B	R	A	■	L	O	S	E	R	S	■	R	U	S	E
L	I	N	C	O	L	N	N	E	B	R	A	S	K	A
E	B	A	Y	■	D	A	D	D	Y	O	■	S	I	C
■	■	■	S	L	A	P	S	■	W	O	R	T	H	■
Z	A	F	T	I	G	■	■	T	O	D	D	■	■	■
E	C	O	■	M	E	R	C	U	R	Y	D	I	M	E
S	T	R	A	P	■	O	O	N	A	■	J	O	I	N
T	I	T	L	E	■	O	M	I	T	■	O	W	E	D
Y	I	E	L	D	■	F	A	C	E	■	B	A	N	S

69

S	L	O	W	■	O	H	I	O	■	Y	U	M	A	■
L	A	M	A	S	■	L	A	W	N	■	O	P	A	L
A	V	E	R	T	■	S	L	O	E	■	G	O	R	E
V	A	N	D	Y	K	E	E	N	T	R	A	N	C	E
■	■	O	L	I	N	■	■	A	I	M	■	■	■	■
G	O	L	F	E	R	S	O	B	S	T	A	C	L	E
A	L	O	F	T	■	P	E	T	■	T	R	I	G	■
M	A	V	■	S	W	A	T	T	E	D	■	E	V	E
A	F	E	W	■	I	D	I	■	■	R	O	P	E	S
L	S	D	I	N	D	U	C	E	D	E	V	E	N	T
■	■	■	S	S	E	■	■	C	A	S	A	■	■	■
L	U	R	E	F	O	R	L	O	B	S	T	E	R	S
I	T	E	M	■	P	E	A	L	■	U	I	N	T	A
N	A	N	A	■	E	L	I	E	■	P	O	R	E	D
T	H	E	N	■	N	O	D	S	■	■	N	Y	S	E

70

L	I	S	A	■	A	C	D	C	■	O	M	A	R	■
U	R	I	C	■	N	O	A	H	■	D	O	P	E	■
N	O	T	H	I	N	G	R	E	C	E	D	E	S	■
A	N	S	E	L	■	N	E	R	O	■	E	M	I	T
T	O	T	■	L	E	A	■	U	N	C	R	A	T	E
I	R	I	S	■	S	C	A	B	■	A	N	N	E	X
C	E	L	L	O	S	■	M	I	A	M	I	■	■	■
■	L	I	K	E	S	U	C	C	E	S	S	■	■	■
■	■	■	D	A	N	E	S	■	T	O	T	E	M	S
C	A	R	E	Y	■	A	E	R	O	■	S	C	O	T
O	V	E	R	S	A	W	■	A	R	E	■	U	S	A
T	O	F	U	■	B	O	S	C	■	S	T	R	E	P
■	W	A	L	T	E	R	W	I	N	C	H	E	L	L
■	A	C	E	D	■	L	A	N	E	■	E	L	L	E
■	L	E	S	S	■	D	Y	E	D	■	E	Y	E	S

71

L	I	E	U		E	T	H	I	C		S	C	A	T
A	S	A	P		S	H	U	N	S		A	H	O	Y
C	A	R	D		T	A	B	C	O	L	L	A	R	S
K	O	L	A		O	R	S		N	E	A	R	T	O
		T	S	P			S	K	A		L	A	N	
H	O	M	E	A	P	P	L	I	A	N	C	E		
O	R	A		T	E	L	E	X		T	A	S	E	R
W	E	L	T		D	I	N	G	Y		M	I	L	E
L	O	T	U	S		E	T	U	I	S		I	A	N
	E	N	T	E	R	O	N	E	S	M	I	N	D	
T	A	D		I	N	S		L	E	A				
O	S	M	A	N	I		T	B	D		D	R	E	D
S	H	I	F	T	G	E	A	R	S		D	O	T	E
C	E	L	T		M	E	R	I	T		E	S	T	A
A	N	K	A		A	L	A	M	O		R	Y	A	N

72

M	P	S		S	T	A	Y	U	P		A	T	E	E
O	A	T		D	O	G	E	A	R		R	O	A	R
T	W	O	F	I	S	H	S	W	I	M	I	N	T	O
E	S	A	U		S	A	M		C	E	A	S	E	S
		N	N	E			R	E	T		I	R	E	
A	C	O	N	C	R	E	T	E	W	A	L	L		
S	A	T	Y	R		V	I	T	A	L	E			
P	R	O	M		L	E	M	U	R		G	L	U	E
		E	L	I	N	O	R		S	H	A	G	S	
	O	N	E	T	U	R	N	S	T	O	T	H	E	
B	T	U		H	E	P			A	E	R			
L	O	T	H	A	R		C	U	L		N	O	S	E
O	T	H	E	R	A	N	D	S	A	Y	S	D	A	M
C	O	I	N		T	O	L	E	D	O		D	I	M
S	E	T	S		I	T	I	S	S	O		S	L	Y

73

B	R	A	V	O		R	H	O		A	D	O	P	T
R	I	V	A	L		S	A	L		D	O	V	E	R
A	G	O	N	Y		V	I	E		E	N	U	R	E
T	A	N		M	Y	P	R	O	B	L	E	M	I	S
		S	P	U	D			A	P	E				
Z	A	F	T	I	G		S	H	A	H		U	S	A
I	N	R	E	C	O	N	C	I	L	I	N	G	M	Y
N	E	E	T			O	A	F			E	L	I	A
G	R	O	S	S	H	A	B	I	T	S	W	I	T	H
S	A	N		H	E	H	S		R	O	S	S	E	S
		B	U	M			G	A	M	Y				
M	Y	N	E	T	I	N	C	O	M	E		R	U	N
A	V	E	R	T		E	O	N		D	O	O	Z	Y
K	E	A	N	E		A	D	Z		A	N	N	I	E
E	S	T	E	R		R	E	O		Y	E	A	S	T

74

R	A	M	P	S		C	L	E	M		S	T	U	N
S	M	A	R	T		A	I	D	A		O	H	N	O
V	I	G	O	R		T	M	E	N		L	O	I	S
P	R	I	V	A	T	E	P	R	O	P	E	R	T	Y
		E	W	E	R	S		F	A	S				
D	E	E		H	A	S		A	W	L		S	S	S
E	L	E	N	A			A	D	A		A	L	T	O
F	I	R	S	T	G	E	N	E	R	A	T	I	O	N
O	T	I	C		E	L	Y			L	E	M	O	N
E	E	E		I	T	S		S	O	L		S	L	Y
		A	D	S			S	T	R	I	A			
C	L	A	S	S	A	C	T	I	O	N	S	U	I	T
O	O	P	S		W	A	R	N		O	C	H	O	A
N	O	S	E		A	L	I	T		N	O	O	N	E
S	T	E	T		Y	I	P	S		E	T	H	E	L

75

M	A	D	E	U	P		L	E	S	S		I	T	O
A	S	I	A	N	S		A	L	T	O		B	U	B
C	H	A	R	T	S		G	A	O	L		A	P	E
		G	L	I	T	T	E	R	P	O	W	D	E	R
P	R	O	S	E		O	R	A	L		H	A	L	O
H	E	N		D	E	M			I	R	O	N	O	N
D	E	A	R		T	E	A		G	O	O			
	F	L	A	S	H	I	N	T	H	E	P	A	N	
		P	E	A		A	R	T		I	N	O	N	
F	A	T	T	E	N		I	S	M		N	U	N	
O	L	E	O		A	R	E	A		A	S	O	N	E
S	P	A	R	K	L	E	P	L	E	N	T	Y		
S	A	C		A	L	S	O		L	A	R	I	A	T
E	C	U		M	E	A	D		U	G	A	N	D	A
Y	A	P		A	N	T	E		L	E	D	G	E	R

76

G	R	E	T	A			T	R	A	M			S	T	A	B
R	O	T	O	R			B	O	S	E			A	R	N	E
O	U	T	O	F	S	I	G	H	T			B	E	N	T	
W	E	E	K		A	L	E		T	H	E	M	E	T		
		T	A	L	L	T	A	L	E		E	X	E			
M	A	S	O	N	S			L	E	A	R	N				
E	M	U		T	A	B	O	O		R	I	D	G	E		
L	A	P	S	E		I	O	N		H	O	O	E	Y		
S	H	E	L	L		T	H	E	S	E		U	N	E		
	R	O	O	S	T			W	A	I	S	T	S			
M	A	D			P	A	S	S	P	O	R	T				
A	M	U	L	E	T		E	A	R		H	O	O	F		
R	I	P	A		I	N	C	R	E	D	I	B	L	E		
I	D	E	S		R	I	T	E		A	N	O	D	E		
S	E	R	E		E	A	S	E		S	K	E	E	T		

77

J	O	K	E		Z	A	I	R	E			E	B	R	O
A	C	E	S		E	R	R	O	L			N	E	O	N
C	H	I	C	K	E	N	O	U	T			R	A	C	E
O	R	T	H	O		O	N	T	O		I	R	K	S	
B	E	H	E	L	D		S	E	N	E	C	A			
		W	A	I	T				S	O	H	O	S		
K	I	S	S		A	R	A	F	A	T		A	K	A	
E	N	E		A	N	I	M	A	L	S		N	I	P	
N	R	A		V	E	X	I	N	G		O	D	E	S	
T	I	L	D	E			G	E	L	T					
	A	O	R	T	A	S		R	A	T	T	L	E		
U	N	D	O		I	R	A	E		C	A	R	A	T	
F	E	E	D		M	O	N	K	E	Y	W	I	T	H	
O	R	A	L		E	S	T	E	R		A	C	H	E	
S	O	L	E		R	E	A	D	S		S	E	E	R	

78

M	O	R	E		P	A	S	O		K	A	S	H	A
B	R	E	N		I	B	A	R		E	Q	U	A	L
A	C	D	C		N	E	V	A		R	U	B	L	E
	C	A	K	E	D	E	C	O	R	A	T	O	R	
S	E	R	M	O	N			L	A	Y		L	E	T
C	R	O	P	D	U	S	T	E	R		F	E	S	S
A	S	S		I	T	C	H		S	A	L			
T	E	S	L	A		H	U	B		C	U	P	P	A
	A	K	A		M	I	T	T		H	O	P		
J	A	M	B		C	A	B	D	R	I	V	E	R	S
O	R	A		E	N	D		A	V	I	A	T	E	
C	A	T	T	L	E	D	E	A	L	E	R	S		
O	B	I	E	S		U	C	L	A		T	A	T	E
S	I	N	A	I		C	O	A	L		U	N	I	T
E	A	G	L	E		E	N	N	A		E	T	C	H

79

B	E	N	D		D	A	L	I	S			S	T	Y	E
O	N	A	N		A	R	E	N	A			Q	U	A	D
S	O	D	A	B	R	E	A	D	S			U	G	L	I
C	C	I		A	N	T	S	Y		B	E	S	E	T	
S	H	A	W	N	E	E		P	I	E					
	A	E	R		P	R	E	T	Z	E	L	S			
	A	R	T	S		P	E	T	P	E	E	V	E	S	
G	L	E	E		Y	E	S	E	S		P	E	N	T	
E	S	P	R	E	S	S	O	S		I	L	L	S		
T	O	O	L	S	E	T	S		A	N	A				
	I	S	R		M	I	D	Y	E	A	R				
A	N	G	L	O		S	H	A	R	I		A	L	A	
M	A	Y	I		B	E	E	R	B	A	T	T	E	R	
E	T	R	E		M	A	R	I	A		R	A	V	E	
R	O	O	S		W	R	O	N	G		I	T	E	R	

80

M	A	N	E	T		S	O	P	H	S		S	A	C
E	L	I	T	E		C	R	E	E	K		I	R	E
M	O	M	E	N	T	A	R	I	L	Y		S	A	D
O	N	O	R	D	E	R		I	M	B	I	B	E	
	G	Y	N		N	E	B		P	A	Y	S		
		A	F	T		A	D	A	P	T	E	R	S	
T	A	B	L	E		I	Z	O	D		E	N	Y	A
E	R	R		D	A	D	A	I	S	M		O	A	F
R	I	O	T		S	E	A	N		B	O	R	N	E
M	A	N	E	A	T	E	R		B	A	T			
	Z	E	R	O		S	E	E		T	E	D		
K	E	E	N	A	N		X	E	R	O	X	E	D	
I	R	A		F	I	R	S	T	F	A	M	I	L	Y
W	I	G		A	S	T	E	R		C	A	L	V	E
I	C	E		T	H	E	T	A		K	N	E	E	S

81

S	T	I	N	T		B	A	M	A		A	M	M	O
T	A	N	G	O		A	V	E	S		T	O	A	D
R	U	N	O	N		R	O	S	H		L	A	M	E
A	P	E	R	S	O	N	W	H	O	H	A	T	E	S
P	E	R		I	C	Y		E	R	A	S			
		C	L	E	A	N	S	E	R		O	A	K	
S	H	O	O		A	R	I		E	L	O	P	E	
T	O	S	P	E	N	D	H	I	S	M	O	N	E	Y
A	L	L	A	N		I	S	U		O	A	R	S	
N	E	O		E	V	I	L	O	M	E	N			
	I	R	A	N		T	U	T		O	P	S		
H	A	S	C	O	S	T	R	O	P	H	O	B	I	A
E	L	I	A		S	O	A	P		E	V	E	N	T
M	O	R	N		A	N	N	E		L	U	S	T	Y
S	U	E	T		L	E	G	S		S	M	E	A	R

82

N	A	V	A	L		G	I	B	E		G	I	S	T
A	T	A	R	I		A	G	U	A		A	M	I	E
M	O	N	T	E		Z	E	S	T		R	A	G	S
E	M	S		S	E	E	T	H	E	L	I	G	H	T
			P	L	E	B		R	E	S	E	T	S	
S	C	H	O	O	L	O	F	F	I	S	H			
W	I	D	O	W		O	W	E	S		Z	E	N	
A	N	T	H		K	U	R	D	S		N	U	K	E
N	E	V		F	A	S	T		R	O	L	E	S	
	B	I	T	E	S	T	H	E	D	U	S	T		
B	R	A	I	N	Y		E	E	N	S				
B	E	D	A	N	D	B	O	A	R	D		M	A	S
G	P	A	S		I	O	N	S		E	N	A	C	T
U	R	G	E		D	O	T	E		R	E	N	T	A
N	O	E	S		S	P	O	T		S	T	E	E	R

83

A	D	A	M	S		S	H	O	W		C	A	D	S
L	E	T	A	T		C	O	C	O		O	M	I	T
E	M	E	R	Y	P	A	P	E	R		L	E	V	Y
C	O	N	C	L	U	D	E	A	S	C	E	N	E	
		O	E	R		N	T	H	S					
R	A	Y	S		P	A	R	S		A	L	U	L	A
E	R	A		M	O	P	E		U	R	A	N	U	S
L	O	W	C	A	R	B	S	A	N	D	W	I	C	H
I	M	P	O	S	T		O	A	K	S		T	E	E
C	A	S	T	E		S	W	A	N		F	E	S	S
	T	R	E	Y		O	H	O						
	S	H	O	U	L	D	E	R	W	A	R	M	E	R
E	L	A	N		U	N	S	A	N	I	T	A	R	Y
M	A	Z	E		D	E	S	I		T	E	R	S	E
S	P	E	D		E	Y	E	D		I	S	L	E	S

84

P	E	S	A	H		F	L	A	W		O	V	I	D
O	C	H	R	E		A	E	R	O	S	P	A	C	E
P	R	O	C	R	A	S	T	I	N	A	T	I	O	N
S	U	R		A	S	T	I		N	I	N	N	Y	
	T	A	T	A		T	A	N	G	O				
B	A	L	L		P	A	B	L	O		N	A	P	A
A	R	I	E	L		S	E	I	N	E		G	I	N
G	I	V	E	S	U	S		N	O	T	H	I	N	G
E	S	E		D	R	U	S	E		C	A	T	E	R
L	E	D	A		G	R	I	S	T		L	A	D	Y
	S	T	E	E	R		H	A	L	T				
I	D	A	H	O		L	O	A	D		E	S	P	
T	O	L	O	O	K	F	O	R	W	A	R	D	T	O
S	T	A	R	T	E	D	I	N		G	A	L	E	S
A	S	W	E		N	A	N	O		E	G	Y	P	T

85

T	O	S	S		A	L	F	I	E		N	A	G	S
L	O	T	T		M	I	L	N	E		O	P	A	L
C	H	E	R	R	Y	P	I	C	K		S	O	L	E
		M	A	O		S	P	A		F	I	L	L	E
S	E	C	T	O	R			S	N	A	R	L	U	P
C	R	E	A	M	O	F	T	H	E	C	R	O	P	
A	I	L		Y	E	A	H		T	E	E			
D	E	L	E		R	I	O			E	S	T	A	
		M	E	W		E	N	G	R		C	A	M	
	A	P	P	L	E	O	F	O	N	E	S	E	Y	E
S	W	O	L	L	E	N		U	S	O	P	E	N	
C	H	L	O	E		F	U	N		E	M	T		
O	I	L	Y		M	I	N	C	E	W	O	R	D	S
F	L	E	E		A	R	I	A	S		Z	E	U	S
F	E	N	D		P	E	T	A	L		A	S	H	E

86

M	A	D	G	E		S	L	O	T			T	A	C	T
O	M	A	H	A		T	I	N	A		A	M	I	D	
R	E	L	O	S		A	V	E	R		C	P	A	S	
A	L	L	S	Y	S	T	E	M	S	G	O				
L	I	A	T		E	E	R	O		P	S	A	L	M	
E	A	S	T	M	A	N		N	E	A		F	O	E	
	O	A	T		M	T	V		C	R	E	W			
O	N	W	I	T	H	T	H	E	S	H	O	W			
L	I	E	N		L	O	N		R	U	E				
A	S	H		T	E	N		M	E	N	A	C	E	S	
S	E	I	K	O		G	M	A	T		T	O	M	E	
	L	O	O	K	O	U	T	B	E	L	O	W			
D	A	L	I		B	O	I	L		A	D	A	T	E	
A	M	E	N		I	N	R	E		Y	O	D	E	L	
B	Y	T	E		E	G	A	D		S	N	A	R	L	

87

W	A	D	E	R		R	E	A	P		D	O	P	E
A	L	O	N	E		O	G	L	E		I	L	E	X
G	O	L	D	D	I	G	G	E	R		A	I	R	E
S	E	E		E	V	E	S		F	A	M	O	U	S
			P	E	E	R		S	U	M	O			
T	O	T	E	M	S		C	O	M	A	N	C	H	E
A	R	R	A	S		G	O	R	E		D	O	O	M
P	A	I	R		S	U	I	T	S		H	A	L	E
E	T	A	L		T	I	N	S		P	E	T	E	R
R	E	D	H	E	A	D	S		B	R	A	S	S	Y
			A	R	G	O		G	O	O	D			
C	H	A	R	G	E		P	I	N	G		S	R	O
H	E	R	B		S	I	L	V	E	R	S	T	A	R
O	R	E	O		E	R	I	E		A	L	I	C	E
P	E	A	R		T	E	E	N		M	O	R	E	L

88

S	L	I	P		S	E	E	M	S		W	R	A	P
T	U	T	U		O	L	L	A	S		I	A	G	O
A	L	I	T		C	E	A	S	E		S	C	A	T
B	U	N	T	S	I	G	N	S		P	E	E	R	S
			P	R	E	Y	S		L	A	S	H		
A	C	Q	U	I	T			S	E	C	T	O	R	S
S	H	U	T		Y	U	P	P	I	E		R	E	O
T	E	E	T	H		S	O	U		R	O	S	S	I
O	R	E		Y	I	E	L	D	S		K	E	E	L
R	I	N	G	E	R	S		E	G	E	S	T	S	
	S	I	N	E		H	E	N	R	Y				
O	L	I	V	A		M	A	J	O	R	D	R	A	G
L	A	Z	E		T	O	N	E	R		O	H	I	O
A	M	E	N		D	A	N	C	E		K	E	R	N
F	E	S	S		S	T	A	T	S		E	A	S	E

89

B	O	O	B		B	E	G	S		S	O	R	T	S
R	U	D	E		E	R	I	E		C	R	O	A	T
A	C	I	D		R	A	F	T		A	B	A	T	E
T	H	E	S	K	Y	S	T	H	E	L	I	M	I	T
			P	A	L	E			N	E	T			
	B	A	R	B		R	A	C	E	D		T	R	E
W	I	S	E	U	P		G	A	R		T	H	U	G
I	T	S	A	L	L	O	R	N	O	T	H	I	N	G
L	E	A	D		E	K	E		S	H	I	R	T	S
D	R	Y		O	A	S	E	S		E	N	D	S	
			S	T	S		L	A	R	K				
B	E	T	T	H	E	H	O	U	S	E	O	N	I	T
A	D	O	R	E		A	L	M	S		V	O	T	E
S	E	D	E	R		R	I	P	E		E	V	E	N
K	N	O	W	S		P	O	S	T		R	A	M	S

90

T	O	A	D		A	C	I	D		S	W	I	P	E
O	S	L	O		B	O	O	R		O	H	A	R	A
T	H	E	B	E	S	T	W	A	Y	T	O	G	E	T
E	A	S	E	L		S	A	G	A		O	O	P	S
			T	L	C			N	A	P				
A	T	O	T	S	A	T	T	E	N	T	I	O	N	
H	O	M	E		B	A	R	R	I	O		B	O	B
E	M	I	R	S		R	U	R		P	L	A	T	O
M	E	T		P	A	S	S	E	D		A	M	I	N
	I	S	T	O	S	I	T	D	O	W	N	A	N	D
		O	T	T			W	E	D					
A	F	R	O		R	E	A	P		S	M	O	C	K
L	O	O	K	C	O	M	F	O	R	T	A	B	L	E
P	A	D	U	A		M	E	R	E		R	O	A	N
S	L	E	P	T		A	W	E	D		K	E	P	T

91

C	A	S	A		A	H	S		M	A	K	E	I	T
E	V	E	R		M	A	E		O	L	I	V	I	A
L	I	N	G		I	S	M		M	I	D	A	I	R
E	A	S	Y	A	S	P	I	E		E	S	S		
S	T	I	L	L	S			L	E	N	T	I	L	S
T	O	N	E	D		P	A	I	R		U	V	E	A
E	R	G		R	E	E	L		I	N	F	E	S	T
			D	I	S	P	O	S	E	O	F			
R	E	R	U	N	S		H	O	S	T		F	O	O
O	P	E	C		A	S	A	P		I	N	L	A	Y
M	I	C	K	E	Y	S		W	O	O	E	R	S	
			A	S	P		N	O	C	O	N	T	E	S	T
G	A	L	O	O	T		A	R	M		A	C	M	E
A	L	L	U	D	E		T	E	A		T	E	A	R
G	A	S	P	E	D		H	E	N		E	R	N	S

92

A	B	E	T		D	A	N	E		E	R	O	D	E
B	O	R	E		A	L	E	X		L	I	V	E	R
C	O	I	N		R	E	N	E		E	V	E	N	S
S	P	E	E	D	Y	R	E	C	O	V	E	R	Y	
			M	E	L	T		S	E	T				
A	L	L	E	N		S	A	T	I	N		T	A	N
W	E	A	N	E	D		G	A	R		A	A	R	E
F	A	S	T	B	A	L	L	P	I	T	C	H	E	R
U	S	E	S		M	O	E		S	E	C	O	N	D
L	E	D		P	A	S	T	E		P	O	E	T	S
			G	A	S		S	T	E	R				
Q	U	I	C	K	O	N	T	H	E	D	R	A	W	
C	U	R	V	E		D	E	A	R		I	O	W	A
E	A	G	E	R		D	A	T	E		O	V	E	N
E	D	E	N	S		S	T	E	W		N	E	S	T

93

B	E	A	D		W	A	S	P		S	H	R	E	D
A	N	N	A		A	G	U	E		Q	U	A	K	E
B	U	T	K	U	S	A	N	D	A	U	S	T	E	N
A	R	I	A	S		G	A	L	A	H	A	D	S	
S	E	C	R	E	T	E		N	O	D				
			E	L	U	T	E		Y	A	K	S		
S	N	O	W	F	A	L	L		M	A	R	I	A	
P	O	W	E	L	L	A	N	D	P	O	W	E	L	L
E	V	E	R	Y		A	I	R	P	L	A	N	E	
W	A	D	E		B	U	R	R	O					
			Y	E	S		E	P	I	T	A	P	H	
E	T	A	G	E	R	E	S		R	O	D	E	O	
M	O	B	Y	A	N	D	C	A	L	A	M	I	T	Y
I	N	E	R	T		T	A	R	A		M	E	A	L
R	I	L	E	S		O	B	E	Y		Y	U	L	E

94

L	I	S	P		M	O	L	T		C	O	M	E	R
O	N	C	E		O	M	O	O		A	V	A	S	T
E	A	R	N		A	N	O	N		M	E	L	T	S
S	P	I	N	E	T	I	N	G	L	E	R			
S	T	P	A	T			S	A	T	I	R	E	S	
			M	A	R	S	H		G	O	C	A	R	T
F	I	N	E	T	U	N	E	D		E	N	N	A	
E	R	O		S	T	O	R	I	E	S		D	I	N
L	E	T	S		B	O	N	E	T	I	R	E	D	
I	N	C	A	S	H		N	E	N	E	S			
D	A	H	L	I	A	S		R	E	U	S	E		
			T	E	L	E	P	H	O	N	E	T	A	G
N	A	D	I	R		V	E	E	R		N	I	N	E
E	L	D	E	R		E	R	L	E		O	L	D	S
T	E	T	R	A		R	P	M	S		W	E	S	T

95

A	P	A	C	E		R	O	L	L		T	R	A	M
B	O	G	U	S		O	G	E	E		R	E	N	O
C	O	U	R	T		U	R	N	S		A	L	I	T
	R	E	V	E	N	G	E	I	S	A	D	I	S	H
			Y	E	A	H		N	O	V	I	C	E	S
O	E	D		M	O	N	A		N	O	T			
I	R	I	S		M	E	S	S		W	I	T	T	Y
L	I	K	E	V	I	C	H	Y	S	S	O	I	S	E
S	C	E	N	E		K	E	N	T		N	E	A	T
			S	I	N		S	T	A	R		S	R	I
A	V	A	I	L	E	D		H		E	S			
B	E	S	T	S	E	R	V	E	D	C	O	L	D	
A	N	T	I		D	Y	E	S		I	D	I	O	M
S	U	E	Z		L	U	T	E		P	A	N	D	A
H	E	R	E		E	P	O	S		E	S	T	O	P

96

S	A	L	E	M	■	O	M	N	I	■	T	Y	P	O
A	B	O	D	E	■	B	E	E	R	■	H	O	O	P
N	A	T	U	R	A	L	G	A	S	■	R	U	L	E
E	S	T	■	I	L	O	■	L	A	T	E	R	O	N
R	E	O	■	N	I	N	O	■	G	O	S	H	■	■
■	■	N	O	T	G	I	V	E	A	H	O	O	T	■
K	I	T	E	S	■	L	I	N	D	■	N	B	A	■
E	G	A	D	■	C	A	R	E	T	■	M	O	O	R
L	O	X	■	G	O	B	I	■	■	E	G	R	E	T
P	R	I	M	A	L	S	C	R	E	A	M	■	■	■
■	S	E	L	L	■	H	A	L	T	■	S	S	W	■
H	O	T	S	E	A	T	■	M	M	E	■	P	T	A
A	L	A	S	■	P	R	I	S	O	N	R	I	O	T
G	E	N	E	■	S	I	R	E	■	U	N	C	L	E
S	O	D	S	■	E	X	E	S	■	P	A	Y	E	R

97

L	I	M	A	■	S	L	A	K	E	■	A	S	E	A
A	S	I	S	■	C	I	T	E	S	■	N	E	O	N
B	A	S	H	T	H	E	O	P	P	O	N	E	N	T
E	I	S	■	I	M	N	O	T	■	V	O	A	■	■
L	A	M	P	P	O	S	T	■	S	A	Y	S	N	O
S	H	E	E	T	■	■	A	L	L	■	H	O	W	■
■	■	T	O	P	E	A	C	E	■	L	O	W	E	■
■	S	P	R	E	A	D	T	H	E	N	E	W	S	■
M	P	A	A	■	R	I	V	E	T	E	D	■	■	■
A	C	S	■	S	E	T	■	■	T	I	L	E	S	■
W	A	S	H	E	S	■	W	A	S	P	N	E	S	T
■	F	A	N	■	I	R	I	N	A	■	A	C	E	■
F	E	A	S	T	O	N	E	S	E	Y	E	S	O	N
O	M	I	T	■	O	C	A	L	A	■	E	E	R	O
R	U	L	E	■	F	A	K	E	D	■	L	S	T	S

98

C	A	F	E	■	E	C	L	A	T	■	S	P	A	S
A	R	I	D	■	S	O	A	R	S	■	N	I	N	E
L	I	F	E	S	T	R	U	C	K	B	I	R	D	S
M	A	I	N	L	A	N	D	■	■	O	P	A	R	T
■	■	■	A	T	E	■	T	V	S	■	T	E	E	■
S	I	C	K	B	E	A	D	S	I	N	S	E	A	T
A	C	C	E	S	S	■	W	A	I	S	T	■	■	■
L	U	C	Y	■	■	P	E	R	■	E	N	D	S	■
■	■	E	A	S	E	L	■	P	R	I	E	S	T	■
H	A	N	D	L	E	S	T	R	I	A	N	G	L	E
E	R	E	■	O	T	T	■	U	L	M	■	■	■	■
L	E	A	S	H	■	■	E	N	G	O	R	G	E	S
L	O	R	N	A	F	F	A	I	R	S	N	E	S	T
O	L	E	O	■	H	O	S	N	I	■	A	N	T	I
S	E	R	B	■	A	B	Y	S	M	■	S	E	E	R

99

K	A	S	E	M	■	A	F	O	O	T	■	A	H	A
I	R	E	N	E	■	U	L	T	R	A	■	J	I	B
T	R	A	C	T	■	R	I	C	K	I	L	A	K	E
H	O	B	O	■	A	A	R	■	P	I	X	E	L	■
S	W	I	M	U	P	S	T	R	E	A	M	■	■	■
■	■	S	I	R	E	■	■	E	R	N	E	S	T	S
N	I	C	A	D	■	C	A	T	S	■	S	H	O	P
L	S	U	■	U	P	A	T	R	E	E	■	O	D	A
E	L	I	A	■	I	D	L	Y	■	A	L	T	O	S
R	A	T	R	A	C	E	■	■	T	R	I	P	■	■
■	■	O	U	T	T	O	P	A	S	T	U	R	E	■
A	F	L	A	T	■	■	Z	A	P	■	I	T	E	R
S	A	C	R	E	D	C	O	W	■	E	N	T	E	R
H	U	D	■	U	C	O	N	N	■	S	T	E	V	E
E	N	S	■	R	I	D	E	S	■	C	O	R	E	D

100

U	R	N	S	■	S	L	A	P	■	M	A	N	G	O
S	E	A	T	■	P	O	L	O	■	A	G	E	R	S
D	A	T	A	■	E	G	O	S	■	N	A	M	E	S
A	P	O	R	T	C	I	T	Y	I	N	I	O	W	A
■	■	■	A	K	C	■	■	S	E	N	■	■	■	■
S	P	O	R	T	S	■	L	A	U	D	■	A	B	A
A	E	I	O	U	■	B	E	N	Z	■	A	T	O	P
C	O	L	U	M	N	O	F	N	U	M	B	E	R	S
K	N	E	E	■	I	N	T	O	■	A	L	I	N	E
S	Y	R	■	S	T	A	Y	■	S	C	E	N	E	S
■	■	■	P	E	R	■	■	S	H	H	■	■	■	■
A	D	V	I	S	O	R	Y	C	O	U	N	C	I	L
L	I	A	N	A	■	E	U	R	O	■	A	U	R	A
B	O	S	O	M	■	A	L	I	T	■	P	R	O	S
A	R	E	T	E	■	L	E	M	S	■	S	E	N	T

101

P	L	A	Y		A	B	I	D	E		M	A	L	E
A	A	R	E		P	O	S	E	R		A	N	I	L
W	H	I	S	P	E	R	I	N	G	P	I	N	E	S
N	R	A		A	M	I	S				O	Z	O	N	E
				F	R	A	N		C	O	O	E	D		
R	O	A	R	I	N	G	S	U	R	F		O	R	G
I	D	L	E	S			P	R	E	S		M	O	A
D	O	P	E		S	H	O	E	S		L	I	S	T
E	R	E		O	L	E	O			E	E	N	I	E
S	S	N		H	O	W	L	I	N	G	W	I	N	D
	H	A	Y	E	S			L	O	R	D			
A	M	O	C	O			A	L	O	E		P	T	A
M	U	R	M	U	R	I	N	G	S	T	R	E	A	M
E	S	N	E		E	S	T	E	E		A	R	N	O
N	E	S	S		P	A	S	T	S		M	U	S	K

102

C	O	T	E		F	E	U	D		M	A	R	S	H
O	D	O	R		U	R	G	E		I	D	A	H	O
H	E	Y	E	R	D	A	H	L		N	A	V	A	L
O	T	B		Y	D	S		P	E	T		E	N	D
S	T	O	L	E			C	H	E	Y	E	N	N	E
T	A	X	I		S	N	A	I	L		N	O	O	R
			B	A	R	A	K			S	T	U	N	S
	H	E	R	S	H	E	Y	B	A	R	S			
A	D	O	R	E			P	I	E	C	E			
R	A	P	T		S	H	A	P	E		A	L	P	S
T	H	E	Y	U	K	O	N			A	T	A	R	I
I	L	L		S	A	M		F	A	A		W	E	E
S	I	E	G	E		I	R	I	S	H	E	Y	E	S
T	A	S	E	R		N	O	S	H		D	E	N	T
E	S	S	E	S		Y	O	K	E		U	R	S	A

103

D	A	R	T		S	K	I	S		T	A	M	P	A
O	L	I	O		T	O	R	O		A	D	I	E	U
R	A	N	T		A	N	O	N		K	A	R	E	N
A	N	G	E	R	M	A	N	A	G	E	M	E	N	T
			M	A	P			R	E	F				
R	A	P		G	A	L	S		M	I	L	E	R	S
A	R	O	N		C	I	T	E		V	A	L	U	E
D	I	R	E	C	T	M	A	R	K	E	T	I	N	G
A	S	T	R	O		A	L	A	I		E	T	T	U
R	E	S	O	R	T		E	T	N	A		E	Y	E
			P	O	P			D	N	A				
V	O	O	D	O	O	E	C	O	N	O	M	I	C	S
A	N	W	A	R		R	O	M	E		P	R	O	P
S	E	L	M	A		I	R	I	S		L	A	L	A
E	A	S	E	L		L	E	T	S		E	N	D	S

104

	D	A	S	H		P	A	C	T	S		A	L	T
	E	D	I	E		A	S	Y	E	T		L	I	I
	L	O	T	I	O	N	A	D	D	I	T	I	V	E
V	O	A		G	T	E				C	R	E	E	D
A	R	N		H	O	L	M		S	K	I	N	N	Y
S	E	N	A	T	E		A	G	R	I		S	S	E
C	A	I	R	O		S	K	I	I	N	G			
O	N	E	O	F		P	E	G		T	R	O	M	P
		O	F	A	R	M	S		H	I	R	E	R	
H	U	G		A	N	Y	A		R	E	T	I	R	E
U	N	R	E	S	T		D	R	A	W		G	I	S
B	R	A	S	H				E	P	A		I	N	S
B	E	T	T	I	N	G	S	E	T	T	I	N	G	
L	A	I		O	R	E	A	D		E	S	A	U	
E	L	S		N	A	T	T	Y		R	O	L	E	

105

N	A	A	C	P		O	L	M	E	C		P	R	Y
A	R	M	O	R		G	U	A	V	A		Y	E	P
H	I	P	P	O	C	R	A	T	E	S		T	A	R
				B	L	E	U		R	I	C	H	I	E
C	A	L	L	O	U	S		S	E	N	I	O	R	S
A	R	I	A	N	E		R	E	A	G	A	N		
P	R	O	V	O		D	E	E	D	S		E	F	T
E	O	N	S		M	E	A	T	Y		T	S	A	R
K	W	H		C	A	R	L	O		P	I	Q	U	E
		E	M	I	N	E	M		M	I	S	U	S	E
N	E	A	T	N	I	K		C	A	C	H	E	T	S
G	A	R	N	E	T		T	I	N	A				
A	R	T		M	O	N	K	E	Y	S	H	I	N	E
I	L	E		A	B	H	O	R		S	E	N	O	R
O	E	D		S	A	L	S	A		O	X	I	D	E

106

```
C O M B   S P A T S   D O T S
H A I R   T A R R Y   A N E W
O T T O   I D I O M   R E P O
P H E W   G R A Y M A T T E R
    N O M E     E C H O E D
C A N O L A   M O T E
A L O U D   B O A R D G A M E
M A S T   T E S T Y   R I O T
P R E S E R V E S   D E M O N
    R A Y S   S I E S T A
S P R A I N   S W A N
W H I T E S A U C E   C O D A
E A S E   M O P E D   A L A I
A S E A   I N O N E   R I L L
T E R M   T E N T S   D O E S
```

107

```
E A T S   R A M S   S C E N E
S L O E   E R I E   H A D I T
S O L E   F I L T H Y R I C H
E E L   B U D D H A   A C H E
    C L O G     M U T T E R
S T A I N E D G L A S S
H A L V E   R E E S E   S T S
O I L Y     O N A   A N E W
E L S   W A L E S   C L A R A
    F O U L S H O O T I N G
A L L I E D     I D O L
N E A T   I M M U N E   M A P
D I R T Y T R I C K   M A L L
E G G E D   E L L E   V I S A
S H E D S   D E A D   P L O Y
```

108

```
S P A   E L G I N   A B A S E
H E D   N O O N E   V A N E S
O D D   T A N K S   O C T E T
W A L K I N G S T I C K
S L E E T     S I E R R A S
    A L E P H   S T E E L E
O A K   E L I O T   S L O G
S T A N D I N G O V A T I O N
C O L A   T A P I R   C F O
A N I M A L   N I M B I
R E F E R E E   O L D I E
    S I T T I N G R O O M S
M A M A S   A D O R E   U P S
A W A K E   P O S I T   S E A
C E D E S   E L E N A   E L Y
```

109

```
J A B S   A B E T   P E A C E
E Z R A   D A T A   O X B O W
W A I L   D I N T   S A R G E
E L D E R S T A T E S M A N
L E A S E     O N E   S O D
S A L   P I A N O S   M I M E
    K A T I E   R A V E N
  S E N I O R C I T I Z E N
M O T O R   K N I F E
A P E X   T A S S E L   S O B
E R R   M O W   E L O P E
  A N C I E N T M A R I N E R
A N I O N   I R O N   T A R T
L O T T O   N E A T   U T A H
A S Y E T   G E N E   P A S S
```

110

```
C A R S   S T R O M   S E A L
I R A N   P A U L O   E D D Y
T I N A   I N T E R   C O D E
R O C K I N G H O R S E
U S H E R     S I E S T A S
S O O   A E R O   S E S A M E
    S T R O K E     I R O N
  P A P E R B A C K B O O K
D E C O   S Y R I A N
D A R K E N   S U N K   A D A
T R E E T O P   E S S E N
  S C I S S O R S K I C K
T E A M   S H A M E   I D O L
A R I A   E A R E D   M E R E
B A R N   S W A N S   P S S T
```

111

P	H	O	T	O		A	N	A	S		S	M	U	G
R	O	P	E	R		P	A	R	A		H	E	M	P
A	N	T	E	D		E	D	G	Y		O	O	P	S
Y	E	S	T	E	R	D	A	Y	S	N	E	W	S	
		E	R	A			L	O	O	S				
S	T	A	R		V	A	L	E		S	H	A	R	P
L	U	G		I	A	G	O		P	H	O	B	I	A
A	T	H	I	N	G	O	F	T	H	E	P	A	S	T
S	T	A	N	C	E		T	O	A	D		S	E	E
H	I	N	D	U		D	Y	E	S		F	E	R	N
		O	B	E	Y			E	T	A				
	A	N	C	I	E	N	T	H	I	S	T	O	R	Y
T	H	A	I		R	A	M	A		A	T	S	E	A
S	O	I	L		I	M	A	M		R	E	S	A	W
P	Y	L	E		E	O	N	S		S	N	A	P	S

112

A	B	Y	S	M		S	P	E	C		S	H	A	D
W	R	O	T	E		L	A	M	A		C	O	C	O
L	A	Y	E	R		A	L	E	C		H	A	R	T
S	T	O	P	G	A	P	M	E	A	S	U	R	E	
	P	E	R				R	O	A	M				
A	B	L	E		E	E	L	S		M	A	I	D	S
T	O	O		A	N	T	I		S	O	N	N	E	T
L	O	O	K	B	A	C	K	I	N	A	N	G	E	R
A	S	S	E	S	S		E	R	I	N		O	R	E
S	T	E	R	E		S	N	A	P		S	T	E	W
		O	N	C	E			E	R	E				
	L	I	S	T	E	N	T	O	R	E	A	S	O	N
M	I	T	E		L	A	R	D		U	S	A	G	E
A	M	E	N		E	T	U	I		S	O	R	E	R
D	O	M	E		B	E	E	N		E	N	D	E	D

113

A	L	O	N	E		S	P	O	T		A	C	M	E
B	E	A	U	X		L	E	A	H		T	H	E	N
E	A	R	T	H	Q	U	A	K	E		K	I	E	V
T	D	S		A	U	N	T		F	L	I	N	T	Y
		F	L	A	K		F	R	A	N	C			
S	O	L	O	E	D		M	O	O	N	S	H	O	T
E	M	I	R	S		R	A	N	G	E		I	C	E
T	A	P	E		V	O	L	T	S		F	L	E	A
U	N	I		L	A	S	T	S		S	O	L	A	R
P	I	Z	Z	E	R	I	A		T	E	X	A	N	S
		Z	O	W	I	E		H	O	A	X			
U	G	A	N	D	A		C	A	W	S		E	V	A
T	A	N	K		B	R	O	W	N	I	E	M	I	X
A	G	E	E		L	U	R	K		C	L	I	N	E
H	A	R	D		E	N	D	S		K	I	T	E	S

114

E	L	I	H	U		F	A	C	T	S		P	A	R
S	I	T	O	N		I	N	U	R	N		A	P	E
P	E	S	T	C	O	N	T	R	O	L		R	O	M
			T	U	R	N	S	T	O		M	T	G	E
E	F	F	E	T	E			S	P	R	A	Y	E	D
A	I	L	S		G	O	B	Y		B	U	S	E	Y
T	R	E	T		A	F	R		S	I	L	T		
S	E	A		E	N	T	A	I	L	S		O	R	B
	M	E	M	O		I	L	E		B	R	I	O	
A	L	A	R	M		I	D	L	E		A	E	O	N
G	E	R	M	A	N	S		P	I	G	S	T	Y	
A	N	K	A		E	R	E	L	O	N	G			
S	T	E		H	E	A	R	I	N	G	A	I	D	S
S	E	T		A	D	E	L	A		O	G	L	E	S
I	N	S		T	Y	L	E	R		T	E	A	M	S

115

G	O	E	R		P	E	R	U		P	E	S	O	S
U	L	E	E		R	O	O	M		G	R	I	T	S
L	I	G	H	T	E	N	U	P		A	R	M	O	R
P	O	S	E	A	S		T	E	E	T	I	M	E	S
		A	C	T	S		D	R	O	N	E			
P	A	T	R	I	O	T	S		R	U	G	R	A	T
A	V	A	S	T		A	P	O	O	R		D	E	E
R	A	K	E		C	H	I	L	L		L	O	R	E
T	I	E		B	A	L	E	D		S	A	W	I	N
S	L	I	P	U	P		S	A	L	T	I	N	E	S
		T	A	T	E	R		S	E	E	D			
M	A	E	S	T	R	O	S		S	N	A	R	L	S
G	R	A	T	E		M	E	L	L	O	W	O	U	T
R	I	S	E	R		A	G	E	E		A	B	B	A
S	L	Y	L	Y		N	O	S	Y		Y	S	E	R

116

M	U	M	P	S			L	A	N	E			R	Y	E	S
A	P	A	R	T			I	D	O	L			E	U	R	O
S	T	R	I	A			E	A	S	T			A	L	A	S
H	O	L	D	Y	O	U	R	H	O	R	S	E	S			
			E	S	P				E	N	O	S				
T	O	Y	S			T	E	N	D			M	I	L	C	H
I	V	E			M	I	M	E			P	A	G	O	D	A
M	I	N	D	Y	O	U	R	M	A	N	N	E	R	S		
I	N	T	E	R	N			V	E	T	O			S	O	P
D	E	A	L	T			G	E	N	E			I	S	M	S
			E	L	S	E			N	O	G					
	B	I	T	E	Y	O	U	R	T	O	N	G	U	E		
M	I	N	I			R	I	V	E			M	O	U	N	D
O	T	T	O			I	D	E	A			P	R	A	T	E
P	E	O	N			A	S	A	P			H	E	R	O	N

117

M	P	H			B	O	O	M			P	A	S	T	E
I	R	A			S	I	L	K	Y			E	W	E	R	S
C	O	L	D	C	R	E	A	M			T	E	E	U	P
A	F	F	O	R	D			P	Y	R	E			R	E	N
			R	A	B	B	I			E	R	A	S			
O	E	D	I	P	A	L			E	X	O	D	U	S		
L	Y	E	S			T	U	R	N			S	O	C	K	S
G	I	N			O	H	F	U	D	G	E			K	O	A
A	N	V	I	L			F	R	E	E			K	E	D	S
	G	E	O	D	E	S			A	N	G	O	R	A	S	
			R	U	S	E			T	R	I	E	D			
A	R	M			A	L	A	R			U	N	A	B	L	E
C	H	I	L	L			F	I	R	S	T	K	I	S	S
T	E	N	E	T			E	P	E	E	S			T	A	P
S	A	T	E	S			W	E	D	S			S	T	Y

118

L	A	I	R			A	T	S	E	A			E	P	O	S
A	L	S	O			L	E	T	U	P			M	U	S	T
G	I	L	D			P	E	A	R	L			I	S	L	E
S	T	E	E	P			M	O	O	N	S	H	O	T		
			T	O	S	S	U	P			M	A	S	T		
P	A	T			S	O	S	O			B	R	A	H	M	S
A	B	E			T	R	E	F			C	R	E	E	K	
P	U	R	R			T	S	A	R	S			Y	E	T	I
A	S	P	E	R			P	A	L	E			N	O	R	
S	E	E	P	E	D			P	R	A	Y			V	O	L
	R	A	N	I			R	E	V	E	R	E				
A	L	F	R	E	S	C	O			S	U	L	K	S		
D	U	E	T			C	A	V	E	D			M	O	N	A
O	N	C	E			U	S	A	G	E			O	P	E	N
S	A	T	E			S	A	L	O	N			R	E	E	D

119

S	O	L	A	R			T	U	B			G	I	S	T	S
O	P	I	N	E			U	R	I			U	N	L	E	T
F	E	E	T	F	I	R	S	T			S	C	O	R	E
A	N	D			U	L	N	A	E			S	H	O	R	E
			L	E	S	T			S	L	E	E	P	E	R	
C	E	R	U	L	E	A	N			E	T	S				
A	L	U	M	S			B	A	R	N			A	T	A	D
L	I	M	B			E	L	I	O	T			L	A	L	O
L	E	S	E			G	E	L	S			W	O	M	E	N
			R	N	A			S	A	M	E	N	E	S	S	
P	L	A	Y	I	N	G			P	I	N	G				
L	I	L	A	C			A	P	A	R	T			O	P	S
A	F	I	R	E			V	E	R	A	M	I	L	E	S
N	E	E	D	S			E	E	K			A	N	G	E	R
E	R	N	S	T			L	P	S			D	E	A	L	S

120

G	T	O	S			E	C	R	U			M	R	B	I	G
R	A	N	T			T	O	E	S			O	O	O	L	A
A	B	I	E			C	R	A	M			T	O	Y	E	D
B	L	O	W	T	H	E	L	I	D	O	F	F				
S	A	N	E	R				N	O	R			R	E	S	
			D	I	G	U	P	T	H	E	D	I	R	T		
B	O	B			P	O	R	E			D	I	E	G	O	
L	U	R	E			O	N	A	I	R			S	N	O	W
A	T	A	R	I			R	O	U	T			D	T	S	
B	R	I	N	G	T	O	L	I	G	H	T					
S	E	N			U	M	A			E	R	A	T	O		
	C	R	A	C	K	W	I	D	E	O	P	E	N			
S	H	E	E	N			L	O	B	E			J	A	R	S
T	U	L	S	A			E	R	I	E			A	C	M	E
P	E	L	T	S			Y	E	S	M			N	E	S	T

121

M	A	M	M	A		I	R	E	N	E		S	T	L
A	L	E	R	T		T	E	X	A	N		T	R	I
E	L	A	S	T	I	C	B	A	N	D		R	A	N
		D	U	R	H	A	M		N	I	E	C	E	
M	A	S	O	N	R	Y		L	O	I	T	E	R	
A	P	P	L	E	S		S	T	A	T	I	C		
L	I	R	E		A	C	U	T	E		H	T	S	
T	A	I		D	A	M	A	G	E	S		L	A	W
A	N	N		E	T	A	T	S		T	I	K	I	
	G	A	M	I	N	S		T	H	A	M	E	S	
S	U	B	D	U	E		S	H	A	R	O	N	S	
A	R	O	A	R		E	A	T	O	U	T			
M	B	A		R	U	B	B	E	R	N	E	C	K	S
O	A	R		E	N	O	L	A		T	S	A	R	S
A	N	D		D	I	N	E	D		S	T	R	A	W

122

W	H	I	P	L	A	S	H	E	S		S	A	G	A
N	O	R	E	A	S	T	E	R	S		E	D	E	N
B	L	O	W	I	N	I	N	T	H	E	W	I	N	D
A	M	C	S		E	C	C	E		A	N	N	I	E
		W	A	K	E	S		R	U	S	E	S		
	S	T	P	A	T			E	S	P				
W	O	O	E	D		P	A	N	E		H	E	S	
J	U	M	P	I	N	J	A	C	K	F	L	A	S	H
M	R	S		E	S	S	O		A	O	R	T	A	
		S	A	T			E	T	U	D	E			
J	A	P	A	N		H	A	U	L	S				
A	B	O	U	T		O	R	L	O		E	L	E	C
P	U	T	T	I	N	O	N	T	H	E	R	I	T	Z
E	T	T	E		T	H	E	R	I	V	I	E	R	A
S	S	S	S		S	A	L	A	M	A	N	D	E	R

123

P	A	N	S		E	G	R	E	T		E	C	C	E
A	B	U	T		G	U	I	L	E		R	O	O	T
R	I	C	O		E	S	S	E	N		A	L	G	A
A	D	L	A	I	S	T	E	V	E	N	S	O	N	
N	E	E		S	T	A		T	I	E	R	O	D	
G	R	I	E	F		V	P	S		P	R	A	M	S
		T	O	E		A	I	L		D	E	O		
	G	E	O	R	G	E	C	L	I	N	T	O	N	
H	E	M		O	A	K		P	O	E				
E	N	O	L	A		U	S	A		T	A	R	P	S
R	E	T	O	S	S		B	B	C		E	R	E	
	R	I	C	H	A	R	D	J	O	H	N	S	O	N
B	O	O	K		R	E	R	U	N		E	A	T	S
R	U	N	E		A	D	O	R	E		S	L	O	E
A	S	S	T		H	O	P	E	S		T	E	N	D

124

L	I	Z	A		J	E	R	K		O	P	A	R	T
A	L	A	N		A	R	E	A		R	E	N	E	E
M	I	N	D	O	N	E	S	P	S	A	N	D	Q	S
P	A	Y	I	N	G		T	O	U	T		A	D	S
		E	E	L	S		K	N	O	B				
G	S	A		T	E	A	M		D	R	U	M	U	P
I	N	L	A	W		C	A	G	E		S	I	R	E
B	O	D	Y	O	F	K	N	O	W	L	E	D	G	E
B	O	E	R		A	S	O	F		E	D	S	E	L
S	T	R	E	A	K		R	A	P	T		T	D	S
		S	T	E	S		R	A	H	S				
A	O	L		R	I	C	E		L	A	L	A	L	A
S	P	I	R	I	T	O	F	S	T	L	O	U	I	S
K	E	A	N	U		T	O	U	R		T	R	A	P
S	C	R	A	M		T	R	E	Y		H	A	M	S

125

M	A	S	T		W	I	S	C		E	D	G	E	D
A	L	T	O		A	R	E	A		R	O	U	T	E
Y	O	U	R	P	L	A	C	E	O	R	M	I	N	E
O	H	D	E	A	R		S	S	T		D	A	M	
R	A	Y		P	U	T		A	I	S	L	E		
		C	A	S	H	O	R	C	R	E	D	I	T	
	S	S	R		E	A	R		A	G	O	R	A	
I	O	T	A		S	W	O	O	P		A	G	A	R
W	O	R	D	Y		N	A	E		T	S	E		
O	N	E	L	U	M	P	O	R	T	W	O			
	S	E	P	A	L		S	S	E		P	A	P	
S	S	S		T	A	G		H	A	I	R	D	O	
C	O	F	F	E	E	T	E	A	O	R	M	I	L	K
A	R	U	B	A		T	R	I	P		A	M	I	E
R	E	L	I	T		E	E	L	S		M	O	B	Y

126

G	A	P	E	■	A	R	E	A	S	■	E	B	A	Y
I	R	O	N	■	S	E	T	T	O	■	W	A	N	D
B	L	T	S	■	T	E	T	O	N	■	E	L	I	S
B	E	A	U	T	I	F	U	L	G	I	R	L	S	■
E	N	T	E	R	■	■	L	S	D	■	R	E	P	■
R	E	O	■	A	H	A	B	■	■	S	C	O	T	T
■	■	C	A	B	L	E	S	■	P	O	T	S	■	■
■	N	E	V	E	R	B	O	T	H	E	R	M	E	■
C	E	D	E	■	P	A	T	R	O	L	■	■	■	■
P	E	G	G	Y	■	■	S	E	R	B	■	L	O	U
A	D	E	■	E	S	S	■	■	■	O	V	O	I	D
■	I	W	I	S	H	T	H	E	Y	W	O	U	L	D
L	E	I	S	■	I	R	A	T	E	■	L	I	M	E
A	S	S	N	■	N	A	V	A	L	■	T	S	A	R
S	T	E	T	■	S	P	E	L	L	■	S	A	N	S

127

S	C	A	R	F	■	H	O	D	■	T	S	A	R	S
P	A	G	E	S	■	I	T	O	■	L	E	V	E	L
A	N	A	D	U	L	T	I	S	■	C	R	E	D	O
■	E	R	R	■	E	L	C	I	D	■	B	R	E	W
■	■	■	A	C	T	I	■	D	O	G	■	A	Y	E
O	N	E	W	H	O	S	N	O	L	O	N	G	E	R
P	O	L	■	A	N	T	I	■	E	L	I	E	■	■
T	W	A	N	G	■	S	E	T	■	F	L	O	S	S
■	■	B	E	R	G	■	C	A	S	T	■	U	K	E
G	R	O	W	I	N	G	E	X	C	E	P	T	I	N
O	A	R	■	N	A	H	■	B	R	E	R	■	■	■
O	V	A	L	■	T	E	R	R	A	■	I	O	U	■
D	A	T	E	S	■	T	H	E	M	I	D	D	L	E
A	G	E	N	T	■	T	E	A	■	C	E	D	E	D
T	E	D	D	Y	■	O	A	K	■	E	S	S	E	S

128

B	L	A	H	■	S	H	E	P	■	H	O	N	O	R
R	E	D	O	■	H	A	Z	E	■	O	M	A	N	I
O	V	E	R	B	O	A	R	D	■	M	E	T	E	D
W	I	N	D	O	W	G	A	R	D	E	N	I	N	G
■	■	■	E	N	T	■	S	O	O	T	■	O	D	E
W	A	S	S	A	I	L	■	■	T	E	E	N	■	■
E	S	Q	■	■	M	E	S	O	■	A	I	W	A	■
D	O	U	B	L	E	I	N	D	E	M	N	I	T	Y
■	F	A	R	E	■	F	L	E	X	■	■	D	O	E
■	■	L	O	S	T	■	■	S	I	C	K	E	N	S
E	L	L	■	T	O	M	B	■	T	A	I	■	■	■
C	O	L	O	R	T	E	L	E	V	I	S	I	O	N
O	U	I	D	A	■	T	I	E	I	N	S	A	L	E
L	I	N	E	D	■	O	N	E	S	■	E	G	G	O
I	S	E	R	E	■	O	D	E	A	■	R	O	A	N

129

M	E	L	D	■	A	M	I	S	H	■	E	R	M	A
I	R	A	E	■	P	I	N	T	O	■	D	E	A	R
M	I	K	E	H	O	L	D	E	R	■	G	E	N	E
I	C	E	■	E	L	K	S	■	S	L	I	D	E	S
C	A	S	U	A	L	■	■	E	E	E	■	■	■	■
■	■	■	G	R	O	V	E	O	F	T	R	E	E	S
S	M	E	L	T	■	E	N	C	L	S	■	R	I	O
L	A	D	Y	■	M	I	N	T	Y	■	B	A	R	D
A	T	E	■	R	A	N	E	E	■	B	U	S	E	S
V	E	N	D	O	R	S	S	T	A	L	L	■	■	■
■	■	■	A	O	L	■	■	C	E	L	E	B	S	■
A	D	D	S	T	O	■	S	E	C	S	■	U	R	E
Y	E	A	H	■	W	I	T	N	E	S	S	B	O	X
E	L	L	E	■	E	T	U	I	S	■	N	I	K	E
S	E	E	D	■	S	E	N	D	S	■	L	E	E	S

130

A	B	B	A	■	J	A	B	B	A	■	S	W	A	P
D	Y	E	R	■	A	U	R	A	S	■	W	H	I	R
A	C	L	E	A	N	D	E	S	K	■	A	E	R	O
P	A	L	■	P	A	R	T	S	■	M	R	E	D	■
T	R	A	P	P	■	E	T	C	■	T	I	E	■	■
■	■	D	E	W	Y	■	L	T	R	■	W	A	G	■
S	O	N	A	T	A	■	P	E	R	U	■	A	S	A
I	S	A	S	I	G	N	O	F	A	M	E	S	S	Y
A	L	I	■	Z	E	E	S	■	S	P	R	I	T	E
M	O	L	■	E	S	P	■	T	H	E	E	■	■	■
■	S	P	R	■	A	M	I	■	T	I	C	K	S	■
J	A	D	E	■	L	U	C	I	E	■	O	N	O	■
U	F	O	S	■	D	E	S	K	D	R	A	W	E	R
N	E	W	T	■	E	S	T	E	E	■	E	L	L	E
O	W	N	S	■	N	E	S	T	S	■	S	S	T	S

131

M	O	U	N	D		P	E	R	E		R	O	A	D
A	B	N	E	R		O	P	E	N		O	N	L	Y
N	O	T	W	O	R	K	I	N	G		O	T	O	E
N	E	O		P	I	E	C	E		E	T	H	E	R
	H	I	N	D	U		A	L	E	E				
E	B	B	I	N	G		R	I	V	E	R	B	E	D
M	I	R	E		M	E	D	I	C		L	E	I	
C	L	O	S	U	R	E		A	S	T	A	I	R	E
E	L	K		S	E	E	P	S		S	N	I	T	
E	Y	E	T	E	E	T	H		S	P	I	K	E	S
	N	E	R	D		A	G	E	R	S				
S	O	D	A	S		E	N	E	R	O		E	F	T
A	D	O	S		O	U	T	O	F	O	R	D	E	R
L	O	W	E		T	R	O	D		F	U	G	U	E
E	R	N	S		T	O	M	E		S	E	E	D	Y

132

R	A	M	P	S		U	N	I	T			F	B	I
A	R	E	A	S		S	I	G	H		P	R	O	M
P	L	A	C	E	V	A	L	U	E		Y	E	L	P
T	O	N	I		C	R	E	E	D		R	E	D	S
		F	I	R	M		S	A	T	E	S			
M	U	S	I	C		Y	D	S		E	X	P	O	S
U	N	I	C	E	F		U	S	P	S		E	L	K
S	I	D		D	R	O	P	O	U	T		E	L	I
E	T	E		T	Y	R	E		G	R	A	C	I	E
D	E	E	R	E		A	D	D		U	S	H	E	R
	F	E	A	S	T		R	A	N	T				
S	O	F	A		I	O	T	A	S		A	S	A	P
O	P	E	C		F	R	O	G	P	R	I	N	C	E
S	E	C	T		T	I	T	O		A	R	O	M	A
A	N	T		S	O	O	N		J	E	W	E	L	

133

O	O	P	S		E	L	M	O		H	O	O	D	S
S	L	E	W		R	O	A	N		A	R	N	I	E
S	A	L	E		E	L	I	E		L	A	I	N	E
O	F	F	E	R	S	A	N	A	P	O	L	O	G	Y
	T	O	T		S	T	A		E	N	Y	A		
L	O	V	E	B	U	G		A	Y	E	S			
O	V	E	N		A	P	T	T	O		V	I	E	
B	E	G	S	F	O	R	G	I	V	E	N	E	S	S
E	R	A		M	A	D	A	M		C	E	L	T	
	E	S	S	E		E	S	C	A	P	E	E		
M	E	S	A		I	N	N		T	E	A			
E	X	P	R	E	S	S	E	S	R	E	G	R	E	T
S	C	E	N	T		P	A	L	E		A	H	M	E
T	O	N	E	R		O	T	I	S		M	E	I	N
A	N	D	R	E		T	O	M	S		E	A	R	S

134

B	E	E	P	S		S	E	A		E	P	I	C	S
O	R	L	O	N		A	M	P		E	R	R	O	L
D	I	E	T	I	N	G	I	S		K	E	A	N	U
E	N	C		T	I	E	R	E	D		S	T	E	M
		T	U	C	K		A	S	S	E	S	S		
F	O	R	T	H	O	S	E	W	H	O				
A	L	O	T		N	A	V	E		A	L	S	O	P
C	A	D	E	T		D	E	N		P	A	L	M	E
E	Y	E	R	S		I	N	C	A		R	Y	A	N
	A	R	E	T	H	I	C	K	A	N	D			
S	A	L	A	R	Y			M	O	S	S			
A	B	E	L		E	I	L	E	E	N		A	N	G
D	O	A	L	L		T	I	R	E	D	O	F	I	T
A	D	R	O	P		E	R	A		O	R	O	N	O
T	E	N	T	S		M	E	T		S	E	X	E	S

135

H	O	A	R	D		A	D	O	S		S	T	A	N
E	R	R	O	R		B	A	R	K		C	O	L	E
N	A	M	B	Y	P	A	M	B	Y		A	P	S	O
S	L	Y		L	A	C	E		D	A	M	S	O	N
	D	A	N	K		H	I	P	P	Y				
S	E	W	I	N	G		L	I	V	E	I	T	U	P
T	R	I	E	D		B	A	K	E	S		U	S	E
E	A	S	T		E	L	D	E	R		T	R	U	E
A	S	H		S	N	E	E	R		R	I	V	A	L
K	E	Y	N	O	T	E	S		B	E	R	Y	L	S
	W	E	I	R	D		M	O	V	E				
F	L	A	T	L	Y		A	I	D	E		B	A	H
L	O	S	T		W	I	L	L	Y	N	I	L	L	Y
A	C	H	E		A	C	M	E		G	R	O	O	M
B	O	Y	D		Y	E	A	R		E	A	T	E	N

136

```
A B C S   S T A I R   X E N A
S O U L   T I N N Y   E L E M
H O P A L O N G C A S S I D Y
    M A L E S   N C O
B A N D W I D T H   H U R O N
A R O U N D     E C O T O N E
R E I N     I G L O O   G E E
  S K I P T O M Y L O U
A L I   L O I N S   C I T E
N E E D L E S     C L O S E R
G A R R I   I N A L A T H E R
    A N O   E L E M I
J U M P I N G O F F P L A C E
I S E E   C A N I T   L I A R
M E N D   E S S E S   O D D S
```

137

```
S A L A D   S P O T   M O R E
A L A M O   T O U R   A M E X
C I G A R   E N T O U R A G E
      P E N N Y P I N C H E R
S A L A M I   U S A   A N T
E V A   I N L E T   B E S T S
C O L A   E A T   A L E
T W O B I T C H I S E L E R S
      A N Y   E R S   S T O W
G L A S S   T R A I T   A L A
A I T   I C E   S U B L E T
S T O P S O N A D I M E
P A N E T E L L A   B R I E F
E N C E   D E A R   L E O N E
D Y E R   S Y N E   E T U D E
```

138

```
S W A G   R A M P S   R Y A N
A R G O   E X I L E   E A S E
P A R K A V E N U E   A R I D
S T E A L   D E N Y   R D A S
  H E R S       G A T E S
    T O D A T E   O N T O P
R E F S   E R R   E N D I V E
A L I   R E C A L L S   C E E
T I E S U P   S I S   W K R P
S A L T S   C H E E S E
    D I T T O   P L A N
A T T N   E L S A   A L T O S
C U R T   P L A I N T O A S T
E R I E   E A G L E   F R E E
S F P D   E R A S E   F I S T
```

139

```
B B S   S H A G G Y   S A K I
R O E   N O R R I S   I M A S
A N T   L U C I L L E B A L L
Y E T I   R E M   R O N E E
  R O N A L D M C D O N A L D
    A N Y   L E S
S P A R K   E L I A   K I T E
T H O M A S J E F F E R S O N
A I L S   H E A T   M A I N E
    T I C   O A K
V I N C E N T V A N G O G H
A C O R N   E M U   W O E S
D A V I D C A R U S O   M I T
I R E S   S U B S E T   E D U
M E L S   A S S E S S   R I B
```

140

```
K N E W   S C O O P   S W A M
A O N E   C H I N A   K O L A
F L E E B A I L E Y   I R O N
K A M P A L A   S I D L E S
A N Y   L E N S   G O D
    J E D G A R H O O V E R
S A G A S   B I E R   I R E
P L A N   P O B O X   R E N E
E E L   O R C A   J E W E L
C E V E R E T T K O O P
  E R A   H E C K   B A A
R E S A L E   L E E W A R D
A C T S   Z C A V A R I C C I
S H O E   R O B I N   P O E T
P O N D   A L A N S   E N D S
```

141

```
L I T H E | B R E D | C H A T
A S W A N | L I P O | L A T H
W R I S T | A G I N | I N T O
  S P R I N G C H I C K E N
I N T | I N C | O O H I N G
M O T H E R H E N | N E E D S
A R I O S O | D O T S |
X M E N | A P I S H | M B A S
  E D I T | E T A L I A
A R R O W | C H O W H O U N D
D A W N O N | P H I | E T E
S T A L K I N G H O R S E
O H N O | P E R U | S A Y A H
R E D A | A R A L | T R E K S
B R A N | T O Y S | S A D A T
```

142

```
L O O M | S P E R M | O D D S
A L L Y | M E L E E | C R O P
M I D S H I P M A N | T A P A
P O S T I T S | S T A G E S
  E Y E | C R A I G
  A B R A | P R O | L O T U S
T R E Y | L I E U T E N A N T
E O E | B E N A T A R | L I E
C S F O R E S T E R | T O T S
H E S S E | O E D | M A N S
  M E A N S | L O P
R E S O D S | O I L I E S T
E V E N | H O R N B L O W E R
D E A D | E D U C E | C O M A
S S T S | N O B E L | A K I M
```

143

```
S O N G | A S A P | S T E N O
O V E R | V A S E | P U L E D
S A R A | I L S A | I L I A D
O L D F L A M E | T R I E R S
  T U T O R | O O P
B A N | C E N T E R | B O D E
A B A C I | S A S | U S E D
S O M E D A Y | R I F L I N G
I D E A | S O B | O B E S E
L E S S | S U I T O R | R E D
  E S E | G R O U P
M I S F I T | F I L M S T A R
U N P I N | I O T A | A R L O
S C A R E | C O O L | L E A D
S H R E W | E T N A | M E N S
```

144

```
S T R E W | B O S S | L A W N
E B O N Y | A N T E | B R I E
A S A L E W H E R E | J I L T
S P R I T E | S I S | R A Y S
  S H E L | P A P A
B A R T | T E A | W A N G L E
A D O | T O A D S | S C R O D
Y O U G E T S O M E T H I N G
O R S O N | T R A L A | P E A
U N E A S E | E S P | H E R R
  L E I S | H A L E
J E E P | F H A | S E R B I A
E X P O | F O R N O D D I N G
T I E S | E R I E | G E N R E
S T E T | L E D A | E D G E S
```

145

```
F A R M | C A N O E | W H O A
A G U A | A G O R A | O U R S
D E B U T S T H I S M O N T H
  S E L A H | E Y E | T E L
  D R A G I N | L I E G E
B E G I N S O N T U E S D A Y
I M O N | S A T | P E P
N O B | S E L E C T S | Z A P
  P U T | R E O | C O D A
S T A R T S I N O N E H O U R
N H L E R | R E S O L E
A R I | A C E | G A M U T
K I C K S O F F T O N I G H T
E L I A | C U O M O | S L U R
S L A Y | A L G I D | T I D Y
```

146

```
L E O N A   A L S O P   R O O
A C T O R   P A T I O   E S P
I H I T T H E B A L L   L A T
N O S E   A M O R   T I K I
    A S H A R D A S I C A N
R U S S I A N   A C H E
O B E Y S   E T H E R N E T
B E T   C I V E T   I L E
B R I S B A N E   A L L I S
    A R I A   E E R I E S T
I F I C A N F I N D I T
T A N K   A N T I   H E R O
S K A   I H I T I T A G A I N
M I N   T E N E T   F O S S E
E R E   E N T R Y   T W E E D
```

147

```
A S T I   A D E L E   G O A D
H O A R   N O L A N   O H N O
A U T O   T A M I L   L I O N
B R A N C H L O C A T I O N
    H A I L   C A M
A P P A L L   T R E S P A S S
T R U N K L I N E S   C U E
W I N D S   O O P   C A R E R
A C T   O U T O N A L I M B
R E S P O N S E   E L U D E S
    E R S   S W I M
    F O R B I D D E N F R U I T
W I G S   G R A D E   O N C E
O S L O   H A L A S   O D E A
W H E N   T W I N S   T O S S
```

148

```
N O V   S H I E L D   P A S S
A L I   P A R L E Y   A R I A
R I G   A G O L F E R W I T H
C O I F   G N A T   A N S E L
    L E I A   A P S E S
A H A N D I C A P I S
L A N C E   A G E D   S P A M
E S T E S   R N A   A T O N E
S H E D   O P E C   M O L D S
    O N E W H O P L A Y S
    C R O A T   U S E R
S H O O T   T A C T   N I C K
W I T H H I S B O S S   Z O O
A L O E   M A L L E T   E L O
N E R D   P R E T T Y   D E L
```

149

```
B B Q S   O D O R   B A M B I
R O U T   P I N A   A L I E N
A T E E   E V E N   T V S E T
W H E N I R E A D T H A T
L A R O S A   D Y E   E A N
    G A N G   D E L R I O
A T V   D E A L   O X B O W
D R I N K I N G I S E V I L I
R I D O F   T O F U   G I S
E N E S C O   E G O S
M I O   L O U   G R A N G E
    G A V E U P R E A D I N G
C R A Z E   T S O S   D E A R
R E M U S   R E N T   A C R E
O V E R T   E T A S   M E L T
```

150

```
N E H R U   F E T C H   L E S
A L O E S   L A U R A   O R A
B O W A N D A R R O W   C V I
S I L L   A G N E W   A K I N
    I S M S   E N T R A N T
M A R S H   H E N   H O N
A R O M A T I C   S E N D E E
R A D   R I P O S T E   K A Y
C L A S P S   N E P A L E S E
    N A E   C O N   S A Y E R
C O D F I S H   T E T S
L U R E   C A B I N   T O M B
A T E   L A W A N D O R D E R
I R E   I L E N E   P O I S E
M E L   P E D A L   S W E A T
```

151

P	E	D	S	■	S	P	L	A	T	■	C	A	R	Y

P E D S ■ S P L A T ■ C A R Y
U L E E ■ K E E P A ■ I P S O
N A T E ■ I R A N I ■ A P T S
D Y E D I N T H E W O O L
I N S Y N C ■ A A R ■ E T E
T E T ■ L A V A ■ N A P P E D
■ S E R E N A ■ A I D S
T I N T E D G L A S S E S
M I N I ■ A L E R T S
E L O P E R ■ E S T E ■ O K D
A L F ■ D O S ■ I A G R E E
■ F R O S T E D F L A K E S
O H I O ■ T E R R A ■ E N N A
F I C A ■ R E L I C ■ L E A D
T E E D ■ A D E P T ■ S Y N E

152

L E T S ■ A C I D ■ E L D E R
I T E M ■ S A D E ■ N O O S E
E U R O ■ T R E E ■ G O R M E
S I N G E R G A R F U N K E L
■ ■ G O O ■ ■ A L S
S T I N G S ■ H A L F ■ G A M
C A C A O ■ B O L D ■ D O P E
A R E I N D A Y S O F Y O R E
P O U R ■ A R L O ■ R E F I T
E S P ■ C R E E ■ B E R Y L S
■ A L E ■ B R O
G A L L E R Y P A I N T I N G
O N A I R ■ E A R N ■ H O A R
S T U C K ■ A G O G ■ E T N A
H I D E S ■ H E N S ■ M A A M

153

S T R A P ■ C A P P ■ C O L D
O H A R E ■ A G E E ■ O B I E
B U C K R O G E R S ■ C O M A
S S E ■ F L E D ■ T A K E O N
■ R I G S ■ S E L A
P A G O D A ■ M A R I N E R S
A L L O Y ■ R A V E ■ D E A L
T A O S ■ J O K E D ■ B R I E
T R O T ■ U S E D ■ G U I L D
I M M E R S E S ■ N O L E S S
■ R U T S ■ V I O L
M A N T R A ■ S I N G ■ R U E
A R I A ■ T O M C O L L I N S
M A L I ■ A R E A ■ E A T I T
A B E L ■ D E E R ■ S P A T E

154

K I T E ■ S C R A P ■ J O L T
A C R E ■ A R E T E ■ O B O E
Y O U L L N E V E R G U E S S
O N E ■ O D E S ■ A S S E T
■ P R E P ■ H A L T E R S
H A T R E D ■ W E L L S
O L I O ■ M E R G E ■ A I M
Y A D D A Y A D D A Y A D D A
A N Y ■ T O N G S ■ W A L L
■ M E L E E ■ E N A M E L
S T R E A K S ■ T R E Y
O R A L S ■ A I R S ■ G I G
D O N T E V E N G O T H E R E
A L E E ■ A L T E R ■ U N I T
S L E D ■ T I E R S ■ M E S S

155

M A T T ■ M E S S ■ P O E M S
A L O E ■ A L T A ■ E N D A T
S C A R ■ R O I L ■ S E U S S
C O M M O N P R A C T I C E
O V A ■ W E E ■ D U L L A R D
T E N O N ■ S C O R E ■ T A I
■ W E D ■ L I V ■ S O T S
G E N E R A L E L E C T R I C
O P U S ■ M A R ■ S A E
D I M ■ S P I K E ■ D W A R F
S L E E T E D ■ L U G ■ P O I
■ O R D I N A R Y P E O P L E
A G A I N ■ W A S P ■ S E L L
M U L C T ■ A G E E ■ S A I D
P E S T S ■ Y S E R ■ O R E S

156

D	E	N	S		A	O	R	T	A		A	L	O	E
E	M	I	T		C	L	U	M	P		G	I	L	A
P	E	T	E	S	E	E	G	E	R		A	G	E	S
T	E	E	T	H			S	N	O	W	S	H	O	E
H	R	S		E	B	B			P	A	S	T		
			P	A	U	L	S	C	O	F	I	E	L	D
H	U	L	A		C	O	A	R	S	E		N	A	Y
E	C	O	L	I		W	W	I		R	O	U	T	E
M	L	S		T	S	E	T	S	E		A	P	E	D
P	A	T	S	C	H	R	O	E	D	E	R			
	H	A	H	A			S	U	M		H	E	X	
T	H	E	B	Y	R	D	S		I	N	A	N	E	
Y	E	A	R		P	A	M	S	H	R	I	V	E	R
P	A	R	E		E	T	U	D	E		N	E	M	O
O	P	T	S		N	A	G	I	N		O	N	Y	X

157

S	O	L	O		C	H	I	A		D	U	S	T	S
E	R	I	N		H	I	L	L		E	N	N	U	I
E	S	K	I	M	O	P	I	E		S	H	O	R	N
T	O	E	T	A	P	P	E	R		T	O	W	N	S
O	N	A		S	P	Y		T	H	R	O	B		
			S	K	Y		S	N	O	O	K	U	M	S
P	U	P	A	S		T	E	E	N	Y		N	Y	C
A	T	O	P		N	U	R	S	E		A	N	N	A
S	A	L		C	A	N	I	S		B	R	Y	A	N
T	H	E	R	A	V	E	N		B	A	T			
	V	O	T	E	S		C	O	Y		A	S	P	
I	P	A	S	S		M	E	L	B	O	U	R	N	E
R	O	U	T	E		I	C	E	B	U	C	K	E	T
A	L	L	E	Y		T	H	A	I		L	I	R	E
N	O	T	R	E		H	O	R	N		A	N	D	S

158

A	B	E	T		S	W	A	B		P	R	O	B	E
R	I	M	E		N	A	I	L		A	A	R	O	N
E	L	A	L		A	L	D	A		S	N	E	A	D
A	L	I	E	N	P	L	A	N	E	T	S			
S	Y	L	V	I	A		C	A	R	O	M	S		
		I	N	T	R	A		T	A	M	A	L	E	
O	P	U	S		A	D	R	E	M		L	E	I	
F	O	R	E	I	G	N	M	I	N	I	S	T	E	R
F	R	I		N	U	K	E	D		T	A	P	E	
S	T	A	N	D	S		N	E	R	V	E			
	S	H	E	E	T	S		A	I	R	I	N	G	
		E	X	O	T	I	C	D	A	N	C	E	R	
A	S	I	D	E		A	L	A	I		E	A	V	E
D	U	R	E	R		M	I	S	S		S	M	E	E
D	E	E	D	S		P	A	T	H		T	E	R	N

159

N	O	T	S	O		I	S	L	A	M		C	O	P
I	M	H	I	P		L	H	A	S	A		A	K	A
S	E	E	T	H	E	L	I	G	H	T		T	R	Y
A	N	T	H	E	M		M	O	L	U	C	C	A	S
N	S	A		L	E	T		S	A	R	A	H		
		F	I	R	E	D		R	E	P	E	L	S	
R	E	F	R	A	I	N	E	D		S	U	S	I	E
A	B	I	E		L	A	P	I	N		L	O	F	T
U	R	G	E	D		M	O	V	E	M	E	N	T	S
L	O	U	D	E	R		T	O	B	I	T			
	R	O	M	E	O		T	U	X		A	R	E	
C	H	E	M	I	S	T	S		L	E	A	V	E	N
R	E	O		G	E	T	T	H	E	D	R	I	F	T
A	R	U		O	D	E	U	M		U	T	T	E	R
M	O	T		D	A	R	N	S		P	E	A	R	Y

160

M	A	P	S		S	T	O	L	E		D	I	S	C
A	L	O	U		T	A	P	E	R		E	C	H	O
S	T	O	P	P	U	T	T	I	N	G	M	E	O	N
C	A	R	P	O	R	T	S			R	A	T	E	S
		O	R	D	O		S	W	A	N				
	A	R	E	Y	O	U	K	I	D	D	I	N	G	
L	A	S	T	S		N	I	N	E		N	E	O	
E	L	K	S		B	R	I	N	E		H	A	I	R
A	T	E		G	O	A	T		M	A	N	L	Y	
N	O	W	I	L	L	T	E	L	L	O	N	E		
		N	E	T	S		L	A	R	D				
A	Z	U	S	A		W	A	T	E	R	L	O	O	
D	O	N	T	M	A	K	E	M	E	L	A	U	G	H
A	L	I	E		D	I	V	A	N		I	T	E	M
R	A	S	P		D	R	E	S	S		L	E	E	S

161

```
L E V I   A Y A H S   S N O W
A C E R   L O C A L   H E R E
T H R O W I N T H E T O W E L
H O B N O B     A E R O S O L
    C R I S P   K O I
  S O L E   T O M   U N T I L
S P C A   D A N A N G   O N E
H E A D F O R T H E H I L L S
I L L   L A R I A T   N E A T
P L A C E   S A L   V A R Y
    R E S   C O T E S
A T T A C H E     R A M B O S
L E A V E I N T H E L U R C H
G A L E   N O N O S   C I T E
A M E N   E S T E S   H O O D
```

162

```
T A S S   S P C A   A S C O T
I R K S   I R A N   B O A R D
A M I N G L I N G   L I M B S
R A W   O L E     S E R B
A D A G E   S Q U A R E O N E
S A X E S   T U R F   E D E N
    N B C   I D E S   I I I
O F B E A R S B U L L S A N D
P R O   D A U B   Y I P
T A U T   Y E L P   P U M A S
S U R E L O S E R   O N I C E
  B E A N     I O U   S O N
F L O S S   B U M S T E E R S
D O N U T   E V E L   D R N O
R A S P S   T A R O   U S S R
```

163

```
C L O T   R E C A P   L E E S
L I L O   U V U L A   E T C H
E M I R   M I R E S   A U R A
F O O T B A L L S T A D I U M
    O A K S     R T E
G E M I N I   B O A R D E R S
A L A S   S A L M I   C I A
B A S E B A L L D I A M O N D
O T T   E V O K E   A L D A
R E S T R I P S   B A R E S T
    O L A   F A R M
B A S K E T B A L L C O U R T
E L L E   O L L I E   S L O E
E T O N   R O V E R   E N O L
R O T S   S T A R S   T A M E
```

164

```
M A C A U   E R G S   J A Z Z
A P I A N   T A R T   E P E E
I N T H E M O N E Y   W E S T
N E E   V A N   A L B E R T A
E A R N E D   U S U A L
    O N E A S Y S T R E E T
C L O G   I D I     H Y D R A
R I M   A T O N E R S   G I G
A M A S S   G O A   H E N S
W O R T H A B U N D L E
  R E V U P   I A M B I C
I N C I S O R   E S T   O N A
N O O K   W E L L H E E L E D
F U M E   E A T S   S W A R D
O N E S   D U D E   T E S T Y
```

165

```
T A M E   L I L Y   U N G E R
A W A Y   I R A E   B I O T A
B A R E   F A L S E A L A R M
B R I D L E   O M A N   T E A
Y E A   E L I   A R G O S
    W O O D E N N I C K E L
A B B A   N O D     C I A O
L E A S   G L E N N   U N T O
I T C H     N A E   L S A T
F A K E P A S S P O R T
  B R O T H   S P Y   E G O
A R E   L O O K   H E A V E N
F U N N Y M O N E Y   G E N E
A D D U P   T I L T   E R I N
R E S T S   S T Y E   D Y E D
```

166

S	T	A	B		B	L	A	B	S		S	T	E	T
H	A	R	E		R	E	S	E	T		M	O	N	O
A	L	G	A		A	W	A	R	E		L	A	S	T
P	L	U	G	A	N	D	P	L	A	Y		D	U	E
E	Y	E	L	I	D			E	L	A	P	S	E	D
	E	M	I	R	S		S	O	O	T				
U	S	E		A	S	T	H	E		L	O	S	T	
P	U	S	H	T	H	E	E	N	V	E	L	O	P	E
S	P	C	A		S	O	C	A	L		L	Y	E	
	A	L	C	S		L	E	G	G	S				
L	A	P	T	O	P	S		R	A	M	O	S	E	
A	L	E		P	I	T	C	H	A	R	O	U	N	D
P	I	P	E		R	O	U	E	N		O	T	I	S
E	C	O	L		A	L	E	R	T		T	I	D	E
L	E	D	S		L	I	R	A	S		H	E	E	L

167

A	M	O	K		S	T	O	A		S	P	E	N	T
C	O	P	E		H	A	M	M		T	A	B	O	O
T	A	T	E		A	C	N	E		R	I	O	T	S
I	T	S	L	O	V	E	I	N	T	E	N	N	I	S
			N	E	T			O	A	T				
A	P	P	L	E	S		G	A	W	K		T	D	S
M	A	R	I	A		T	O	L	E		H	A	R	E
B	E	E	T	L	E	B	A	I	L	E	Y	P	A	L
L	A	S	E		R	A	P	T		S	P	I	K	E
E	N	S		S	U	R	E		A	T	O	N	E	S
		R	E	P			S	N	O					
W	W	I	I	A	T	T	A	C	K	P	L	A	N	E
H	A	D	A	T		A	W	O	L		E	L	A	L
O	R	A	T	E		M	A	R	E		G	O	S	H
A	S	S	A	D		E	Y	E	S		S	E	T	I

168

C	A	L	M	S		T	W	E	R	P		A	L	P
O	N	I	O	N		E	I	D	E	R		N	O	R
O	N	C	L	O	U	D	N	I	N	E		T	I	E
T	A	K	E	O	N		S	E	T	T	L	E	R	S
		D	E	C		E	R	O	D	E	S			
M	A	G	I		A	L	G	E	R	I	A			
I	C	O	N		S	O	O	T		A	D	A	G	E
T	H	E	S	K	Y	S	T	H	E	L	I	M	I	T
E	E	R	I	E		E	T	A	S		N	O	G	O
	P	R	O	T	O	N	S		G	R	I	N		
O	N	F	I	R	E			E	E	G				
S	A	R	D	I	N	I	A		N	O	U	G	A	T
A	D	O		G	O	O	D	H	E	A	V	E	N	S
K	I	N		A	N	W	A	R		L	E	N	D	A
A	R	T		N	E	A	R	S		S	A	T	Y	R

169

A	C	N	E		A	R	O	S	E		C	A	L	L
R	O	E	S		S	U	D	A	N		O	L	E	O
O	R	E	S		S	T	I	N	G		A	D	D	S
U	N	D	E	R	T	H	E	T	A	B	L	E		
S	E	N	S	E			A	G	O		R	D	A	
E	A	T		R	E	B	A		E	N	A	M	E	L
		P	U	N	I	S	H		F	A	L	L		
B	E	H	I	N	D	T	H	E	S	C	E	N	E	S
A	L	I	T		S	E	E	S	A	W				
B	I	G	S	U	R		S	L	I	T		M	S	S
Y	A	H		R	O	O			E	L	E	C	T	
	B	E	L	O	W	T	H	E	R	A	D	A	R	
H	E	R	A		S	L	O	O	P		T	U	N	E
A	G	E	S		T	E	R	S	E		I	S	T	S
M	O	D	E		S	T	A	T	E		N	A	Y	S

170

R	O	M	A	N		B	L	U	R		S	P	A	R
I	N	A	N	E		R	O	T	H		I	O	T	A
P	O	R	T	A		I	N	T	O		L	O	T	S
	Z	I	P	A	D	E	E	D	O	O	D	A	H	
D	O	I		S	R	A		R	A	P		L	I	E
N	A	P	A		E	L	H	I		T	E	E	N	S
A	R	A	F	A	T		I	N	O	I	L			
	N	O	T	H	I	N	G	D	O	W	N			
	O	R	A	T	E		E	N	A	B	L	E		
G	E	S	T	E		S	S	R	S		Y	A	L	L
A	L	E		S	T	A		E	S	C		T	D	S
Z	E	R	O	T	O	L	E	R	A	N	C	E		
E	V	E	R		G	I	V	E		O	H	A	R	A
B	E	N	E		A	V	I	A		T	I	M	E	S
O	N	E	S		S	E	E	D		E	A	S	T	S

171

```
A P E D   S C R I P T   I R A
R U S E   T R E M O R   D O N
G R A N N Y A P P L E   T U E
O R I G A M I     B R A G S
      F I G U R E E I G H T
A D E S T E   P A R K S
C O T T A   A S T A   O D D S
E S A U   K I T E S   T R A P
S E L F   I M A S   S T A R R
      F I L E R   S C O T T Y
C H A I N L E T T E R
Y A L T A       I V O R I E S
C L I   S Q U A R E D A N C E
L E V   E I S N E R   M E R E
E Y E   C D C A S E   A Z U R
```

172

```
S P E C   P A W A T   B L E D
W A X Y   E L O P E   L O V E
A T T N   R A M I E   A R A B
M I R I A M   B E N E D I C T
P O A C H E D   C I N E
      S A U T E E D   A S K
M A A M   T M I   A D L A I
E G G P R E P A R A T I O N S
E R A S E   R E S   N E S S
T A R   C L E A N S E
      M U O N   D E V I L E D
O V E R E A S Y   S E N I L E
H E R B   D U E T S   B E A M
M A G I   E R N I E   E T T U
S L O G   R E S O D   D O E R
```

173

```
C A P   T E N O R   S T A L E
U M A   A L A M O   W A F E R
R O C K O F G I B R A L T A R
S E M I S     T O A T E E
E B A N   T E S T S   R I O
S A N D B O X   S P I N A C H
    L U M P Y   S E L E S
  S C I S S O R S V A U L T
S P R E E     S P E A R
H O A R D E D   I N C O M E S
E T S   D I A N A   T O R I
    H A B I T S   A I D A N
P A P E R T H I N E X C U S E
T I A R A   E D I L E   L E W
A D D O N   R E A M S   E S S
```

174

```
S T A R   W A K E   S T I L E
O R L E   E V I L   T I D A L
R I L E   I O W A   A L E C K
T O Y F O R W I N D Y D A Y S
      A D S   R O E
P O T A T O   G M A N   R P M
S H O R E   B O O K   T H A I
H A W K R E L A T E D B I R D
A R E S   R O P E   R A N K S
W E D   L U T E   R A R E S T
      T I P   S U M
T O M O F T H E P G A T O U R
O V E R T   E M I R   O R S O
M A T T E   N I N A   W E E D
B L E E D   S T E T   N O D E
```

175

```
C A N O E   A T L A S   S E A
A L O U D   C H I R P   T A X
C O T T O N C A N D Y   E S E
A N E W   O U T D O   J E T S
O E D I P U S   E R R O L
    T A R T A N   N E W T S
S O B   R I O T   S A L O O N
E G O S   S M A R T   S O F A
P E S A C H   R E E F   L U G
T E S L A   C I T R U S
    T O N T O   A I R P O R T
D O W N   A B O I L   E S A I
A V E   F L A N N E L C A K E
L E E   D O L C E   B I K E R
E N D   A N T E D   S E A R S
```

176

W	E	A	R	Y		R	A	H		L	A	M	A	S
A	R	N	I	E		E	C	O		S	C	A	L	E
S	T	E	A	M	B	A	T	H		T	O	X	I	N
P	E	W		E	A	T	O	U	T		R	E	B	A
		O	N	E	A	R	M	B	A	N	D	I	T	
B	E	S	T	I	R			I	V	S				
E	T	U	I			E	C	O	L	I		S	I	R
M	A	L	C	O	L	M	B	A	L	D	R	I	G	E
A	S	K		J	O	U	S	T			I	Z	O	D
		S	A	O				A	S	T	E	R	S	
G	O	C	L	I	M	B	A	T	R	E	E			
A	C	R	E		S	I	D	E	A	S		S	L	Y
S	T	I	E	S		J	I	M	B	A	C	K	U	S
P	E	E	V	E		O	O	P		M	A	I	N	E
S	T	R	E	W		U	S	O			E	L	D	E	R

177

O	N	C	E		A	N	T	I	C		G	A	L	A
S	E	A	S		C	A	I	R	O		A	M	I	S
L	A	S	T	S	U	P	P	E	R		L	E	E	K
O	P	E	R	A	T	E	S		R	H	E	S	U	S
			O	W	E			J	U	A	N			
	P	A	G	E		S	T	O	P	W	A	T	C	H
M	I	R	E	D		P	A	C	T	S		W	E	I
A	X	O	N		L	I	M	O	S		S	I	L	T
R	I	M		H	I	R	E	S		S	E	L	L	S
C	E	A	S	E	F	I	R	E		H	A	L	O	
			W	A	T	T			D	A	B			
T	O	M	A	T	O		A	M	E	R	I	C	A	S
O	N	I	T		F	I	N	A	L	D	R	A	F	T
M	Y	T	H		F	R	O	S	T		D	R	A	Y
E	X	E	S		S	A	N	T	A		S	E	R	E

178

A	L	M	A		M	A	T	C	H		B	E	A	M
L	O	A	D		I	D	A	H	O		E	X	P	O
B	U	Z	Z	A	L	D	R	I	N		L	A	S	S
E	I	D	E	R		L	A	P		V	I	C	E	S
E	S	A		R	A	E		S	L	E	E	T		
		B	O	B	S	C	H	I	E	F	F	E	R	
A	L	L	O	W	S		R	O	B	S		A	X	E
R	U	E	D		E	M	O	T	E		W	R	E	N
A	L	F		O	N	E	S		R	A	R	E	S	T
B	U	T	C	H	C	A	S	S	I	D	Y			
	O	L	M	E	C		H	A	L		A	B	A	
C	A	V	E	S		U	M	A		A	A	R	O	N
U	S	E	R		F	L	I	P	W	I	L	S	O	N
B	E	R	G		A	P	N	E	A		T	O	T	E
E	A	S	Y		D	A	D	D	Y		O	N	Y	X

179

P	O	W	E	R		T	E	A	M		A	S	T	O
A	N	I	T	A		E	A	S	E		S	W	A	B
P	U	N	C	H	I	N	G	I	N		S	I	R	E
A	S	K		R	O	S	E	S		S	U	N	N	Y
			C	A	N	E	R		B	U	R	G		
T	O	R	A	H	S		L	A	R	G	E	S	S	E
A	V	I	S			S	Y	R	I	A		H	I	M
M	I	N	A	R	E	T		T	E	R	M	I	T	E
E	N	G		E	R	A	S	E		A	F	A	R	
R	E	L	E	V	A	N	T		S	E	N	T	R	Y
		E	X	E	S		E	N	T	R	Y			
G	R	A	I	L		R	A	Y	O	N		S	L	O
R	E	D	S		B	E	L	L	P	E	P	P	E	R
A	B	E	T		I	N	T	O		S	T	I	N	G
B	A	R	S		B	E	H	N		T	A	T	T	Y

180

B	I	D	S		T	E	N	S		F	A	C	T	S
E	C	R	U		A	X	E	L		R	E	L	I	C
T	O	U	R		L	U	R	E		A	R	O	M	A
A	N	G	E	L	C	L	O	W	N	T	I	G	E	R
			O	U	T		U	S	E					
B	A	R	N	U	M		D	E	B		S	H	A	D
A	G	A	I	N		P	U	R	I	M		A	G	A
S	A	I	L	G	O	L	D	R	A	I	N	B	O	W
I	T	S		E	P	E	E	S		M	O	I	R	E
L	E	E	S		A	D	S		A	O	R	T	A	S
		E	L	L		P	C	S						
J	E	L	L	Y	S	T	A	R	C	A	T	R	E	D
A	L	I	E	N		A	L	E	E		R	O	A	R
B	L	A	N	C		R	O	E	S		A	L	S	O
S	A	R	A	H		E	E	N	S		P	E	E	P

181

S	C	U	D			I	D	E	A		M	E	S	H	
O	U	Z	O			O	O	R	T		I	S	E	E	
W	E	I	G	H	T	W	I	L	L	S	N	A	C	K	
		D	E	A	N		A	S	S	E	N	T	S		
P	R	I	O	R		P	O	S	T			C	A	T	
H	A	M	M		T	L	C		S	O	N	O	R	A	
I	M	P		C	O	A	T	S		C	A	N	E	R	
		U	P	O	N	Y	O	U	W	H	E	N			
S	T	L	E	O		S	P	I	E	S		E	G	O	
C	A	S	T	L	E		U	T	E		D	R	A	W	
A	P	E		V	I	S	A		M	A	Y	B	E		
L	I	B	E	L	E	D		T	S	A	R				
Y	O	U	R	E	N	O	T	L	O	O	K	I	N	G	
	C	Y	S	T		L	E	A	N		E	R	I	E	
	A	S	T	O		S	E	W	S		N	E	X	T	

182

B	R	E	W	S		M	O	W	S		A	M	P	S	
R	E	M	I	T		A	K	I	N		G	U	A	M	
I	M	P	L	Y		G	I	N	A		O	G	L	E	
B	O	T	T	L	E	N	E	C	K	S		S	O	L	
E	R	O	S	I	V	E		E	Y	E	S	H	O	T	
E	A	R		I	S	I	S		C	O	O	K	E	
		R	U	N	I	N		G	U	I	T	A	R	
	C	A	N	C	A	N	G	I	R	L	S			
S	O	U	R	C	E		E	L	V	E	S			
E	X	P	E	L		T	R	E	E			B	A	A	
M	I	C	R	O	B	E		E	T	C	H	E	R	S	
I	D	A		G	L	A	S	S	H	O	U	S	E	S	
T	A	K	E		O	S	L	O		A	M	I	N	E	
I	T	E	M		T	E	A	M		S	O	D	A	S	
C	E	S	T		S	T	Y	E		T	R	E	S	S	

183

S	C	A	B		P	O	E	T		S	C	R	A	M	
N	A	P	E		A	P	S	E		T	H	E	R	E	
A	N	O	D		L	E	A	N		R	E	A	C	T	
C	O	O	K	I	E	C	U	T	T	E	R				
K	E	R	N	S			H	E	A	V	E	H	O		
		O	L	M	O	S		E	M	I	L	I	A	
E	G	G	B	E	A	T	E	R		L	I	N	T	
S	I	R		S	H	I	N	E	T	O		A	G	E	
T	R	E	S		C	A	N	O	P	E	N	E	R	
E	L	A	T	E	S		T	O	N	E	R			
S	T	A	T	E	S			R	A	T	S	O			
		P	O	T	A	T	O	M	A	S	H	E	R	
C	H	I	L	I		L	I	K	E		U	R	N	S	
D	O	W	E	L		A	R	I	A		R	E	D	O	
S	T	O	R	E		D	E	E	D		E	W	A	N	

184

E	R	A	S	E		C	O	E	D		S	N	O	W	
R	E	B	A	G		A	R	L	O		P	E	L	E	
I	C	A	C	O		B	A	I	O		A	W	E	D	
C	O	C	K	T	A	I	L	D	R	E	S	S			
A	N	A		R	U	N		E	M	O		M	S	G	
		O	I	D			A	N	G	E	L	A			
P	O	R	K	P	I	E	H	A	T		O	D	E	S	
A	R	I	A	S		M	O	M		S	T	I	P	E	
T	I	N	Y		S	U	G	A	R	C	O	A	T	S	
T	O	S	S	U	P			I	O	N					
I	N	E		R	E	C		V	C	R		E	S	E	
		D	I	N	N	E	R	J	A	C	K	E	T	S	
B	M	O	C		C	L	O	D		H	E	R	A	T	
L	I	F	E		E	L	S	A		E	L	I	T	E	
T	A	F	T		R	O	S	Y		S	T	E	E	R	

185

D	A	D		P	A	I	L	S		A	F	I	R	E	
U	T	A		I	S	S	U	E		G	A	M	U	T	
C	O	R	N	C	H	I	P	S		O	L	S	E	N	
A	N	I	O	N		T	E	A	R		S	O	D	A	
T	E	N	N	I	S		M	A	T	E	S				
		C	O	F	F	E	E	S	H	O	P	S			
T	A	M	P		O	U	R		K	O	R	E	A		
A	R	I	E		T	R	I	E	D		O	R	E	S	
L	L	A	N	O		A	L	I		D	Y	N	E		
C	O	M	I	C	S	T	R	I	P	S					
		I	N	T	E	R		S	E	N	A	T	E	
R	A	H	S		E	A	S	E		A	I	R	E	S	
O	N	E	U	P		C	O	L	D	S	N	A	P	S	
S	T	A	L	E		T	A	B	O	O		B	E	E	
S	I	T	A	R		S	P	A	W	N		S	E	X	

186

A	R	G	O	T	■	A	G	F	A	■	■	G	A	P
L	E	O	N	A	■	L	A	I	D	■	A	O	N	E
T	R	U	C	K	■	A	I	R	J	O	R	D	A	N
H	U	R	L	E	D	I	N	S	U	L	T	S	■	■
E	N	D	E	A	R	■	■	T	R	A	I	P	S	E
A	S	S	■	B	E	B	R	I	E	F	■	E	A	R
■	■	B	U	G	L	E	S	■	■	H	E	W	N	■
■	T	O	S	S	E	D	S	A	L	A	D	■	■	■
A	G	O	G	■	■	M	O	U	L	I	N	■	■	■
R	O	W	■	G	U	I	N	E	A	N	■	A	M	S
C	A	N	C	A	N	S	■	■	M	E	S	S	U	P
■	P	I	T	C	H	E	D	B	A	T	T	L	E	■
S	O	L	I	T	A	I	R	E	■	G	O	U	D	A
K	W	A	I	■	S	N	O	B	■	E	N	T	E	R
Y	E	N	■	■	E	G	O	S	■	S	E	E	R	S

187

■	B	A	R	T	■	A	B	E	L	■	S	A	S	H
■	O	L	E	O	■	N	E	R	O	■	P	I	T	A
■	L	A	D	O	D	G	E	R	S	N	I	D	E	R
D	I	B	S	■	E	O	N	■	I	N	E	R	T	■
E	V	A	■	T	A	R	■	S	E	C	E	D	E	S
F	I	S	T	I	N	A	F	I	G	H	T	■	■	■
E	A	T	O	N	■	U	R	G	E	■	L	E	E	■
A	N	E	W	■	M	A	N	E	S	■	P	U	M	A
T	O	R	■	D	O	U	G	■	E	L	M	O	S	■
■	■	R	A	N	K	I	N	G	N	O	B	L	E	■
A	S	C	E	N	T	S	■	O	R	E	■	E	L	L
L	I	L	A	C	■	E	R	A	■	K	R	I	S	■
U	N	I	V	E	R	S	I	T	Y	N	A	M	E	■
M	A	M	E	■	H	E	R	O	■	E	L	A	N	■
S	I	B	S	■	O	W	E	N	■	T	E	N	T	■

188

A	R	F	■	A	V	E	R	S	■	B	R	I	S	K
N	E	L	■	M	A	X	I	M	■	L	E	T	O	N
I	H	A	V	E	N	T	G	O	T	A	C	L	U	E
M	A	R	I	N	E	R	■	G	A	Z	E	L	L	E
A	B	E	S	■	S	A	M	■	K	E	N	■	■	■
■	■	O	K	S	■	A	P	E	■	T	B	A	R	■
Y	O	U	R	E	A	S	K	I	N	G	■	E	C	O
E	R	N	S	T	■	T	E	E	■	E	A	R	L	S
L	E	D	■	T	H	E	W	R	O	N	G	G	U	Y
L	O	O	K	■	E	P	A	■	B	A	H	■	■	■
■	A	L	A	■	Y	E	S	■	A	S	T	O	■	■
D	E	P	R	I	V	E	■	B	E	E	S	W	A	X
I	T	S	A	M	Y	S	T	E	R	Y	T	O	M	E
G	U	S	T	O	■	S	E	R	V	E	■	R	E	Y
S	I	T	E	S	■	O	A	T	E	S	■	E	S	E

189

S	T	A	G	E	■	A	N	N	■	F	E	T	A	L
A	R	B	O	R	■	T	I	O	■	E	M	O	T	E
C	O	L	O	R	C	A	S	T	■	S	E	T	O	N
S	T	Y	■	■	O	L	E	S	■	T	R	E	N	D
■	■	■	M	I	L	L	I	O	N	A	I	R	E	S
A	G	R	E	E	D	■	■	E	L	L	■	■	■	■
F	L	A	I	R	■	N	A	P	A	■	■	A	Y	E
R	E	F	R	I	G	E	R	A	T	O	R	C	A	R
O	N	T	■	M	E	E	T	■	■	J	I	N	K	S
■	■	P	G	A	■	■	S	A	F	E	S	T	■	■
M	I	C	R	O	C	I	R	C	U	I	T	■	■	■
I	N	L	A	W	■	M	E	R	E	■	■	P	A	N
S	L	A	I	N	■	B	E	A	R	N	A	I	S	E
T	E	R	S	E	■	U	S	C	■	A	G	A	I	N
S	T	E	E	D	■	E	E	K	■	G	A	F	F	E

190

A	L	G	A	E	■	P	A	R	T	■	T	A	C	O
G	I	R	L	S	■	A	L	O	E	■	R	E	A	P
H	E	A	L	T	H	Y	A	S	A	H	O	R	S	E
A	N	D	S	■	E	O	N	S	■	A	L	I	E	N
■	■	■	T	U	R	F	■	A	L	L	E	Y	S	■
F	I	T	A	S	A	F	I	D	D	L	E	■	■	■
A	D	O	R	E	■	N	O	D	■	Y	O	G	A	■
D	O	N	■	R	E	Q	U	E	S	T	■	M	O	M
S	L	I	T	■	C	U	R	■	E	L	A	T	E	■
■	■	S	T	R	O	N	G	A	S	A	N	O	X	■
G	A	T	E	A	U	■	A	R	T	Y	■	■	■	■
A	Z	O	T	E	■	S	Y	N	C	■	A	S	E	A
R	U	N	S	L	I	K	E	T	H	E	W	I	N	D
T	R	E	E	■	R	E	A	R	■	L	A	R	G	O
H	E	R	S	■	A	W	R	Y	■	M	Y	E	R	S

191

E	A	R	N	S		S	O	C	K		J	A	B	S
S	N	O	O	P		P	A	I	N		A	T	O	M
S	T	O	V	E		O	T	T	O		R	O	N	A
	I	F	A	L	L	T	H	E	W	O	R	L	D	S
			L	O	T	S			W	E	L	S	H	
R	E	A	L	I	T	Y		M	E	L	D			
O	R	I	E	N	T		W	A	R			T	R	A
A	S	T	A	G	E	W	H	E	R	E	D	O	E	S
R	E	S			R	E	Y		A	L	U	M	N	A
		B	E	Y	S		S	T	A	B	B	E	D	
S	W	A	R	M		S	U	I	T					
T	H	E	A	U	D	I	E	N	C	E	S	I	T	
R	I	T	Z		A	R	T	S		D	A	M	O	N
A	N	N	E		N	O	T	E		L	L	A	M	A
D	E	A	N		K	N	O	T		Y	E	M	E	N

192

A	L	S	O		A	R	E	A		R	E	W	E	T
Y	E	A	H		G	E	A	R		A	L	A	M	O
A	V	I	D		E	A	R	N		N	I	X	O	N
H	I	D	E	A	N	D	S	E	E	K		A	T	E
			A	T	T	Y			P	E	N	N	E	D
A	L	E	R	T			E	L	I	D	E	D		
M	A	B		A	T	O	M	I	C		S	W	A	N
B	I	B	B		A	D	I	N	A		T	A	M	E
O	R	A	L		H	O	T	E	L	S		N	O	T
		N	A	D	I	R	S			L	E	E	K	S
			R	E	D	H	A	T		B	E	E	S	
E	L	F		G	I	V	E	A	N	D	T	A	K	E
G	U	L	A	G		E	A	S	T		A	R	I	A
A	D	O	B	E		E	V	E	R		T	I	N	S
N	E	W	E	R		R	E	L	Y		E	D	D	Y

193

G	A	M	E	Y		S	E	T	S		C	A	L	M
A	L	O	N	E		C	L	A	W		O	D	I	E
M	I	N	D	O	N	E	S	M	A	N	N	E	R	S
E	V	E		M	I	N	E		H	Y	E	N	A	S
R	E	T	R	A	C	E		T	I	L				
			I	N	K		C	O	L	O	S	S	A	L
B	R	I	G		S	T	A	Y	I	N	L	I	N	E
E	I	G	H	T		I	R	E		S	A	L	E	S
T	O	E	T	H	E	M	A	R	K		V	O	W	S
A	T	T	O	R	N	E	Y		A	M	I			
			I	N	S		A	T	E	C	R	O	W	
M	O	N	A	C	O		A	S	I	T		I	V	E
A	B	I	D	E	B	Y	T	H	E	R	U	L	E	S
K	E	N	O		L	A	T	E		I	N	E	R	T
E	Y	E	S		E	M	U	S		C	O	S	T	S

194

M	O	U	S	E		R	E	R	A	N		S	E	W
P	H	N	O	M		E	T	U	D	E		L	E	I
G	O	D	D	A	U	G	H	T	E	R		E	Y	E
			E	A	G	R	E			N	O	T	I	O	N
E	R	R		S	I	N	K	S		O	G	R	E	
L	O	A	D		S	T	E	P	F	A	T	H	E	R
M	A	G	I	C		G	U	I	L	E				
O	N	E	C	A	L	L		D	R	I	B	B	L	E
			T	R	I	E	D			T	A	R	A	S
G	R	E	A	T	U	N	C	L	E		G	A	S	P
R	A	N	T		S	L	I	M	E		S	H	Y	
E	G	R	E	S	S		M	I	N	U	S			
A	L	A		H	A	L	F	B	R	O	T	H	E	R
S	A	G		A	G	I	L	E		L	E	A	S	E
E	N	E		M	O	T	O	R		A	P	T	L	Y

195

P	I	L	A	F		A	S	A	P		F	L	O	G
A	R	U	R	U		B	I	L	L		I	O	T	A
P	A	L	M	S	U	N	D	A	Y		N	U	T	S
E	N	L		T	R	E	E		B	I	G	T	O	P
R	I	S	K	I	E	R		T	O	T	E			
			N	A	Y		Q	U	A	T	R	A	I	N
C	A	J	U	N		B	U	R	R		P	E	R	E
O	P	E	C		E	L	A	N	D		R	O	M	A
M	I	L	K		M	A	C	S		F	I	N	A	L
B	A	L	L	P	A	R	K		V	I	N			
		E	R	N	E		C	E	N	T	E	R	S	
B	A	L	B	O	A		M	O	R	E		G	E	E
A	R	I	A		T	H	U	M	B	S	C	R	E	W
R	E	E	L		E	A	S	E		S	I	E	V	E
S	A	U	L		S	T	E	T		E	A	T	E	R

196

S	I	R	S		M	A	T	C	H		A	L	A	S
A	C	U	P		E	C	O	L	I		C	O	R	E
L	E	D	A		A	U	D	E	N		T	A	C	T
A	M	O	M	E	N	T	O	F	T	R	U	T	H	
M	E	L		L	Y	E				A	P	H	I	D
I	N	F	R	A		S	T	E	M		I	V	Y	
		O	N	P	A	P	E	R		K	N	E	E	
	D	A	D	D	Y	L	O	N	G	L	E	G	S	
E	R	I	E		R	E	I	S	S	U	E			
E	E	R		F	E	E	L			G	N	A	S	H
K	A	B	O	B			S	S	E		S	H	Y	
	R	O	B	I	N	S	O	N	C	R	U	S	O	E
D	I	R	E		A	T	S	E	A		T	U	R	N
D	E	N	S		P	A	L	E	R		A	R	E	A
T	R	E	E		S	T	O	R	E		H	E	S	S

197

S	E	R	U	M		J	O	V	E		L	O	P	E
A	T	O	N	E		U	R	I	S		A	P	E	X
S	H	O	O	T	C	R	A	P	S		M	E	R	E
H	O	T		R	O	I	L			B	A	N	K	S
A	S	S	A	I	L	S		T	B	I	R	D		
			S	C	A	T	T	E	R	B	R	A	I	N
A	C	T	I			I	R	I	S		T	O	O	
I	R	A	S		V	I	T	A	E		S	E	W	S
L	O	X		S	I	L	L			I	S	A	Y	
S	C	R	A	M	B	L	E	D	E	G	G			
	E	P	E	E	S		I	R	O	N	B	A	R	
A	L	B	E	E		E	V	I	L		O	N	A	
L	O	A	M		O	U	T	I	N	F	R	O	N	T
T	O	T	E		O	M	A	N		E	E	R	I	E
O	M	E	N		H	A	L	E		R	O	S	E	S

198

F	E	R	R	I	S		E	C	H	O		F	A	T
G	R	E	E	C	E		X	L	I	I		O	T	S
H	E	L	P	I	N	G	H	A	N	D		R	T	E
		O	N	T	O	A	S	T		T	W	I	T	
R	E	C		G	R	O	U	P		C	H	A	R	S
O	L	A	F		Y	D	S		S	I	R	R	E	E
O	L	L	I	E		S	T	I	R	R	E	D		
F	A	L	L	S	T	O		C	I	C	A	D	A	S
		I	T	S	O	N	M	E		A	D	E	L	E
L	I	N	E	A	R		A	D	S		S	C	O	W
A	N	G	R	Y		A	N	T	I	S		K	E	N
S	A	C	S		S	C	I	E	N	C	E			
S	R	A		P	A	C	K	A	G	E	D	E	A	L
O	U	R		A	G	R	I		E	N	E	R	G	Y
S	T	D		L	E	A	N		S	E	N	A	T	E

199

C	R	U	S	T		C	A	A	N		H	I	S	S
C	A	M	E	O		A	R	C	O		A	C	H	E
S	H	A	T	T	E	R	E	D	V	I	S	I	O	N
			U	S	E	R		C	A	N	T	E	R	S
S	L	A	P		L	O	P			C	A	S	T	E
P	I	G		E	S	T	A	T	E		T	A	S	
A	M	A	H	L			M	A	L	E	S			
	B	R	O	K	E	N	P	R	O	M	I	S	E	
			E	S	T	E	E		I	R	O	N	Y	
M	T	V		A	T	R	E	S	T		R	O	E	
A	R	I	E	S		S	A	P		P	E	S	T	
D	I	O	R	A	M	A		T	I	N	E			
S	P	L	I	T	I	N	F	I	N	I	T	I	V	E
E	L	A	N		S	T	U	N		P	A	R	E	S
N	E	S	S		S	I	N	G		S	L	A	T	S

200

S	P	A	N	S		A	R	I	A		O	O	P	S
M	E	L	E	E		B	A	N	G		L	O	U	T
I	A	L	W	A	Y	S	T	H	O	U	G	H	T	A
R	C	A		S	O	U	S	A		N	A	S	T	Y
K	E	Y		C	U	R		L	E	I				
		Y	A	R	D	W	A	S	T	H	R	E	E	
C	A	N	A	P	E		A	N	T		A	U	R	A
A	L	I	C	E		S	I	T		D	I	N	G	S
L	O	C	H		G	A	S		R	E	T	E	S	T
F	E	E	T	B	U	T	T	H	E	N	I			
			E	M	U		A	N	D		V	O	W	
O	A	S	I	S		R	A	R	E	R		A	V	A
S	T	A	R	T	E	D	M	O	W	I	N	G	I	T
L	O	L	A		W	A	I	L		T	A	U	N	T
O	M	E	N		E	Y	E	D		E	P	E	E	S

Can't get enough of *USA TODAY* puzzles?

You can play more *USA TODAY* puzzles:

- In your daily *USA TODAY* newspaper

- On USATODAY.com at
  puzzles.usatoday.com

- On mobile phones (certain puzzles only—
  check with your individual carrier)